At Sea with Bishop John Bede Polding

C. F. Fowler

At Sea with Bishop John Bede Polding

The Journals of Lewis Harding

1835 (Liverpool to Sydney)
1846 (Sydney to London)

Transcribed and edited with an introduction

by

C. F. Fowler

ATF THEOLOGY

Adelaide
2019

Front cover photo supplied by Downside Abbey with thanks to Simon Johnson

978-1-925872-73-6 soft
978-1-925872-74-3 hard
978-1-925872-75-0 epub
978-1-925872-76-7 pdf

Published by:

An imprint of the ATF Press Publishing Group owned by ATF (Australia) Ltd.
PO Box 504
Hindmarsh, SA 5007
ABN 90 116 359 963
www.atfpress.com
Making a lasting impact

Dedicated to

John Hugh Baron

friar, francophile, friend

Un simple commerce avec une âme élevée modifie la nôtre; il nous élève. On ne peut s'approcher des grands coeurs sans qu'il s'exhale d'eux quelque chose qui pénètre jusqu'à nous et nous rend plus dignes de leur contact.

(Henri-Dominique Lacordaire, *Vingt-septième Conférence de Notre-Dame*, Carême 1844)

Table of Contents

Acknowledgements

I wish to acknowledge with gratitude all the assistance received in this project. Ms Jo Robertson, former archivist at the Sydney Archdiocesan Archives (SAA), alerted me to the existence of the manuscript of the 1846 Harding journal. It was the receipt of the digitised text that initiated the project. Her successor, Ms Lienntje Cornelisson, and Mr Ronnie Borg, have continued to provide the assistance and encouragement of the Archives.

Dr Simon Johnson, Director of Heritage at Downside Abbey, Somerset, gave new life to the project in revealing that Harding's 1835 Journal, contrary to rumours of its loss, was in good condition in the Abbey archives. He provided a clear digitised copy, and his continued assistance and encouragement towards publication have been indispensable.

My Dominican confrere, Rev Dr Denis Minns, applied his skills to disentangling many of Harding's indecipherable words and phrases in the 1846 text, especially those in Latin.

I am grateful to the Doyen among historians of Sydney's monks, Br Terry Kavenagh OSB, who read a draft of the introduction and suggested wise adjustments. I am honoured by his acceptance of the invitation to launch the book.

Sister Lia van Haren of the Good Samaritan Archives and her successor Ms Joanna Mead have been most helpful in all things Benedictine.

Mr Jeremy Rowett Johns, director of Polperro Heritage Press, was of great assistance in all matters regarding Lewis Harding's Cornwall connections.

I owe a particular debt of gratitude to Mr Hilary Regan for accepting the text for publication by ATF Press. His patience and advice have been crucial in guiding the project into print.

Finally, I acknowledge the generosity of Downside Abbey, Sydney Archdiocese and the Good Samaritan Sisters in facilitating the publication by their commitment to purchasing copies of the book.

Abbreviations

Adjutor Deus	M. Xavier Compton et al (eds), *Adjutor Deus. Documents and resource material relating to the episcopacy of Archbishop John Bede Polding OSB*, 2 vols, Sydney, 2000.
Birt	Henry Norbert Birt, *Benedictine Pioneers in Australia*. 2 vols, London, 1911.
HRA	Frederick Watson (ed), *Historical Records of Australia. Series I: Governors' despatches to and from England, 1788–1848*. 26 vols., Library Committee of the Commonwealth Parliament, Sydney, 1914-1925.
Polding Letters:	M. Xavier Compton et al (eds), *The Letters of John Bede Polding OSB*, 3 vols, Sydney, 1994.
SAA	Sydney Archdiocesan Archives

Figures

Introduction

I THE BISHOP

Figure 1. The newly consecrated Bishop of Hiero-Caesarea, Vicar Apostolic of New Holland and Van Diemen's Land.

John Bede Polding, during his more than forty years as a bishop, tallied a total number of days at sea equivalent to almost four years. In addition to the four-month duration of his inaugural voyage in 1835, he sailed to and from Europe four times. Twice on the voyages to Europe the passage was eastward and around Cape Horn (1840 and 1846); twice the ship sailed across the Indian Ocean to the Red Sea

– in March 1854 on the barque-rigged screw-steamship *Chusan* and in November 1865 on the Royal Mail Steam Ship *Bombay* to Suez, thence overland to Alexandria and then by sea to Naples via Malta.[1] The four return voyages to Australia were via the Cape of Good Hope.[2] The slowest of the voyages was six months from November 1840 to May 1841. Polding and company sailed on the *Orion* from Sydney to Chile via New Zealand, thence on a French whaler around Cape Horn to Le Havre and finally across the Channel to London; he returned from that voyage as Archbishop of Sydney, having shed the foreign title of Hiero-Caesarea, which was the cause of much embarrassment and the ridicule of Protestants. The fastest passage was that of 1855–56 on the *Phoenix* from London to Sydney non-stop – 92 days. These four voyages to and from Europe kept the Bishop at sea for approximately 35 months. In addition, he sailed several times to and from ports within his Province – Newcastle, Hobart, Melbourne, Adelaide, Brisbane, Albany and Perth. When in Europe he regularly criss-crossed the Irish Sea and the English Channel. In his old age, in October 1869, he undertook a final voyage intending to reach Europe in time for the opening of the Vatican Council at Rome in December. The P&O Mail Steamer *Malta* sailed via Melbourne and Albany into the Indian Ocean, thence to the Red Sea and Suez Canal, which was due to open in November. However, the Archbishop, sick and exhausted, turned back after reaching the port of Aden, arriving in Sydney via Bombay, Galle and Melbourne on Christmas Eve 1869.

During his first ocean crossing of 1835 Polding had established a pattern of shipboard life that he later recommended to others. A fellow passenger in 1835, Sizar Elliot, a Protestant layman, was greatly impressed by his first encounter with a Roman Catholic bishop, praising Polding's preaching, but especially delighting in the warmth of his personality, as he recalled fifty years later: 'But the conducting of sermons was not the Bishop's only strong point. He was a most social and kindly man; he joined in whist parties, and invited us to his cabin once a week for a social evening, singing and music. He was fond of

1. The 'Overland Route' involved a 100-mile trek by camel or horse-drawn carriage from Suez to Cairo, followed by a journey down the Nile by river steamer, thence to Alexandria by canal barge.
2. On Polding's voyages see Miriam Theresa Starkey, 'J. B. Polding – Ships', manuscript, 1977, Good Samaritan Archives, Sydney.

a bit of quiet fun and amusement.'[3] In both Harding journals Polding emerges as a most charming and generous host, regularly entertaining in his cabin, playing at cards, joining in fun, though not extending his participation to the rowdy activities associated with 'crossing the line'. He revealed his self-deprecating humour in a letter written on board the *Oriental* in May 1835: 'To my shame, I must say, I am as much inclined to laugh when I ought to be serious, by sea as by land: indeed, more so. Such queer things do sometimes happen. For instance, I was giving the blessing at Prime on Easter Sunday, and just as I said the word *disponat* the ship gave a lurch and seated me on the floor of my cabin.'[4]

By the conclusion of the difficult and slow 1846 *Ratcliff* passage of 129 days, Polding had become a seasoned seafarer. He had boasted towards the end of the voyage: 'I enjoy my leisure exceedingly and feel not the lassitude and tedium of which my fellow passengers continually complain.'[5] He was confident of giving advice to those undertaking the long voyage to Australia for the first time. In November 1846 he farewelled and issued instructions to three priests, two of whom had only experienced shipboard life during their single crossing of the Irish Sea; the other had crossed the Atlantic:

> My dear children in Christ,
> I regret exceedingly that I am deprived of the gratification of accompanying you on board and of imparting to you my blessing. In this exigence, I must endeavour to supply by writing, some of those instructions and suggestions which, in my anxiety for your welfare, I should have given you. These will refer rather to your sojourn on shipboard than to your conduct on landing. For the time of the voyage is most valuable; during it, studies may be matured, attention given

3. Elliott (see Appendix I below)
4. Polding to L.B.Barber OSB, 3 May 1835 (*Polding Letters* I.53–54; see Appendix I below). Perhaps the Bishop was thrown to the floor while reciting this part of a long prayer: '... *etiam abundantiam omnium bonorum spiritualium et corporalium et gratiam Spiritus Sancti qui me bene per omnia disponat* . . .' ('Obtain also an abundance of all good things, spiritual and bodily, and the grace of the Holy Spirit so He may set all things in good order for me.') He wittily played on the meaning of 'disponat'/'set'.
5. Polding to Bishop Willson, 5 June 1846 (*Polding Letters* II.53).

> to the interior life, habits of order, recollection and piety strengthened in a very discernible degree.[6]
> ... [F]rom unaccustomedness with the sea, it is probable that sickness will come on and continue for some days. During this time if, as is often the case, the recitation of the Divine Office be exceedingly burdensome, without scruple substitute the three parts of the rosary or even one if the sickness be very oppressive. The rosary may be said lying in your berth; you will find the recumbent posture most easy...
> I do not object to your joining, in this spirit, any games that may be played, chess, backgammon, even cards, though from the moment you reach Sydney, these are never to be touched. But on shipboard it is virtue to contribute to the amusement of others, even by these unusual modes of clerical relaxation ... It will be advantageous to you if you keep a log-book as it is called. I do not mean for the purpose of merely notifying the incidents, trifling or otherwise, which may occur, but more particularly to note down the remarks you have made in the course of the day's reading ... A day of strict retirement occasionally will be of service ... [T]ake at least some hours, say four, of active exercise each day. By taking relaxation at proper times, observing silence at other times, you will find the voyage exceedingly pleasant and improving.

He gave strict and specific instructions about when and how to celebrate Mass at sea:

> As regards the celebration of the Mystery, this can only take place when the vessel is steady, sailing with the wind on lee beam. To prevent scruples, whenever you doubt whether you can without difficulty celebrate, in all cases of doubt decide you will not celebrate. Let every precaution to prevent

6. In the midst of the 1846 voyage, Harding was less sanguine about the advantages of shipboard life: 'We have reason to remark that whoever imagines that a sea voyage will afford a season for mental exertion, for literary acquirement, for a making up of past deficiencies or for preparing the means for more successful efforts for the future, has only to experience the cold, contrary winds, fogs, gales with the delightful never-failing accompaniment of sea sickness, which such a voyage as ours has abounded with, and he will be radically cured of the sweet delusion' (*1846 Journal*, 64).

> accident be used; the priest assisting should have his hand on the chalice whenever the celebrant has not. Take care that there are no drafts or currents passing over the altar. This may be constructed that the priest at the *Dominus Vobiscum* will not be required to turn around. I would recommend Mass always be celebrated in the cabin below.[7]

Even on that most hazardous of his voyages in 1846, Polding put into practice, throughout the long weeks and months of treacherous seas, the wisdom of maintaining a sensible balance of reflection, relaxation and social amiability, combining religious duty with 'unusual modes of clerical relaxation'. However, he gave a rather negative assessment of the voyage in a letter to Cardinal Fransoni, perhaps in the expectation of a sympathetic hearing when in Rome: 'a long and painful voyage of nearly 129 days during which, as well as inevitable troubles of cold and heat, I had also to suffer rather severe privations.'[8]

The one recommendation he did not seem to keep was that of maintaining a logbook; there is no record of his having done so. However, his fellow passengers often did. There are five extant diaries kept of voyages with Polding onboard. Apart from the two transcribed in this volume, there were two kept on the 1847–48 return voyage to Australia on the *St Vincent* by Brother Edmund Moore OSB and Sister Scholastica Gregory OSB[9], and one on the 1855–56 passage to Australia on the *Phoenix* by Myles Athy.[10] In addition to the Harding journal of 1835 there are the later reminiscences of two other passengers on the *Oriental*.[11]

---

7. Polding to Priests Embarking for Australia, 16 November 1846 (*Polding Letters* II.65–66; see Appendix II below).
8. Polding to Cardinal Fransoni, 15 July 1846 (*Polding Letters* II.57; see Appendix II below).
9. See G. D. (ed), 'With Dr Polding to Australia, 1847', *Downside Review*, 32(1913), 69–92, 314–327, republished in Tjurunga 6(1974) 109–124, 7(1974) 77–92, 9(1975), 105–119; M. G. Forster (ed), 'Fragment of a Diary', *Tjurunga. An Australian Benedictine Review*. 26(1984), 60
10. See Anne Wark, *Journal of a Voyage to Australia 1855–56: Myles Athy, a recruit for St Mary's Monastery Sydney*, ATF Press, Adelaide, 2017.
11. See Appendix II below.

II THE MISSIONERS

Accompanying the young Bishop Polding was an unusual collection of monks, priests, seminarians and catechists. In February 1834, at the recommendation of Governor Richard Bourke, the Colonial Office had approved the funding of an additional four priests for New South Wales; a further stipulation was that these priests be Englishmen.[12] Bishop Bramston of the London District, tasked with providing these clergymen, turned for help to the English Benedictine Congregation:

> It was also positively suggested to me that the clergymen to be sent should be Englishmen and the Minister for Colonies in accordance with this proposal asked me to choose four clergymen born in England. Alerted by this petition, as I had no more among my own subjects whom I could send, I discussed this matter of such importance with John Birdsall, the very Reverend President of the English Benedictine monks, since I judged that, among the clergy of the Order, four could easily be found possessed of high qualifications and suitable for this ministry.[13]

Bramston concluded his letter to the Cardinal Prefect of Propaganda Fide by proposing that John Bede Polding be one of the four approved clergy and that he be consecrated Bishop and appointed Vicar-Apostolic of New Holland and Van Diemen's Land. The Pope agreed and the Colonial Office concurred. That left the selection of three English Benedictines to complete the missionary team.

Polding's hope was to recruit them from among the 'Gregorians', monks belonging to the Priory of St Gregory at Downside and to establish a branch of the English Congregation in his new Vicariate Apostolic.[14] Many of the Downside monks had been Polding's stu-

12. Right Hon. E. G. Stanley to Governor Bourke, 15 February 1834 (HRA XVII.371).
13. Bishop Bramston to Cardinal Pedicini, 26 April 1834 (*Adjutor Deus* I. 7–8; see Appendix I below).
14. The Gregorians were one of four groups of English Benedictines originating from communities exiled to the Continent after the English Reformation. Expelled during the French Revolution, the monks of St Gregory's at Douai in Flanders, founded in 1605, eventually settled at Downside; the community of St Edmund's in Paris, founded in 1615, returned to France in 1823 and settled at Douai until again expelled in 1903, when they established Douai Abbey at Woolhampton in Berkshire; the monks of St Lawrence's at Dieulouard in Lorraine, also expelled

dents, one of whom, Bernard Ullathorne, was already in New South Wales as Vicar-General. In this he did not succeed, due to a combination of the unwillingness of individuals and the reluctance of superiors to lose monks to a distant mission.[15] Opposition to Polding's plan was sharply expressed by Dom Barber in a letter to the Provincial of Canterbury:

> Polding has received his appointment as Vic. Ap. of New South Wales, and is to be consecrated Bishop of Hiero-Caesarea *in partibus*. It is not unlikely that you will be receiving an application from Duck to go out with him. Do me the favour to agree with me and put a decided veto upon it. We are weakening ourselves at home to serve missions abroad.[16]

In the eight months between his consecration as bishop in June 1834 and embarkation in March 1835, Polding was able to recruit only one English Benedictine priest, newly ordained Ambrose Cotham, not a Gregorian but belonging to the community of St Edmund's at Douai, and about whom the Father President had serious misgivings: 'It is

---

in 1789, finally, in 1802, founded a priory at Ampleforth in Yorkshire; the community of Ss. Adrian and Denis at Lambspringe in Westphalia, an Abbey given to English monks in 1644, was expelled by the Prussian Government in 1803 and briefly established a priory at Broadway in Worcestershire (1826–1834). See page 37 of the 1846 Journal for Polding's explanation of how he and his cousins were distributed among three of the houses of the EBC by their uncle President Dom Bede Brewer.

15. On the reluctance of the EBC to assent to Polding's plans see T. Kavenagh, 'J. B. Polding and the English Benedictine Congregation, 1834–1843', introduction to 'The 1855 Monastic Declarations of St Mary's, Sydney: adapting the "RB" to Colonial Australia', *Tjurunga* 34(1988), pp 65–69.
16. Luke Bernard Barber OSB to James Benedict Deday OSB, 6 June 1834 (Birt I.232; see Appendix I below).
    Luke Bernard Barber OSB (1790–1850), monk of Downside, Prior 1818–1830; Vicar of nuns and resident chaplain at Salford 1830–1838 and at Stanbrook 1838 to 1850; President-General of the English Benedictine Congregation 1842–1850.
    James Benedict Deday OSB (1773–1845), Downside monk, ordained priest 1800; Provincial of Canterbury 1826–1834.
    James Ambrose Duck OSB (1797–1848), professed at Downside, 1816, ordained priest 1824.
    The biographical details of the monks of the English Benedictine Congregation, here and throughout, are taken from Henry Norbert Birt's *Obit Book of the English Benedictines, 1600–1912*, Edinburgh, 1913.

no other than a suspicious symptom, in Mr Cotham, to be speaking about Canon Law: if his duties and his rights are to be determined, or were discussed by Canon Laws, you may calculate upon no little trouble with him.'[17] To complete the allocation of priests, Polding had to turn to an Irish Dominican, James Corcoran, and a sickly Liverpool priest, Clement Fisher.

Polding was also raising with the Colonial Office the need for teachers to undertake the education of Catholic children in the Colony. In August he had gained a commitment to fund the voyage of two catechists.[18] Failing to secure stipends for them, he turned to a public appeal and directly to the Palace.[19] He wrote to King William's Private Secretary explaining his appeal and requesting a contribution, suggesting that a royal donation would go far to quelling rebelliousness among his flock of Irish convicts:

> May I indulge the hope that His Majesty will cause me and them to rejoice in being considered deserving objects of His Royal Bounty. I ask this great favour to be extended to us, not only to be enabled by this means to render essential service to the cause of Morality, but also that I may urge as a most powerful argument in the event of disturbance (which may God in his mercy prevent) for loyalty and peaceable bearing - the positive proof of the wise and beneficence of our Sovereign in the relief He will vouchsafe to grant us.[20]

In February of 1835 the State Secretary for Colonies, Lord Aberdeen, wrote to Governor Bourke naming the three priests to accompany Polding and detailing the financial arrangements regarding their appointment. They were Revd Mr Cotham, Revd Mr Corcoran, Revd Mr Sumner. Sumner was in fact a sub-deacon, not yet ordained

---

17. Birdsall to Polding, 17 March 1835 (*Adjutor Deus* I.17; see Appendix I).
    James Ambrose Cotham OSB (1810–1883), educated at St Edmund's, Douai; professed 1830; ordained December 1834.
18. Polding to J. A. Birdsall OSB, 14 August 1834 (*Polding Letters* I.40; see Appendix I below).
19. The appeal to the public was made through Charity Sermons and via the distribution of a pamphlet (see documents for August 1834 in Appendix I below).
20. Polding to Sir Herbert Taylor, 18 August 1834 (*Polding Letters* I.41; see Appendix I below).

priest.[21] The four named, including Polding, were each granted a travel allowance of £150, and on arrival were to be given an annual stipend of £150. Polding was not granted a larger stipend, because Ullathorne as the current resident superior was already receiving the higher stipend of £200. Aberdeen offered Bourke a way of avoiding an awkward situation: 'I, therefore, propose that Mr Ullathorne should be removed to Van Diemen's Land upon the same rate of pay as he now receives, when, if you deem it advisable, Dr Polding's Salary might be augmented to £200 per annum.'[22]

The result of Polding's request to include seminarians/catechists in his party had resulted disappointingly in an increase to just three, not the six he had sought, and with no commitment to salaries on arrival:

> Dr Polding will be accompanied by three Students, Messrs. Gregory, Spencer and Kenny, who are in course of preparation for Holy Orders, but who are intended to act for the present as Catechists. The Colonial Agent has issued to each of them the sum of £100, in aid of the expenses of their passage to the Colony; but no expectation has been held out to any of them by this Department, that they will receive any salary or allowance whatever from the Government.[23]

On the eve of embarkation from Liverpool, Polding gave an updated list of the members of his party in a letter to the Cardinal Prefect of Propaganda Fide.

> Coming out with me are three priests and the same number of choir religious, two of whom are already in Orders, and also a young Scotsman desirous of embracing the clerical state, all of them having a good testimonial from their Ordinaries and regular Superiors, and who say they are burning with zeal for souls. Of the priests, the senior is a Secular, a former student of the English College in Rome, Father Clement Fisher, who when back in his Mother country was so afflicted with poor health that, after a short time on the English Mission, being

21. *Joseph Bede Sumner* OSB (1803–1871): clothed at Downside 1831; professed 1833; ordained priest at Sydney 1836.
22. Earl of Aberdeen to Sir Richard Bourke, 20 February 1835 (*HRA* XVII.682–683). Ullathorne commented amusingly on the proposed financial arrangements in his autobiography ((Ullathorne, *Autobiography*, pp 88–89).
23. Aberdeen to Bourke, op. cit.

> unwell, he has left and his Bishop, on the advice of the doctors has granted him the permission to seek the healthier region of New Holland with me. The second is Mr Corcoran, of the Irish branch of the Dominican Fathers, who was formerly attached to the community of St Clement in Rome.[24]

The sub-deacon, Bede Sumner, was removed from the list of priests and replaced by the ailing Fr Clement Fisher, and relocated among the young seminarians, Gregory, Spencer and Kenny. Henry Gregory Gregory OSB, aged 21, a student at Downside but a member of the Broadway priory, and John Benedict Spencer OSB of Downside, aged 31, were junior monks, not long in vows, and both had been students of Polding; John Kenny was a 19-year-old Scottish seminarian.[25] Of the eight named members of the mission team, three, including Polding, were Downside monks, two were members of other Benedictine groups, Cotham from Douai and Gregory from Broadway, and three were not Benedictines. However, at the time of embarkation on March 27, there were two more members on board without any Government funding – the young layman John Lewis Harding and a boy, John Gorman, taken at the request of his father to be trained for the priesthood and subsidised by a London priest, Father Jones. This was far from the ideal team of Gregorians that Polding originally had in mind.

The fragility of the group was manifest within two months of embarkation with the death of Clement Fisher onboard.[26] As for

24. Corcoran prepared for the priesthood in Rome, living at the Irish Convent of San Clemente, and was ordained in that city in 1825. He was assigned to Dominican convents in Perugia in 1827 and then Lucca in 1829 where he pursued further studies. In 1831 he returned to the British Isles and took up a private chaplaincy in the Trelawny household.

25. Henry Gregory Gregory OSB (1813–1877) was educated at St Edmund's, Douay, and Downside, received habit as monk of Broadway priory 1833, professed June 1834, ordained priest at Sydney in 1837.
John Benedict Spencer OSB (1803–1864): clothed at Downside 1824; professed November 1825; ordained sub-deacon 1827; at Trappist abbey of Du Garde, France, 1831–1833; ordained deacon at Sydney 1836; sent back to England 1837, having caused dissension in the Benedictine community and scandal in Sydney.
John Kenny (1816–1886): born in Fife, Scotland, and educated by Benedictines; catechist in Hobart Town 1835–1836; ordained priest in Sydney 1843.

26. 'Died: On the 28th of May last, on board the Oriental, the Rev. Clement Fisher, late of St Anthony's Chapel, in this town' (*Liverpool Mercury*, September 4, 1835).

Ambrose Cotham, his focus seemed to be to join his brother Lawrence recently arrived in Hobart. He was left there by Polding. He sailed to Sydney just once, accompanying Bishop Willson to the First Provincial Synod in September 1844. He returned to England in 1851. On the very day of the arrival of the *Oriental* in Sydney, 13 September 1835, deep misgivings emerged about John Benedict Spencer, as recorded by Bernard Ullathorne in his autobiography:

> Knowing that the Bishop had brought with him one person who had been a perpetual failure, the first thing I did when I met him in the harbour was to strive to impress upon him very solemnly the duty of sending that person back on the very first opportunity. After which we had our cordial and affectionate greeting. That person was unfortunately retained for two or three years on one ground or another until he got the Bishop into a good deal of trouble, and was then shipped off. He was the very man against whose profession we young religious had protested in vain. His coming damped my joy in the Bishop's arrival considerably as, in a Colony, every folly and weakness gets to be known everywhere.[27]

In 1838 Spencer and Gorman were sent back to England following the predictable scandals. Another member of the original team, James Vincent Corcoran, had been killed in a carriage accident in September 1837.

When in 1841 Polding sailed back to England with Ullathorne and Gregory on a recruiting mission, there was just one Benedictine remaining in Sydney, Bede Sumner. However, five years later, at the time of his second return voyage to Europe on the *Ratcliff*, he was able to report proudly on the local Sydney community to the General Chapter of the English Congregation: 'Our little Community consists of six Professed for the Mission and eight Lay Brothers. We have also nine Postulants – five of whom will shortly take the Habit – the others are very young. All however intended for the Choir assist at the Divine Office . . . The Archbishop, Father Henry Gregory Gregory, the Procu-

27. William Bernard Ullathorne, *The Devil is a Jackass: being the dying words of the autobiographer William Bernard Ullathorne 1806–1889* (edited by Leo Madigan), Downside Abbey Publications Bath, 1995, page 129.

rator, Father Bede Sumner, live in common with the Community.'[28] The impressive growth was due mostly to local recruiting. Polding was aware that the community lacked senior monks for 'offices of trust' – Ullathorne, already disillusioned with Polding's Benedictine dream, had not returned – so the Archbishop requested the General Chapter to send such brethren to Australia: '[S]o, Venerable Fathers, do we in confidence inspired by filial affection look to you for aid in our present exigencies. We require some Brethren, zealous for discipline, whom we may place in offices of trust. Those of our own growth, of course, have not had time to reach maturity and sufficient strength.'[29] He modelled the desired relationship between the English Benedictines and the Australian mission on that of St Andrew's Monastery on the Caelian Hill in Rome and the English mission of St Augustine, which continued to receive monks from Rome into the seventh century. An implied comparison was between Archbishop Augustine of Canterbury and Archbishop John Bede of Sydney, and perhaps even a flattering hint at a comparison between Pope Gregory the Great and the President of the English Congregation. However, the General Chapter, likely cautioned by Ullathorne, gave a very limited response to Polding's request. For his Coadjutor they released Charles Henry Davis of Downside, one of Polding's novices, who had expressed disappointment at not being chosen to accompany the bishop and his classmate Henry Gregory in 1835, and whom Polding had requested as Coadjutor when in England in 1847.[30] Davis was ordained bishop in February 1848 and arrived in Sydney in December that year.

Despite failing to gain the full assistance he sought from the English Congregation, Polding managed to recruit five monks for Sydney

28. Polding to the General Chapter of the English Congregation, 11 July (*Polding Letters* II, 56).

29. Ibid. Polding summarised the qualities needed in a letter to the Rector of the English College in Rome: 'zealous, good and true Religious, capable of governing by example as much as by advice' (Polding to Thomas Grant, 11 August 1847 (Polding Letters II. 80).

30. Charles Henry Davis OSB (1815–1854) was educated at Downside 1826–33, professed with Henry Gregory in 1834, ordained priest 1840 and bishop 1848.
See Appendix I below: Charles Davis to Edwin Davis, 24 July 1834 (Birt I.241–242).
Polding to Fr. Thomas Grant, op. cit.
See also Graeme Pender, 'The life and contribution of Bishop Charles Henry Davis OSB (1815–1854) to the Catholic Church in Australia' *Journal of the Australian Catholic Historical Society*, 39(2018), 29–44.

during his visit of 1846–1847; they sailed with him in October 1847: Ruggiero Emmanuele, an ordained Sicilian monk of the Cassinese Congregation, who was at Downside learning English in 1847; Jean Gourbeillon, an ordained French monk of Solesmes Abbey; Edmund Moore, a Downside monk; blood-brothers Thomas Edmund and John Bernard Caldwell, junior monks of Douai. The three English monks, aged 23, 25 and 19, were not in Holy Orders. The five arrived at Sydney with Polding in February 1848 and by 1859 they had all returned to Europe for various reasons reflecting poorly either on St Mary's or themselves.[31] The first to leave were the youngest, Edmund Moore and Bernard Caldwell; they sailed in May 1849, just fifteen months after arrival.[32] In April Moore had written to a classmate at Downside commenting: 'I despair of ever seeing St Mary's made a happy Religious House.'[33] None of the five Benedictine recruits of 1847 proved capable of filling offices of trust, and some of them seemed incapable of any task. The Irish priest Michael Corish, who sailed for Australia in November 1846, joined the monastery on arrival in Sydney; in 1854 he sailed to Rome to argue unsuccessfully against the validity of his vows.[34]

The one Downside monk who had the potential to fill 'offices of trust' was Charles Henry Davis. He was given the crucial role of directing the formation of the monks, while his classmate Henry Gregory retained responsibility for administration. He soon concluded that 'the good Archbishop made a slip in the last importation of labourers', naming Gourbeillon, Edmund Caldwell and Edmund Moore as

31. For details of these monks see T. Kavenagh, 'Polding's Monks', *Tjurunga* 8(1974), Appendix 1, pp i–xviii. On the dismissal of Jean Gourbeillon see John Hosie, 'Letters of Jean Gourbeillon', *Tjurunga* 12(1976), 143–155 and J. Brian Butler, 'Jean Gourbeillon: a French Sculptor in Nineteenth-Century Sydney', *Tjurunga* 67(2004), 35–47.
32. 'Departure: May 20, *Sobraon*, ship, 379 tons, Captain Nicol, for London. Passengers – . . . Mr. Caldwell and Mr. Moore.' (*Shipping Gazette and Sydney General Trade*, 26 May 1849, p 140)
33. Moore to Dom Alphonsus Morrall, 18 April 1849 (quoted in T. Kavenagh, 'My Dear Alphonsus, selections from the Sydney letters of Abbot Edmund Moore', *Tjurunga* 10(1975), p 52).
34. On the crisis about the validity of vows in the Sydney monastery see Mary Shanahan, *Out of Time, Out of Place: Henry Gregory and the Benedictine Order in Colonial Australia*, ANU Press, Canberra, 1970, pp 57–62.

failures.[35] In the absence of Gregory in Europe from 1850 to 1853, Davis was obliged to assume the administrative work of the Archdiocese as well as the governance of the monastery. However, his health proved fragile and he became a convalescent; he died in May 1854, while Polding and Gregory were again absent in Europe. In 1860 a heavy blow was dealt the Archbishop when his beloved confidante of twenty-five years, Abbot Gregory, was recalled by the President of the English Congregation, Dom Placid Burchall, on instructions from Rome, supposedly 'on account of accusations which ill become a religious person'.[36]

The impact of the inability or unwillingness of the English Congregation to provide sufficient monks capable of filling 'offices of trust' in Sydney was manifest in the statistics of profession of vows from 1845 to 1877: from 1845 to 1852 there were 28 professions; from 1853 to 1877 just eight, and in that same period six monks quit the monastery, some creating scandal.[37] Polding's Benedictine dream had become a nightmare for his Gregorian Coadjutor, Roger Bede Vaughan, who arrived in Sydney in 1873. On succeeding to the archdiocese in 1877 after Polding's death, Vaughan acted quickly, dismantling the monastic establishment and assigning the few remaining monks to parish ministry.[38]

Just three years earlier, in 1874, a different note had been struck in a secular newspaper. The *Sydney Mail and NSW Advertiser* honoured the eightieth birthday of the Archbishop by publishing an article accompanied by a portrait. It was effusive in its appreciation of Polding's contribution to the religious and civic life of the Colony, highlighting the impact of his Benedictine qualities:

---

35. Davis to Prior Wilson, 28 February 1849 (quoted in Frances O'Donoghue, *The Bishop of Botany Bay: the life of John Bede Polding, Australia's first Catholic Archbishop*, Sydney, Angus & Robertson, 1982, p 95).

36. Cardinal Barnabo to Polding 30 July 1860 (Adjutor Deus II.45). On the recall see Shanahan, op. cit. chapter IX, 165–178.

37. See T. Kavenagh, 'Profession dates (and others) of the monks of St Mary's, Sydney', *Tjurunga* 48(1985), 69–75.

38. Roger Bede Vaughan OSB (1834–1883) professed at Downside 1854, ordained 1859, Coadjutor of Sydney 1873, succeeded as Archbishop March 1877. On the dismantling of the monastery see T. Kavenagh, 'Vaughan and the Monks of Sydney', *Tjurunga* 25(1983), 147–233, and 'The end of the Sydney Benedictines', *Tjurunga* 52(1997), 31–42. In 1971 the then Lord Abbot of Downside described St Mary's, Sydney, as 'a monastery which never really got off the ground' ('Abbot Gregory Gregory [1813–1877]', *Downside Review*, 89(1971), p 191).

> On the foundation of the University of Sydney [1850] he addressed a pastoral letter to his flock on the necessity for the establishment of a Roman Catholic College within the University. And his view of the results of university-training was precisely what might have been expected from a man of refinement and varied culture, and from a member, however humble, of that countless company of scholars, statesmen, and pontiffs which has upheld the greatness of the Benedictine Order since it first issued, thirteen centuries ago from the Grotto of Subiaco and the hillside of Monte Cassino.[39]

This was an appreciation towards the end of Polding's life which echoed the news sent from England forty years before: 'A Catholic Bishop has been consecrated for your Colony and you may expect him over very shortly. He is a Monk of the Benedictine Order, the best and most rational of all the Catholic Orders.'[40]

Figure 2: The 1869 collage of Archbishop Polding surrounded by his Clergy. The only 1835 veterans present were Polding and Dean John Kenny (front row, extreme left). Seven of the 45 priests were Benedictines; two monks were unaccountably missing – Bede Sumner, a veteran of 1835, and Myles Edmund Athy.[41]

39. *The Sydney Mail and NSW Advertiser*, 8 August 1874, p 169.
40. Extract from a private letter of 8 November 1834 (*Australian*, 17 March 1835, page 3; see Appendix I below)
41. The other known surviving veterans of 1835 in 1869 were Dom Henry Gregory, Cathedral Canon of the Welsh Diocese of Newport and Menevia, and Dom Ambrose Cotham, missioner at Cheltenham.

The last of Polding's monks, Austin Sheehy, died in 1910.[42] However, the 'best of all the Catholic Orders' did not die in the Antipodes. Polding's Nuns and Polding's Sisters continue the tradition – the Benedictine Nuns of the Presentation Abbey, founded in 1849, and the Sisters of the Good Samaritan of the Order of St Benedict, founded in 1857, now spread throughout Australia and with foundations in Japan, the Philippines and Kiribati. These Polding foundations, together with the monks of New Norcia in Western Australia, founded in 1847 by Spanish Benedictines, and the mid-twentieth Century arrivals, the Tyburn nuns and the Sylvestrine and Cistercian monks, now form the Benedictine Union of Australia and New Zealand.

III THE VOYAGES

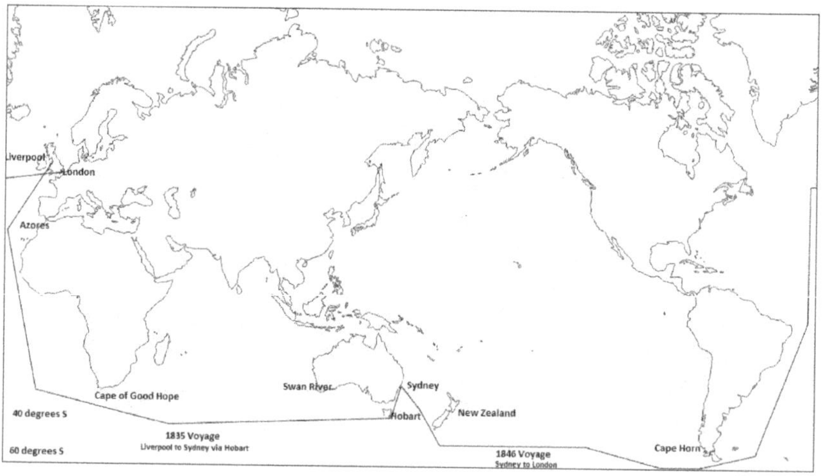

Figure 3

42. Samuel Austin Sheehy (1827–1910), born in Australia, was received as a choir postulant in 1845, professed in 1848 and ordained priest in 1852. He was President of the Seminary 1852–56 and of Lyndhurst College 1861–64. In November 1866, by Papal Brief, he was elected Bishop of Bethsaida and appointed Coadjutor to Polding. Acting on objections from Irish bishops in Australia, Propaganda Fide delayed his consecration and an investigation was begun. Declining the appointment, Sheehy returned the Papal Bull to Rome in August 1867 (*Adjutor Deus* II.175–176). See Figure 2 above – Sheehy: front row, third from right.

The first passage from England to Botany Bay was that of the First Fleet under the command of Captain Arthur Phillip, leaving Spithead in May 1787 and arriving more than six months later in January 1788. The convoy consisted of two Royal Navy vessels, three store ships and six convict transports. Initially the fleet followed a route already well established by the ships of the East India Company sailing around the Cape of Good Hope into the Indian Ocean. The passage began by sailing down the northern coast of Africa to pick up the favourable trade winds and then south-west across the Atlantic to Rio de Janeiro for replenishing supplies of food and water. The ships then sailed in a south-easterly direction towards the Dutch colony of Cape Town, where they lingered for a month, taking on board supplies of plants, seeds and livestock. Rounding the Cape of Good Hope, they followed the long final stretch of the passage across the southern Indian Ocean, assisted by the gales of the 'Roaring Forties' at latitudes below the 40th parallel.

This remained the pattern of voyaging to Australia until the opening of the Suez Canal in 1869. The duration could be significantly reduced by the elimination of ports of call. However, delays in the doldrums in the equatorial zone could add to the time taken and also place a strain upon provisions, especially water. The 1835 voyage of the *Oriental* followed the established pattern, taking 102 days to reach Hobart Town, without calling at any ports along the way. The southernmost latitude recorded by Lewis was 40°45' on 7 July. However, he had left blank the latitudes on the following days as the ship approached Hobart Town at latitude 42°52'S.[43]

A mid-nineteenth Century development led to faster passages. The 'Great Circle' route from the Cape of Good Hope to Australia, curving down to 60 degrees south, was significantly shorter, and also offered much stronger prevailing westerly winds. However, there were the added risks associated with icebergs. The voyage from England to Australia following this course was sometimes reduced by as much as a whole month. On his return voyage of 1855–1856, Archbishop Polding onboard the *Phoenix* completed the passage to Sydney along the 'Great Circle' route in 92 days.

43. Harding, *1835 Journal*, pp 102–104. The distance represented by one degree of latitude is 60 nautical miles or approximately 110km.

The homeward passage from the eastern coast of Australia to England was most often eastward across the Pacific Ocean and around Cape Horn at a southern latitude of 56 degrees into the South Atlantic. Most ships stayed north of this latitude while sailing cross the Pacific, dipping south into the ice zone as they approached the Horn. In February 1846, the *Ratcliff* sailed from Sydney towards New Zealand; avoiding the dangerous Cook Strait, it rounded the South Island at latitude 47° and headed even further south into the Southern Ocean.[44] On 29 March 1846, the *Ratcliff* was as far south as 61°20'.[45] On 4 April, as the ship approached the Horn, Harding recorded:

> Lat 60°16'S; Long 78°12'W. Strong breezes, thick weather, hail, snow and squally. Hens freezing; fling snow balls at each other. The hen coops are covered with sheets of ice. A large heavy swell follows us from the west[war]d. It appears evident that a strong current from the N. sets in towards the S., of which it behoves all navigators to be aware, though this is not mentioned in chart or publication. Indeed, there has been great remissness on the part of Government in this matter. The passage from N.S. Wales and the Australian Colonies in general to England is made by Cape Horn. The distance to the Cape from Sydney has been accomplished by a very slow sailing vessel, the *Achilles*, from Hobart Town in 28 days, by the *General Huet* from Sydney in 32 days, whilst the *Everetta* was employed 73 days in accomplishing the same distance. We shall probably be more than 50 days, and this I conceive to be about the average.[46]

Cape Horn was a source of fear for ship captains and crew. The strong winds and currents, which flow around the Southern Ocean, are funneled by the Horn into the narrow Drake Passage and, coupled with turbulent winds coming off the Andes and the shallow water near the Horn, these conditions created deadly hazards for sailing ships. Vessels which survived the rounding of the Cape continued their passage up the Atlantic, driven by the winds of the eastern South Atlantic; after the Doldrums, they entered into the western regions of the

44. The Southern Ocean is generally regarded as the waters below the latitude of 60 degrees.
45. Harding, *1846 Journal*, p 51.
46. Ibid. p 54.

North Atlantic driven by the Trade Winds. A good run for the 23,750 km from Australia to England was approximately 100 days. The *Ratcliff*, which experienced all the hazards of the route, took 129 days to complete its voyage.

After the experience of the slow and hazardous 1846 passage around Cape Horn, Bishop Polding resolved never again to take that homeward course. The advent of steam had made a westward passage faster and safer than the Horn route. His subsequent voyages to Europe took him across the Indian Ocean to the Red Sea, thence overland from Suez to the Mediterranean. The combination of the advent of steamers and the opening of the Suez Canal in November 1869 finally marked the end of homeward passages via Cape Horn.

IV THE DIARIST[47]

Figure 4: Lewis Harding and family – the only known photo of Lewis, taken at the entrance of Trelawne House circa 1856:

left to right: Lewis's father, sister, sister-in-law, Lewis with niece on lap, mother, brother (top-hatted and obscured).
From the Harding Collection, courtesy of the Royal Institution of Cornwall.

47. Earlier versions of this section have appeared in the *Journal of the Australian Catholic Historical Society* 2018 and in the *Journal of the Cornwall Association of Local Historians* 2019.

The name of John Lewis Harding has not been well-known in the history of the Catholic Church in Australia. There have only been passing references to him as a junior member of Polding's 1835 missionary band.[48] His slow rescue from obscurity began with the research of the late Philip Correll, who in the year 2000 published a book focusing on Lewis as 'Cornwall's pioneer photographer'.[49] In that book Correll briefly outlined Lewis' career in Australia between 1835 and 1846. In a typed document, a copy of which he lodged in the State Library of New South Wales, he gave much more extensive treatment to the Australian years. In the bibliography of that text he noted the existence of the 1835 journal but recorded it as 'unaccountably missing' from the archives of Downside Abbey in Somerset.[50] The earliest citation from the journal is found in the *Downside Review* of 1881, in an anonymous article on Polding, the second in a series entitled, 'Memoirs of Distinguished Gregorians'. A more extensive reference is found in Dom Henry Norbert Birt's *Benedictine Pioneers in Australia*, in which the author quoted brief passages from the manuscript, referring to the rest as 'a mass of trivialities'.[51]

In 1840 Harding's name had been inscribed on a metal commemorative plate. On 25 July 1840, the feast of St James the Great, foundation stones were laid for the building of the first churches, Anglican and Roman Catholic, at the convict settlement of Norfolk Island, 1000 kilometres north-east of Sydney. The day was chosen to honour the patron saint of the Anglican chapel. The Catholic chapel was dedicated to the Blessed Virgin Mary and St Vincent de Paul, invoked as patron saint of prisoners, because of his ministry among convicts sentenced to service on the French galleys. Sydney's Catholic newspaper, the *Australasian Chronicle*, gave an extensive report of the event,

48. In a list of 'Polding's monks', the name 'Br. Lewis' is recorded with the comment: 'One would expect "Louis". Perhaps this is a surname' (T. Kavenagh, 'Polding's monks', *Tjurunga* 8[1974], Appendix 1, p xv).
49. Philip M. Correll, *Lewis Harding: Cornwall's pioneer photographer*, Polperro, Polperro Heritage Press, 2000.
50. Philip Correll, *Lewis Harding: photographer of Polperro*, typescript, 1996.
51. Anon., 'The Most Reverend John Bede Polding, D.D., O.S.B., First Archbishop of Sydney', *Downside Review* 1(1881), p 68; Birt I.253. Dom Birt was probably the author of the 1881 article.

including an English translation of the Latin text inscribed on the copper plate attached to the foundation stone of the Catholic chapel:

The Foundation Stone
of this edifice,
in honour of the Most Holy Trinity,
and dedicated to the Blessed Virgin Mary and
St Vincent of Paul,
was laid by Alexander Maconochie, R. N.,
Knight of the Guelphic Order of Hanover,
Superintendent of Norfolk Island,
the sacred rites
having been performed by the Rev. John MacEncroe,
assisted by the Rev. P. Farrelly and J.A.H.I. Harding,
under the authority of
the Right Reverend John Bede, Bishop
and Vicar Apostolic
of New Holland and Van Diemen's Land,
Sir George Gipps, Knight,
being Governor,
and Vicegerent of her Majesty,
Victoria, Queen of Great Britain,
whom may God long preserve.
25th July,
1840.[52]

The only name in the inscription not accompanied by a title is that of 'J.A.H.I.Harding'. The first two initials stand for 'Johannes Aloysius', while the 'H.I.' remains a mystery.

John Aloysius Harding, known in the family as Lewis, the English form of Aloysius, was the first child of John Cooke Harding and his wife Mary Trelawny. He was born on 13 April 1807 in London and baptised at the Catholic chapel of St Aloysius in Somers Town. Both parents were Catholic converts. Mary, daughter of the Reverend Sir Harry Trelawny, seventh baronet Trelawne, had converted at an early age through the influence of an émigré French priest sheltered at Tre-

52. *Australasian Chronicle*, 29 August 1840, page 4. Established in 1839, the *Chronicle* was Sydney's first Catholic newspaper. See C. F. Fowler, 'Anti-Catholic polemic at the origins of Australia's first Catholic newspaper', *Journal of the Australian Catholic Historical Society*, 37 (2016), 147–160.

lawne House in Cornwall.[53] The baron himself would convert and be ordained at Rome in 1830 at the age of 64. He had begun his ministry as a Presbyterian in 1777 at the age of 21, then drifted into Unitarianism, returning to Anglicanism and receiving holy orders in 1781.

In 1814, following the abdication of Emperor Napoleon and the restoration of the French Monarchy, the Harding family took up residence in Brittany. After a brief return to Cornwall following Napoleon's escape from Elba, the family re-established itself in France, where Lewis boarded at a Catholic college in Auray.[54] It was there that Lewis showed the first signs of erratic behaviour. In 1818 the family received a school report from Lewis' Jesuit master:

> He is a good child, and there is even something solid in him. But we think we have never seen a child as active and quick-tempered as he is. He is to be watched all the time . . . If we had any number like him, it would be impossible to get on. Happily, we do not note any tendency towards vice, which, together with a basic faith we observe in him, consoles us somewhat, and gives us hope that little by little, this unceasing tumult will die down.[55]

After his conversion, Sir Harry established a Catholic Mission at Trelawne and in 1831 engaged an Irish Dominican, James Vincent Corcoran, as chaplain. In 1834 the Dominican friar volunteered to join a group of Benedictine monks from Downside Priory in neighbouring Somerset, who were preparing to sail to New Holland. It is likely that Corcoran proposed Lewis as a late addition to Polding's

53. The Abbé Arzell was said to have frequented Trelawne House, 'when Sir Harry Trelawny was tending to Roman Catholicism' (Thomas Quiller Couch, 'A sketch of the life of Jonathan Couch' in Jonathan Couch, *The History of Polperro: a fishing town on the South coast of Cornwall,* Truro, 1871, p 5.)

54. The Harding parents kept a diary which provides much information about the family's life from 1812 to 1818. For the first year's entries see Philip Correll, 'John Cooke Harding's Journal', *South Western Catholic History,* 13(1995), 15ff. Napoleon's 'Hundred Days' put an end to the Downside monks' decision to return to France. Young Bede Polding had been opposed to the idea of return. See Birt, *Downside the history of St. Gregory's School from its commencement at Douay to the present time,* London, 1902, p. 169.

55. Philip Correll, *Lewis Harding: Cornwall's Pioneer Photographer,* Polperro, 2000, p 15. An expert in autism might be able to discern in this school report and in elements of the journals the presence of this condition in Harding.

missionary band. Harding was described as an 'ecclesiastical student' by fellow passenger John Kenny in his 1886 history of Australian Catholicism.[56] In his 1835 journal one can sense Lewis' excitement at being part of Bishop Polding's monastery-at-sea:

> On Sundays, prayers in the Bishop's cabin, read out of *Garden of the Soul*, the *Venite Exultemus* sung and played on the piano, terminating with a meditation and an instruction by the Bishop, always 'veramente bella e propria alla nostra situazione'[truly fine and appropriate for our needs]. In the evening the Compline and Litany of BVM [Blessed Virgin Mary] were sung with accompaniment. Also the Blessed Sacrament was kept in Mr. Fisher's cabin as long as he lived (about two months), where we met for night prayers, and afterwards in the Oratory that was made up.[57]

It was not all 'bells and smells' on board the *Oriental*; the ship was turned into a floating theological college, as described by Polding five weeks into the journey: 'I have commenced a course of Moral Theology with the young men; and the priests and myself hold a conference on the Sacraments three times each week.'[58]

Lewis several times referred nostalgically to Cornwall. He noted that on 21 April, the Tuesday evening of Easter week, at one of the many festive gatherings in Bishop Polding's cabin, 'the bowl went round to the health of those at Downside and Salford and Liverpool, and the scenes of olden times recorded . . . Nor was I unmindful in chiming in with a "here's a toast to friends in Cornwall" as well.' As the ship approached Hobart Town, Lewis commented: 'The low broken cliffs of Bruny Island on our right as far as Tasman's Head resemble very much that part of the coast between Looe and Polperro, beautiful as the Ausonian vales.'[59]

---

56. John Kenny, *A History of the Commencement and Progress of Catholicity in Australia up to the Year 1840*, Sydney 1886, p 68.
57. Ibid, volume 1, 255. Rev. Clement Fisher died at sea on 28 May. He joined the voyage seeking a warmer climate for health reasons, possibly consumption, as did many immigrants during the 19th Century.
58. Polding to Dom Luke Barber, 3 May 1835, 21 deg. W. Long., 5 deg. N. Lat. (Polding Letters I.53–54)..
59. Lewis Harding, *1835 Journal*, entries: 21 April 1835 & 3 August 1835.

The *Oriental* sailed through Sydney Heads on 13 September 1835. Harding concluded his journal: 'Anchored at 20 past 1 pm . . . Mr Plunkett sent his carriage for Dr Polding. At 3pm all went ashore. Dr Polding was cheered by the sailors who were ordered to have their extra glass.'[60]

Life in Sydney for the ecclesiastical students involved continuation of theological studies, teaching in the school, which Polding established at his Woollomooloo residence, and participation in the instruction of incoming convicts, an arrangement which Governor Bourke had approved at the request of the bishop. Vicar-General Bernard Ullathorne outlined the process:

> The catholic prisoners, who are about one third of those who arrive . . . remain ten days in Sydney before they are assigned, for the purpose of obtaining religious and other instruction . . . Our ecclesiastical students act as catechists . . . and after they [convicts] have gone through a series of religious exercises and through a series of individual converse with the clergy, they then . . . go through another series of instruction as regards their condition as prisoners . . . After this they proceed to their assignment.[61]

Harding also assisted the Bishop in his administrative tasks, especially during Ullathorne's absence in Europe in 1837 and 1838. Nor did Lewis neglect his familial bonds - on 30 April 1837, he shipped two cases of Australian butterfly and insect specimens to his father, addressed to 'J. C. Harding Esq., Trelawny, Polperro, Cornwall, care of Dr Couch, forward by Capt. Rowett, per *Statesman*.'[62]

On 15 March 1838, Harding was mentioned in a letter from the Bishop to the Colonial Secretary, Edward Deas Thomson, 'in reference to the appointment of the Reverend Mr. Harding to be Catechist of the Roman Catholic Prisoners at Norfolk Island':

> I have the honor to mention that he is prepared to proceed to his destination by the first conveyance . . . the services of Mr Harding at Norfolk Island will be most valuable in instructing, and consoling the Prison Population, and in preparing them

60. Birt I.257.
61. Quoted in Kenny op. cit., 75.
62. Correll 1996, op. cit., 58.

> for those ordinances of religion which only a Priest can administer, but which for various reasons, they could not for some time be permitted to participate.[63]

After requesting that Governor Gipps approve an annual salary of one hundred pounds, Polding stated that 'in the course of three or four months I shall be enabled to send a Priest to remain permanently at Norfolk Island'.

By this time the failure of the Bishop to provide a chaplain for the distant penal colony had become a source of great irritation to the Government. Within a few months after Governor Richard Bourke's arrival in December 1831, he had raised with Viscount Goderick the problem of the lack of any clergy on Norfolk Island.[64] Two years later it was Lord Stanley whom Bourke addressed:

> I take the liberty of again bringing under the notice of H. M. Government a matter of the greatest importance to this Penal Settlement, namely, the absolute necessity, as solicited in former despatches, both of a Protestant and a Roman Catholic Chaplain for Norfolk Island, where there is now no minister of Religion. I have felt continued regret at my inability to supply this deficiency.[65]

After almost another two years, the then Secretary for the Colonies in London, Lord Glenelg, despairing of the inability of the colony's Anglican Archdeacon, William Grant Broughton, to provide a chaplain, announced to Bourke that he would 'obtain the services of a Clergyman of some other denomination'.[66] The Reverend Thomas Atkins, an 'Independent Minister' arrived at the island in November 1836 and left in the following January, having condemned the system in place under Commandant Joseph Anderson.[67] In June 1836, Broughton, now 'Lord Bishop of Australia', managed to make a tem-

63. Polding to Colonial Secretary, 15 March 1838 (*Polding Letters* I.100).
64. Bourke to Goderick, 28 February 1832 (HRA XVI.542).
65. Bourke to Stanley, 15 January 1834 (HRA XVII.327–328).
66. Glenelg to Bourke, 30 November 1835 (HRA XVIII.204).
67. K. J. Cable, 'Atkins, Thomas (1808–1860)', *Australian Dictionary of Biography*, National Centre of Biography, Australian National University, http://adb.anu.edu.au/biography/atkins-thomas-1724/text1889, published first in hardcopy 1966, accessed online 4 July 2018.

porary appointment, sending Rev Thomas Sharpe to Norfolk island 'for the recovery of his health'. Sharpe would remain as chaplain until October 1841.

At the beginning of 1838 there was still no resident Catholic chaplain. Two Catholic priests had been prisoners at the first Norfolk Island penal settlement, having been banished from Ireland following the 1798 rising: James Harold, 1801–1808, and Peter O'Neil, 1801–1803. Both were recruited as teachers while prisoners on the island, and they engaged in unofficial ministry among their fellow Catholic prisoners. The second penal establishment, begun in 1825 after a gap of 11 years, received only a few passing visits from Catholic clergy sent to assist condemned prisoners to prepare for their executions. In September 1833 Father John Joseph Therry, still under formal Government suspension, joined Judge James Dowling in sailing to the island for the trial of prisoners accused of capital offences. Following the sentence of death Therry was present at the execution of two prisoners, as reported in the *Sydney Gazette*: 'On Monday morning, at the hour of nine, the whole of the prisoners on the island were placed in front of the scaffold, about two hundred yards from it; at right angles with them the soldiers were all drawn out; Connor looked very frightened, they knelt down, the priest between them, and sang a long hymn, and then prayed some time.'[68] On two separate occasions Father Bernard Ullathorne performed a similarly grim task, in September 1834 and again in November 1835. It was the impact of these experiences that led him to write so alarmingly of the horrors of Norfolk Island and witness so effectively at the Molesworth Commission of the House of Commons in 1838. Ullathorne's major concern, shared by clergy, Secretaries for the colonies and governors, was with 'the great evil', his oblique reference to sodomy. In his autobiography he recalled:

> Soon after my return to Sydney I placed the state of the convicts at Norfolk Island before Sir Richard Bourke, and strongly represented the great evil of their being locked up at night in the dark, without any division between the men and any watchman to control their conduct. I earnestly pointed out the necessity of partitions, lights, and watchmen under proper superintendence. But that was not effected until long

68. *Sydney Gazette*, 29 October 1833.

> afterwards, when the representations of Bishop Willson prevailed. But I put my attempt on record in my evidence before Sir William Molesworth's Committee in 1838.[69]

In the absence of permanent chaplains, the various commandants of Norfolk Island had made arrangements for Divine Service for their prisoners, soldiers, officials and families. From March to May 1835 two Quaker missionaries, James Backhouse and George Washington Walker lived on the island and participated in the Sunday services of Protestants and Roman Catholics. In his 1843 book, *A Narrative of a visit to the Australian Colonies,* Backhouse related his participation in a Catholic Sunday service:

> At two o'clock, we went with Major Anderson to the public worship of the Roman Catholic prisoners, which commences at the same hours as that of the Protestants, in a mess-room, in what is designated a Lumber-yard. The prayers were read by a prisoner, in English, except one, near the close, in Latin. This man is also said to have been educated for the ministry; he seems likewise to have some practical knowledge of the inward work of grace. He also read a well-arranged address, of his own preparing, inciting to practical piety; and which, in point of doctrine, would not, I suppose, have been considered faulty, by any Protestant congregation.[70]

The name of the prisoner said to have trained for the priesthood remains unknown. Backhouse reported that the address he was invited to give at the conclusion of the service was well received by the prisoners. The free residents of the Island, military and civilian, gathered separately in the military barracks and the Catholic service was led by a serjeant of the 50th regiment.

Ullathorne's principal reason for sailing to Europe in 1837 was the recruitment of clergy for the Vicariate of New Holland. He especially set himself to enlist a chaplain for Norfolk Island. He engaged Father John Brady, an experienced missionary, and proposed his appointment to Lord Glenelg, who wrote to Governor Bourke with the good news: 'As Mr. Brady is intended to officiate at Norfolk Island, his sal-

69. William Bernard Ullathorne, *Autobiography*, London 1891, 108–109.
70. James Backhouse, *A Narrative of a visit to the Australian Colonies*, London, 1843, 253.

ary of £150 per annum will be paid out of the Convict Fund.'[71] In April 1838, the new Governor, Sir George Gipps, had disappointing news for His Lordship in London - Brady, who had arrived on the same ship as Gipps, causally informed His Excellency 'that the Roman Catholic Archbishop, instead of sending him to Norfolk Island, had appointed him to the do duty at Windsor'[72]. On demanding an explanation from Polding, Gipps was told that Mr. Brady 'was not aware, till he arrived in the Colony, of the confined range of Duty on Norfolk Island; he has been accustomed to a more active life which he prefers.' Polding tried to appease the affronted Governor by claiming he had another priest, who 'has long desired to retire to a situation less arduous than that which circumstances required him to occupy' and who would proceed to Norfolk Island 'in the course of a short time.'[73] This priest was the Dominican Christopher Vincent Dowling, whose only wish was to stay put at Newcastle, where indeed he completed his ministry in 1873, dying at the age of 84.

It was in this awkward situation that Polding turned to Harding as an interim solution for Norfolk Island, as Gipps reported to Glenelg in his April despatch: '[T]he want of a Roman Catholic Clergyman will be in the meantime the less felt, as Mr. Harding, a Catechist of the Roman Catholic Church, has been very recently despatched to Norfolk Island from Sydney.'[74] Lord Glenelg replied sternly to the Brady saga in August, stipulating that 'Her Majesty's Government considered that Dr Ullathorne had become pledged by the arrangement respecting Mr. Brady', and that Brady would not receive any portion of the £150 salary if he remained in New South Wales, and that 'the £100 advanced for his passage must be repaid'.[75] By this time Harding was well settled on the island, having sailed from Sydney on 18 March.

Lord Glenelg was later informed by Gipps that two priests had sailed to Norfolk Island in August:

> I have the honor to report to your Lordship that two Roman Catholic Clergymen, the Revd. Mr. McEncroe and the Revd.

71. Glenelg to Bourke, 2 October 1837 (HRA XIX,110).
72. Gipps to Glenelg, 7 April 1838 (HRA XIX, 362).
73. Polding to Gipps, 15 March 1838 (HRA XIX, 362).
74. Gipps to Glenelg, 7 April 1838 (HRA XIX, 362).
75. Glenelg to Gipps, 28 August 1838 (HRA XIX, 560).

> Mr. Gregory, were sent by their Bishop (Dr Polding) to Norfolk Island in the Government Vessel, which sailed from Sydney on the 19th August last. I have sanctioned the issue of rations to both Clergymen, as well as to Mr. Harding the Catechist . . . but it is distinctly understood that they are to have among them no more than the Salary of £150 authorised by your Lordship's despatch of the 2nd Oct, 1837.[76]

Polding had asked for a stipend of £200, 'which Stipend I believe the Revd. Sharp receives'. He based his application for the increase on the need to support two priests, there being a reluctance on the part of his clergy to be alone on the island, 'inasmuch as by reason of his distant situation he will there be deprived of the ministrations and Consolations of a Brother Clergyman'. This was an ideal to which the bishop aspired so that no priest would be without the opportunity of receiving absolution in the confessional. The ideal was rarely achieved; one wit among the colonial clergy commented that he was so far from his neighbouring priest that to travel for confession was 'too distant for a venial sin and too dangerous for a mortal'.

Polding had obviously been informed by Harding about the state of accommodation at the settlement, for he complained to the Governor that Rev. Sharpe had moved into the house built for the Catholic chaplain: 'To prevent misunderstanding, I submit to your excellency's consideration that in as much as the several Dwellings were erected for their distinct purposes – directions may be given to enable the R.C. Chaplain to occupy the House erected to be his residence if he think fit.'[77] Perhaps it was because of Gipps' refusal to grant the higher stipend, that the chaplains did not depart in August, as Gipps had informed London, but were kept back until 17 October: 'The brig Governor Phillip, for Norfolk Island. Passengers — The Rev. Messrs M'Encroe and Gregory, R. C. C., Mr Stewart, one officer, a detachment of soldiers, and seventy prisoners of the crown.'[78]

Nor did Gipps act on Polding's request regarding the clergy housing. Major Thomas Bunbury, who took over as commandant in Janu-

---

76. Gipps to Glenelg, 28 November 1838 (HRA XIX, 686). McEncroe and Gregory left Sydney aboard the Government brig, *Governor Phillip*, on 17 October 1838 (*Australian* 18 October 1838, p2).
77. Polding to Gipps, July-August 1838 (Polding Letters, I.108–109).
78. *Australian*, 18 October 1838, p2.

ary 1839, inherited the unresolved controversy. In his Reminiscences he recounted how he dealt with the conflict between the Protestant and Catholic chaplains: 'Besides the Protestant clergyman, we had two Catholic priests and a coadjutor . . . The ministers of religion on the island did not however agree together.' He cited 'attempted proselytism and jealousy' as the underlying problems, exacerbated by the controversy over accommodation. On his arrival, the Catholic party requested 'an immediate ejectment' of the Rev. Sharpe and his family from the house originally designated for the Catholic chaplain. Bunbury found a solution in the fact that as well as houses, gardens had also been supplied for chaplains. The Catholic garden grant in possession of Rev. McEncroe far exceeded in quality that of Rev. Sharpe. Bunbury explained to McEncroe that if he persisted in obtaining Sharpe's house, he would have also to exchange gardens. After some discussion McEncroe 'preferred remaining as he was.' Bunbury concluded by commenting that 'the disputants attended the parties at Government House at first in rotation, but afterwards together, and I was glad to see that they latterly became greater friends.'[79] Bunbury's brief appointment came to an end in September 1839, following a soldiers' mutiny. He was succeeded by Major Ryan, well known to McEncroe.

Contrary to Bunbury's claim of friendship between chaplains, the Reverend Thomas Sharpe's extensive diary indicated the continuation of clergy conflict over 'attempted proselytism and jealousy'. Soon after Harding's arrival, Sharpe, having described him as 'quiet and friendly', commented with some relief: 'Notwithstanding Mr Harding's arrival, the R.C. in the Jail attend Divine Service as usual.'[80] He would soon lose that section of his congregation and more. He commented on the arrival of McEncroe and Gregory: 'We have two Romanist priests here, who are great favourites.'[81] This jealousy persisted throughout his stay on the island; the diary is peppered with complaints about favours granted to the Romanist clergy, to Catholic convicts appointed as overseers, and alarm at members of his flock

79. Thomas Bunbury, *Reminiscences of a veteran: being personal and military adventures in Portugal, Spain, France, Malta, New South Wales, Norfolk Island, New Zealand, Andaman Islands, and India*, 3 vols., London, 1861, volume 2, 320–322.

80. Thomas Sharpe, *Journal on Norfolk Island, 1837–1840*, manuscript, NSW State Library (B 217–B 218), entry for 10 April 1838, p 264.

81. Sharpe, *Journal*, entry for 30 November 1838, 299.

being 'anew baptised by the popish priests'.[82] In October 1839 he again referred to Harding:

> The Romanist priests, here as elsewhere, have a wonderful propensity to make proselytes and to shew favour to those who embrace their opinions, as a means of inducing others to imitate their example. A young man some time ago notorious for infamous conduct, since the arrival of Mr. Harding became a Romanist.[83]

Such repeated whinging did not endear him to the settlement's officials.

One of those officials was the assistant-surgeon Dr James Stuart (1802–1842). Stuart was an Irish surgeon and naturalist, who arrived in the Colony in 1834 and was appointed to Sydney's North Head Quarantine Station. In 1839 he was sent to Norfolk Island, returning to Sydney in January 1841. He illustrated many species of birds, insects and fish during his time at the penal settlement. In February 1840 the *Sydney Gazette* reported:

> We have been favored by Dr Stuart, Colonial Assistant Surgeon of New South Wales, with a sight of all the natural curiosities of Norfolk Island, amongst which are drawings of above one hundred kinds of fish, beautifully executed and entirely different from anything of the kind we have ever seen. Besides these, we have seen drawings of reptiles and birds, beautifully executed and as different.[84]

It was probably Stuart who encouraged Harding's interest in natural science, which led to the encyclopedic knowledge which Lewis displayed in his 1846 Journal. His scientific knowledge and sharp observation and sketches of birds and marine life during that voyage probably owed much to Stuart's influence. In May 1842 Stuart died of typhus contracted from passengers on disease-ridden ships, whom he attended at the quarantine station.

---

82. Sharpe, *Journal*, entry for 10 December 1838, 307.
83. Sharpe, *Journal*, entry for 19 October 1839. 509.
84. *Sydney Gazette and New South Wales Advertiser*, 13 February 1840, page 2. Many of his paintings are held by the New South Wales Archives and by the Mitchell Library. See A. Musgrave, *Dr James Stuart: Artist Naturalist*, Sydney, 1955.

The prominence given to the name of Alexander Maconochie in the inscription of the chapel foundation stone was an expression of the honour in which he was held by the Catholic chaplains. He had been welcomed as a reforming superintendent of the penal colony of Norfolk Island, which over the past fifteen years had the reputation of being 'Hell in Paradise'.[85] In a footnote to the *Chronicle*, its scholarly editor, William Augustine Duncan, compared pre-Maconochie Norfolk Island to the Aegean island of Patmos, 'the penal settlement of ancient Imperial Rome, about twenty miles in circumference, just the size of its modern rival'. The more common comparison was with Sodom and Gomorrah of the Book of Genesis.[86]

The provision of the island's first places of worship was an early sign of the changes Maconochie would bring. Governor George Gipps, not uncritical of the new superintendent's penal system, in his report to Lord Stanley following his much-delayed visit to Norfolk Island in March 1843, noted with approval the two chapels built by Captain Maconochie; he commented that 'though the erection of them without authority was made a matter of charge against him, I cannot but speak in terms of commendation of them, and bear witness to the humanizing effect, which attendance at them seems to be producing in the minds of the Prisoners.'[87]

In 1837 Captain Maconochie had accompanied Lieutenant-Governor Sir John Franklin to Van Diemen's land as his private secretary. Before sailing, he had been commissioned by the Society for the Improvement of Prison Discipline to report on the treatment of convicts. His report was published in London as a parliamentary paper

85. On Maconochie's reforms see J. V. Barry, *Alexander Maconochie of Norfolk Island – a study of a pioneer in penal reform*, OUP, Melbourne, 1958.

86. The *Monitor* referred to Norfolk Island as 'Gomorrah Island' (*Monitor*, 6 April 1827, p 4).

87. Sir George Gipps to Lord Stanley, 1 April 1843 (HDA, XXII, 632). A detailed description of the Catholic chapel was sent to the *Chronicle* from 'Alumnus' and published in two articles (10 & 12 August 1841, p 2). Joseph Spruson, in a summary of the history of Norfolk Island prepared for Governor Loftus in 1885, noted that the chapels 'have long since fallen into decay'. [*Norfolk Island: outline of its history from 1788 to 1884*, Sydney 1885, p 24]. In undated notes by Fr. Harry Moore on events and clergy on the island, the following comments are found on the year 1870: 'pulpit from St Vincent de Paul chapel to Lifou Is., New Caledonia'; 'dark marble holy water font moved to St Barnabas Melanesian Chapel' (Norfolk Island file, Sydney Archdiocesan Archives [SAA]).

and tabled at the Molesworth committee in 1838. His criticism of official policy led to his dismissal by Franklin. However, the Select Committee was impressed with his proposed 'new system' and recommended that it be trialled. The Marquess of Normanby, Secretary for the Colonies in the new Whig ministry, proposed to Governor George Gipps that Maconochie be appointed as superintendent of Norfolk Island. Though doubtful of the new system producing any great results among the island's convicts, Gipps expressed 'great faith in the principles on which his experiments are to be founded'.[88]

Those principles were succinctly expressed in Maconochie's address to the group of 199 Irish convicts who landed at the island with him and his family on 6 March 1840. In April the text was forwarded to the editor of the *Australasian Chronicle* by 'Nautilus', 'your obedient servant'. This was the first of many letters and documents sent to William Augustine Duncan during Maconochie's term of office from March 1840 to February 1844. The covering letter began and ended enthusiastically:

> I enclose for you a copy of the 'Exposition', given by Captain Maconochie to the prisoners at Norfolk Island, of the practical working of his system. It explains in a few pages the end and object of his views on prison discipline. No reflecting man can doubt of its ultimate success . . . A new era has certainly commenced where 'no order, but perpetual horror, used to dwell' - one proof at least of the utility of trying 'the social system'.[89]

Maconochie's 'exposition' set forth the object of the new system to improve and reform the prisoners. There were to be two stages in this process – punishment for the past and probation or training for the future. Good conduct at each stage would be rewarded by the granting of 'marks', the accumulation of which would lead eventually to freedom; bad conduct would lead to loss of marks. The 'mark system' served both as a form of wages for labour and a fine for misbehaviour. The system provided hope and incentive for advancing from punishment to probation to ultimate release. The new system placed the fate of the prisoner 'entirely in his own hands'. A final element led to

88. Gipps to Normanby, 33 November 1839 (HRA XX, 403).
89. *Australasian Chronicle*, 17 April 1840, p 2.

the plan initially being called the 'social system' - the probation stage would involve forming prisoners into groups of six, who would be held 'severally responsible for each other's conduct and will gain or lose marks according to the behaviour of each': 'The superintendent trusts that, among all, it will restrain the evil-disposed, and give influence and authority to the well-disposed, beyond any other means that he can devise.'

He concluded his address with confidence in transforming Norfolk Island: 'In conclusion, the object and purport of the whole system will thus be seen to be the conversion of this whole penal settlement from a scene of prolonged suffering, too often degenerating into a scene of aggravated and continued misconduct, into a field of moral reform and probation, for an early return to society.' He also had a message of hope for the 'old hands' on the island, the doubly or triply convicted – he intended 'at the earliest possible period' to bring them under the new system.[90] He quickly pressed ahead with this commitment, despite not receiving government permission; it was a decision that led to his eventual dismissal and abandonment of the 'Merits System of Penal Discipline'.

The Catholic newspaper the *Australasian Chronicle* was forthright in its support for the new system. The editor regularly published letters from 'our Norfolk Island correspondent' during Maconochie's administration. Father John McEncroe was the most obvious source of this regular reporting. Letters from the island sometimes carried a pseudonym: 'Nautilus' (5 March 1840, p 2; 3 April 1840, p 2); 'An Eyewitness' (17 March 1840, p 2); 'Vivat Victoria' (23 June 1840, p 2); 'Vindex Junior' (27 June 1840, p 2). 'Nautilus' was most likely the pseudonym of the deputy-surgeon, James Aquinas Reid, recruited by Maconochie more for his musical skills than for his medical prowess, and who arrived at the island aboard the ship *Nautilus*, in company with the superintendent.[91] 'Vindex Junior' was possibly Lewis Harding, the junior member of the Catholic chaplaincy team. McEncroe, the 'esteemed correspondent', also kept the *Chronicle*'s editor supplied with copies of Captain Maconochie's regular addresses and 'orders' to

---

90. Ibid.
91. Maconochie, Reid and Duncan were Scots; Reid and Duncan were Catholics. For the importance of music in Maconochie's 'System' see Alan Maddox, 'On the machinery of moral improvement: music and prison reform in the penal colony of Norfolk Island', *Musicology Australia*, 34(2012), 185–205.

prisoners. Within a period of three weeks, beginning on 29 August 1840, six such documents were published in the *Chronicle*.[92] Even though most Sydney newspapers abandoned support for Maconochie after his 'indulgences' to the convicts at the celebration of Queen Victoria's birthday on 25 May 1840, the *Chronicle* and its Norfolk Island correspondents remained supportive.[93]

However, the attitude of W. A. Duncan's newspaper to the reforming superintendent underwent a dramatic change in 1842. Reports of the seizure of the brig *Governor Philip* by convicts in June 1842, during which one soldier and five convict-pirates were killed, led to an intensification of hostility in Sydney to the Maconochie experiment, and to a change of heart of his few remaining supporters. Even Duncan now expressed doubts about the new system:

> We regret to state that the accounts of the relapsed state of this settlement recently published are but too well confirmed by the intelligence just received by the 'Governor Phillip' . . . Indeed, from all we can learn, Captain Maconochie's philanthropic effort is destined to terminate in a manner very different from that which every good man must have wished. For our own part, we can truly say our disappointment is great in the extreme.[94]

Governor Gipps, however, was surprisingly sanguine about the 'piracy' in his report to Lord Stanley. Unlike the Sydney press, he did not blame the Maconochie system: 'The late attempt to take the Government Brig . . . was I believe only a solitary act of desperation.' He interpreted the mutiny as arising from the 'irksome restraint' still in place on the island, 'notwithstanding the relaxed nature of the discipline to which the Prisoners are now subject'.[95] Of no surprise was the very different interpretation of the cause of the mutiny given by the *Sydney Morning Herald* at the conclusion of the trial: '[T]he main feature of this atrocious affair . . . is that it is one of the practical fruits of

92. *Australasian Chronicle*, 29 August, 1840; 3, 5, 10, 12, 15 September 1840.
93. Sydney's *Commercial Journal and Advertiser* (4 July 1840) also remained supportive. The *Herald* listed the Queen's birthday 'indulgences': 'delectable climate and fruits, cricket matches, Hogsheads of Lemonade with libations of Rum, plays, idleness, speeches, bands of music' (*Herald*, Supplement, 1 July 1840, 1).
94. *Australasian Chronicle*, 16 July 1842 page 2.
95. Sir George Gipps to Lord Stanley, 15 August 1840 (HRA, XXII, 207–208).

that wildest of all wild theories of penal nursery-government hatched by this mawkish sentimentalism of Captain Maconochie.'[96]

Duncan's misgivings about Maconochie's system had first been revealed in the *Chronicle* in April 1842:

> NORFOLK ISLAND -We regret to learn, by communications from this settlement, that Captain Maconochie's indulgence has been entirely lost on many of the hardened wretches there confined, and that robberies, violence, and unnatural crimes are now nearly as prevalent as they were under the old regime. It is thought even by those who were most friendly to the Captain, and the warmest supporters of his system, that he has pushed indulgence beyond the bounds of discretion.[97]

In May Duncan repeated his growing concern in response to a correspondent, *Humanidad*, who defended Maconochie against the increasing criticism:

> We are as anxious as Captain Maconochie himself can be to see the triumph of his humane system, which we believe to be the best ever yet tried, but we cannot consent to a suppression of facts; and we are assured by a gentleman residing on the island, who is incapable of deceiving us, that on no occasion since the formation of the settlement 'have there been so many daring robberies as within the last few weeks'.[98]

The 'gentleman residing on the island' was Father McEncroe, formerly 'most friendly to the Captain'. In March 1842 McEncroe had gathered together three letters written to Maconochie and six to Governor Gipps with the intention of having them published as a pamphlet.[99]

96. *Sydney Morning Herald*, 21 October 1842, page 2.

97. *Australasian Chronicle*, 28 April 1842, page 2. The communications from Norfolk Island included McEncroe's draft of a pamphlet for publication, which was severely critical of Maconochie.

98. *Australasian Chronicle*, 7 May 1842, page 2. The letter of 'Humanidad' carried the Latin heading, *Audi alteram partem* ('Let the other side be heard').

99. For the letters to Gipps see R. A. Daly, 'Archdeacon McEncroe on Norfolk Island, 1838–42', *Australasian Catholic Record*, 36(1959), 285–305; for those to Maconochie see the editor's article in a forthcoming number of *Australasian Catholic Record*.

He explained his motive in a brief preface to the appendix of the draft pamphlet:

> Every person, in whose heart the feelings of Religion and humanity are not extinguished, is bound to use his best efforts towards the suppression of those crimes that cry to heaven for vengeance. The following letters were written under the influence of such feelings. No step has been taken, as yet, in this momentous matter; it is then, in order to call the attention of the public authorities to this crying evil, that the letters are given to the public through the medium of the Press.[100]

The proposed title page graphically revealed the theme of the correspondence:

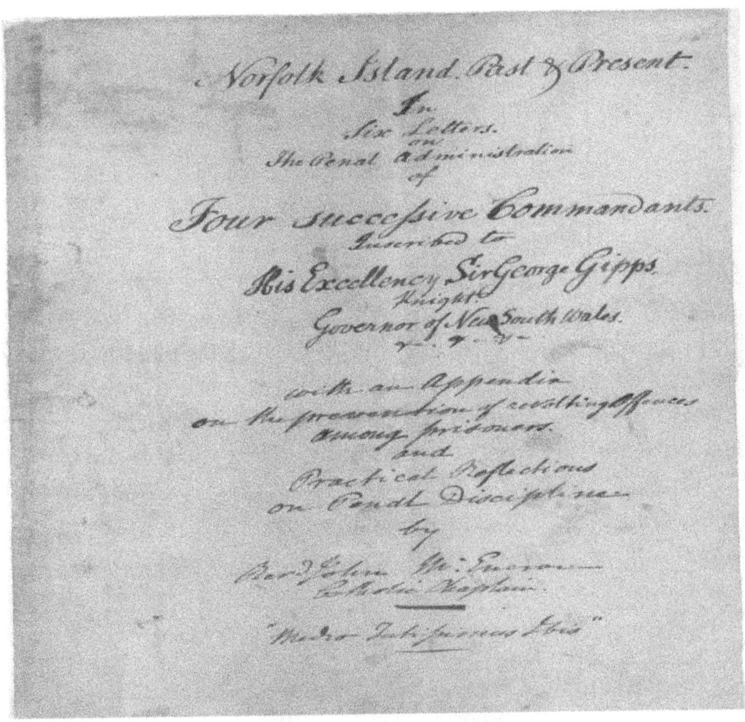
Norfolk Island Past & Present.
In
Six Letters
on
The Penal Administration
of
Four successive Commandants.
Inscribed to
His Excellency Sir George Gipps
Knight
Governor of New South Wales.
&c. &c. &c.
with an Appendix
on the prevention of revolting offences
among prisoners
and
Practical Reflections
on Penal Discipline
by
Revd John McEncroe
Catholic Chaplain
"Medio Tutissimus Ibis"

Figure 5: title page of John McEncroe's 1842 draft pamphlet in handwriting of Lewis Harding (compare with Figures 8, 10, 11)

100. The manuscript is held in the SAA, Box A0388.

Norfolk Island Past & Present.
In
Six Letters
on
The Penal Administration
of
Four successive Commandants.
Inscribed to
His Excellency Sir George Gipps,
Knight.
Governor of New South Wales.
&c &c &c
with an Appendix
on the prevention of revolting offences
among prisoners
and
Practical Reflections
on Penal Discipline
by
Revd John McEncroe
Catholic Chaplain

'Medio Tutissimus Ibis'[101]

The appendix contained the three letters to Maconochie, the first of which was written as early as August 1840. The writing in the manuscript pamphlet is not that of McEncroe; the title page and first letter are clearly from the hand of Lewis Harding.[102] The other letters were perhaps transcribed by the assistant chaplain, Richard Walsh.[103] The manuscript was most probably submitted for publication to William Duncan at the *Chronicle*, who in 1841 had published McEncroe's collection of letters written on Norfolk Island, *The wanderings of the human mind in searching the scriptures . . . in a series of letters to a*

101. 'In the middle you will go most safely' (Ovid, *Metamorphoses*, Book II, line 137). The three letters to Maconochie were dated 10 August 1840, 22 March and 28 June 1841.

102. Compare with Figures 8, 10 and 11 below.

103. Richard Walsh (1815–1868), recruited for Sydney from Waterford Seminary in 1838; ordained 1839; on Norfolk Island 1841–1845.

candid inquirer after truth.[104] However, the pamphlet did not make it into print.

Duncan's growing disillusionment was compounded by a letter received from Lewis Harding at Norfolk Island and published in the *Chronicle* three days after the report of the attempted seizure of the brig *Governor Philip*. Harding concluded his saga of the mutiny: 'The game is up, if it be acknowledged there is any mischief in the atrocities daily perpetrated here, besides the present instance.'[105] The letter was published anonymously; its provenance was later explained by Duncan and Harding himself. Duncan stated that the letter had been sent by 'a resident on the island to a gentleman in Sydney, who presented it to us for publication, requesting us at the same time to strike out the writer's name.'[106] Harding explained that he had sent it to a friend, 'who had been for some time in an official capacity' on Norfolk Island.[107] A likely recipient of the private letter was Dr Patrick Harnett, the Catholic surgeon on Norfolk Island at the time of Harding's arrival there in March 1838.[108]

The impact of the publication of the letter was summarised by deputy-surgeon Dr James Reid in a letter to a colleague in Sydney:

> You must have seen the papers teeming with articles on the subject of the late attempt to seize the Governor Philip here. One of these was by its bombastic style supposed to be the production of the R. Catholic catechist of this place, who is remarkable for his flowery and absurd language. He admitted it partly and was instantly suspended and ordered off the island by Captain Maconochie. The Revd. Mr. McEncroe, R. C. Clergyman, was not a little indignant, and determined

---

104. John McEncroe, *The Wanderings of the Human Mind in Searching the Scriptures, being a concise history of the origin, progress and condemnation of the principal heresies that have arisen in the several ages of Christianity from the private interpretation of the Holy Bible, in a series of letters to a candid inquirer after truth*, W.A. Duncan, Sydney, 1841.
105. *Australasian Chronicle*, 19 July 1842, page 2.
106. *Australasian Chronicle*, 6 October 1842 page 2.
107. L. Harding to the Editor, *Australasian Chronicle*, 8 October 1842 page 1.
108. Patrick Harnett had arrived on the island in October 1836 as assistant-surgeon; he returned to Sydney as Colonial Surgeon with his wife and child in December 1838 (*Sydney Gazette and New South Wales Advertiser*, 4 December 1838, p 2). He died suddenly in September 1844; the jury at the inquest returned a verdict of 'Died by the Visitation of God' (*Morning Chronicle*, 18 September 1844, page 2).

> to proceed himself to Sydney to lay the case before Sir G. G. [Governor Sir George Gipps].[109]

A week after the arrival of McEncroe and Harding back in Sydney in October 1842, the Vicar-General, Father Francis Murphy, wrote to the Colonial Secretary, Edward Deas Thomson, in defence of Harding:

> After carefully comparing the minute of Captain Maconochie, charging Mr. Harding with a 'moral official and malicious Libel', Mr. Harding's answer to the same, and the evidence taken before His Honor the Chief Justice on the trial of the Mutineers, I can see no just grounds for the arbitrary order of Captain Maconochie by which Mr. Harding has been sent away from Norfolk Island. If there be any libel in the case, it appears to me to have been incurred by Captain Maconochie in publishing an Official Document not sustained by Facts and Evidence, which has cast a most serious imputation on the Roman Catholic Catechist, who has conducted himself for several years without reproach at that Penal settlement.
> Therefore, although Mr. Harding has no wish to return to the Island, yet in regard to the imputation attempted officially to be fixed on his character, I beg respectfully to submit to the consideration of His Excellency the Governor, the propriety of causing the Order to be rescinded, by which Captain Maconochie caused Mr. Harding to be removed without any just or sufficient cause.[110]

Father Richard Walsh, the assistant chaplain on the island, gave his version of the affair in a letter to Father Patrick Geoghegan in Melbourne:

> Norfolk Island at present is in a very unsettled state. Captain Maconochie is sending Mr. Harding off the Island for writing an article in the *Chronicle* about the taking of the Brig. He has endeavoured to injure him in every way and even exposed his

109. James Aquinas Reid (Norfolk Island) to Henry Curzon Allport (Kissing Point), 27 September 1842; State Library of New South Wales, ML, MS Ar26/3 (Document 3 in Dr Graeme Skinner's website 'Australharmony': http://sydney.edu.au/paradisec/australharmony/reid-james-aquinas.php [accessed 30 July 2018]).

110. Murphy to Colonial Secretary, 20 October 1842 (SAA, P Books [transcribed P71], Letter 374).

> life to the fury of prisoners by circulating among them that Mr. Harding was their enemy and that he was writing against them. I hope he will pay for this, as Mr. Harding is to take an action against him. Rev. Mr. McEncroe is returning to Sydney by the same Barque and I fear he will not come back as he is disgusted with the old Captain's management of the prisoners, so that I am left alone to do the best I can.[111]

Harding did not take legal action, but he did continue a 'bombastic' exchange of letters with Maconochie in the *Australasian Chronicle*.[112]

Back in Sydney, Harding resumed his teaching at St Mary's Seminary, as recollected by Dr Frederick Milford in his memoirs. Reminiscing about his school days at St Mary's, he recalled that he and his brothers were 'principally instructed' by 'a Mr. Harding who had taken deacon's orders but could not be prevailed upon to become a priest'; 'he paid us every attention holding catechism classes and giving us good advice of all kinds'; 'Mr. Hardinge was a great favourite with all the family'.[113]

In August 1845, on behalf of the Archbishop, Lewis wrote a letter to the English agent of the Archdiocese, Dom Paulinus Heptonstall: 'The Archbishop being so much preoccupied with affairs at this present moment has desired me to write to you the few following commissieres by the ship *Ganges* which sails this evening for London.'[114]

111. Rev. Richard Walsh to Geoghegan 21/9/1842 (Brian Condon, *Letters and Documents in 19th Century Australian Catholic History* [*http://www.library.unisa.edu.au/condon/CatholicLetters*; accessed 30 January 2018]).
Patrick Bonaventure Geoghegan (1805–1864), Franciscan friar, arrived in Sydney in 1837 and sent the following year to open the first mission at Port Philip, later Melbourne; in 1858 appointed second bishop of Adelaide.
112. *Australasian Chronicle*, 6 & 8 October, 20 & 22 December 1842.
113. *Reminiscences of Frederick Milford* (V3051/31), University of New England and Regional Archives (AO465), n.d. The widow, Eliza Milford, was among a group of wives of prominent Sydney Catholics who came to the monastery the day before embarkation with provisions for the Archbishop and Lewis (see J. Lewis Harding, *1846 Journal*, 4.)
114. Harding to D. Heptonstall OSB, 16 August 1845 (cited in Philip Correll, 'Lewis Harding: photographer of Polperro', typescript, 1996 [Mitchell Library MLMSS 6119], 73–74).
Thomas Paulinus Heptonstall OSB (1798–1869): a cousin of Polding, educated at Acton Burnell and ordained priest at Downside in 1827. He was for many years the English agent for Archbishop Polding and other Australian bishops. Polding affectionately called him 'Hep'.

He followed the business matters of the letter with local news, concluding with reference to unwelcome changes at Norfolk Island:

> The Home Government are introducing new regulations regarding Catholic Clergymen entrusted with the care of the Prisoners in Van Diemen's Land and Norfolk Island, quite repugnant to the spirit and discipline of the Catholic Church and robbing it of its spiritual rights . . .[115]
>
> I have the honor to be
> Dear Reverend Sir,
> Your very humble obedient servant,
> L. Harding.

Sickness was a theme of Lewis' life, and was perhaps the reason he did not persevere in his ecclesiastical vocation.[116] Chronic illness seems to have set in after his return from Norfolk Island. Frederick Milford, who at the time of writing his memoirs was a renowned Sydney surgeon, recalled that it was about twelve months after the arrival of the Milford family in January 1843 that Lewis contracted rheumatic fever and that 'he was laid up during three months and after the fever left him he was crippled by heart affection having had a bad attack of pericarditis during the progress of his illness.'[117]

His condition was noted in his own words during his brief term as chronicler at St Mary's Monastery. The entry dated 8 October 1845

115. In September 1844, following the cessation of transportation to New South Wales, administration of Norfolk Island was transferred to Van Diemen's Land. The Lieutenant-Governor placed chaplains employed in the convict department under the civil authorities, causing much conflict with the Anglican and Catholic bishops. On his arrival in England Polding wrote to Bishop Willson of Hobart summarising the origins of the 'the infraction of Church Discipline involved in the present regulations for the Convict Department . . . [It] is of the greatest advantage to us that Lord Grey is in office and not Lord Stanley, for as these Regulations were devised by the latter and he is proverbially obstinate and has adopted as a maxim that whosoever is paid by the State is a servant of the State, under its control and to do its bidding, there can be no room for doubt as to the difficulties which would have been in our way.' See Appendix II: Polding to Bishop Willson, 24 August 1846 (*Polding Letters* II.61–62).

116. The theme emerges throughout the 1846 Journal.

117. Pericarditis is the inflammation of the thin tissue sac that surrounds the heart. The main symptom is chest pain, which can radiate towards the neck, shoulders, arms and back.

began: 'Br Lewis, who commences this day to write this book, is weak and sickly; [he] recommends himself to the prayers of the reader'. Written vertically was the heading 'Sickness', and the whole entry took up the gloomy theme:

> Revd Mr Hallinan taken ill and confined to bed.
> Revd Mr Geoghegan at present dangerously ill from an inflammation of the lungs, occasioned by the heavy ministerial duties imposed upon him in consequence of the recent departure of the Revd Mr Walsh.
> Lewis Duncan, 10 yrs old, formerly of the Seminary, son of W. A. Duncan, formerly editor of the Chronicle, died this morning of palpitations.
> Bishop Pompallier who arrived here from New Zealand is beginning to recover from a dangerous attack of pleuresy which was thought very dangerous a few days ago.
> The Revd Young likewise has just escaped the jaws of death.
> Dr Gregory is also sickly and fainted last Sunday while making his speech at St Patrick's Meeting.[118]

The next entry in the journal, dated 12 October 1845, was in another hand - Lewis' crabbed handwriting was replaced by a more florid style. On Monday, 16 February 1846, the monastic chronicler recorded: 'The Archbishop and the Rev. Mr. Harding sailed for Europe in the Ratcliffe.'[119]

There was speculation in newspapers about the reason for Polding's return to Europe so soon after his last visit. The Reverend John Dunmore Lang repeated one rumour in a ranting letter against papal ambitions in Australia and the Pacific: 'He has since been in Europe about five years ago and was made an Archbishop. He is now on his

118. *Ecclesiastical Transactions of the Archdiocese of Sydney* ('Benedictine Journal 1843–1860'), SAA.

119. There has been speculation about Harding's ecclesiastical status. The fact that he acted as monastery chronicler, even though briefly, indicates that he was a member of the Benedictine community, as does his styling himself 'B. Lewis' (Brother Lewis). He was often referred to as 'Reverend' - as early as March 1838 in a Polding letter and as late as February 1846 in the Benedictine Journal - suggesting that he had received some form of Holy Orders, either minor or diaconal. However, there is no record either of profession of vows or ordination. See T. Kavenagh, 'Profession dates (and others) of the monks of St Mary's, Sydney', *Tjurunga* 48(1985), 69–75.

way thither again, for a Cardinal's or 'scarlet coloured' hat, it is said, but certainly to strengthen and extend Romish influence with a view to Romish domination in these uttermost parts of the earth.'[120]

The *Ratcliff*, also spelt *Radcliffe*, a wooden ship of 740 tons, was a relatively new vessel, built at Whitby in 1842.[121] She was engaged as a convict ship under the command of Captain James Gilbert with surgeon-superintendent Dr Robert Dobie. She sailed from Dublin in May 1845 transporting 215 Irish male prisoners and 47 rank and file of the 11th regiment to Van Diemen's Land, arriving in Hobart Town at the end of August.[122] She sailed for Sydney after three weeks, having swapped her human cargo for local products including 10 boxes of sperm candles, 20 hogsheads of brandy, 4 casks of porter, 1 case of kangaroo skins and 11 casks of bottled beer, part of the original Irish cargo.[123] The *Ratcliff*'s departure from Sydney was announced early in January: 'FOR LONDON THE FINE SHIP RATCLIFF: James Gilbert, commander, has one stern and two side cabins disengaged, and carries an experienced Surgeon. For freight of wool, or passage, apply to the Captain, on board.'[124] Archbishop Polding booked the stern cabin for himself and Lewis.[125] The ship finally sailed on 16 February with five passengers, including Dr Dobie. The cargo consisted of 2336 bales of wool, 1000 hides, 80 bags of bark, 36 casks of tallow, 2 tons of coconut oil and 40 tons of bones and horns.[126]

Two days before embarkation advertisements appeared offering places on steamers which would accompany the *Ratcliff* to the Heads. One offer included onboard dancing:

120. Letter to editor, *Sydney Morning Herald*, 14 March 1846, 3; also *The Sentinel*, 19 February 1846, 2.
121. Bateson, Charles, *The Convict Ships 1787–1868*, Glasgow, 1939, p 270. The ship's name was variously spelt 'Radcliffe', 'Ratcliff' and Radcliff'.
122. *Courier* (Hobart Town), 3 September 1845, p 2.
123. *Courier*, 24 September 1845, p 2.
124. *Sydney Morning Herald*, 6 January 1846.
125. Polding regretted the choice of the stern cabin: 'The Archbishop remarks about his stern cabin that he would advise no one to take that cabin from experience. His Grace says it is the most uncomfortable part of the ship, being the furthest removed from the centre of motion, it consequently rises up and down through the greatest space; the noise of the chains at the wheel is incessant' (Harding, *1846 Journal*, entry: 28 February 1846, p 23).
126. *Sydney Morning Herald*, 31 January 1846.

DEPARTURE OP HIS GRACE THE ARCHBISHOP OF SYDNEY.

> EDWARD BERMINGHAM begs to inform his friends and the public generally that he has engaged the fine steamer COMET, for the purpose of accompanying His Lordship outside the Heads, on Monday next. To leave the Circular Wharf at ten o'clock A.M.
> Refreshments can be had on board on reasonable terms.
> Double tickets 5s. 0d. Single tickets 2s. 6d. Children half-price.
> A first-rate Quadrille Band will be in attendance.[127]

Harding began writing his journal at St Mary's monastery the day before sailing.

Eleven weeks into the voyage, which, at that stage, Lewis found 'irksome in the extreme', he began to excuse himself as 'too unwell to write' and even despaired of his 'complaint':

> The heat and food and altogether seems to have so far disagreed with me also, as to bring on again the attacks of my complaint, which I had some slight hope the voyage would have removed. The Archbishop now tells me the doctor thinks <u>7 years</u> may not bring an end to this my purgatory. It will require that time at least to effect a sensible recovery with proper care and precautions. Meanwhile my weakness prevents me standing on my legs with sufficient firmness to walk or to counteract the motion of the ship when the breeze blows and metics and pills and <u>this prospect of 7 more weeks</u> here make me feel indeed not too sure of reaching home yet.[128]

Towards the end of the long arduous voyage around Cape Horn, as the ship approached the English Channel on the evening of 22 June, Lewis commented excitedly on his first glimpse of Cornwall after eleven years in the antipodes:

> About 7 o'clock a Cowes boat approached in the view of landing passengers and of taking the mail. Of the former none were disposed to accept his offer, and the vessel hove to for the purpose of delivering the latter. But the fellow most awkwardly dropped astern, not before however he had imparted the most satisfactory intelligence that we were just 13 miles E.N.E. of

127. *Sydney Morning Herald*, 14 February 1846.
128. Ibid, entry 9 May, 80.

> the Lizard, the revolving lights of which, we had the happiness to discern some few minutes afterwards. And like mariners of the olden times might well on first sight of land, after such a voyage, give thanks to God in chanting the *Salve Regina*, which seamen used in times of distress and joy alike, we were now about to embrace our friends.

He accompanied the entry with a drawing: 'Lizard N. by W. 4 Leagues; 22 June, Monday at sun down'.[129]

On his arrival in Cornwall, Lewis was reported as having returned from a distant climate to Trelawne 'in a very imperfect state of health'. Dr Jonathan Couch, Polperro doctor and Harding family friend, devised a novel therapeutic regime for the invalid, as recalled by his son:

> The Trelawny family, especially, had not only the fullest confidence in his [Dr Couch] abilities, but admitted him to their intimate friendship at the old mansion of Trelawne, where he often engaged himself in the deciphering and transcribing the archives of the house . . . A member of the family [Lewis Harding] had returned from a distant clime in a very imperfect state of health, and it became necessary to prescribe for him a sort and degree of occupation which should direct his mind without overstraining it, and not entail bodily fatigue. Mr. Couch set him such a pleasant task, by requesting him to observe and keep a daily diary of the inhabitants of the old rookery. The result was the improved health of the patient and, for the doctor, a very interesting MS. Volume entitled 'Life in a Rookery'.[130]

Lewis was already a close observer of nature; his shipboard journals are evidence of his interest in and encyclopedic knowledge of birds and marine life. He undertook the prescribed programme over a period of twelve months, beginning in August 1847, assiduously recording his daily observations. The therapy resulted in the diary which Dr Couch had bound and treasured in his library. Some years later Lewis turned to photography as a means of 'amusement', and

129. Lewis Harding, *1846 Journal*, entry 22 June, 121.
The Lizard: the most southerly promontory of England surmounted by two lighthouses; the first land seen by ships on entering the English Channel.
130. Thomas Quiller Couch, op. cit., p 12.

perhaps as an extension of Dr Couch's therapy. He developed his hobby into a major occupation, producing a vast array of portrait and landscape collodion photographs at the fishing village of Polperro, and becoming celebrated as 'Cornwall's pioneer photographer'.[131]
Lewis' health remained fragile; in 1870, Dr Couch's son, Dr Thomas Quiller Couch described him as 'a great invalid'.[132] However, he lived to the age of 86, dying in October 1893. He was buried in the grounds of Sclerder Abbey near Polperro, a convent founded by his family in 1843.

V THE MANUSCRIPTS

In May 2015 I was forwarded a series of digitised manuscripts, catalogued at the Sydney Archdiocesan Archives as 'Priests' Diaries', for consideration regarding transcription and editing. The only one that captured my interest was the 1846 'Ship Journal of Lewis Harding'; the name of the diarist was little known to me. Initial research on Harding led to the book of Philip Correll and through his research to the existence of Harding's 1835 journal, supposedly 'unaccountably missing' from Downside Abbey archives. In July 2018 an enquiry to the Downside archivist about the catalogue entry for the 'missing' journal, brought the happy news that the manuscript was safely shelved in the collection and 'in good condition'. Simon Johnson then generously forwarded a digitised copy of the journal with permission and encouragement to proceed with transcription. With copies of both manuscripts accessible, the happy prospect emerged of publishing them together. The work of transcribing and editing began in earnest in July 2018.

The first thing noticed about both journals is that they are sewn and bound books. Any notion that they were written in blank exercise books during the voyage is contradicted by the fact that each concludes on the final page of the book. No writer could have so carefully structured a diary so as to conclude in this way. Further evidence against shipboard writing is the evenness of the script in both journals, showing no sign of having been written at sea. There is no difference in the quality of writing penned in calm or rough conditions,

131. See Correll, *Lewis Harding: Cornwall's pioneer photographer*, op. cit.
132. Andrew Lanyon, *The Rooks of Trelawne*, The Photographers Gallery, London, 1976 (no pagination).

in the doldrums or in the roaring forties. To be noted is the contrast between a draft sermon written by Polding onboard the *Ratcliff* in 1846 and Lewis' writing in the journal – see figures 6 and 7 below.[133]

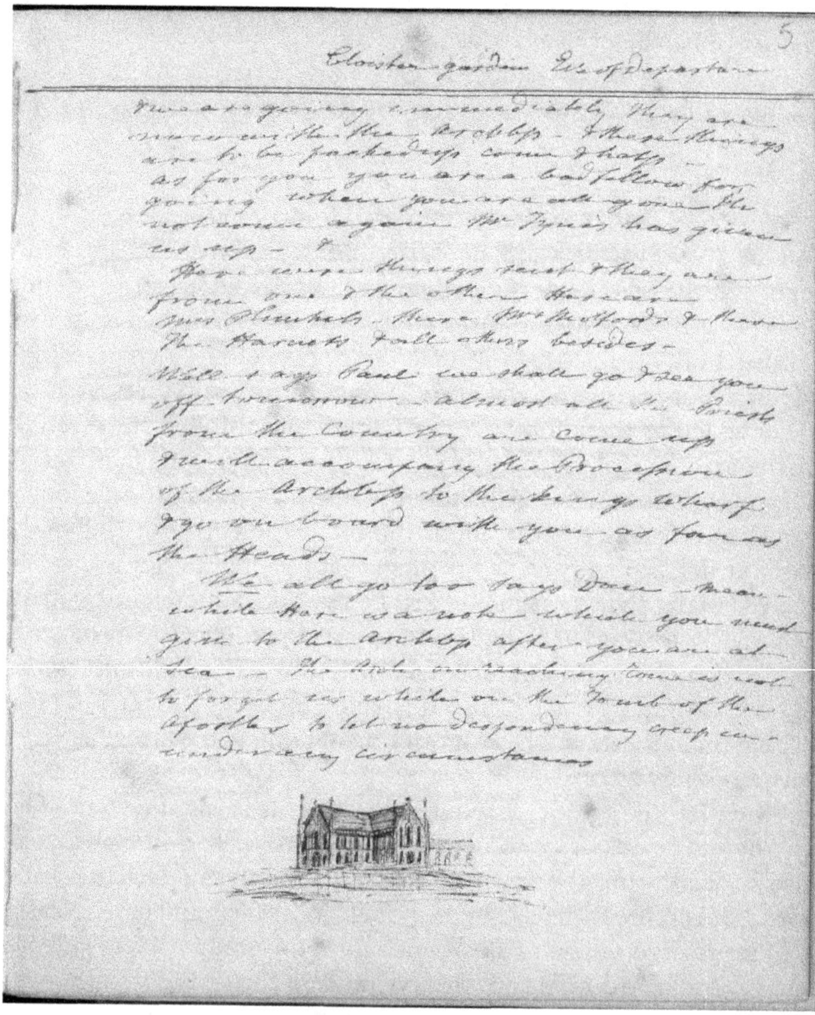
5
Cloister garden Eve of Departure
[illegible] are going immediately. They are
[illegible] with the Archbp - & these things
are to be packed up come & help -
as for you you are a bad fellow for
going when you are all gone [illegible]
not come again Mr [illegible] has given
us up - &
[illegible] these things [illegible] & they are
from one & the other. Here are
[illegible] Plunketts. Here Mrs [illegible] & there
the Harnetts & all others besides -
Well says Paul we shall go & see you
off tomorrow - almost all the Priests
from the Country are come up
& will accompany the Procession
of the Archbp to the Kings wharf
& go on board with you as far as
the Heads -
We all go too says Dan - mean-
while Here is a note which you need
give to the Archbp after you are at
sea - [illegible] is not
to forget us while on the Tomb of the
Apostles to let no despondency creep in -
under any circumstances

Figure 6: 1846 Journal page 5 with drawing of St Mary's Cathedral

133. At the end of letter written at sea during the 1835 voyage, Polding commented: 'My hand is shaking with the heat and the motion of the vessel is so great I am afraid you will scarcely make out this.' See Appendix I: Polding to L. B. Barber OSB, 3 May 1835 (Polding Letters I.53–54).

Figure 7: Draft of a sermon for 25 March, written by Archbishop Polding onboard the Ratcliff.[134]

134. On 15 May, Lewis commented: 'His Grace has completed 20 sermons written on board, 32 remaining to be written, being one for every Sunday of the year' (1846 Journal, 86).

The process involved in creating a journal, common in nautical compositions, was the keeping of a log at sea followed by the writing-up of the journal on land. The clearest evidence for this process in writing the 1835 Journal is the entry for 5 April on page 15, where there is a reference to an event that would take place in May:

> In the evening the compline and litany of the B.V.M. were sung with accompaniment, also the B[lessed] S[acrament] was kept in Mr. Fisher's room, as long as he lived (about 2 months), where we met for night prayers and afterwards in the oratorio which was made up.

There is internal evidence in the 1846 journal, where Lewis referred to having with him the log, not the journal, of the 1835 voyage:

> By a strange coincidence, turning over a former log, I perceive that on this day 11 years we crossed the Line in the ship *Oriental* (Captain Allen) on our way to Sydney. We then crossed it in Longitude 20°8', far to the eastward of our present position. By a coincidence not less remarkable, we find that the same number of days (84) has been spent in sailing from Sydney here, that we required to take us from the Line to Hobart Town (via Cape Good Hope). [81]

The log was a blank notebook in which were recorded the date, latitude and longitude, weather conditions and any other observations which would become the basis of writing an expanded journal. Official logs were kept by the ship's captain and surgeon. Writing the journal on land would have enabled Lewis to expand his references in the 1846 journal to the many books cited, but unlikely to be part of a shipboard library. The finely drawn images would have been made from rough sketches in the logbook.

The process involved in creating the journals in book form began with large blank sheets of paper folded twice to create four leaves or eight faces of the dimensions found in the 1835 and 1846 books. As the writing progressed, completed leaves were inserted into each other and finally these gathered sheets, called signatures or fascicules, were sewn together and bound, thus creating the books as they now appear.[135]

The 1835 journal was addressed by Lewis to his father John. He recalled experiences of events, persons and places which they shared. Lewis mentioned that he had kept a sketch-book onboard: 'I send with the journal sketches of plans and drawings I made, which will suffice to give you an idea of what went on.'[136] The journal made its way from the Harding family to the Downside archives; there is no record of the sketch book at Downside.

The 1846 journal was dedicated to Archbishop Polding, Doctor Gregory and friends. It is supposed that it remained in the possession of the Sydney Benedictines and eventually found its way into the archives of the Archdiocese of Sydney.

Physical description of manuscripts

1835 Journal

The major recorded reference to the journal between 1835 and 2018 was that by Dom Henry Norbert Birt OSB, who quoted briefly from it in his *Benedictine Pioneers in Australia*. His pencil lines can be seen against the reporting of Fr Fisher's death on page [26] of the journal, which he quotes in full (see Figure 9 below). Birt referred dismissively to the rest of the journal as 'a mass of trivialities'.[137]

The transcription was done exclusively from the digitised copy. The catalogue entry for the manuscript in the Downside Archives is as follows:

'Journal of Voyage from England to New South Wales: M. Harding, 1835'

The characteristics of the manuscript not discernible from the copy have been provided by the Downside archivist:

- page size: 20cm × 13 cm
- Sewn and bound signatures

135. See Franziska Morlok and Miriam Waszelewski, *Bookbinding: a comprehensive guide to folding, sewing & binding*, translated by Caroline Waight, Princeton Architectural Press, New York, 2018. The log-journal distinction is referred to on the dedication page of the 1846 journal; see reproduction above.

136. 1835 Journal, p [117].

137. Birt I.253.

- Leather spine
- plain fly leaves
- Unlined paper
- 125 pages unnumbered; pagination has been added in the transcript, beginning with the first page of text [1].
- Running heading – month of the year.

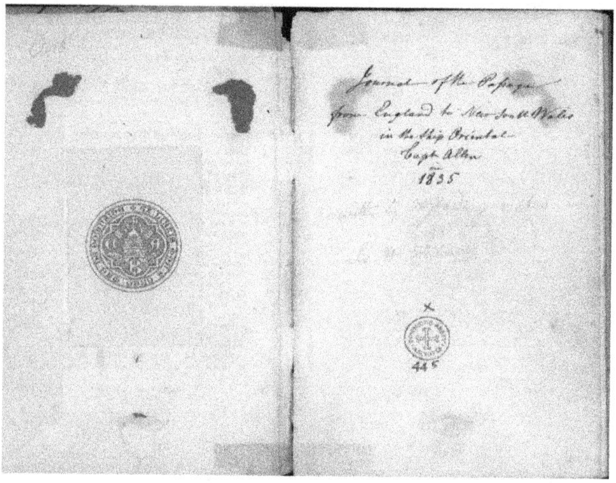

Figure 8: 1835 Journal title page; inscribed in pencil, probably by Dom Birt: 'written by Mr. Harding, nephew of Sir. H. Trelawny'.[138]

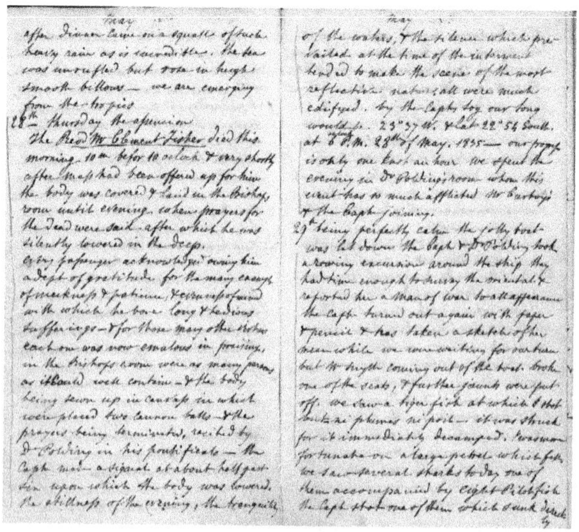

Figure 9: 1835 Journal pages 26–27 – death of Rev Fisher

138. Lewis was the grandson, not nephew, of Rev. Sir Harry Trelawny.

1846 Journal

No published references to this journal have been found. The manuscript, as part of the McGovern Collection, was absent from SAA until 2008.[139]

Limited access to the manuscript was available at the Sydney Archdiocesan Archives. The bulk of the transcribing was done from the digitised copy.

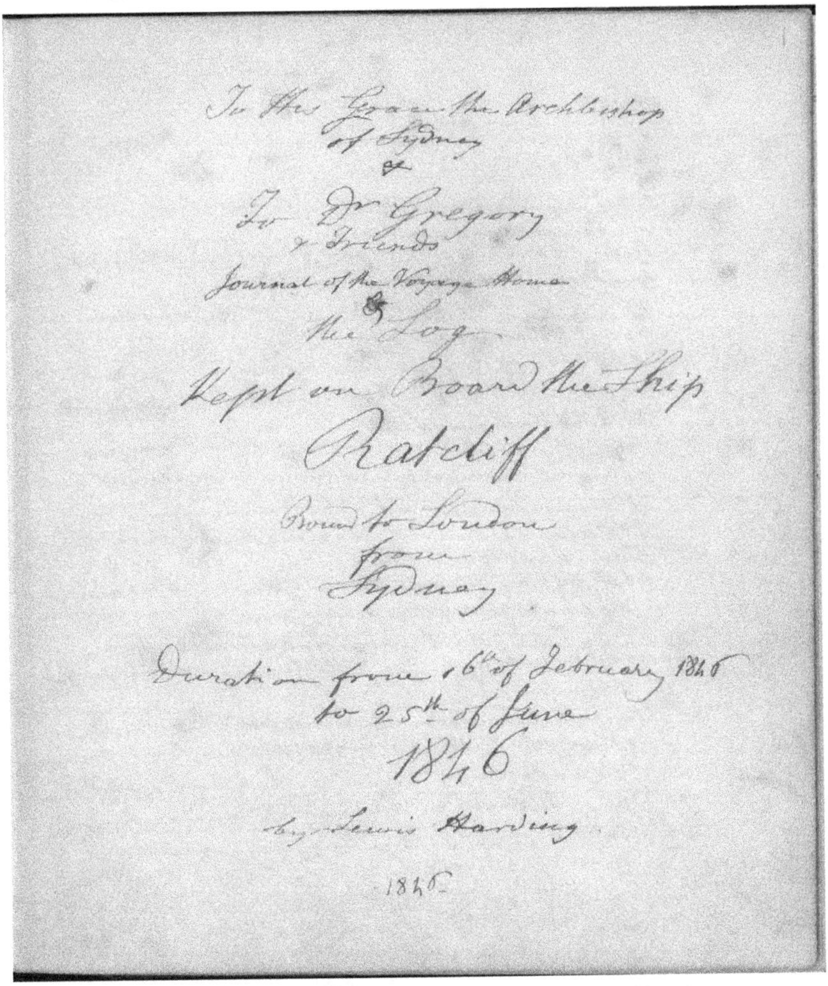
To His Grace the Archbishop
of Sydney
&
To Dr Gregory
& Friends
Journal of the Voyage Home
&
the Log
Kept on Board the Ship
Ratcliff
Bound to London
from
Sydney
Duration from 16th of February 1846
to 25th of June
1846
by Lewis Harding
1846

Figure 10: Dedication page of 1846 Journal

139. Rev. Joseph J. McGovern was Sydney Archdiocesan Archivist from 1938 to 1940 and from 1947 to 1964.

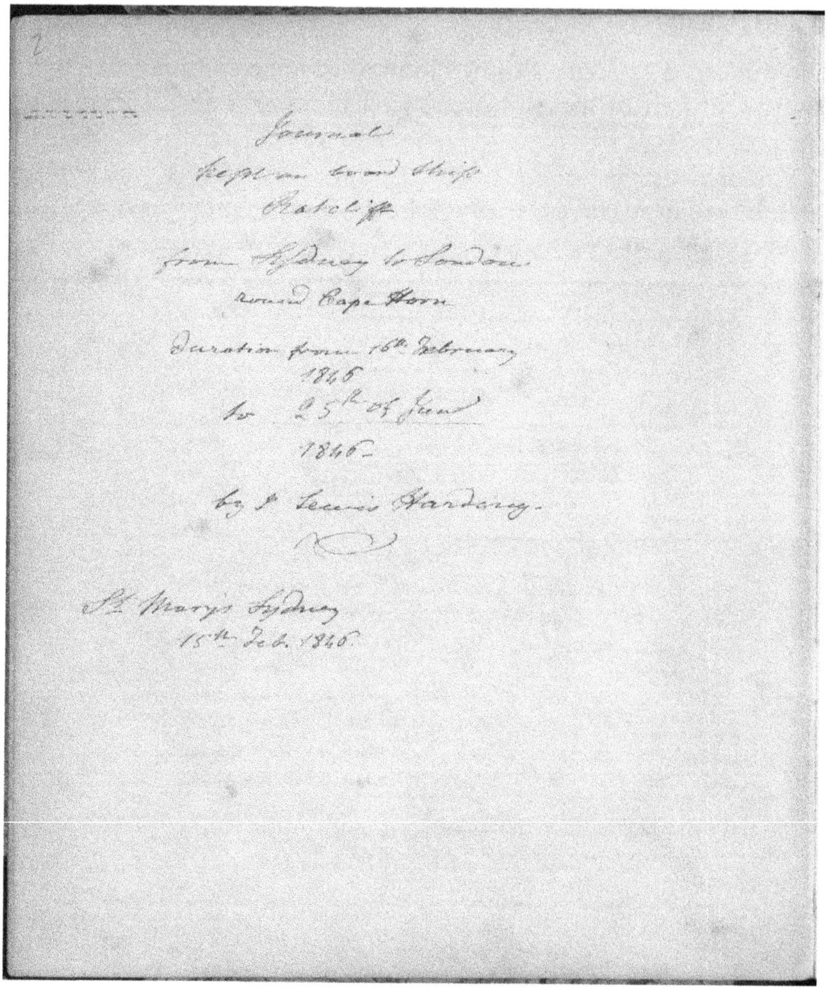

Journal
kept on board Ship
Ratcliff
from Sydney to London
round Cape Horn
Duration from 16th February
1846
to 25th of June
1846
by [illegible] Lewis Harding.

St Mary's Sydney
15th Feb. 1846

Figure 11: Title page of 1846 Journal

The catalogue entry for the manuscript in the Sydney Archdiocesan Archives is as follows:

> # Polding - Ship Journal of Lewis Harding on board the ship Ratcliff from Sydney to London 6th February 1846 to 25th June 1846, addressed to His Grace the Archbishop of Sydney and to Dr Gregory and friends (hand illustrated); a bound volume exercise type book. Microfilmed and digitised Feb 2012.[140]

140. The date of sailing is mistaken – 6th not 16th February.

Manuscript characteristics:

standard quarto size volume (23cm × 18.5cm)
Sewn and abound signatures
Leather spine and corners
Marbled boards and fly leaves
Unlined paper
130 pages numbered by Harding or another hand
page margins of 3cm
Pages are numbered, though whether by Lewis or subsequently is uncertain.
Black ink
Some areas of faded ink, perhaps through dilution
Consistent writing throughout, except for dedication and title pages in large cursive style
Page headings – topic of the page underlined by ruled double lines

VI THE TRANSCRIPTIONS

It became clear that if the published Journals were to be read with any comfort, then some adjustments had to be made to Harding's texts in transcribing them, but not so many as to lose the flavour of his rapid-running mind and pen. The following practices were, therefore, adopted:

- Paragraphing, largely absent in the manuscripts, has been imposed to assist in the reading of the texts.
- Abbreviations are sometimes replaced by the full word (eg bishop for bp; captain for capt).
- The ampersand is consistently replaced.
- Harding's erratic use of capitals is standardised – imposed on proper nouns and eliminated from others.
- His minimal use of punctuation is expanded, especially when comprehension is at stake.
- The dash was Harding's favourite punctuating device, lavishly used and tending to bespatter the page and divert the eye; in the transcriptions the dash is often replaced by a semi-colon, of whose usefulness Lewis seems to have been unaware.
- His use of the long 's' throughout is eliminated.

- Where no confusion occurs, spelling peculiar to the diarist is left unchanged and the intrusive use of [sic] is avoided (eg 'stuard' for steward).
- Underlinings and vertical lines, thick and in pencil in the 1835 journal, seem to have been added later, probably by Dom Birt (see Figure 9 above); they have not been reproduced. Those in ink in the 1846 journal have been taken as original and have been retained.
- deletions have not been transcribed.
- indecipherable words have been square-bracketed with clear letters, if any, printed and obscure ones marked with *.
- uncertain transcriptions are followed by [?]
- the pagination of the manuscripts is placed in square brackets.

The editing process has involved much footnoting; the purpose of the footnotes is multiple:

- to translate words and phrases in foreign languages
- to identify names persons and places
- to explain geographical, historical, literary, astronomical, nautical, botanical, zoological, mythological, hagiographical, liturgical and other references reflecting Lewis Harding's encyclopedic knowledge.

The sketches in the 1846 journal are reproduced on the pages on which Lewis drew them and adjacent to the related text, but not always in the exact position found in the manuscript.

Journal of the Passage from England to New South Wales in the Ship Oriental Captn Allen in 1835

March

We left Liverpool on Friday the 27th of March, 1835, and sure there were great works and confusion that same day, but as the good dam at the Hotel in London once told you, it was 'all in the way of business, Sir'.[1] We were made to hasten, one after the other, at the Brunswick docks,[2] for 'there she lay', and push our way through a dense crowd met to witness the departure and cheer away their friends.

Several other ships were lying in the basin near the *Oriental* preparing to sail also.[3] Their clearing occasioning some delay, it was about eleven o'clock when she moved out slowly and majestically. Her figurehead, which represents a lady of the East draped in rich profusion, was so elevated and prominent that it passed very near as if seeking to take leave of the spectators on the quay. On her smiling countenance sat a supernatural serenity, which imparted an instant and irresistible impulse of confidence to the beholder. It must, I thought, be one of Thetis's race

[2]

on an embassy to escort us across her wild unbounded dominions.[4] So, paying her homage, I was reminded to jump onboard.

1. The journal seems to have been addressed to Harding's father, John Cooke Harding (1781–1868).
2. The Brunswick dock had been constructed between 1827 and 1832.
3. The *Oriental* was a 507-ton teak sailing ship built at Cochin in 1830, an old East Indiaman plying the China trade; this was her first voyage to Sydney.
4. *Thetis*: one of the sea-nymphs of Greek mythology.

I found the cuddy[5] and every in and out crowded – more than fifty or sixty persons present to accompany us down the river some 20 miles. I can only describe to you the cheers and huzzas given and returned as the steamer was preparing to tow us on leaving the basin – but by reminding you of the account given by the du Dresnays[6] and Messrs Gowes etc gave of their departure from Roscoff.[7] We started, led in triumph by the *Martha Tranmere* lashed alongside, her pigmy proportions contrasting singularly with the towering height of our poop – such a diminutive body containing such vast power; ours registered 500 tons but carried 1,000.[8] The weather was clear and calm; the panorama and its 'mille carine'[9] concealed something melancholy, as we slowly receded. On nearing the Black Rock and Fort[10], the scene became very *pittoresque* and interesting to me, at least from the

[3]

scenes it recalled. The chateau standing solitary and fearless on the plain of waters strikingly resembled the chateau du Taureau[11] and the deception increased as we carried on and distinguished the low sandy shores of Cheshire bright with the warmest tints. To westward, from Paddy's land[12], came a mist rolling perceptibly on towards us

---

5. *Cuddy*: a saloon cabin at the stern of ships, where wealthy passengers could gather in greater comfort than those in steerage below.
6. The du Dresnay family were members of the ancient nobility of Brittany. One of Lewis' sisters, Maria Anna (1818–1851), married into the family, becoming Countess du Dresnay.
7. Roscoff is a Breton port across the Channel from Cornwall.
8. Steam ferries had been operating along the Mersey river, from Liverpool to Tranmere, since 1817. *poop*: a superstructure at the stern of a sailing ship.
9. 'mille carine': 'thousands of dear ones'; Lewis occasionally turns to Italian and regularly to French.
10. Black Rock, at the Mersey Estuary, is cut off at high tide. A defensive fort, mounted with 18 guns and known as the Perch Rock Battery, was constructed there in 1829.
11. Chateau du Taureau is an island fortress-prison at the entrance to the bay of Morlaix in Brittany. Its construction dates back to the sixteenth century. The Hardings were very familiar with sailing between Cornwall and Brittany, where they were resident and Lewis at boarding school from 1818.
12. *Paddy* (from *Patrick*): an often derogatory term used by the English for the Irish.

and magnified like a lense the numerous ships and steamers, which crowded on the icy surface.

Indeed, our setting off resembled more the description given of Cleopatra's set-out on the river Cydnus to meet Anthony, than to poor fellows fleeing home and country, fond companions and favourite household gods.[13] Our hearts were cheered by the voice of song and the harmony of music and airs well known to you and often echoed in the chapels of St Acheul, St Anne and Trelawny and which have often graced little Johnny's lips, resounded on our departure on board the *Oriental* for Hobart Town and Sydney.[14]

We were hardly out of soundings[15], than Mr. Corcoran (pull away you knave) had already many a fishing line thrown out and so eager

[4]

deja.[16] The steamer was casting off, those who came to accompany us left, stepping into her – about sixty in number. They gave three cheers, which were heartily returned. After moving off some distance, she returned again, as if loath to leave us, and rounding-to described

13. The river Cydnus had its headwaters in the Tarsos Mountains in the Cilicia and flowed into the Mediterranean near the city of Tarsus. In 41BC Cleopatra, summoned by Antony, sailed from Egypt to Tarsus. As she made the final leg of her journey up the river Cydnus, she traveled in a magnificent barge filled with flowers and scented with exotic perfumes while she reclined on deck surrounded by her servants and trappings of gold, as described in Plutarch's *Life of Antony.*
14. Saint-Acheul was a former monastery near Amiens, turned into a Jesuit college from 1816 to 1830; the Jesuit college of St Anne near Auray, Brittany, was Lewis' boarding school from 1818; the chapel at Trelawne was converted to Catholic use by Lewis' grandfather, Rev. Sir Harry Trelawny.
    'Little Johnny': Lewis' younger brother Jonathan (1825–1874).
15. *Soundings*: water shallow enough for depth measurements to be taken by a hand line.
16. *Mr Corcoran*: James Vincent Corcoran, Irish Dominican priest, who had been chaplain to the Trelawny household. He was probably responsible for introducing Lewis as a very late addition to Polding's missionary band. Harding's name does not occur in any of the lists of missionaries prior to sailing from Liverpool. In September 1837 Corc, as Polding affectionately called him, was tragically killed in a gig accident while travelling to Sydney from his mission station at Windsor.

a graceful sweep about the ship, when the cheering recommenced. I saw a tear trickling down some cheeks as we lost her and the sight of the land, to which she was returning, disappearing for ever – it was one o'clock; all sails set.

We immediately, with different minds, set to work regulating our berths, lashing our boxes down with ropes fastened to iron bolts screwed in the deck and at the sides. The carpenter lending us a hand, we had our cots to suspend and beds to make, which took us some hours of serious employment, whilst all hands were engaged without, making clear for sea service.

Our room was next to Dr Polding and Mr. Gregory, and the Captain's, which two were alike, having large windows, which extended across the

[5]

whole length of the stern of the ship. They were the largest; ours was about ten feet on every side and 7 feet high, which after a little time we found sufficiently spacious. Mr. Corcoran had his sea couch; my cot caused him sometimes great alarm. Our corresponding berth was taken by Mr. Roberts. Those two right and left on entering the cuddy, which are smaller than the others, were occupied, the one by Messrs. Sumner and Spencer, the other by Smyth, brother to A.B. Smyth and Co., Sydney.[17] Below in one room was the Revd. Mr. Fisher; adjoining

---

17. *Joseph Bede Sumner* OSB (1803–1871): clothed at Downside 1831; professed 1833; ordained priest at Sydney 1836; retired to nuns' monastery at Subiaco, Parramatta, in 1868.
The biographical details of the monks of the English Benedictine Congregation, here and throughout, are taken from Henry Norbert Birt's *Obit Book of the English Benedictines, 1600–1912*, Edinburgh, 1913.
John Benedict Spencer OSB (1803–1864): clothed at Downside 1824; ordained deacon 1836; choir-master at St Mary's Cathedral; sent back to England 1837, having caused dissension in the Benedictine community and scandal in Sydney. Ordained priest circa 1839, he wandered between monasteries in England and France, and was expelled from the Benedictines in 1851 and secularised in 1852. In June1860 it was widely reported in the English press that 'John Benedict Spencer, the ex-Catholic priest, who kept a school as Hackney, has been fully committed to Newgate on five separate indictments for abominable offences' (*Preston Chronicle*, 23 June 1860). He died in Dartmoor gaol in 1864
A.B. Smyth and Co: a shipping agency in George St., Sydney.

were Rev. Mr. Cotham, Mr. Kenny, a Scotchman, a young catechist and John Gorman, who came from the Revd. Mr. Jones in London.[18] These gentlemen were all from or had been trained at Downside, and as you were disposed to send Johnny thither, I heard with great interest, as we met on different occasions in the Bishop's room, accounts of gone-by events in that peaceful abode, which also brought me back to days of other years at Auray.[19]

The stranger passengers were not many – there is Signor Curtoise, a Spaniard, with his wife, a person from the Isle of Man, a baby (of the boy kind) and a servant maid.[20] Mr. Curtoise and Mr. Spencer

[6]

are music amateurs and play on the piano in our evening meetings, which are spent, when we are together, much as *Ma Tante* would have them at her organ and books with Sam. J. Jago, Jane Mary Knight etc by her side preparing for the Sunday following.

Dr Sampson is the 'experienced surgeon on board'; Mr. Roberts, Mr. Elliot and Mr. Smyth, the two last on their way from America; the latter appears a forward, blustering kind of fellow, who might shine

18. Clement Fisher (died 1835): young priest-in-charge of St Anthony's, Scotland Road, Liverpool, at the time of the church's opening in 1833; he joined the expedition for reasons of health, as explained in a letter of 6 March 1835 from Polding to the Colonial Office (*Letters* I.49–50). He died on the voyage on 28 May and was buried at sea.
James Ambrose Cotham OSB (1810–1883): clothed at Douay, France, 1829; ordained priest 1834; missioner in Van Diemen's Land; returned to England 1851; retired to Douay 1873; retired to Belmont 1882.
John Kenny (1816–1886): born in Fife, Scotland, and educated by Benedictines; catechist in Hobart Town 1835–1836; ordained priest in Sydney 1843, engaged in parish ministry; author of *A History of the Commencement and Progress of Catholicity in Australia, Up to the Year 1840* (Sydney, 1886).
John Gorman: this boy, whom Polding hoped would become a monk and priest, came under the influence of Spencer and left Australia in disgrace in 1838 (see T. J. Kavenagh, 'Polding's Monks' *Tjurunga* 8[1974], Appendix I, ii).
19. The Jesuit college of St Anne near Auray, Brittany, was Lewis' boarding school from 1818.
20. *Curtoise* (later spelt Curtoys): the family took up residence in Sydney at 1 Fort-street, near Dawes' Battery.

in a tap room.[21] Our little captain is captain-like as well – Captain Allen is from Waterford; he appears obliging and likes fun and wit of any kind. He wears a gilt watch chain as regularly over his waistcoat, gracefully folded in and out the pocket and buttonholes as if it were a badge of his office. He had served formerly on board an East Indiaman.[22] Prudence shews itself uppermost of his other qualifications.

At four o'clock, the appointed hour, we sat down to dinner – about eighteen in number. Looking around, as it were, to reconnoitre each other's features,

[7]

'We shall soon know each other' vociferated Smythe with a hoarse laugh. We were no more disturbed by the motion of the ship than if we had been dining at home, and the conversation was animated. The first and second mate have their places at each end of the table and carve. The Captain and the Doctor opposite each other do the honour. A pair of blacks wait on and have the care of the cuddy. One of them is the Stuard, a catholic; he is from Bombay, married and been on the ship ever since it was built. The other plays the fiddle and was taken partly on that account, and his services in that way are called for on extraordinary days, when the reaching of some new latitude or our approach to some land, or else to fall in with some homeward-bound, or perhaps in escape from pirates, to be celebrated by an evening's revelry, dance and song.

The fare onboard is passable when once you get accustomed to it and come to table with a good appetite. It breaks one well into the good old spartan custom of making shift with anything. It is all laid out, however, with great taste. Over the table is a large skylight, two round trays are fastened to the poop beams above

21. *Mr. Elliot*: Sizar Elliott (1814–1901) was taken at 4, after his father died, to New Brunswick, Canada. He celebrated his 21st birthday on the voyage to Australia. In 1887 he published 'Fifty Years of Colonial Life', in which he reminisced about the 1835 voyage (see Appendix I).
    Tap room: a room or establishment where alcoholic drinks are served.
22. *East Indiaman*: general name for any sailing ship operating under charter to the East India Company.

[8]

containing jugs and tumblers, which swing with the motion of the ship. From the center depend a Barometer and a Thermometer with a handsome lamp on each side. Sitting at table you have a view, through the glass partition extending across the deck, of the whole ship and gang ways forward (pronounced *forad*).

The hours for meals, that is breakfast at half past eight, lunch at twelve, dinner at four and tea at six or seven, are regulated at noon each day, when the observations are taken and the moment of the sun's passing the meridian ascertained. Then eight bells are sounded, the nautical day begins and is divided into six watches, four hours each. Then follows –

at half past twelve the order is given: 'Strike one Bell';
at one o'clock – two bells
at half past one – three bells
at two – four bells
at half past two – five bells
at three – six bells
half past three – seven
at four o'clock – 'Strike bell Eight'.
When the second watch begins, observe in the

[9]

same order in the management of the bell. Thus the word 'Strike bell eight' is called out at four, eight and twelve o'clock. At noon each one has to set his watch, if he wish, to the apparent time, or by leaving it, if a good one, its difference of time will enable him to make out the distance in longitude sufficiently correct, reckoning, of course, four minutes to a degree or fifteen for an hour. We have thus ourselves kept a pretty good longitude independent of the Captain's, who would not give us his during the voyage.[23]

Comparing the different altitudes taken with the Captain's observations, I find the instrument we had at Coxe's to differ four minutes from his, but this difference always happening in the same way,

23. Perhaps the captain jealously guarded the more accurate calculations achieved by the use of the ship's chronometer, while Harding relied on his watch and sextant.

I was quite satisfied with it and its only fault being its extreme delicacy requiring very tender treatment and frequent adjustments.

We shortly made Holyhead, where we fell in with the wind and ranged swiftly along and in sight of the Wicklow and Wexford coasts, the Captain casting a wishful look towards his native hills and pointing to us, the next day, the direction of his home.

[10]

We made Cork at the distance of 10 miles only, as we steered westward.

The 30th in long. 9°2', a ship was in sight and being desired to let no opportunity pass by which we might get ourselves reported in Liverpool, the Captain hoisted a signal and lay-to. In half an hour the ship was close to us and recognised to be the 'Catherine of Belfast' from New Orleans.[24] She promised to have our name in the list of ships spoken to. We dwell with pleasure on the thought of our friends hearing of us.

On the 31st the wind increased as stiff as when going over with Gambel to St Paul.[25] I suspected old Neptune might have been bribed to drive us back. We were nearly all sick and considering the last trip, I could not have believed it.

The 1st of April in lat. 50°39'; long. 11°12'. Made a sail again, the . . . bound for London from St Michael.[26] She understood and answered our signals on the wing, as she shot passed us rapidly before the wind. She as smaller than ours and although at no great distance, the intervening waves conceiled altogether at times her main yards and topsails.

[11] April

As night came on it blew harder and in the morning of 2nd of April, as we viewed a small portion of her light bulwarks carried away and the sea entering through the portholes and rushing across the deck

24. The *Catherine* was an Irish migrant ship crossing the Atlantic.
25. *St Paul*: Saint-Pol-de-Léon is an cathedral town in Brittany. The Harding family lived in a chateau close to Saint-Pol from 1818 to 1830.
26. *St Michaels*: a shipbuilding town in Maryland.

like a weir, we thought, being yet green, that we had rode a storm. We were too sick to enjoy at this time the *quelle* scene before us – the breakfast cups, jugs, beef, ham, coffee, pratties[27] etc. etc. all swept off the table in one fell swoop. And 'John!', says Smyth, 'bring me over my top boots flung across in that Gent's cabin yonder'; another enquiring for his box, which had been made to take a voyage. And as we rolled heavily, 'What is going on', says Mr. Solids, peeping out of his bed (a Gent who received this appellation for his cautioning the rest to lay in a good foundation of solids as the only specific for sea sickness and had joined example to precepts by engulphing two or three plates of pork and cold chicken). 'Have you fresh horses, Captain, that we are bowling on at this rate?'

But Dr Sampson was the worst and most unfortunate in his tumbles and bruises; he stormed loudly against Mr. Porter for not having secured him a convenient berth. Mr. Roberts offered

[12]

to share his cabin, but his hospitality was near becoming fatal, for having settled his cot there, he was no sooner in than it broke down and threw him on his head against a jar of blacking. He came out in a miserable condition and lay flat on the floor holding round to the mizzen mast (pronounced *must*). This was not the only cot accident, but they took place through mere carelessness, and, after all, a cot is a real luxury. I hope you will always have one in your future jaunts to Roscoff. As I recall, yours cannot be rightly suspended, but the usual cot etc etc made to suspend, as they commonly are, are preferable to anything. Hammocks may be warmer, but one is apt to fall from them.

I was only slightly seasick, but otherwise weak and my arm was still very painful. The Bishop was very bad and so was Mr. Corcoran, who would not own it.
The 3rd. Lat 49°19'; Long 11°30'

Towards evening the wind moderated and the sea went down. It blew fair and after all the tacking, the ship went straight again, as Maister Cockum says, the change was so welcome that at the end of dinner, when the mate on watch announced the fair wind, more wine

27. *pratties*: boiled or roasted potatoes in their jackets complete with eyes.

[13]

was called for and those who could sing had to give their song. Dr Sampson, bad as he was, being pressed to come out, took his seat and gave a long song about 'it's all my eye and Betty Martin', which was very loudly applauded.[28] Master Kenny delivered a speech taken from Anthony's oration at the death of Caesar, which classical strain made the Captain stare.[29] He laughed at the exploits of Brutus or Anthony or Cassius; they were names nowhere to be met with in nautical annals or magazines. Paganini's fiddle was in request the greater part of the night and our spirits were roused by its reviving notes and the quick tread of gallopades and quadrilles in which Smith was foremost.[30]

The Captain, on the 4th, read to us several letters written to him by the owners of the ship *New Ross*, of which he had been commander, giving him a good deal of praise for his ingenious invention of a new rudder, when his was carried away by another ship running foul of them in a dark night, during a gale of wind on their way from Quebec.

[14]

5th Sunday. It sounds strange, but would you believe that out here we awake every morning by the noise of ducks quacking, cocks crowing and all the sounds which may issue from a farmyard. The day was fine and calm and the gravity of some faces and their formal dress indicated it to be Sunday. Even Mr. Corcoran paraded in a coat; you would not have recognised him again. His pair of thick worsted stockings and buckles at his knees added some twenty or thirty years to his age.[31]

At 10 o'clock the bell tolled solemnly for Prayers. I thought of little Johnny and Thomas ringing for the same purpose, perhaps at the same moment; it sounded so alike. The Captain officiated for the other passengers and sailors assembled in the cuddy. We heard him

---

28. *It's all my eye and Betty Martin*: a seventeenth century idiom indicating nonsense talk.
29. *Anthony's oration*: the speech of Mark Antony in Shakespeare's *Julius Caesar*, Act III, Scene 2, which begins: 'Friends, Romans, countrymen, lend me your ears'.
30. *Paganini's fiddle*: Lewis playfully applies the name of the great violinist and composer, Niccolò Paganini (1782–1840), to the ship's Indian fiddler. He is later given the name 'Harry' (p. 17).
31. James Vincent Corcoran was 34 at the time of sailing.

reading very parson-like. Mr. Curtoyn, the stuard and two Irishmen in steerage joined us in the Bishop's room. We had not Mass today, but in general oftener than we had expected at first, as well in calm weather, as going at the rate of 8 or 9 knots. When deprived of it, prayers were read out of the 'Garden of the Soul', the *Venite Exultemus* sung and played on the piano terminating with a meditation and an

[15]

instruction by the Bishop, always 'veramente bella e propria alla nostra situazione'.[32] In the evening the compline and litany of the B.V.M. were sung with accompaniment, also the B.S. was kept in Mr. Fisher's room, as long as he lived (about 2 months), where we met for night prayers and afterwards in the oratorio which was made up.[33]

As the weather was fine, we admired each day some new beauty on ocean's fair but variable face. Today it was a sun setting amidst glorious colours and long streaks of gilt-edged clouds succeeded by a clear light horizon contrasting strongly with a dark bank of calm sea beneath. Another day it was a clear blue sky behind the well-defined edges of some fantastical clouds representing hills and valleys and trees, or some huge monster. Across this a solitary bird taking his flight would appear coming from the land or winging it from one hill to another.

We had several shots at porpoises and other things. Dr Polding had rifles, but we were not successful. Mr. Sumner was the best shot; we were too sick to stir ourselves to shoot. Some, to dispel their drowsiness and inclination to be sick

[16]

would occupy themselves with the manoeuvres of the ship and run up the rigging, but the sailors were instantly after them and considering it an invasion of their rights would lash down the offender to the

---

32. 'Truly beautiful and appropriate to our situation'.
33. *B.V.M.*: Blessed Virgin Mary.
    B.S.: Blessed Sacrament.
    Lewis' parenthetic comment about the date of Clement Fisher's death indicates that parts of the journal, if not the whole, were written, not on the dates indicated, but at a later time.

spot where he was caught. I made some attempts at occupying myself, but the feel of sickness and giddiness was too overpowering to admit of long or serious reading.

On the 9th at 10 in the morning (we were in Lat 42°56'; Long 12°50') the word 'pirate' was hallo'ed out and flew from mouth to mouth. It came from the sailor on watch at the forecastle[34], either seriously or in a joke, as the sudden appearance of a sail lying to only a mile right ahead (unnoticed before on account of the thick-set sails) had given some alarm. Everyone was instantly on the poop. And who should have the spying glass? There were but two. These latitudes swarm with pirates and this one appeared rather bold. On her masthead a long red pennant stretched in the wind; her sails gracefully set were counteracting each other (the method of lying to) and 6 or 7 guns appeared projecting from their poop. It was the British sloop of war, the 'Fair Rosamond', belonging to the

[17]

Lisbon station and on her cruizing ground.[35] One of her officers in uniform hailed us with a speaking trumpet and enquiring who we were, whither bound etc, in the usual way. Then offering an apology and saluting us with his hand, darted off *instanter*, and they were out of sight in half an hour, leaving us reflecting on Old England, her glory and might.

Here we were basking in the sunny clime of old Troy, Greece and Italy too; admired the same sky you there did with *ma tante* and Letty, for that was all I could admire.[36] The same moon, which was so friendly to the perfidious Greeks behind Tenedos[37], now shone to better purpose and favoured the evening dance as the sounds of Harry's fiddle

34. *Forecastle* (pronounced fo'c'sle): the upper deck of a sailing ship forward of the foremast, or the forward part of a ship with the sailors' living quarters.
35. The sloop *Rosamund* was built in 1807.
    The Lisbon Station was a formation of the British Navy operating off the coast of Portugal from 1779–1841.
36. *Ma Tante*: possibly Anne Letitia, sister of Lewis' mother Mary.
    Letty: Lewis' sister Maria Angela Letitia (1815–1884).
37. Tenedos, mentioned in both the *Iliad* and the *Aeneid*, was the island where the 'perfidious' Greeks hid their fleet near the end of the Trojan War in order to trick the Trojans into believing the war was over and into taking the Trojan Horse within their city walls.

mingled with the creaking of the main tack and in the breeze, which drove us steadily on 7 or 8 knots an hour. This evening was the most lively we had. There was a pleasure in the idea or connection you could fancy between our situation making our way through the vast waves and the village dance on a Sunday evening.

On the 11th we discovered a distant sail, which kept in sight apparently dodging us the whole day and night. When she was again perceived the following morning, when it was declared to be suspicious, returning us no answer to

[18]

the Captain's signals, our conversation was of sea fights. It was said she had better beware of the fair Rosamond in whose honour we had lowered the foretop gallant stunsails[38] and were talking of saluting this one with a broadside. Accordingly, and to be *semper parati* (Mr Gill's mother), the carpenter and some hands were at work clearing the guns and a whole day was taken up in scraping and mounting two of them (we had four of them and two wooden ones) with their accompaniments of rammers and sponges.[39]

On the 11th, our lat. being 39°21', long. 15°30', we saw for the first time what the sailors called Portuguese Men-of-War and for a description of which *vide* the Bridgewater treatises.[40] Floating innumerable, driven onwards like a feather by the slightest wind, they reflected the brightest colours and several of them were taken up by letting down a bucket with a rope. The doctor, with a view no doubt to increase the 'lights of science', certainly added to his own, for he was seriously stung or burnt or bit by merely touching one and his hands covered with bladders over. The same effect was produced by touching a rope or anything that had been in contact with them.

38. *Stunsail* or *studsail*: an extra sail hoisted alongside a square-rigged sail on an extension of its yardarm, providing extra speed in fine weather.
39. *semper parati*: ever ready.
40. *Bridgewater Treatises*: These publications derive their origin and title from the Rev. Francis Henry Egerton, 8th Earl of Bridgewater (1756–1829), who directed in his will that £8,000 be invested in the public funds to be applied to the production of treatises on the 'Power, Wisdom and Goodness of God as manifested in Creation'. Three works had been produced by 1835, the third being: 'History, Habits, and Instincts of Animals', by William Kirby (1835). This contained descriptions of the Portuguese Man-of-War jellyfish.

[19]

The 13th. We saw a swallow flying about; it appeared tired and often rested itself on a mast or yard. The Captain says they come from the Cape de Verd or the Western Islands. This one was on her voyage to England no doubt; as Dr C. knew someone who understood their language this bird may give some information.

Some passengers this evening, wishing to play on our *officier de santé*[41] and try the courage of others as well, began after everyone had retired to rouse the whole ship with an outcry of 'Pirates'. They imitated the yells of men ready to board us. Calling at the same time on the Stuard for powder. The doctor was called up, but would not move, he said, until some broken bones were brought to him to mend. Mr. Cotham enquired half asleep whether it was the same pirate we had seen. Mr. Corcoran, Marcey, Harding, where are your guns now?

Bowling on, the finest weather attended, the thermometer averaging 66°, but the heat of the days encreased with the declination of the sun nearing us daily, already our side of the line, on its way to Cancer.[42] Our bread is nearly done and biscuits succeed; the water is now portioned out, but the market stocked with praities[43], and we are to have fresh

[20]

meat all the voyage.

We are now gradually recovering and better enabled to employ the day writing or reading. Mr. Elliot took in his head to read French to me. Our doctor was not remiss in daily visiting his patients and once or twice threw out hints of some dangerous sickness lurking on board. On the 14th, being confined himself to his bed, a trial of his professional solicitude was made yesterday. One of the sailors had bruised his foot by falling and the doctor said he might possibly have a locked jaw. One of the undermates hearing this, affrighted the poor doctor at an early hour whilst fast asleep and giving him no time to enquire, made off, leaving the words 'poor man' and 'lock jaw' and 'be quick' to reverberate in his ears. Away trundled the doctor imme-

41. *Officier de santé*: health officer.
42. *The line*: the equator.
43. *Praities*: potatoes, from the Irish *pratai*.

diately and, although disconcerted at the breakfast table about it, he won great applause. He attends also Mr. Fisher.

We saw two Tortoises in the course of the day; they were floating past the ship quite near.

Mr. Roberts at dinner time accuses Smythe of harping always on the same string and that his conversation is stale, flat and unprofitable. Well, Paganini, you know, plays always on one string.

[21]

Our lat. is 36°48' and long 16°55' and the thermometer is at 75°. Our progress is about 7 or 8 knots.

This time was Holy Week, very different, though, from yours. We had Low Mass on the 16th, Holy Thursday, when we performed our Easter duties, joining *corde et animo* with you more favoured.[44] I began a letter home expecting to meet some ship, which is likely enough about here, being now on the latitude of Madeira. The Captain, who would not let us have his longitude, amused himself, *à nos dépends*[45], and made us strain our eyes to see the 'haze over the land', when we must have been about 100 miles to the westward. It was a great event – a petition was got up among some signed by the D.M. stating how sick we were and how desirable it would be to make Madeira, only anchor in the roads and send in the boat for fresh fruit.[46] Hitherto our private supplies of fruit, figs, almonds, oranges and excellent wine appeared indispensable in the weak state to which we were reduced and we expected to renew our stock at Madeira. But it was all in vain, as the ship was insured differently. But the Captain, to amuse us, kept everyone on the lookout. 'Boats do

[22]

ply', he says, 'thus far to meet with ships. In the morning perhaps some may be seen sailing around laden deep with lots of golden fruit of the Hesperides';[47] and we dreamt at night we were already

44. *corde et animo*: in heart and soul.
45. *à nos dépends*: at our expense.
46. D.M.: Doctor Medicinae; *roads*: a sheltered body of water where ships can anchor reasonably safely.
47. *Hesperides*: in Greek mythology the nymphs of evening tended a lush garden in a far western corner of the world, located near the Atlas mountains in North Africa.

scampering over its woody hills and stretching our legs with a race through its gardens.

17th in lat. 30°37', long. 20°2'. The Captain, taking his usual observation for the apparent time at 9 o'clock, remarked, he told us, a spot of the shape of a ✓ on the lower part of the sun's disk. Thus ✓ which I took from his log.

The day was squally and on the 18th it became more so. We rolled dreadfully. Mr. Corcoran was in great tribulation at not being able to adjust his couch. He removed it to another part of the room. The framework is fixed by means of screws and is made to be converted to a sopha in the daytime. He could not admire it at all, as it was not as solid as a *lit-clos.*[48] Mr. Gregory endeavoured in vain to point out to him the beauty and convenience of it: 'Ah, what a beauty indeed to see my bed all to pieces and never keep a moment

[23]

together.' He then began to stud it over with immense nails.

We fired with our rifles today at bottles, which we threw out; Mr. Spencer hit on the first shot. We let fly at some porpoises to no effect. Mr. Slater says they are 'delicious eating, sea beef in fact.'[49]

Our lat. is 29°30' N and long. W 20°42'. The rain has poured down in torrents and the lightning appears in the horizon quite vivid. The carpenter and joiner, who have been occupied at making a framework, at length fix it in the cuddy at each end, containing rows of muskets, boarding pikes and cutlasses.

On the 19th Lat. 27°54' N, Long. 20°17', and gradually entering the first of the two permanent trade winds, which blow, the one in the northern hemisphere from N.E., the other in the Southern from the S.E., perpetually in the same direction following the direction of the sun the whole year and varying merely a point or two from this course, thus forming two currents constantly the same, which meeting obliquely on or near the line, by neutralising each other, cause a prevailing calm more or less which extends perhaps 7 or 8 degrees

48. *lit-clos*: the enclosed bed or box-bed is closed on all sides by panels of wood.
49. William Slater: second mate on the Oriental.

[24]

on either side of the line, in which ships are detained; the Captain says sometimes 6 weeks.[50] Within this space are usually very heavy rains accompanyed with strong thunder and lightning, and on the weather we shall meet with here, he says, will depend in great measure the quickness of our voyage. For these two trades once crossed as in the high northern latitudes so in the southern, constant westerly winds again blow as if to counteract the last – and quite different from the main trades, extending the same influence more or less round the globe, are other local ones, some prevailing in the Indian seas, blowing half the year one way and the other half another, or others confined to still narrower limits – so much for my dear Tish and Johnny to make out on their globes.[51]

It was Easter Sunday, very squally and much rolling, the Captain and sailors read prayers on benches and chairs firmly lashed. We, as yet the veriest Tyros[52] in nautical life, could not assemble without being rolled and pitched on each other in

[25]

anything like a blowing breeze, so we desisted.

A ship in the morning had been perceived steering apparently in our course. Towards evening she hoisted a signal; we answered by giving our number and discovered her by hers to be the *Connecticut*, an American merchantman and on her way thither. On the 20th we saw her again disappearing on the horizon ahead of us.

We crossed today the Tropic (of Cancer) in long.21°41'. The weather having become very warm and sultry, pieces of canvas were distributed to the men for cloathing. We have yet rather a rough and tumbling sea, but the ship's motion was much steadier, being driven on by the trade at a uniform rate.

Several, for some time back, were taken ill and complaining of headache and giddiness owing in great measure to the heat and it was

50. *The line:* the equator.
51. *Tish and Johnny*: Letitia and Jonathan, Lewis' sister and brother.
52. *Tyro*: beginner or novice.

dangerous to sit in the sun. The doctor gave them blue pills, and medicines to nearly everyone, but the sickness was still tending to make its round, when today Mr. Corcoran was taken bad at dinner time. He went to bed and was bled. We were for an hour or two in great alarm, when the doctor said that by his promptitude [he] had

[26]

been the means of saving his life. The heat appeared to be daily adding strength to Mr. Fisher. He was daily able to come up in the Bishop's room. A sopha was daily placed for him on the deck, on which he might recline for a good part of the day. He could see the sailors at their work or be read to, which he was fond of. We begin to flatter ourselves that he may still recover. Mr. Gregory has undertaken to be his infirmarian and I could almost resign myself to be in Mr. Fisher's place to have such a one.[53] Although I have weathered the prevailing contagion myself so far, I feel weak and stupefied and my arm is painful.[54]

We were raffling it on at the steady rate of 7 or 8 knots, when on the 21 fancy us already in the latitude of the Celestial Empire – of Delhi and Agra, where the Major was only a short while ago. I can imagine I see him on his elephant pacing it heavily along in Aurengzeb's road with a few servile 'vilains' scorched by the fierce sun, which we now feel ourselves.[55]

I gazed on the sea which was blue and fresh and which the breeze curled up into white breakers. I pitied the poor travellers as well on their elephants, as those in tackrevans[?] on a camel's back journeying in caravans and wished them a puff of the trades,

[27]

which filled our sails. But if they had to guard against the attacks of some roving tribe, so had we, and this day had been appointed for a general muster of the crew, and the passengers had volunteered as well,

---

53. *Infirmarian*: monastic term for the monk given responsibility for sick members of the community.
54. Lewis experienced ill health throughout his life. Symptoms of rheumatic fever were later observed.
55. *Aurengzeb* (1658–1707): last of the great Mughal emperors.
Vilain (French): peasant.

for in the case of pirates we have to depend on our own resources. The name of each person was called out, his respective station assigned him in case of a surprise. Our party were made small arms men and the Bishop with Dr Sampson would attend to the dying and wounded in the Cockpit. Some were distributed about the rigging and 4 or 5 of the men were appointed to have the management of one great gun and were exercised on the spot. The guns were wheeled backwards and forwards at the word of command given by their Captain.[56]

The day was pleasant and the evening more so, spent in Dr Polding's room. This was one of the convivial meetings, where we met in spirit with friends at home. The bowl went round to the health of those at Downside and Salford and Liverpool, and scenes of olden times recorded. Today was talked of a memorable fire, which took place once in Mr. Ulathorn's room (now G. Vicar at Sydney) which threatened destruction to the college.[57] There was a bucket of water thrown over a Reverend

[28]

and now a Right Revd. personage.[58] Abbé Boideffre's wig also figured in the flames. Mr. Barber's health (a name in great favour among the party) was proposed[59] (and it was added from a spot on the ocean, on which for the first time the name had been called). Nor was I unmindful in chiming in with a 'here's a toast to friends in Cornwall as well'.

The Captain on the 23rd let down the Jolly boat.[60] The day was quite calm and Dr Polding with him launched forth and were enabled to take a

56. A complete list of assigned defence duties was given by passenger Sizar Elliott in his reminiscences of the voyage in 'Fifty Years of Colonial Life'(see Appendix I).
57. William Bernard Ullathorne OSB (1806–1889): clothed at Downside 1824 and professed 1825; ordained priest 1831; in 1833 sent to Australia as Vicar-General of Bishop Morris of Mauritius; returned to England in 1840; first bishop of Birmingham in 1850.
58. The 'Right Revd. Personage' was Bishop Polding himself. He had been Ullathorne's prefect and director from 1823 to 1831 and was the most likely source of the story about the fire, including the self-deprecating detail about getting wet.
59. Luke Bernard Barber OSB (1790–1850) was educated at Acton Burnell and ordained priest at Downside in 1815. He was president of the English Benedictine Congregation and vicar of the nuns at Stanbrook from 1842 until death.
60. *jolly boat*: a small boat used mainly to ferry personnel to and from the ship.

survey of the ship. There is always a swell in the greatest calm and when the boat was at the distance of about 3 or 4 hundred yards, every succeeding wave would conceal her from our view standing on the poop 20 feet above the water. The Captain praised his ship and said it was like a man-of-war, that he would go again and take a sketch of her, when we might accompany in turns. The Doctor and I engaged to have a dip.

At sunrise on the 24th we saw a sail on the horizon and by breakfast time it was discovered to be French, having a tricolore flag. The 1st mate and one of the men had some words, which ended by the man receiving and returning some blows. As they were about

[29]

to seize the man, he swore he should not be taken nor be made offer an apology. He endeavoured to escape and ran towards the poop, then along the spanker boom,[61] and as he held on by the feet ropes, threatened, if they laid hands on him, to drop overboard. After remaining there an hour, Dr Polding and Mr. Corcoran persuaded him to return to his duty and the indulgence he got was to be handcuffed by the Captain himself and he was then confined.

The sun's altitude at noon was 82° (very near vertical) while our latitude on the 25th was but 18°13' N. The heat rendered the deck no longer tenable but for an awning, which was extended yesterday over the poop, and which now converts it to a cool and shady walk.

'We are about 2,500 miles from home' (this is from someone's journal) 'where our fond parents take many a deep thought in their silent moments on the departure of the fond youth over whom they doted and who now, far removed from their gaze, they eagerly ponder over our destiny.' I would say something, but might get engulphed . . . We find our time to pass very cheerily, when we are well and able to employ ourselves. We are now on the point of reaching the second stage

[30]

of our voyage, the Cape de Verd islands, the old seat of the Gorgons! with rain over them with Ovid and Pausanias. Their next discovery

61. *spanker boom*: the mast extension to which the spanker sail, the aftermost in a sailing vessel, is attached.

by Antonio de Noli in 1440, Sir Francis Drake taking possession of them in 1585, Sir Anthony Sherley's expedition hither in 1595, were talked of like the news of the day.[62] We thought on the *Sir Thomas Munro* wrecked here on some of these infamous scopuli a few weeks ago only, and here we are ourselves called up on Sunday morning the 26th with the joyful sound of 'Land, land ahoy! On the larboard bow'.[63] It was St Anthonio, the northward of these islands[64], *dont la tête*, I say literally, *se cache dans un bourbillon de frimats glacés*, and only twelve miles off, its astonishing height above the clouds made me doubt for some time whether it could be land.[65] The sketch I have taken and which I shall send you, as they say on board, is correct and resembling.[66] I can give you only an imperfect idea of the reality – numerous birds we had not yet seen and seagulls were flying in every direction like swallows, and shoals of flying fish, pursued by the dolphin and bonitoes[67], keep rising out of the water but to no

[31]

purpose, for they are instantly pounced upon by these birds.

---

62. *Gorgons*: term commonly referring to the three sisters of Greek mythology who had hair made of living, venomous snakes. They were said to dwell on the Gorgades islands, identified by some as the Cape Verde islands.
Ovid and Pausinias: both these classical authors wrote about the Gorgons.
Antonio de Noli (1415–1497): a fifteenth century Genoese nobleman and navigator; he discovered some of the Cape Verde islands and was made first Governor by King Afonso V of Portugal.
Sir Francis Drake (1540–1596): English privateer, who twice sacked the islands in 1585.
Sir Anthony Sherley (1565–1635): English adventurer.
63. *Sirenum scopuli*: three small rocky islands where the Sirens of Greek mythology lived and lured sailors to their deaths.
Sir Thomas Munro: ship wrecked on Boa Vista, Cape Verde Islands, 9 December 1834 with the loss of two of the 70 people on board. She was on a voyage from London to Hobart. See Appendix I for newspaper reports that Polding was aboard the Sir Thomas Munro.
64. *Santo Antao* (Portuguese for 'Saint Anthony'): the north-western island of Cape Verde, its highest point rising to 744 metres
65. *dont la tête se cache dans un bourbillon de frimats glacés*: 'whose summit is hidden in frozen fogs'.
66. Lewis' sketch book does not seem to have survived.
67. *bonitos*: school of medium-sized, ray-finned predatory fish.

We had Mass for the second time onboard today. Mr Kenny related to me at great length everything he knew of Charles X. He saw them every Sunday at St Mary's chapel in Edinburgh during a year and a half. Little Henry V ran habitually into the vestry after the service, remaining for some time there and talking to them in French. He was of a very open disposition, lively and sprightly and was particularly beloved by all.[68] The clergymen who attended there were the Revd. Mr. Badenoch, James Gillis, J. McKay and McPhearson.[69] Did not Emilie mention having seen him when at Paris last at the Duke of Orleans? I recollect at St Anne the guns being fired at his birth and the rejoicing which took place.

On the 27th we were still in sight of some of the islands all the morning. The sun's altitude at noon was 87°48'. We expected it to be vertical tomorrow. Our lat. is 15°38' and long. 26°19'. For the first time we beheld this evening the Southern Cross, still keeping a pretty good sight of the North pole star and great bear.

[32]

We saluted with great enthusiasm our southern constellations – *Crux Orion, Corona Australis* – and as we descryed them in the heavens and on our charts by the light of the binacle.[70]

---

68. Charles X (1757–1836): King of France from 1824 until 1830, when deposed and succeeded by Louis-Philippe, Duke of Orleans. The Bourbon royals fled to England and were given accommodation at Holyrood Castle in Edinburgh until 1832, when the family moved to Prague. After Charles' death in Gorizia, his grandson, born on 29 September 1820, succeeded as Bourbon pretender, claiming the title Henri V. The Bourbons were never restored to the French throne.
   St Mary's chapel was opened for worship in 1814; after much embellishment over the years, on the restoration of the Scottish hierarchy in 1878, it became the pro-cathedral of the new Archdiocese of St Andrews and Edinburgh.
69. *James Gillis* (1802–1864): ordained 1827; in 1838 consecrated at Edinburgh as Coadjutor of the Eastern District, succeeding as Vicar-Apostolic in 1852; in 1857 he preached in Orléans cathedral an eloquent panegyric of Joan of Arc, receiving in return from the Mayor of Orléans the heart of King Henry II of England, who had died at Chinon in 1189.
70. *Binnacle*: a waist-high case or stand on the deck of a ship, generally mounted in front of the helmsman to hold the ship's magnetic compass, mounted in gimbals to keep it level while the ship pitched and rolled.

On the 18th we carry on still pretty steadily at the rate of 7 or 8 knots, having scarcely shifted a sail since we entered the trade. The flying fish appear in immense shoals some thousands strong. They rise around the ship like larks put up by the dogs, *à la chasse des perdreaux*, when you call out 'alouette'.[71] One of them flew in Mr. Curtoys room through the window and was caught. It was about 7 or 8 inches long and their finny wings are glassy and transparent. Stormy petrels and Mother Carey's chickens now make their first appearance. There are different species of them; those we saw here resembled the swift in size and mode of flight and skim along the surface in great numbers and following in the wake of the ship.

The sun was as near vertical as possible today and in my sextant I made it travel all the way round and on the very verge of the horizon, which was very beautiful. The heat was so great that no one attempted to work beyond the awning. Our latitude at noon was 13°5' N.

[33]

We had begun to use baths of every description except the right one, which would be to jump overboard, which the Captain endeavoured to prevent on account of the sharks. There were shower baths both in the Captain's and Dr Polding's room, and every morning, when they were washing the decks, we went and might have a dozen buckets of water poured on us or stand under the pumps and let the water run over for half an hour, all which methods we found refreshing.

Our past suffering appeared light as we got accostomed to the sea. Nought material has yet occurred to destroy our peaceful harmony, save sometimes hurrying poor Harry, who won't give us water sufficient to drink our soda powders in.

'Unconscious of danger we have hitherto roamed' (as I take it from the same journal) 'upon the waters and such security has almost prevented us from anticipating any danger to assail us, but have we not heard of the mighty tempests which have summoned the sea and sky to dismal war and have engulphed the stately ship in their dreadful contest. May the all-protecting preserve us from such a fate, but stop my pen! We may have

71. à la chasse des perdreaux: 'at a partridge hunt'.
alouette (French): lark.

[34]

yet to recount a bold battle with the outrageous waters etc. etc.'

And indeed other battles of longer endurance, if not so fierce, may perhaps be told, which were brought on by a little, ugly, 'diseased' terrier pup having been tip't overboard.

[35]

May

May the 1st – this morning a sail was in sight – an outward bound. The Captain hoisted colours but she did not return the compliment. A bonitoe which had been caught yesterday was cooked for breakfast. It tasted rather like mullet.

After the usual salutations, the Captain's first query is: 'Well Doctor, how are your patients this morning?' One of the men was in a pitiable condition; a chain cable had fallen on his foot and the Doctor expects his toe is fractured. This was the second accident of the kind. Some of them make use of artifice by conceiling any disease they may have when they come onboard, waiting to be laid up when on the voyage and by that means escape working.

Our latitude at noon was 7°17' and long. 23°13'.

There are generally one or two parties of whist players in the evening, who play now with their coats off. Dr Polding took a shower bath this evening at 10 o'clock.

On the 2nd the sailors were again exercised at the cannon. We have lost the trade wind and are becalmed.

On the 3rd a sail appeared, which the Captain took for a homeward bound and desired everyone to be quick, who intended writing to their friends. But we were disappointed,

[36]

after having written, to find her suddenly altering her course and bearing away westward.[72]

72. Bishop Polding's only extant letter on the voyage was dated May 3rd: +J.B. Polding, aboard *Oriental*, to Rev. L.B. Barber OSB, Downside (Polding, *Letters*, volume 1, 53–54).

We were rolling disagreeably the whole day without making any progress. At three o'clock the weather became exceeding close and sultry; thundering clouds gathered dense and dark. A black streak appeared on the horizon occasioned by the rain falling on the sea, which gradually widening as it approached us and contrasted strongly with the intermediate sea, which was light and smooth, while this advanced in rude and angry waves covered with breakers. Deep expectation pervaded everyone, whilst the Captain watched this suspicious aspect. 'All hands' were suddenly called. Some drops of rain had already fallen, when –

'Main gallant hallyards all clear – fore gallant hallyards clear – all clear, Sir – Let go – furl – haul away main stay – all hands – belay – lower mizen top sail. How is her head – Northeast by north.'[73]

As the men were at this work, we were called to dinner and nothing more than those torrents of the heaviest rain I ever saw and the dark shade of the cloud passed over us, instead of the squall of wind as we expected. This was succeeded by a clear and serene sky – we

[37]

paced the deck until late, admiring the bright corruscations, which covered the surface of the waves around the ship, and reconnoitering those constellations, which were perhaps in future to guide us through the bush. We remarked the moon going her course with her horns perpendicularly upwards, not at all relined as when viewed in high latitudes.[74]

On the 4th I was aroused early by the crash of thunder and the rain pouring on the deck in absolute torrents never was such. I found nearly everyone up and sheets and awnings spread out to collect the water, which was reserved for the ducks and fowls and for washing. About four hogsheads were thus saved.[75] We remained, most of us, puddling in the rain and torrents flowing on deck, splashing it at one

73. *halyard or halliard*: rope used to hoist sails; term comes from the cry, 'Haul yards'. *mizzen-mast*: the aft-most mast.
74. *her horns*: the ends of the crescent moon; the direction of the horns varies according to seasons and is mirror-reversed in northern and southern hemispheres.
75. *Hogshead*: a measure of capacity for beer equal to 54 imperial gallons.

another and washing our clothes until breakfast time, with only light trousers on.

A large shark made its appearance for the first time and made off; in the evening five or six collected round the ship. A large iron hook fastened to a rope was thrown out with a piece of pork attached to it and everyone watched with breathless expectation the enemy attracted by the bait and then retiring. After some fruitless attempts, at last, turning

[38]

on his back, smelling for some time, then opening its jaws and closing its treble row of teeth on the hook, this fellow was hoisted up in triumph in spite of a powerful resistance. He kicked and flapped the deck until one of the men with a rope got a reef knot round its tail, when he was dragged with loud shoutings from the poop to the forecastle. It is measured six ft and weighs a hundred pounds. The backbone and jaws were preserved, the latter 13 inches wide. Each of these sharks was accompanied by other fish called Pilot fish, which formed like a retinue around him. The Captain says the shark is never seen without at least 3 or 4 of these. They are beautifully marked, something like a zebra. We could not catch one of them; they appear about 2 feet long and shaped not unlike a trout. Firmly fastened to the shark was a sucker (or remora[76]) described in a number of the (penny) Saterdays magazines, wherein we found the description to tally, except in one point – they place the sucking part on the crown of the head; we found it to be under. I have sketched it in different positions and preserved the fish in a decanter of rum. We undoubtedly conclude this to be the species alluded to and inaccurately

[39]

described in the Saterdays magazines.[77]

Our latitude today was 4°50' and long 20°30', and on the 5th we were again baiting sharks the whole day and firing at them with rifles, but had no success.

---

76. *Remora*: a suckerfish with sucker on its head; from Latin meaning 'delay': in antiquity the remora was believed to stop a ship from sailing.
77. Perhaps the *Saturday Magazine*, a British magazine published from 1832 to 1844 by the Society for Promoting Christian Knowledge.

We had one or two severe squalls during which we went at the rate of 9 knots. Mr. Gregory and I spent some time reading Johnny's *Souvenirs de Saint-Acheul.*[78] He invited us all this evening to a reunion to celebrate his sister's professsion day which took place yesterday at Cheltenham.[79]

A swallow was remarked flying about the rigging. On the 6th the weather continues more squally; at one moment it is like a violent hurricane and storm of rain driving us 9 knots, then a calm in which we roll over majestic smooth undulating waves without a breath of wind to keep her sails steady. The immense swell overspreads itself instantly with white foaming spray. No horizon is distinguishable, but clouds and sea appear to meet. The thermometer is 80°. The barometer, the captain says, is no service here. Our latitude is 4°0' N., and they expect we are about entering the second trade, meeting it thus early (or on this side of the line) on account of the sun's declivity being at present so far north. Mr. Roberts and I were comparing the Welch and Breton – he

[40]

has a Welch bible. It appeared that the difference was greater in the pronunciation than in the words themselves as they were written, for instance the pater[80] and several other prayers, although his pronunciation was strange, when I read them my own way, I could scarce

78. This is an indication that Jonathan Harding was a student at the Jesuit College at Saint-Acheul in Picardy.
79. Henry Gregory's sister Anne (1818–1857) was a Dominican nun. The English Dominican nuns at Brussels fled to England during the French revolution and settled at Hartpury Court, near Cheltenham in Gloucestershire, until 1839, when the community established the Convent of the Rosary at Atherstone. Cheltenham was the hometown of the Gregory family, converts of Dom Augustine Birdsall OSB, missioner at Cheltenham from 1809. An obituary notice in the Sydney *Freeman's Journal* of 23 May 1857 recorded the death from consumption of Sister Catherine Teresa, sister of Abbot Gregory. The community relocated to Carisbrooke on the Isle of Wight in 1866.
   Another sister, Jane (1817–1850), joined the Benedictines at Princethorpe in 1842 and as Sister Scholastica sailed to Australia with Polding in 1848 to establish a community with Dame Magdalene de Clerc of Stanbrook Abbey. Scholastica also died of consumption in 1850 aged 33.
80. *The Pater*: the Lord's Prayer.

find a difference. He is from Abegelly or the North of Wales, where pronunciation may be very different.[81]

The 7th: the weather continues much the same. I shot a few stormy petrels; it rained very heavily.

The 8th: still squally. The ship rides steadily and with ease through the blast; it is not so bad as we anticipated. We rather wish for squalls now, as they drive us on and the Captain says one knot here is better than five elsewhere. Each time he goes on the poop, his first words are sure to be: 'How is her head?' And if her is not satisfied: 'Keep her one point more or less one way or t'other.'

The general topic now is Neptune's visit onboard, which is to take place the day we cross the line and each is anxious to find out what may befall him on that day. Today we caught a shark larger than the first; its length was 6 feet 7 inches; its breadth of fins from tip to tip was 4 feet 3 inches; it weighed 120 pounds.

At day dawn, the

[41]

9th, a sail came in sight, said to be a pirate and then the *Jane Goudie* (a barque that was said to have sailed from Liverpool a few days after we left).[82] The morning having been fine, most of us, as usual, had brought our cots out and spread about the cloathes; a sudden squall of rain coming, it was ridiculous to see us bundling them down at so short a notice, and the mates vociferating on their side to close all the ports.

The doctor has dissected the shark's fins and is cleaning them in hopes to preserve them. The sails continuing in sight, the men were exercised at their guns and were very busy the rest of the day making preparations, not to resist the pirate, but for Neptune's reception.

Our latitude is 2°6' N and long W 17°48'. They had appointed this evening for the celestial messenger to come and announce the God's approach. After tea a rumbling noise was heard and cries of Pirates.

---

81. *Abergele*: a small market town situated on the north coast of Wales.
82. *Jane Goudie*: a barque, tonnage 234, Captain David Simpson; arrived Sydney 31 August, having left Liverpool 2 April and Rio de Janeiro 2 June.

Those who understood and cared not for ducking bolted out of the cuddy. We were received by the sailors, who were conceiled in the rigging, heaving down on us their buckets of water, ready stowed away in the main and mizen tops. We were soon drenched and found the way of retorting by dashing tubsfull at each other,

[42]

until Neptune's messenger arrived. He was led up and familiarly shook hands with the Captain, assured him of the God's protection and friendship. Captain Allen, he said, was an old and tried friend of his majesty and an Irishman, that like poetry. He evinced by the alacrity, with which he had prepared for his reception, should be rewarded by an early visit of the divinity on Monday following – *sic fatus*[83] – and he retired dripping, as if he were melting into water, and was no sooner overboard than he assumed he shape of a ball of fire (in a tar bucket that had been set ablaze), rising and falling on the waves and vanished at the last far away in the horizon.

Sunday the 10th: *la Messe* à *lendemain.*[84]

Mr. Fisher had a severe crisis and was not expected to live.

This evening was beautiful and calm like one of Cuyp's paintings with his stream 'slumbering' in the light of the moon, which shone this evening bright and vertical.[85] The horns, as she moves through her course, point right up equally, as on St Sophia.[86] A flying fish occasionally darts along like a silvery arrow and numerous petrels, like swallows gathered around some solitary ruins, lead my roaming fancy homewards.

Latitude 1°56' N only.

[43] *+ing the_*[crossing the line] **May**

May 11th: day of crossing the line – a grand day but for discord, who had hitherto kept a very jealous eye on the peaceful Oriental and had now determined that we should not pass the threshold of her hemi-

83. *Sic fatus* (Latin): 'so saying'.
84. *la Messe à lendemain*: 'Mass tomorrow'.
85. *Aelbert Jacobsz Cuyp* (1620–1691): Dutch landscape painter.
86. Perhaps a reference to the crescent moon on Hagia Sophia at Istanbul.

sphere in such quiet and good order. She had tricked Amphitrite[87] into a consent to let her preside at the ceremony and thought no less than snatching away all the honours of the day to herself by means of one of the stranger passengers, who had resolved to be revenged on another for the loss of his little dog, which had been thrown overboard, perhaps not altogether in the most polite fashion. However, *saepe rixatur de lana caprina*[88], and this was an instance. The culprit had barricaded himself in his room resolved to stand his ground, *vi et armis*[89], until 10 o'clock, when the Captain, at his request, pledged himself that nothing more should be done to him than to any other and that he should receive no extra touch, which the sailors had been bribed most shamefully in their night drinking parties with this passenger, to bestow on him largely.

The day was fine. The preparations completed, the main sheet was spread between the longboat and gangways so as to contain 4 or 5 ft of water

[44]

and near which was placed a throne. About 11 o'clock Neptune and Amphitrite sitting on a gun carriage were drawn by a great black bear chained to the car. A dozen men covered with sheep skins and skins of all sorts, with their faces and legs tarred and blacked, marched before and behind, each brandishing a spar and making with it all the noise they could. The Captain and clergy were on deck; I was in the cuddy with a few others and Mr. Kenny, and held up Mr. Fisher to let him have a sight of the procession. He was excessively weak and spent.

No sooner was the throne occupied and the names called out than the cuddy was closed and we could obtain no further sight. Our ears were assailed with shoutings and lurid laughter and the trampling of feet as each in his turn was tossed, *sans ceremonie*, head over tip into the water contained in the sail. In momentary expectation of hearing our names called out, some, who had remained in, began to use the

87. Perhaps a confusion between Amphridite, wife of Poseidon and queen of the sea, with Aphrodite. Discord's interference had resulted in the destruction of Troy brought about by Paris' awarding of the golden apple to Aphrodite.
88. *Saepe rixatur de lana caprina* (Horace): 'He often quarrels over goat's hair' – to quibble (fabric woven of wool was prized, fabric woven of goat's hair disdained).
89. *vi et armis*: legal term used of a trespass to person or property.

bottle pretty freely and to be so excited as to make an attempt to force their way to the poop through Neptune's armed police, who were the themselves half-seas over.[90] Their intentions were to have forced down some individuals there, but they were made to retreat

[45]

during the affray.

Dr Sampson was called and returned in a few moments with a swelling in the right temple and apparently exhausted. He said he had been struck and insulted and swore vengeance. We guessed things were turning out badly and just consulting what to do, when the passenger who was to have received the main daubing was called. Shortly after came Mr. Corcoran, who desired us not to go up in our turn, but rather defend ourselves. The men were drunk, he remarked, and there appeared no more subordination. Retiring to our rooms, we promptly got all to rights, resolved to resist the expected assault. Not answering the call, Mr. Corcoran told them our door was wide open; they might fetch us out at their peril. While the culprit above mentioned was up, the Captain was down. He made enquiries if there were arms and if people meant to use them. He received no answer and returned. Shortly everything was put an end to suddenly. The Captain complained his orders of offering no indignity to any passenger had been disobeyed. It was expected to have ended worse, but order was restored by degrees. The master of the day has retired to bed; the men are deprived of their allowance of grog.[91]

[46]

We went to dinner, where no one brought up any occurrences of the day.

In the morning of the 12th we had at breakfast a fish called Skip-Jack. A sail kept in sight all the morning. The day was spent reading. I

90. '*half-seas over*' (slang): intoxicated (the phrase likely alludes to the staggering gait of one who is drunk).

91. *Grog*: the word originally referred to a drink made with rum and water, which Admiral Vernon introduced into the naval squadron he commanded in the West Indies in 1740. Vernon wore a coat of grogram cloth and was nicknamed Old Grog.

felicitated myself aloud of having crossed the line and escaped the shaving, but as it is remarked, you must have done a thing once before you can flatter yourself of doing well. We all agree now that should such circumstances ever take place again, none of us would undergo the formality. Let anyone about to undertake such a voyage show his determination from the first to resist with promptitude and firmness what is really nothing else than an assault on his person. He will find the others to join him. A few enemies of the kind would put down this ridiculous custom of shaving, practiced onboard all these outward bound. I would not so much as promise anything to the men by way of bribe, but merely give them something afterwards if properly behaved. Nor can anyone be too particular in binding down both Captains and owner by a written engagement to fulfill whatever bargain has been struck in this or in the way of room and conveniences, specifying that damages shall be recovered

[47]

in law in case of any infringement.

The passengers should always have a store of their own consisting of tea or coffee and sugar, spice cakes, cheese, hams, pickles and preserves, oatmeal or arrowroot and sago, soda powders in abundance, lemon juice and good wine and some tin cans of preserved meat and fish and about ten wax candles a week

The 13th: the deck presented a busy scene – all hands at different occupations, sail making/mending, making ropes, worming and salving old ones[92], then covering them with canvas. We are becalmed and tacking. The Captain's latitude is still only 0°43' North–we make it 0°37' South.

In the evening, while at tea, a brilliant light appeared outside, so bright that it suddenly shone like full moon. The mate and his sailors told us it was a meteor or ball of fire with a blue tail three times the length of its diameter, which appeared to be two feet. It rose about a mile off apparently from the larboard yardarm, darted across with great rapidity, lighting up distinctly every thread of the rigging and

92. *worming and salving*: worming, serving, parceling and slushing were techniques of protecting ropes against chafing and deterioration.

after passing the larboard quarter split in two, each part going on awhile in different directions, then vanished.

14th: the first thing in the morning we found a

[48]

blue shark caught by one of the lines, which had been left out and dragging with it. It was immediately taken up and placed on a cask for inspection. You may see the outline in my sketch book; it was smaller than the other kind of shark. Mr. Slater stuffed it with hay well steeped in spirits and camphor and it is meant for the Downside museum.

The sun's altitude at midday was 71°15'.

The 15th a beautiful day; at 11 o'clock a great confusion forward, the men were drawing in an Albacore.[93] Mr. Curtoy's drawing of it in my book may give you an idea of its size and shape only; the colours were beautiful and brilliant and every moment changing as it flapped about in its blue element and on the ridges of the white spray as it was hoisted from the bows of the ship cutting on at 5 or 6 knots. It was 4 feet in length and weighed 120 pounds. The doctor is endeavouring to preserve it.

Day after day we have had the finest weather and the evenings so beautiful that we remain sometimes until 10 o'clock pacing on the poop, admiring how she dashes through with a steady breeze or trade sporting over the waves, which come sometimes tumbling against her sides and white in her

[49]

path as they fall back far and near. Riding in the dark she raises millions of sparkling lights, which crowd and meet in the eddy of her wake like balls of fire forming a long stream of corruscant light fit for the Gods to tread on. If this be the froth of the sea, I don't wonder they should have made Venus to spring from it.

Sunday 17: Mass as usual this morning.

93. *Albacore*: a species of tuna found in temperate and tropical waters.

An albacore was observed keeping by the side of the ship a few yards off only, going like a dart without any effort or apparent motion, as we were sailing 7 or 8 knots. Several attempts were made to strike it with the grains fastened to a line.[94]

Our latitude 3°6' South, long 22°6'.

18th: sailing with great speed; the trade blew strongest at night towards 11 o'clock. A great sea struck her, which she shipped, and came pouring down the hatchways, which were open, and into our cabins.[95]

We remarked an albacore, perhaps the same, keeping us steady company.

Lat 5°1' S, long 23°4' W.

20th: spent the morning in my usual Geodesic[96] meditations and making my usual tribute of an hour's reading to Mr. Fisher, who appears to like it and awaits impatiently the moment

[50]

of my calling in. He has been for some time confined to his bed without being able to come at meals, which the stuard takes him in his room.

The day was fine and uncommonly calm. We were all called on deck to view the beauties of the sun setting; the sky was light above, gradually deepening to a yellow ochre towards the horizon, when long streaks of white clouds like wreaths of steam kept varying their distinct outlines on a ground of light saffron. The colouring was very unusual and called for some poetical effusions. Such aspects were the introduction, we supposed, to still more resplendent visions, which abound in these tropical climes, where books say that nature is arrayed in all her pride and glory – *sed omne ignotum magnificatur.*[97]

94. *Grains*: Lewis gives explanation of this word on 52: a pole with 3 iron darts fastened to a line.
95. *Ship* (verb): to take in water over the side.
96. *Geodesic*: the shortest route between two points on the Earth's surface; perhaps referring the brevity of Lewis' meditation.
97. but everything unknown appears magnificent.

Some said they had seen just as fine in England; there was no need of going from home in hopes of finding anything new or beauty in any respect more attractive. No sooner was the sun set than all these fine colours darkened, rain began to fall and in encreased torrents a squall came on, and whilst we were at tea, the Captain was called out by the mate on watch to give his orders, as the breeze had stiffened

[51]

to a deafening roar. The cry of 'all hands' pierced through in the dark and was answered, 'Aye, Aye, Sir. Ease her head there; Gallant, Halyards clear; down foresail and jib; square the yards. Let run the Halyards you, ease off topsails, clue up, two reefs shift the helm—luff up[98] – all hands man the weather braces – which they set about singing 'All together ahio cheerly man. Come pull her ahio cheerly man, for she is heavy ahio, all together cheerly man, she's frisky ahio, cheerly man, oh, oh, ahio. She's a dandy, ahio; well wash her, ahio, cheerly man, well swab her, ahio all ahio.'

We turned in at 10 o'clock, 'suspicious' of what was to follow.

21: it moderated in the daytime; the night was bad. We had shipped two or three heavy seas. One wave, which had broken over the deck, poured down the hatchways deluging our cabins. The rolling, smashing of plates, bottles, glass of every description in the stuard's lockers at every lurch kept us on the alert the whole night. After some louder crash than usual, Mr. Roberts' tiny voice was heard repeated by the Doctor 'Here's a lark!', succeeded by laughs and screams let us know that

[52]

there was still life somewhere in the midst of the surrounding darkness and confusion.

The weather, although not at all mild in the daytime was very warm, the thermometer being at 82–83, being its usual height since we entered the tropics.

98. *Luff up*: alter course to windward

24 Sunday: stiff breeze still. We have run 1,000 miles this last week and to judge of appearances we are likely to get on as well this week. A flying fish was caught today which entrapped itself into one of the portholes whilst flying.

25th Monday: the wind seems spent and the sea is calm. Mr. Fisher is so weakened that the Doctor now despairs of his recovery. Mr. Corcoran staid up with him last night, remaining on the sopha in the cuddy.

Our latitude is 19°33' and long 28°2'.

During dinner the Captain sent someone to the masthead and shortly after we heard 'Land, land ahoy'. It was the island of Trinidada on our Leebow – but a barren rock visible only from the masthead.[99] Henry's fiddle soon cheered up. It was grog day and the men made merry forward, while on the poop and below the boards shook with the dancing, and those who could not dance jumped. Smyth and boy bently figured

[53]

among the most determined – Archilochus should have been here to have handed round the punch and exalt the glories of the victors at the games we were at until 12 o'clock.[100]

27th Wednesday: at 11 o'clock adjusting my sextant, I remarked that the sun was partly eclipsed. On enquiring of the Captain below what he knew of it, everyone soon came up. It was very cloudy and unusually dark. The almanacks were searched to account for this unprepared for event and by the help of coloured glasses we observed the emersion, as one late to make out the beginning of this eclipse, which is annual and visible at the Cape. When first noticed the sun's disk was three parts conceiled. By observing the time of the emersion as well as dark black clouds passing across would allow us, I found our longitude to be 26°33' 35" thus:

99. Trindade and Martin Vaz: an archipelago in the Southern Atlantic.
100. *Archilochus* (680–645 BC): a Greek lyric poet.

Moon's emersion appointed time	12h 22' 40"
Time at the Cape	4h 5'
diff.	3h 27' 40"
equals	45° 33' 35"
deduct for the distance of longitude	
between the Greenwich & the Cape	18° 23' 35"
longitude in	26° 33' 35" W
our latitude at noon being	22° 12' South

[54]

After dinner came on a squall of such heavy rain as is incredible. The sea was unrufled but rose in high smooth billow. We are emerging from the tropics.

28th Thursday, the Ascension.

The Revd. Mr. Clement Fisher died this morning 10am and very shortly after Mass had been offered up for him. The body was covered and laid in the Bishop's room until evening, when prayers for the dead were said, after which he was silently lowered in the deep. Every passenger acknowledged owing him a debt of gratitude for the many examples of meekness and patience and evenness of mind, with which he bore long and tedious sufferings and for those many other virtues. Each one was now emulous in praising. In the Bishop's room were as many persons as it could well contain; and the body being sewn up in canvass, in which were placed two cannon balls – the prayers being terminated, recited by Dr Polding in his pontificals – the Captain made a signal at about half past six, upon which the body was lowered.[101] The stillness of the evening, the tranquility

[55]

of the waters and the silence, which prevailed at the time of the interment, tended to make the scene of the most reflective nature. All were much edyfied.

By the Captain's log our longitude would be 23°37' W and latitude 22°54' South at 6 o'clock pm.

101. *Pontificals*: episcopal regalia.

28th of May 1835: our progress is only one knot an hour. We spent the evening in Dr Polding's room, whom this event has so much afflicted, Mr. Curtoys and the Captain joining.

29th being perfectly calm the jolly boat was let down. The Captain and Dr Polding took a rowing excursion around the ship. They had time enough to survey the Oriental and reported her a man-of-war to all appearances. The Captain turned out again with paper and pencil and has taken a sketch of her. Meanwhile we were waiting for our turn, but Mr. Smyth coming out of the boat broke one of the seats and further jaunts were put off.

We saw a tiger fish at which I shot; it was struck, for it immediately decamped. I was more fortunate on a large petrel which fell. We saw several sharks today, one of them accompanied by eight pilot fish. The Captain shot one of them, which sank directly.

[56]

The shark was caught, speared with the grains (a pole with 3 iron darts fastened to a line) very dexterously by Mr. Slater, the 2nd mate. It was 3 feet long. It would have made ladies shed a tear to see the distress in which were the poor pilot fish at the loss of their patron. Their agitation was visible by the manner with which they appeared to search in every direction; their hurried movements to and fro could not but excite a sympathy.

30: sudden squalls and calms alternately, now 9 knots then 1 & ½, as we emerged from the trade and we expected variable and inconstant winds. It resembles the weather at Penenrue in those high westerly winds, which come on in sudden gusts.[102] It blows in the sails for the space of half and hour or an hour with incredible fury and deafening roar, preceded and followed by rain in torrents appalling. The sea is agitated and rears in fierce breakers. There is generally a warning and at a moment's notice the top gallant sails, mizen top and spanker, gibs and foretops more or less are furled or reefed in. The light ship

102. *Penenrue*: the old chateau near St Pol-de-Léon purchased by the Hardings in 1814.

[57]

sports over wave after wave assailing her bows in vain, with clouds of dense spray no sooner poured on deck than carried off – the wind spends itself suddenly – no longer any which surf, and billows smooth and glassy roll with majestic swell, rising and falling with slow dignity, the nearest obstructing all from view. And as we glide along its deep trough every drop of rain is visible on its stretched surface, and the pleasure of a swim over one or two such.

Lat 23°33' S; Long 23°7' W.

31: a fine day – the sun's altitude 43°59'; no Mass, but prayers, being Sunday. Numerous porpoises keep alongside. We feel it getting colder.

I have been occupied with you the greater part of this last month of May and with your *souvenirs de St Acheul*, which Mr. Gregory and I read together.[103] Mr. Spencer knows several of them, having been a long time at Amiens. He was at the Abbey du Gard, where Philips went and was particularly acquainted with the Père St Germain and received his last adieu before he died.[104]

[58] June

Now hold on, Ladies and Gentlemen.

1st June: out latitude at noon was 24°8' S and long 19°10' W; the morning was most lovely, as was, last night, the sunset. The sky was like a furnace and the most brilliant colours enriched the horizon for half an hour afterwards. The greater part of the day was employed cleaning and washing our guns, premeditating more slaughter. It must be owned we were very bad shots, but Mr. Sumner was the most successful.

Having no wind, we rolled greatly; all the boxes and trunks heaped in Mr. Kenny's room tumbled on every side. My washstand, well lashed, too fetched away in a lurch. The Captain greets the helmsman

103. See page 36 above.
104. *Abbaye du Gard*: Notre Dame du Gard, a Trappist monastery in the vicinity of Amiens reoccupied by monks following the restoration of the Bourbon monarchy in 1815. Spencer was at the abbey 1831–1833 (see T. J. Kavenagh, op. cit.). Dom Germain was abbot of the reestablished monastery.

each time he goes on the poop with a 'How is her head', to which he answers accordingly, 'S by E or SE by S as it is'. A breeze sprung in the afternoon, when we saw a whale not more than 50 yards from us: 'There she spouts'. I should not wonder if I were at the topmast of a whaler some day shouting the like within the Southern Antarctic circle. This one appeared a fine booty. Alas, we

[59]

had no harpoon. It was the first we had seen.

This evening was squally to the southward with lightning; sun's altitude was 43°43' 30".

2nd: we were roused in the morning by a musket shot and halloo's of a 'Ship ahead'. The gun had been fired by the Captain as a signal for her to approach. Mr. Corcoran and I were soon up, as everyone else, and in great excitement on the lookout fore and aft. The boat had been lowered; the 2nd mate and two men were halfway towards her as she lay a mile ahead. We all set to work at writing home. While thus engaged, the mate returned, passed through the cuddy (with more than a sailor's walk than usual, blue dressed, a 'flare-up' hat, which hardly covered his head) without condescending to inform anyone, but went to the Captain to deliver his important embassy. The ship was called *The Brook's*, the captain's name was Stubs. She had left Valparaiso about the same time we sailed from Liverpool. She was laden with log wood and specie and bound to London.[105] The Captain would take charge of our letter and asked to purchase a cask of beef, which was sent to him with a large parcel of letters and an invitation to the Captain to come and breakfast with us, which he however declined,

[60]

as a breeze sprang up about the time. She stretched away, leaving us to think on you – I thought when and where you would receive my letter, which I directed to you care of Wright's, uncertain whether you might be at Trelawny at the time or in France. The ship remained near us for about two hours. I was too much agitated to write a long letter and this evening can hardly recollect what I have written about.

105. *Specie*: coined money.

Our latitude at noon was 24°22' South and long 19°W.

The 3rd: although oct[ave] day, Dr Polding kept his feast today.[106] All the passengers were invited and the Captain and 1st mate and Mr. Slater. The evening was spent in merriment and dance was prolonged till late. The sailors were given grog; we had punch on the poop and songs were sung and each one endeavoured to contribute to the amusement of the rest. The night was fine and the stars numerous and brilliant and the moon far to the west when we 'turned in'.

4th: turned a new leaf reading about the Colonies of N.S.Wales and the exploration parties and resolved to lead one myself; Mr. Corcoran and Mr. Spencer very animated at their card playing – they lose, but it was a hard battle.[107]

[61]

5th Friday: the morning was fine and a fresh wind had sprung up in the night. We go at 7 or 8 knots and are still said to be a fortnight's sail from the Cape. Our latitude is 28°14' South, long 17°54' W.

We had fresh salmon for Lunch in Dr Polding's room – claret and muscella. The wind rises in the evening. The boat on the poop upset and threw the helmsman over the hen coops; a dark sky and lightning.

6th: the night has been very boisterous and calamitous, the cuddy fore and aft offering a scene of wreck and disaster. We thought in the night time every bit of glass onboard had been smashed and were kept awake by the noise of boxes rolling and the fetching away of every loose article. The worst was the water washing over the deck. It tore up the tarpauling which was nailed down to one of the hatchways and fell in cascades below. Mr. Corcoran's boxes got wet through. We had to call down some boys to swab up the water. Returning to my cot after the operation, the rolling became so heavy as to rock it up to the ceil-

---

106. *Octave day*: eight days after 27 May, the date of the feast of St Bede, Polding's patron.

107. Concerning clergy playing at cards, Polding gave the following advice and warning as he farewelled two recruits from England in November 1846: 'I do not object to you joining in this spirit any games that may be played, chess, backgammon, even cards, though from the moment you reach Sydney, these are never to be touched.' (*Polding Letters* II.65 [see Appendix I])

ing at each swing; however, it kept high above the wet. The morning was darkly clouded and the wind drove us on 8 knots. A cape pigeon

[62]

was seen the first that made its appearance. The sea continued very rough and a heavy pitch snapped the gib-boom in two.

Latitude at noon 29°17' S, long 15°56'.

7th. Whitsunday: gale or half gale, as they call it, continues. Majestic waves; proceeding under furled royals; Gallant sails and top sails reefed. Numerous Cape pigeons and albatrosses, which we now saw for the first time, were flying around the ship. It was new company. Mr. Corcoran talking at table about O'Connell after dinner.[108] We had wine in Dr Polding's room.

8th: wind and waves continue rough and boisterous. We were all engaged firing at albatrosses. Six guns were at once fired at one and all missed. They have very thick and close feathers. Either the rocking of the ship or a great deception in our judgment of distance prevent our killing. Three birds only were shot after long firing. The Cape pigeons offer an easy shot; they follow about innumerable following in the wake. They appear the tamest of all birds. They are a too easy prey to attend to.

(Lat 31°21' S, long 11°15' W.)

[63]

Albatrosses are very large, Mr. Slater says, having caught some measuring 14 feet across the winds from tip to tip. They appear heavy and fly slowly, hardly ever flap their wings, but undulate across the air with a gentle but easy motion, sometimes skimming the surface or ranging along the broken ridges of the vast waves, then rising and presenting their broad wings to the gale, let themselves be carried away, as it were, by the winds. These, the Cape pigeons, Petrels and other oceanic birds remain in large flocks floating peaceably on the calm sea and pick up an easy prey on or very little below the surface, until perhaps the storm arises 'awakening the deep'. They then take to their wings and being

108. Daniel O'Connell (1775–1847) was known in Ireland as the Liberator. In 1835 the 'Tithe War', campaign against the payment of a tax to the Established Church by Irish Catholics, was at its peak (1830–1836).

prevented from fishing content themselves with whatever chance offers. We see them in the trough of a gigantic wave darting on some stray fish, keeping their wings extended right up, then with the fish in their bills tread over the surface two or three yards before they can rise.

In the afternoon the wind strengthened, blew away a studding sail, which was picked up again. At 9 pm, the half gale,

[64]

as we were all alive at card playing, encreased with unprecedented fury. The royal gallant sails were furled and topsails reefed. We saw from the poop the whole expanse covered with breakers. The rugged white surface contrasts with the darkness of the hour and black squally clouds. The rain, as I write, has just poured, not in rain, but in buckets-full and enters the portholes like a cascade rushing over the deck and sweeps all before it from side to side. You might as well attempt to ford a waterfall as bounce across the deck at this moment. *Le plus hardi marin n'y passe qu'en tremblant.*[109] The ship rolls dreadfully and many are sick. Now and then a wave breaks itself against the sides and the clap it makes resounds along fore and aft as if 5 or 6 canons had just been fired. *Insonuere cava genituque dedere cavernae.*[110]

At 10 we go to bed. The wind does not appear to abate, on the contrary the men are waiting to take in another reef. Although these two hours it has been roaring like thunder in the topsails, it is lightening on the weather bow and all portends a storm.

[65]

9th: stopped up last night some hours. Smyth all alive with the sailors reefing and shortening sail every half hour to attempt a description of what we saw or endeavour to relate what forcible ideas of awe and delight at the same time crowded in our minds would be a failure. Each remark this morning, whatever descriptions they had read of storms, is far below or different from impressions which the reality now leaves. I remarked with my pencil in hand noting there were

109. 'The boldest sailor could only pass in trembling.'

110. insonuere cavae gemitumque dedere cavernae: 'The caverns moaned loudly and the caves gave forth a groan' (Virgil, Aeneid II.53).

only 3 sails up; they close reefed (or presenting but the smallest surface of canvass they could be reduced to) in these and through the shrouds the wind whistled and blew with such roar that had there been any thunder it could not have been heard.[111] The moon shone bright at intervals between black clouds which raced past its disk. I should guess 20 knots an hour; we went 8. The guns, at every roll of the ship, dipped into the water their black snouts, which was as a signal for a wave, such as break on a sandy beach on a lee shore, to break through the ports and over the bulwarks

[66]

and lay all that side fore and aft right under water. But don't think that at this moment the side opposite is dry; it is indeed worse than the other to be at, for the hight and exposed flanks of the weather side are beaten against with the swell as if she had struck a rock, which towers aloft and falls in a cloud of dense heavy spray and you think the deck itself is or must be stove in. This over, a laborious effort rights her once more. The sea on deck knee deep as it follows the motion rushes carrying with it every loose tackle. All follow together with the corresponding roll and so on turn after turn. A man standing by us on a heap of coiled ropes we saw disappear, suddenly born off by a wave in one of these rolls, coils and all, across the deck and back in the twinkling of an eye, a moment; he was given up. Some, and among them Mr. Corcoran, came out complaining they could not sleep: 'The ship was as if it were tearing to pieces.'

At 3 o'clock I lay on the cuddy sopha to take some rest, the doctor in another, after lashing 2 or 3 chairs to prevent being thrown out.

[67]

The repeated strokes of the tumbling waves against her sides caused such frequent loud and sudden reports, succeeded by a quivering of the whole ship, prevented all sleep, and the water, moreover, breaking through the skylight and splashing over us – chairs, boxes and glass fractured, whirled from starboard to larboard. The occasional voices of those below, as if issuing from a grave in an interval of momen-

111. *shrouds*: set of ropes forming part of the standing rigging of a sailing ship.

tary lull, and other noises, you may well think, kept us from any long sleep. My thoughts turned on you, where you were and what doing. I fancied being snug in my bed and wondered old Betty did not bring me up my frico.[112] Rose at 5 in hopes of finding the weather moderated or contemplate its pleasing and terrifying grandeur with more light on the subject. The sea was running awfully high and I had not been looking on five minutes when an unusual black cloud of spray suddenly envelloped all forward. I involuntarily moved a few steps sideways, when down came that part of the cuddy front near which I stood, letting in an irresistible flood, which swamped for

[68]

a moment the cuddy, Smyth's cabin, the Captain's cot and sopha, on which he was, carrying on with it the fragments of the cuddy door, loose floating timber and spars, chairs and benches and with all the fury of an explosion. The Captain had only left his cot the moment before; as for Smyth he bolted out of his cabin and staring wildly around for a short time, when he saw me laugh as I repeated to him his own words: 'Who would not sell his farm and go to sea'. He then began to dance, recommencing his usual shouting. He thought he had been washed overboard through his window whilst fast asleep. Some hands were instantly called to clear away and fence in the cuddy and swat out the water in buckets. Everyone was soon up and at breakfast time everyone was more employed in guarding against a fall than anything else. I wish you could have seen us at breakfast – nothing could be kept on the table; we were collected at one end supporting one another and holding in one hand a roll of bread and some fried bacon and in the other a cup of coffee, which you were reminded to drink off and not scold your next neighbour,

[69]

without appetite, sick and giddy. And 'Who would not sell his farm and go to sea', shouts Smyth.

At 11 o'clock we were able to crawl and scramble somehow or other on the poop and there, holding with both hands to the irons on the

---

112. *frico*: dish of heated cheese and potatoes.

mizen mast, to look around and admire. Dr Polding went up also at his usual hour after breakfast, then looks at his plants, which are all in flower and full verdure at least and doing well. There are about 200 different kinds. We fear the seawater, which has got to them today may injure them.

The wind was cold and sharp and soon drove us down. Mr. Sumner and Mr. Spencer were caught, standing on the poop, by a sea, which unmoored in its passage thither a boat suspended on the starboard quarter at least 20 feet above the water, overtook them. They had quickly to come down and change. But the troubled sea, in spite of such, was worth looking at. In the trough, the dark blue wave moving out before us and concealing all horizon was crowned with a snow-white rolling surf keeping pace with it for a time, then, left behind, it spread itself out in long irregular streaks of milky froth. As we reached the

[70]

summit and envelloped in the foaming breaker, the view extended no further than to a few of these undulating hills. Pigeons, cape hens and every sized petrel collected appear in the distance like whole flocks grazing in some deep and solitary meadow, while the slow albatross with its white bosom glided along the snow-clad summits like the spirit of the wave.

At dinner time assembled as merry as grigs, but we had to hold our plates and eat with our fingers.[113] The table, although fitted purposely to hold dishes on such occasions still, the greater part of the *appareil gastronomique* was strewed, spilt and broken about the room. Our chairs slid away under us and our plates, unless we held them tight, would travel across the table to some other body. Mr. Spencer was near coming out of his cabin through the blind, leaving in it a round hole the size of his head. The Doctor appears the worst hand in avoiding slips and falls, which are too numerous to note down. He related of some friends of his giving an account of what they called a sea voyage from London to Margate in a steamer

113. *Merry as a grig* (idiom): carefree, lively, full of fun.

[71]

and to be sure how they spoke of the raging mane and the boat would go up one wave and down another[114] – it was awful. 'But now, when I meet', he says, 'one of these fellows in coach or otherwhere before strangers, I'll let him go on and spin out his yarn and then put a stopper; only see what these fellows know about it, letting them talk for some time – and then –'

The gale this evening does not appear to abate. We met in Dr Polding's room, where songs were sung to drive away sickness and dull care. Mr. Curtoys played beautifully the:

Oh Pilot, 'tis a fearful night
There's danger on the deep – I'll come and
pace the deck with thee etc. etc. –[115]

Our latitude was 32°10' South; Long 8°35' W.

10th Wednesday: gale moderated by degrees the whole day. We employed shooting – only one or two were killed. The evening brought calm, which continued on the 11th. Our latitude today 33°1' South; Long 5°39' W; rolling rather bad still. The men were employed at repairs. The boom had been cast a good bit to starboard; posts were placed up to strengthen the cuddy front;

[72]

a second binacle was placed on the poop for convenience. Mr. Roberts fired a pistol he had taken from Mr. Corcoran; it burst in his hands, luckily without injury.

12: a large sea and rolling, but no wind in lat 33°30' South, long 4°50' W. We are nearly in the depth of winter; you now enjoying summer as we steer to colder climes. But we have now the same hours of the day in common with you, so that we can follow your occupations, although on the other side of the sun. A breeze sets in towards evening, which stops the rolling, and we are stretching away at 7 or 8 knots.

114. *mane*(sic): main sea, the open sea.
115. Song composed by Thomas Haynes Bayley (1797–1839), English lyric poet.

No whist game this evening. We meet in Dr Polding's room to take wine and song: 'This night we had a revelry etc. etc.'; 'Come haste then to share in the fairy's gay festival sports, for this is the hour of high frolic and revelry, fa la la la' etc.

13th Saturday: the breeze was fresh all night. She occasionally shipped a sea, which broke with great fury over the deck partly entering our room. Mr. Corcoran greatly displeased and attacked the captain about it at breakfast time, as his

[73]

things were continually getting wet. The barometer lowered sensibly in the morning, which gave us [to] suspect another gale. Towards evening, however, it rose again to 30.2 – 29.5 or 29.6, we have noticed, is the point for gales and rough weather.

We are near opposite the Cape by our latitude. Beyond, they say, at this season we are to expect nothing but storms, gales and intense cold – we shall see.

Dr Polding proposes Thursday for singing, music and convivial meeting. But Saturday being the Captain's day and which is kept in the navy, that day was also put aside for festive purposes. Smyth's mode of singing we found to be this evening more than usually extravagant and fantastic. He certainly has done much to keep up the sport, but he shows such a revengeful and susceptible temper that he undoes by his manner the good effects his clamorous merriment might otherwise in such circumstances produce.

Our latitude is 34°37' South, long 2°23' W.

14th Trinity Sunday: the thermometer lowered 10° since yesterday; cold and some heavy rolls during Mass; a few Cape pigeons and albatrosses were caught with a fishing line.

[74]

We were glad to have so near a view of them. They have three joints in their wings, which are of great strength and very long. When placed on the deck, the extreme length of their wings prevent them from rising, so they are let free and can't escape. One of them was a white albatross. Cape pigeons were the size of a common pigeon.

Today was Mr. Curtoys' birthday and he gave wine for dinner. Dr Polding proposed a musical party in the evening and the social bowl went round. Mr. Curtoys played the music of 'We've weathered out the gale, our bark has reached the port', the 'Lady fair', the 'Marseillaise' and other airs. These concerts are charming considering the place and circumstance, our distance from such scenes on land, to which they bring us back, and the continued warnings, as we roughly tumble over one another, that we are girt far and wide with the boisterous ocean.

15th: stiff breeze; barometer 30.4; 7 knots. Mr. Spencer was the only one on board who took the alt[titude] today, which he found to be 31°52', which would make our latitude to be 35°38' South.

The Doctor poisoned the birds caught yesterday by giving them on their tongued one drop

[75]

of prussic acid, which deprived them of life in one minute.[116]

16th: passed latitude of the Cape in longitude 6°2' E. We are in the latitude of the Hottentots.[117] Travelling 9 knots all the morning we have gone over 230 miles since yesterday at noon. Within the 2½ hours after tea all invited by Dr Polding in his room to rake a bowl of punch, where we remained until 11. The Captain made a bet with everyone, of one shilling each, that not one would give the same answer or answer the same word <u>three times following</u> to any three questions he might propose. Among 20 of us who took the bet the Captain was winner of a shilling only. What caused some merriment was that everyone was so sure he was able to repeat a word of his own choosing 3 times; Mr. Cotham was so certain that he scrupled to take up the bet, but being prevailed on, he lost. My examination ran thus: 'The ship is going steadily' – answer: 'Noboclish' – 'How is the wind?' – 'Noboclish'. Then he rose us triumphantly and said: 'Ah! Now you have lost the bet!'; I answered: 'How?' instead of repeating the word I had begun to use. One or two having chosen 'Indeed' for

116. *Prussic acid*: hydrogen cyanide, first prepared from Prussian blue by the Swedish chemist Carl Wilhelm Scheele in 1782; in English, it became known popularly as *prussic acid.*

117. *Hottentot*: Dutch term applied to the Khoikhoi people of southern Africa.

[76]

an answer, they won by accident, but without knowing it.

Lat 36°44' S; long 6°2' east.

17th Wednesday: the wind changed during the night, but still we are making good way dashing through the surf in the afternoon. A dark bronze tint overspread the rough wilderness reflected from a stormy and deep red sky. Our lat 37°35' S, long 9°52' East.

18th: anniversary of my feast since 1819. I gave 3 bottles of wine at the reunion in Dr Polding's room and figs and raisins etc. etc. and sent some to John Kenny.[118]

19: birds very numerous about, but everyone seems disgusted with shooting, having had hitherto so little success. 7 or 8 of us fired in a volley at an albatross not 40 yards off, which did not so much as make it stir an inch from its course. Mr. Lancaster (the 3rd mate) relates having been detained, in the spot we now were, on a former voyage for nearly 3 weeks by contrary weather and successive gales.

Our latitude is 37°36' and long 13°2' east of Greenwich; barometer 30.8; thermometer 66°; rate 7 or 8 knots.

In the evening a beautiful meteor passed over us.

[77]

20th: travelling steadily all the forenoon; turned squally at dinner time, when we went 9 knots. We all agreed during dinner to form a lottery and make tickets to value of 10/- on the day we should arrive in Hobart Town.

Lat 37°2' and long 18°36'

21st: Sunday and St Louis de Gonzague.[119] The day fine; at night lightning. The sea has a dark green or dirty greyish colour indicative of our

118. Lewis' patron was St Louis Gonzaga, whose feast day is 21 June. There must have been some family reason why, since 1819, he celebrated his name day on 18 June.

119. St Aloysius de Gonzague (1568–1591): an Italian aristocrat who joined the Jesuits in Rome; while still a student, he died as a result of caring for the victims of a serious epidemic; he was canonised in 1726. The Harding family had a

near approach to land-the African coast beyond the Cape. It blows, but the barometer is 30.6, so it's all right. Lat 36°50', long 19°49' E.

22nd: tolerable breeze all day; a rough squall or two at 5 o'clock. At dinner time the lottery was arranged and the numbers registered. We drew our tickets paying 10/- each. The lottery amounted to 9£. On each card was inscribed a day in the month of Aug.; the whole month of July was to form one. And whatever day a pilot from Hobart Town should set his foot onboard to take charge of the ship, the owner of the ticket for that day was to win. On my ticket is inscribed the 8th and the forenoon of the 23rd.

Lat 37°15', long 21°34' E. and Hobart Town is 147° E.

23rd Tuesday: morning fresh; at noon

[78]

clouds set in and it blew fresher. We dash onwards with crowded sails at the rate of 9 knots. Mr. Sumner and I shot a few Cape pigeons. I now begin to have the knack of shooting from a poop. Sitting at dinner as we look a yard or two out through the windows, porpoises were rolling in great numbers over the passing billows. An occasional wave strikes the side of the ship as if to smash them. Then the Captain gives his usual warning 'Hold on, Ladies and Gentlemen'. We begin to feel it cold and have 7,000 miles yet to go. The barometer 30; thermometer 63°; lat 28°2' S, long 23°35' E.[120]

24th Wednesday: last night was dark and squally and we rolled very heavily. Mr. Corcoran groaning now and then as he lay in his bed, his feet at times far above his head, and the sea rushed along the deck, immediately over us, like a river. In the morning the sea continued running very high. Numerous porpoises about and birds different from any we had yet seen, of the petrel species with blue streaks under their wings and others white; they flew about in endless confusion like bees. The breakfast things were tossed about and it was useless

---

special devotion to the saint: in 1818 John Harding, writing to Lewis' Jesuit headmaster, explained that Lewis had been born on the day of the laying of the foundation stone of the chapel of St Aloysius in Somers Town, London. (Correll p.45)

120. Lewis was mistaken in recording the latitude-28°2' S instead of 38°2' S.

[79] *24 June: votre fête*

to sit down to attempt to write. This they call but a breeze in winter off the Cape. Our lat is 38°7', long 27°30'. It appears by our diff. of longitude we have gone 160 miles since yesterday noon in the 24 hours.

Today is St John the Baptist – I wish you a happy feast – a mind as calm as the seas we have past when basking in the warm climes of the parallels of the Peloponesius and Italy – and that looking forward to many happy returns of this joyous day time to come may present itself to your imagination dyed in tints as bright and lovely as the sky and clouds we there admired.

Mr. Curtoys says he is black all over with the thumps and falls in the rolling. Dr Polding remarks he shall want a new back bone at the end of the voyage.

A Cape pigeon came on the deck. It was soon caught and let go with a ribbon tied to its leg. At dinner time it continued a strong wind and a large sea. The dishes, rice, potatoes and liquids were travelling from one to another. Dr Sampson, while tearing with his teeth a greasy wing of a goose he held, the plate was sliding from the table onto the floor and from the

[80]

floor to Smyth's cabin. The Captain, to comfort us, brought out after dinner an old nautical book, in which the Doctor read out an article guarding sailors against the prevailing storms and sudden squalls of hail and thunder in our present latitude, as I enquired of the helmsman what he thought of the weather and the night: 'Did it threaten a gale?' 'Oh! Not a bit', said he, 'Good wholesome weather this.' The thermometer at 64; barometer 29°. She was driving at 9 knots. The high waves in every direction appeared rising as if trying their power while a thundering wind swept away their towering crests into wreaths of snow, on which the rays of the lowering sun, piercing through wild and bronze hued clouds, produced the colour of the rainbow.

Today was Mr. Gregory's profession day also.[121] Mr. Spencer sang *Cantiques* this evening and the *Benissons a jamais.*[122]

25: Squally still; much rocking in the night – numerous birds and albatrosses; the Doctor engaged writing in the Captain's room. An unusual heavy roll came in the height of the squall, fetched table and books, chairs away, hove out an enormous

[81]

box from its place behind which the Doctor got jammed against the sides of the ship. The deck was deluged in waves and spray, and some sailors adjusting a part of the rigging stood up to their waists in water. Squalls encrease as the day advances. A sea came in Mr. Sumner's cabin; swamped all his traps. An *assemblé* in Dr Polding's room, as it was Mr. Sumner's profession day. He treated us with punch and we continued to past 11.

Thermometer today was 65; barometer 28.8; lat 38°50', long 31°6'.

26 Friday: a fearful night has passed over. Mr. Sumner, having to get up in the night time to put his boxes in a safer place from the water, cut his hand very bad. Mr. Corcoran and I having taken our present cabin and which is preferable in some respects, still is exactly where we hear, and feel too, the very fiercest conflicts of waves on deck immediately overhead, striving to overcome and swallow up the craft. Squalls succeeded each other every half hour and large bolts everywhere groaned and sighed, as she lay along, with weight of the

121. First anniversary of Henry Gregory's profession at Downside.

122. *Cantiques*: the evening canticles are the *Magnificat* and the *Nunc dimittis*. *Bénissons à jamais*: *Les perfections divines* (canticle of St Louis-Marie Grignion de Montfort [1673–1716]):
Bénissons à jamais
Le Seigneur dans ses bienfaits;
Exaltons à jamais
Le Seigneur dans ses hauts faits!
Adorons à jamais
Le Seigneur dans ce qu'il est;
Bénissons à jamais
Le Seigneur dans ses beaux faits!

[82]

main tack and masts and the rush of the heavy sea flowing in tuns on these frail supports. Owing to her being so deeply laden, carrying a 1,000 tuns for 500, instead of riding over the wave, she labours through and often so heavily that the rolling billow heaves over her bows its towering crest, which washes right across the deck.[123] When this occurs the men themselves are cautious how they will venture to ford the torrent to attend their duty, and we have often seen them in their passage from the forecastle to the cuddy in water up to their waists. In the interval of such squalls a lull, an awful stillness would prevail for a short time, when we turned in our beds endeavouring to snatch a moment's slumber. All was silence then, excepting perhaps the cheering sound of the helmsman's voice, the quick tread of the mate on watch pacing the poop or the slow quiet slow tolling of the bell, which in our quiet solitude, forgetting where we were, invited by its church-like sounding, our

[83]

thoughts to roam over years of old and days of chivalry, when similar peals awoke monks to matins or directed the steps of some weary knight in safety through the tractless wilderness perhaps to the Halls of his fair Dona.

The morning was moderate; making 7 or 8 knots; encreased shortly after to 9. There was probably too great a press of sails as a top mast yardarm and sail were carried away. Our lat 39°1' S, long 34°17' E.

27th Saturday: sun shone at intervals on a cold wintery and high-running sea till 11 o'clock, when it became finer; our rate steady at 8 knots. Mr. Corcoran unwell and remained in bed until 11. The sun's altitude at noon was 27°23'. The deck was so slippery by the flying spray that two men very involuntarily measured their lengths on it. A meteor appeared on a boom end for some moments. It was called a blue light. A Saturday's evening in the captain's cabin as usual. Mr. Slater gives us every evening a new song, but always the same air. Lat 39°7', long 37°12'.

28th Sunday: Therm. 63°, Barom. 29.8. Mr. Spencer sang on the piano the Litany of the B.V. and some cantiques.

123. Items from the *Oriental's* general cargo were advertised soon after arrival in Hobart Town: 'Superior Malt Whiskey, Gin in hogsheads, Pale Sherry in hogsheads and quarter-casks, Madeira in quarter-casks, Prime Irish Mess Pork, Gunpowder and Shot . . .' (*Colonial Times*, 11 August 1835, page 8).

[84]

29th Monday: Dr Polding's consecration day.[124] We lunch in his room on fresh salmon, wine and preserves. The Captain being ill the reunion for the evening was transferred to the morrow. The sailors were given grog. At two o'clock a whale was said to be in sight. The day rainy. lat 39°14' S, long 43°13'.

30th Tuesday: the day has been delightful. Therm. 64, B. 30.1. Dr Polding gave wine after dinner – 5 bottles. Mr. Slater and Mr. Lancaster wished 'multos annos'[125] and the sailors cheered from outside. We stopped up till 12 o'clock. The bowl circulated and toasts were given, while Mr. Curtoys on the piano gave: 'This night we hold a revelry', 'Behold far o'er the troubled tide you gallant skiff' and some French airs. Each one gave his song. I gave a short speech meant for the 'Pip, pip, pip hurrah' of the millions, whom this day sends a chief Pastor. The evening ended in a chorus of 'God save the king'.[126]

lat. 39°16' S, long. 45°13' East.

[85]

July

1st July: a dead calm in the early part of the day. The sun rose for us 3 hours and some minutes before it could light your gallery window or shed a ray in the green room. The rest of the day was fine. The log time after breakfast indicated we were going at 7 knots, which rate we kept the whole day. Mr. Corcoran had his line out and caught a sea snake, but which escaped as they were hauling it up, carrying the hook with it. Our lat. 39°18' S and long. 47°45'.

2: a splendid day and a frosty morning; Lady Day and Mass was said.[127] Therm. 58 and Bar. 30.3; the therm. was 52 at sunrise. The captain expresses his astonishment at the fine weather we have here,

124. John Bede Polding was consecrated bishop on the feast of Saints Peter and Paul, 29 June 1834, in the tiny private chapel of the Vicar-Apostolic of the London District, James Bramston. The recently appointed Vicar-Apostolic of Eastern Oceania, Etienne Rouchouze, was one of the co-consecrators. Rouchouze perished at sea in 1843 on a voyage from France to the Sandwich Islands via Cape Horn.

125. Ad multos annos: toast-'to many years to come!'

126. *The king*: William IV (reigned 1830–1837).

127. Lady Day: 2 July feast of the Visitation.

which he says is very unusual, even in summer; much more in this line in the depth of winter. I have been much occupied all day giving lessons at rifle shooting to Mr. Cotham. He is the greatest stranger, without excepting Mr. Corcoran, I ever saw in management of a gun. He had a rifle with every necessary appendage. I had to

[86]

instruct him not only in the manner of loading, shouldering and pointing it, but also in cleaning, mounting and disposing it, the use of the caps, turnscrews etc., which were elements of science he had not the most distant idea of.

3rd: a strong wind arose during the night; a snorter it has been termed.[128] It snapped a stunsail boom. The morning was rough and we were making 10 knots. An immense sea at one time swept over the deck covering the cuddy over, although the door was shut. Mr. Spencer and Smyth got drenched and had to change immediately. A shoal of porpoises were seen playing around the bows. A sail came in sight supposed to be a whaler and sure it would be luck for us, for there was no oil left onboard to burn and we had few candles left. Our lat 39°33', long. 54°53'; Therm. 67 and B. 30.2. The two front cabins, Smyth's and Sumner's, got full with water, as we are playing at cards. Every prospect of a rough night.

4th: the Doctor called on us in the night, desiring a light to prepare some poison to give to his dog and in a plaintive tone complained

[87]

of the Captain's stern order to throw it overboard, as it made great noise. I, however, advised him to conceil it in the long boat on a bed of hay, of which he was very glad afterwards having done, as it saved him his pup. The morning was sombre and rough; broke a studding sail and stay sheet, but no further damage. Mr. Slater and I got drenched in a heavy spray. The captain in bed with toothache. At 7 o'clock the wind shifted and abated altogether. Great rolling in the evening. The Barom. lowered from 30.2 to 29. lat. 39°37' S, long 59°30'.

128. 'a snorter': a thing that is a remarkable example of its kind, especially for its strength or severity.

5th Sunday: calm till 8, but no Mass, nor prayers in the cuddy either, the captain being confined to his bed. Mr. Corcoran, who at prayer time read the five *Laudates* in English and lays a peculiar Paddy emphasis on the verse 'Praise the Lord, ye whales' etc.[129] After breakfast a flowing sheet carried us at 8 knots the rest of the day. Mr. Corcoran gave wine this evening; the last goose was eaten. lat 40°6' S, long 60°7'.

6th: Dark clouds and rough sea. At 7 they commenced reefing; at 10 a 2nd reef in the top sails; the Therm. 60°, Barom. 29.7. []

[88]

with an ominous appearance. The poor goat Nanny died after an illness of two weeks. I was interested in the fate of the poor goat and recollected having accompanied Mr. Philips through every street and at every ship victualling agent and other rearers of poultry etc, in search of one.[130] Its milk was of great service to Mr. Fisher during his illness. The Captain was worse today and Mr. Gregory and little John were 'took bad'.[131] lat. 40°17' S, long. 62°53'.

7th Tuesday: the morning was rough again, but nothing to what it encreased during the day. We call it a gale, although the Captain does not acknowledge it. The Bishop says he calculated during the night time having travelled 3 miles by the mere motion of his cot swinging to and fro, allowing a yard for each swing. At dinner times everything, except what each one held in his hand, was sent rolling clean off from the table. Only four sails up; double reefed as she lurches to leeward, her yards bow to the water and righting herself. The sails then bear up against a roaring blast, which

[89]

then serves as a check to the given impulse, which otherwise joined to the corresponding heave, would apparently stretch her on her beam ends. This is the second real gale we have had; I think stronger than the

129. *Laudates*: the psalms 145–150 beginning 'Praise the Lord'; Irishman Corcoran would have improvised in reading 'whales' in place of 'monsters of the deep' in Psalm 148.

130. *Mr. Philips*: Samuel Maurus Philips OSB (1794–1855), ordained 1819, on mission at Liverpool in 1835 assisting in the preparation of Polding's departure.

131. *Little John*: John Gorman.

first, although not so large a sea. It beats, however, against her sides now and then with such report that a cannon ball fired in them could not make more noise. We wonder sometimes she does not 'all scattabroad'. Only outside the cuddy door. The torrent sweeps over the gangways knee deep, whirling itself impetuously into wreaths of foam. I was sitting in my room with Mr. Roberts, when the ladder leading up to the poop was wrenched from its mooring and thrown from its heigth by a wave on the deck overhead. We were too accostomed to these trifles now to take notice of them, when at another time, we should have imagined the deck stove in. At tea time the scene was unique. Unable to sit, each one held his cup of tea holding fast at some corner with straddled legs. It rolled so unusually that, in spite of all our efforts, many were scalded with their tea and boiling water. The waiters, as they served,

[90]

slid across the cuddy loosening others from their holds, who followed. Even Vick (the Captain's dog), with its fore paws stretched forward, was seen, at every roll, in the wake of some sliding party; it was like a skating match. I was scalded with the rest and afterwards sitting with Mr. Cotham on the sopha, the sea came banging at our backs, enough to carry away the whole cuddy, causing a lurch which made him disappear instantly under the table and whirled me half way over it. We shortly after left the cuddy and spent a more pleasant hour in Dr Polding's room talking and eating nuts. It was their time for saying office but which they were obliged to dispense with this evening. The Captain all the while was in bed, but doing better. At 10, after night prayers, which I said very fervently, we turned in. At night we had to call for a couple of hands to come and secure our porthole, which had got loose. The barometer was at 29.5; our lat. 40°45' S, long. 66°27' E.

8th: the wind has gone down, but not the sea. She shipped great quantities and rolled extraordinarily. Mr. Corcoran, who had slept in my cot last night very comfortably,

[91]

was surprised on our waking in the morning to find how much it rocked him. 'Oh, mercy; and was I carried in this way all the night?' He reminded me of Md de Persi sitting in your chair once. I shot 4 or

5 albatrosses today, as did Mr. Sumner. The Captain is much better. The oil being all consumed, slush was used in the lamps this evening.[132] Therm. 58° and Barom 29.8; lat 40°32' S, long. 69°18' E.

9th. Rough sea and high wind still but favourable. We expect to pass St Paul and Amsterdam tomorrow.[133] The captain came to dinner for the first time since Saturday last. Therm. 62° and Barom. 29.9.

Eastward the moon appeared remarkably bright, darting rays like the sun and seemed travelling across dark scattered and wild clouds at the rate of 50 knots an hour. The sun has set deep red, its crimson colour expending to the zenith. lat in 39°12', long 72°11'.

10th: since yesterday noon in the 24 h. we have travelled 178 knots. Mr. Curtoys shot 7 birds. The boy Jimmy Duck (who feeds the fowls and has the office of farmer boy) was caught in a sea that came over the

[92]

bulwarks; nothing but his head appeared above the surge, which hurled him on several yards, as if bourn on a cloud. We were deeply engaged fishing for birds all day. A piece of pork is fastened to the hook, and the lines being a mere thread, floats; Albatross and Pigeons soon catch it and are hauled up like fish. The Captain did not come to dinner. Shortly after, the starboard fore topmast stunsail broke down. Therm. 63° and Barom. 29.8; lat 39°28' S, long 75°52' E.

11th: Rather a rough sea broke over the poop once or twice; had Mass early. The breeze resumes its strength, blows nearly aft, carrying us about 10 knots. Gigantic waves roll behind us and the spray drives on the wind in every direction whitening the billows like hills fast covering with pelting hail, while the colours of the rainbow flash across each rising wreath of surf in a direct line aft. Ever so far the sky is clear and blue and the horizon not 3 miles off, well defined and like the edge of a great saw. The men have been occupied incessantly cutting bottles; they are cut in two. Both ends, one of them

132. *Slush*: nautical grease or fat discarded from a ship's galley.
133. *St Paul and Amsterdam*: pair of uninhabited islands in the Southern Ocean at lat. 38°43' S & long. 77°31' E, a point at which captains heading to Australia would often begin to veer north.

[93]

being corked, are used to hold slush and are suspended as lamps. The way they have of cutting these bottles is by doubling a string round them, which is drawn backwards and forwards until the glass in that part is greatly heated. It is then immersed immediately in cold water and separates as clean as if cut with a knife. Mr. Cotham this evening, while standing on the Poop to Leeward, the ship gave a weather roll and the boling bridle, by a flap of the main sail, whirled round and struck badly on the nose.[134]

12th: Calm as is remarked most every Sunday. Walking on the poop remarked several large banks of seaweed, which are drifted by the westerly winds from the islands of St Paul and Amsterdam, and float away eastwards. Towards evening the breeze stiffened to a gale driving us 10 knots. Mr. Cotham forgetting to shut his porthole, his cabin was filled ancle deep by a wave suddenly rushing in. A great part of his things got wet. My large box happened to be in the way, which broke the force of the water and not a drop entered in. Mr. Cotham lays

[94]

the fault of his things getting wet on Mr. Gregory and says Gregory: 'I'll never trust you again as long as I am board.' lat. 39°1', long. 83°26'.

13th: woke in the morning with the rough motion; found the weather rough and the sea fierce; only 3 sails up, close reefed. Towards 12 the wind and sea increase to an awful pitch, a more tremendous sea than we had yet seen nearly crushed and drowned Harry crossing the gangways – madness to go on the poop. Dr Polding was much hurt on the poop and nearly sent overboard. Mr. Corcoran got wet peeping out of the cuddy door. Two heavy showers of hail succeeded each other; breakfast pell-mell. One sea came down the skylight like a flood over the cuddy. The wind increases every moment till it got beyond everything we had ever yet seen or heard. At 3 o'clock the whole ship was enveloped in a typhoon. Smyth's cabin altogether and part of the front of the cuddy was washed away. Goods, chattels and all flew in the torrent. The cabins in the cuddy were broke in by the water and it rushed

---

134. *Bridle*: a line secured at both ends to distribute a strain between two points.

[95]

for some time down the main hatching like a waterfall. I was below and some others; none of us could get up and every cabin to leeward was filling fast; those who were in them having water up to their waists. We shall never forget this. At dinner no plates or forks etc, and we dined with water up to our knees. All hands were as busy as the confusion would allow until night bucketing up the water and striving with every effort to shut out the sea from the cuddy, in which was the open hatch, where a brass balustrade prevented its being covered, but which was at last nailed in with boards and surrounded with canvas 3 feet high, leaving only a small room, where one man could just wedge down. While this was going on, the cook having to come in got crushed among the broken boards and spars floating around Smyth's cabin and was taken for dead. Dr Polding and the Doctor remained with him for an hour; he was without pulse. After much care he returned to himself. A great many things were damaged. Mr and Mrs Curtoys spent the rest of the evening in Dr Polding's room, where we had some

[96]

peppermint water and singing until eleven. The wind kept up all night. We lay-to 10 hours and many heavy waves rolled over the deck.[135]

The barom. was 29.3, Therm. 59°; lat 39°3' S, long 83°26' E.

14th: only one sail up. A spare mast fastened to the side of the ship with iron cramps was broken off in the night, but secured again; everyone nearly in bed till 8 or 9. Immense sea, yet the gale blows from the S.W. The gib boom in a tremendous pitch broke short 5 or 6 feet from the bows. Breakfast as each one could catch it; who would not sell their farm and go to sea? Card playing in the evening. Reported this evening that the water in the pump is black and extremely salty; said that some casks of wine must have been stove in and that the water has got to the salts, a great quantity of it being stowed about the pump wells.

135. *Lay-to*: check a ship's forward motion by bringing the bow into the wind.

The captain said he would not sail again to Sydney under the same circumstances; talked of scudding down to the Swan river.[136]

Lat. about the same, long. 92°2' E.

15th: to go from below to the cuddy is now like climbing up a chimney. The carpenters are employed rebuilding Smyth's cabin and the cuddy front.

[97]

We were kept awake the whole of the night watch with the noise of the pumps. One of them is disabled and they were pumping for hours. A talk of having sprung a leak and the quantity of salt water alarms the Captain. A mention is made of running the ship into Swan river. Alternate rain and sunshine; afternoon better appearance, but heavy rolling. Began to shoot at birds and cleaning the guns. Mr Curtoys discovers all his books to be spoiled with the wet. The joiner mending up the cuddy seats. I killed one albatross.

Lat. 39°8' S, long. 92°30' East.

16th: the men were employed placing up a new bowsprit and Gibboom and setting up the bow-stays and shrouds.[137] The Captain appears perfectly recovered and the cook is brought round so far as to begin to do duty. I feel a bad cold in my head and pain in my ears. Smyth is obliged to sleep below until his cabin can be got up again; Dr Polding has lent him mattress and bed clothes. We have been going 8 knots all day. We had figs for lunch. We use a number of mugs at dinner for glasses; a wonder there was anything not broke.

Long. 95°10' E, lat. 39°50' S,.

[98]

17th: sea lightly furrowed; men spreading out sails and yards to dry, stowing away broken and shivered spars; 3 knots per hour; lat 40°15' S, long 97°6' E.

---

136. *Scud*: to run before a gale with little or no sail set.
Swan River: the Swan River Colony, founded in 1829, was the closest settlement at latitude 31°56' S and longitude 115°50' E, a distance of approximately 2,150 kms.

137. *bowsprit*: a spar extending forward from the vessel's prow;
gib-boom: a spar used to extend the length of a bowsprit.

18th: a beautiful day; shot 3 albatrosses; Captain very well; had a 'flare-up' in his room, it being Saturday evening as usual; Therm. 58°, barom. 30.8, long 99°16'.

19th: Mass in the morning; fine weather continues; boy Heath sent up to the gallant yardarm, his penance for drinking. 3 hours later he was called down and condemned to be flogged. The Steward, who had been ill, recovered. Smyth's cabin is refitted; he was looking over his things, which he found greatly damaged and his gun rusted all over.

Therm. 64°, Bar. 30.3 – lat. 39°39' S, long. 102°33' E.

20th Monday: making good way. Jimmy Ducks was flogged; he received 18 stripes from the boatswain.[138]
Lat 39°54', long 107°3'.

21st Tuesday: a gale in the night time. The Captain was up all night. The mizen backstay snapped in a ¼ hour. The wind turned every point of the compass. The Captain thinking the ship would not obey the helm, not knowing what was

[99]

the matter for some time. It continued brisk the whole day. lat 39°18', long 110°21'.

22nd Wednesday: moderate; got very cold; the thermometer at freezing point; Bar. 30.3 – lat 39°7' S – long 112°3'.

23rd: Calm and cold. Mr Cotham and I jumped overboard; we were no sooner in the water than a breeze sprang up and we had hard matter to keep up, the ship going at 2½ knots or 3, and they had much difficulty in taking us out again. The water was very warm and comfortable. *Assemblé* in the evening in Dr Polding's room.
Lat. 39°40' South, long 112°50' E.

24th: fine, breeze; porpoises abundant.
lat 39°27', long 114°7' E.

25th: Mr. Corcoran's birthday and vigil of St Anne; solemnised his anniversary this evening; he did the honours and sent wine around. We had preserves and wine for lunch.

---

138. *boatswain*: a ship's officer in charge of equipment and crew.

26th St Anne. What is going on at St Anne now?[139] It is rather far to make a pilgrimage there now from here. I recollect the time they used to assemble and pitch their tents like a camp over the surrounding country. Mr. Spencer and I

[100]

talking these things over now in lat 38°57' S and long 121°15' E.

27th: we saw an albatross with a ribbon round its wing. Two or three lights were seen last night on the sea, one particularly bright floating on the waves, apparently 200 yards only to the starboard. Unlike phosphorous it shone with a bright and steady light.

Therm. 58°; Barom. 30.1 – lat 39°1' S – long 124°35' E.

28th Tuesday: rough and noisy the whole night. Lights were again seen floating. The Captain did not know what to make of it. It was conjectured to be decayed blubber from whale. Still it was said to shine too large and bright to be that. The captain had never read or heard of such before. The Doctor had again jammed his feet behind some boxes in his room in a stumble. He has always some good story of the kind in the morning, when he comes up. The wind abates in the evening. Cold in my head and face again. Therm. 54°; Barom 29.3; lat 39°6', – long 128°5' E.

[101]

29th Wednesday: great rolling last night. Mr. Cotham and Mr. Gregory, whom I can't get so often with me now, are busy at their philosophy, when I go to see them. They remind me of Tully in his moral ends disputing with all the elegance and courtesy and pleasantry imaginable. Today St Martha, patron of infirmarians.[140] Dr Polding having held that office at Downside, it was made his feast, which we

139. The village of Sainte-Anne-d'Auray, where Lewis attended a Jesuit College, was a popular place of pilgrimage, where a miraculous image of St Anne had been located. The image was destroyed during the Revolution, but pilgrimages continued and increased.

140. Martha served, while her sister Mary sat listening to Jesus.

solemnised as usual by a reunion in his room.[141] The day was cloudy and rough.

The Therm. 54°, Barom. 29.5, lat 40°17' S, long 131°29' E.

30th: took out what cloaths I thought I should want for Hobart Town. We have another week yet of it – cold in my head worse – raw and wet weather. The wind rises in the evening with squalls. They all spend the evening merrily in Dr Polding's room, while I was in bed; Mr. Gregory brought down some punch. Mick, one of the 2 Irish forward, whom Mr. Corcoran has taken as a servant, comes down and tells me that all the quicksilver in the barometer had fallen to the very bottom

[102]

of the glass, that the thermometer and chronometer were all gone bad and that the captain was out on deck and did not know how to manage. That is Paddy's story again; I thought to take no account of it.

Therm 56°, Barom. 29.8 – lat 40°20' S – long 133°14' E.

31st Friday: remained in my room. The Doctor had been to see me last night and given me something which relieved the pain; don't feel well yet. Mr. Corcoran with me reading extracts from a journal he had written 20 years ago, when on a voyage from Liverpool to Naples. In a great storm the Captain called him up and showed him the top-mast broken and the raging mane. His dismay was such that he could not even repeat the *pater*, but kept thinking on his mother and sisters. Near Gibraltar he heard the cannon. He described very comically how he was struck on arriving at the appearance of a doctor and two priests, who came on board, and the manner they underwent twelve days of quarantine – how mad the Captain was,

141. Polding was well remembered for his role as infirmarian at Downside as recalled by a former student: 'As infirmarian, none ever surpassed Dr Polding; and it was perhaps peculiarly an office in accord with his natural humanity and benevolence.' (*Downside Review* volume 1, p, 91)
He himself described watching through the night with the sick and dying as 'my own true and real vocation – Night Caps not Mitres were meant for me.' (Polding to Hepstonstall, 19 June 1849 [Polding Letters II.137]).

[103]

the curses he uttered against all the officers and quarantines – Smyth comes in fishing to know what we shall do with our money if we win the ticket and tells us it is usual to make presents to the Captain. He is, however, too interested a personage in the matter to heed what he says.
Lat 40°30' S, long 135°22' E.

[104]

August

1st August, Saturday: rough and stiff breeze; the main topsail leach lines break;[142] great conjecture about the day of landing. We rolled heavily and took a great deal of water on deck. All in the Captain's room celebrating, we fancy, the last Saturday. The Captain won't give us his longitude. I suspect that if he is as correct as he says he is and that he could be sure of seeing the land within an hour or two, he could not conceal it.

Therm 58°, Barom. 29.6, lat – , long 138°44'.

2nd-Sunday: *point de Messe*[143] – too much rolling. I kept my room. The Captain was to have told us the longitude today at dinner. When the time came he said: 'Well Gents, as you are desirous of knowing where we are, I have the pleasure of informing you that you are on the *Oriental*.' Mr. Spencer tells him we shall see land tomorrow morning at daylight – may it be so.

Therm. 60°; Barom. 29.7, lat – , long 143°13'.

3rd – Monday: At day dawn cry of 'Land!'. Here we are off SW Cape. The captain

[105]

was surprised in the morning when Mr. Slater came down telling him land was in sight. He said we had drifted 50 miles in the night and that there was a very strong current here and so there was – S W Cape at last, which and some rocks in the distance appear like sugar loaves;

142. *Leach*: the aft or trailing edge of a fore-and-aft sail.
143. 'No Mass'.

black clouds overhanging them. At last we arrive. They are taking out the chain cables; men and carpenters busy preparing to get into Port; taking down the beams and spars that had been put up in the cuddy as supports in times of storms and gales and each one getting ready to land.

12 o'clock: we range along a fine bold coast, many parts resembling very much the English western coast. Between S W Cape and S Cape we can distinguish nothing on the land, although from the ideas we had formed, we fancy woods and fields. Ahead of us streaks of snow cover some high mountains. A land breeze wafts us 6 or 7 knots. The sun being in our eyes prevents us distinguishing anything, but at the same time blends its rays in the mist and

[106]

fog over the land in such a manner as to make what we do see most pittoresque and romantic. At 2 or 3 o'clock we remark the water to be of a greyish colour, no more the blue and the land becomes more distinct and we see trees very plainly along the outlines of the hills; others higher covered with snow half way down on our side or the southern. Smyth unwell in bed. All getting ready their trunks to take on shore. The Captain says if he had but 6 hours more of daylight, we should run in this evening. In four hence we shall have passed S. Cape. At dinner time – better dinner than usual; nothing wanting now and every underling as attenttive, as if they had been so all the voyage.

Our course is no more taken by observations of lunars or latitudes, but drawn on a chart from angles and bearings to the different headlands and rocks.[144] After dinner we admired as beautiful a sunset as was ever beheld!

[107]

We are now not more than 4 or 5 miles from the shore, gliding over a dirty gray or green wave, as we steer at the entrance of Entrecasteau's

144. *lunars*: 'lunar distances' were used to determine longitude at sea in the period from about 1767 until 1850, when it was superseded by the marine chronometer.

channel.[145] The low broken cliffs of Bruny island on our right as far as Tasmans head resemble very much that part of the coast between Looe and Polperro, beautiful as the Ausonian vales.[146]

To the left of the land is high and mountainous. All feel more or less excited. Today was Mr. Sumner's day for the ticket; tomorrow is Mrs. Curtoise and it is said she will win it. My day is the 18th. This evening we spend in Dr Polding's room gayly enough. We are lying-to for the night about 5 miles off Tasman Head.
It is a fine moonlight night. Everyone gives a song as Mr Curtoys accompanies on the piano. At 12 went to bed. Mick slept in our room.

4th Tuesday: St Dominic. Mr. Corcoran was very anxious to get in today. He often said during the voyage that we should be in by today. Early we rise and on the poop to descry new lands.

[108]

Mr. Corcoran says, as we dress early by candle light, that wherever you are you think of us this day.
Light winds from the N.N.E.; tacking on the skirts of Storm bay until dinner time, when a strong breeze sets in from the same quarters. Towards evening the breeze stiffens from the N. and gets very strong. We think we shall have to run out to sea again. Thus end our hopes of getting in today and we must tack to and fro. At 12 o'clock at night I leave he Captain's room as we lay off about 8 miles from Cape Raoul.[147] The Captain says we might now run in, but the wind might also change and caution forbids venturing.

---

145. d'Entrecasteaux Channel named after Antoine Raymond Joseph de Bruni d'Entrecasteaux (1737–1793), French naval officer and explorer, best known for his exploration of the Australian coast in 1792, while searching for the La Pérouse expedition.

146. *Tasman's Head*: Tasman Peninsula;
Looe and Polperro: fishing villages on southern coast of Cornwall, Harding's home district;
Ausonian: from Latin *Ausonia* – Lower Italy; extended poetically to the whole of Italy.

147. *Cape Raoul*: situated at the southernmost part of the Tasman Peninsula; named after d'Entrecasteaux's pilot.

5th Wednesday: B.M. ad Nives.[148] We don't appear to have advanced much in the bay. Today Smyth's day, tomorrow Mr Corcoran's for the tickets. We perceive two whalers near fluted cape with great smoke issuing from their craft.

At 9 o'clock comes heavy rain and the wind is ahead.

12 o'clock the rain ceased; it has not changed the wind. A small skiff appears in the distance. Cry of 'pilot boat'.

[109]

At 1 o'clock the Pilot comes on board – a jolly fat fellow with ruddy countenance. He wore a broad brimmed white hat and a blue jacket. His name is Lawrence; his boat is sharp at each end like a whalers.

At 2 o'clock advance tolerably well. The Pilot's house begins to appear – white cottage and low. Every hill which rises higher and higher inland is covered thickly with timber – one continued forest, which reaches to the water's edge. Cliffs moderately high, but very precipitous, divided here and there by a wide perpendicular fissure. Very cold. As we near the Pilot's house and farm, the only spot of cultivation to be seen around, each one says he could live happy there. He has 350 acres of land, of which 8 or 10 appear tilled. A second house appears standing lower down in a small valley connected with the first by a wooden paling. The whole of this little green spot is surrounded by the tractless forest. At the upper end of the bay, as we advance, the rocks appear very different; they resemble those about the Isle de Bas, high stratified masses.[149] The Pilot says that the Captain of the

[110]

ship . . . a short time ago had taken the situation of his house and several other points, which were imperfectly marked or omitted in the charts, and about to publish the same on his return to England. He says ships call in on average once a fortnight. It is not good to have two trades, otherwise, besides his pilotage, he would be a whaler. He occasionally lends a hand to his neighbours who are whalers and catch whales even in the bay and as far up as the mouth of the Der-

148. *B.M. ad Nives*: feast of Our Lady of Snows.
149. Île de Batz, an island off Roscoff in Brittany very familiar to Lewis.

went River. They were the same we had seen and had captured a whale the day before yesterday on the spot we now were. Whales yield oil from 4, 5 to 14 ton –there are no tides in the bay.

At 5 o'clock we remarked the lighthouse; it appeared a poor concern and was built very low.[150] Therm. stands 55° and the barometer 30°. Within the last twelve months 5 ships were lost at the entrance of this bay in Entrecasteaux channel (a misfortune unheard of before) one of them, the *Enchantress*, in which Dr Polding

[111]

intended at first to have come in.[151] Another was lost off Tasman's Head where we lay-to. She struck on one of the projecting reefs. Only the Captain, Doctor and one or two passengers escaped in the gig.[152] They managed to push out, while the crew were employed clearing away the long boat. The ship sank her bows foremost and all of them perished. Our Captain says that not one out of 20 ships has had finer weather hither (not altogether favourable in a nautical sense he did not mean), but finer weather than we have had, having experienced, I may say, but two or three bad days and which is the more striking, being off the Cape and in the southern latitudes of 40° and more south in the depth of winter.

At 7 o'clock: the anchor was dropped in a bay of Bruny Island.

6th – Thursday: at 4 o'clock in the morning got under weigh. Heaving the anchor was a ceremony of great moment. The trampling of twenty

---

150. This lighthouse, the first in Tasmania, was erected at the mouth of the Derwent River in 1832.

151. Charles Bateson lists the following ships as wrecked in that period in that location: *Amelia*, 11 June 1833; *Thomas*, 21 September 1833; *Prince Regent*, 9 April 1834; *Porpoise*, 9 August 1834; *Australian*, October 1834; *Enchantress*, 17 July 1835 (*Australian Shipwrecks*, 1622–1850, Sydney, 1972).
The *Enchantress*: a barque of 376 tons, built at Bristol in 1826, and registered at London, had been a regular trader between London, Sydney and Hobart since 1832, carrying convicts. On the evening of 16 July 1835, having sailed from London on 20 March, she was tacking offshore from Bruny Island when she struck heavily on uncharted rocks and sank; an officer, fifteen of the crew, and a passenger were drowned in the long boat, when it was crushed by the sinking ship.

152. *Gig*: a long light ship's boat, usually reserved for use by the ship's captain.

of the men beating round in measured steps as they turned round the capstan, singing in loud chorus to tunes well known and having a magical influence on the mind of every jolly tar.[153]

[112]

The tune was everything – the words as I could catch them were:[154]

Solo

Get ready your chests and your hammocks
 for we will go ashore
 for we will go ashore
I don't care for the captain
 for we will go ashore
Nor for the chief mate
 for we will go ashore
We came into this country to know
what it is and we will go ashore.
I don't care for we will go ashore
on shore in Hobart Town
For I will go ashore in Hobart Town.

And again:

Oh how I love a bottle of rum.
The sailors in the morning think nothing
of the bottle oh.
a bottle of gin
and a bottle of rum
and a bottle of cherry brandy oh.

153. *Jolly tar*: this expression for a British sailor occurs in the chorus of the 'Heart of Oak', the official march of the Royal Navy, composed in the eighteenth century:
'Heart of Oak are our ships,
Jolly Tars are our men,
We always are ready: Steady, boys, Steady!
We'll fight and we'll conquer again and again.'

154. There follow various improvised sea shanties, songs with alternating solo and chorus sung by sailors performing physical labor together

Chorus:

So early in the morning
the sailors lie the bottle oh
the bottle oh, the bottle oh
the bottle of whiskey oh
Give me a bottle of rum
I'd drink the rum
and break the bottle oh.

[113]

And again:

Bonny lassy, Highland lassy (pronounced Heeland)
Where have you been all the day?
Up the hills and down the braies
Bonny highland lassy.
Why did you leave me
Bonny lassy, Highland lassy?
I've been ginning in Aberdeen
Bonny Highland lassy.

The anchor being hove up, the fore main and mizen top sails are set to the song of 'cheerly man', as when all hands in the gale haul in the weather braces.

At breakfast time we were near the lighthouse. Three sails appear in the offing; two of them are whalers. They have harpooned a whale this morning and are now giving over the chase. We advanced to the mouth of the river by short tacks. We all admire the beauty of the country. The numerous inlets and points of land covered with trees. In this wide range we have as yet seen but two or three cultivated spots. On the top of a hill is a watch house and signal – reminds me of the one in Polperro.

[114]

At ½ past 4: while at dinner, turned up the river and as we approached the shore, we could not help exclaiming at the beauty of the scenery – small hills around, bending down their sides in curves as Hogarth's line of beauty covered with stately trees with, here and there, openings of green turf[155] – all is simple nature as when first formed and bid encrease and multiply. Approaching a line of smoke indicates the situation of the town. *Et iam summa procul villarum culmina fumant.*[156] Table Mount appears on the left behind the town, its top covered with streaks of snow and just meets the clouds, which prevent us, defining its long level table-like summit, its dark blue sides broken in deep ridges contrasts with the intermediate green hills.[157] The Bishop sent Mr. Corcoran and Mr. Sumner with a letter to Revd. Mr. Connolly.[158] Mr. Corcoran had great fun this evening-introduced himself as the bishop and gave us a long and lively description of Mr. Connolly, his house, the chapel, the town and everything they saw. Mr. Cotham's brother came onboard and the evening was spent in Dr Polding's room,

[115]

as in the open ocean, in festivity and song. We slept on board and the following morning at 9 o'clock on the 7th the anchor was dropped in Sullivans Cove. We had a full view of the Town, the Governor Colonel Arthur's residence, the Captain of the Port, Moriatie, an Irishman, on the left, to the right Kangaroo Point, from which two small steamers, the size of a barge, were hourly plying.[159]

---

155. *Hogarth's line of beauty*: a theory in art used to describe an S-shaped or serpentine line appearing within an object or as the boundary line of an object. This theory originated with William Hogarth, English painter (1697–1764) and is an essential part of his theory of aesthetics as described in his *Analysis of Beauty* (1753). According to this theory, curved lines signify liveliness and activity and excite the attention of the viewer as contrasted with straight lines, which signify stasis or inanimate objects.
156. 'And already there is smoke coming from the roofs of farmsteads' (Virgil, *Eclogues* I.83).
157. *Table Mountain*: Matthew Flinders had given this name in 1798; it remained its common name until in 1832 it was renamed in honour of the Duke of Wellington.
158. Mr. Connolly: Philip Conolly (1786–1839), pioneer priest in Van Diemen's Land, arrived in Hobart in 1821.
159. On this day a local newspaper announced that Captain Moriarty RN had been appointed to a subcommittee 'to survey the south coast and report on the most eligible site for a light house, at or near the entrance of D'Entrecasteaux's Channel' (*Hobart Town Courier*, Friday 7 August 1835, page 2). The same edition carried ecclesiastical news: 'The Rev. Mr. Ullathorne, the talented Roman Catholic

At 10 o'clock Captain Forth came from the Governor's to receive Dr Polding and take him onshore, where a carriage was in waiting.[160] We shortly afterwards landed and walked up to the chapel to return thanks for our arrival and preservation from all dangers, which was a most pleasing task to perform.

Here stops my journal; and I have written to you an account of what took place here and given you a description of the town and manner of living here. I went to see the natives at a Mr. Robinson's, who keeps some for show.[161] He speaks their language and has, it is said, rendered great services to the Colony by conciliating them, for which he has a particular tact. They are fond of him and follow him and in general do all he desires

[116]

of them. There were paintings and drawings of chiefs of different tribes and a very handsome bust of one. Among other curiosities was a fine large 4 or 5 rowed necklace of strung shells and hunting bags made exceedingly well of the fibres of different trees. These natives have their hair thickly smeared with grease and ochre. They were all

clergyman now at Sydney, is we learn about to become permanently resident in Van Diemen's land'; this did not eventuate. 'His Majesty's government has decided that the Australian colonies of New South Wales and Van Diemen's until now forming an archdeaconry, subject to the see of Calcutta, shall be erected into a separate and independent Bishoprick, the seat of which will be fixed at Sydney. The appointment has been offered to Archdeacon Broughton, now in this country, who, it is expected, will he consecrated to the episcopal office previous to his return to Australia'; this did eventuate.

160. At a meeting of the Catholic Committee on that evening the following resolutions were moved: 'That the warmest thanks of the Catholic Community are due to His Excellency Lieutenant Governor Arthur, for his uniform and zealous attention to their interests, and for the very handsome manner in which His Excellency was pleased to receive their Prelate, on his arrival this day' and 'That as a mark of their gratitude and attachment, His Excellency be respectfully requested to accept a Piece of Plate of the highest value their funds will admit' (*Colonial Times*, Tuesday 11 August 1835, page 3).

161. George Augustus Robinson (1791–1866), protector of Aboriginals. In February 1835 Robinson had been called 'a second Las Casas', after the Dominican missionary, Bartolomé de Las Casas (1474–1566), who was the first to expose the oppression of indigenous peoples by Europeans in the Americas and to call for the abolition of slavery there (*Hobart Town Courier*, 6 February 1835, 2).

huddling together round a fire. I asked them to show some feat with their spears which they did by throwing them at the distance of 60 to 70 yards, very true and with great strength, hitting a stick which was pocked in the ground. They appear extremely dirty and filthy, and the chief's only distinction from the rest was that he had a greater share of dirt and grease about his person and his face was tattooed.

Travelling in the interior I found the roads good and coaches plying over them as regular as at home. Crammed on the outside with passengers continually changing as they go from one to the other of their scattered farms, makes it appear as if you were travelling in an omnibus. The horses are very good and no one thinks anything of a ride of 20 or 30 miles before breakfast. They appear to know but two

[117]

paces – a walk and a gallop – in the bush over the wild rugged path or no path at all. They walk with very sure foot and on the road gallop on up hill and down. I could hardly believe myself riding from Richmond to Kangaroo Point, a distance of 25 miles, to find it done in a little more than two hours without even requiring to strike the horse.

About a fortnight after our arrival there was a ball at the governor's. Having called there before, I received an invitation and went. I was struck at finding such a numerous assembly and little expected to find so much beauty and fashion in this town. The beauty however all lay in the dress, in the silk gowns, ribbons and flowers. There were few countenances I thought pretty and they all appeared so old. It was crowded with officers as well. I am not a minute having already written you these things.

The country is very well supplied with game – kangaroos and different sorts of quails – but found the kangaroos of more difficult access. I was out but two or three days shooting and I reserve bird shooting for those, to whom I promised to send some, until I arrive at Sydney, as well as the collection of seaweed specimens etc. etc. I send with the journal sketches of plans and drawings I made, which will suffice to give you an idea of what went on. Mr. Cotham

[118]

and Mr. Kenny were left at Hobart Town. We have 2 passengers to Sydney more – Lieut. Creswell and Mr. Flowers.[162]

5th of September. After a month's residence at Hobart Town, this morning the signal gun was fired at 9 o'clock to give notice to the passengers on shore. Something occurred which prevented our sailing and we slept onboard this night in the harbour. There were several strangers at dinner and Captain Moriati and the Pilot and Mr. Corcoran contributed to the merriment of the evening.[163]

6th: weighed anchor, which caused much music among the sailors. In the evening we doubled Cape Pillar.[164]

7th: calm till ten o'clock in the morning. At 3pm half a gale; two reefs in the top sails; mizen top furled.

8th: wind high and sea heavy. One of the guns was broken away from its moorings and was rolled about the deck for some time, which caused great noise and confusion. I began a letter home, which I mean to send off on arriving. Mr. Curtoys unwell. We saw two whales. A reunion in Dr Polding's room.

9th – Wednesday: going at 8 knots. The fore-studding sail broke down; much pitching.

[119]

At 5 o'clock: the gale renewed. The mizen topsail not being furled quick enough broke its buntings and flapped like thunder. The ship rolled and gale blew dreadfully.

At 10 o'clock tremendous rolling; 9 knots all night.

10th: continuing 9 knots; a great deal of water shipped. Dr Polding had his deadlights put down on account of the sea breaking over aft. At 2 o'clock three sails up all reefed.

---

162. *Lieut. Creswell*: Lieutenant William Caswell R.N., a veteran of the American War of Independence.

163. A trio of jolly Irishmen.

164. *Cape Pillar*: a prominent feature of the Dolerite landscape of the Tasman Peninsula.

11th: fine morning; saw many whales sporting about; wind contrary; fine moonshine; saw land early.

12th: expecting to get in yesterday. A foul wind succeeded yesterday's calm. Sighted Botany Bay; two ships in sight, one for Sydney, the other for Hobart Town; saw more whales. It appears very barren around Botany Bay; saw the revolving light.[165]

13th: sun rose beautiful; moderate breeze till 7, when it came on a gale. We got into the headlands about 9 o'clock, but ran out again for an hour. The gale increased. The Captain agitated and, as he said, afterwards, never felt

[120]

so anxious. In beating back, keeping the weather coast as much as possible, the Captain kept in all sails, which were not absolutely necessary for moving and had just determined to venture in and begged all passengers to lend a hand, when we spied the Pilot, which made his heart leap for joy. The Pilot set his foot onboard at ½ past 11. We were then inside the Heads. We beat up 7 miles to the Harbour, the passengers lending their services at the spanker boom. We had several critical tacks and nice manouvering, which called for as many claps of applause from the pilot to the men. We anchored at 20 minutes past 1pm to the great joy of Captain and the crowds of spectators. Mr. Sumner came on board and Mr Plunkett, who sent his carriage for Dr Polding.[166] At 3 o'clock we all went on shore. Dr Polding was cheered out by the men, who were ordered to have their extra glass. The *Oriental* remained in this port a month, when she sailed on the [14th of October] for Bombay.

165. *revolving light*: Macquarie Tower lighthouse on South Head opened in 1818, demolished and replaced in 1887.

166. It seems that Sumner had preceded the missionary party from Hobart to Sydney.
Mr. Plunkett: John Hubert Plunkett (1802–1869), arrived in New South Wales in 1832 as solicitor-general. He was the first Catholic appointed to high civil office in the colony.

Journal of the Passage from Autralia to England in the Ship Ratcliff 1846

[1] To His Grace the Archbishop
of Sydney
&
to Dr Gregory
& Friends.
Journal of the Voyage Home
&
the Log
kept on Board the Ship
Ratcliff
bound to London
from
Sydney
duration from 16th of February 1846
to 25th of June
1846
by Lewis Harding

1846

[v23 etc] Ps cviii[1]

[23] *Qui descenderunt mare in navibus, facientes operationem in aquis multis,*

[They that went down to the sea in ships, doing business in the great waters,]

[24] *Ipsi viderunt opera Domini, et mirabilia ejus in profundo.*

[These have seen the works of the Lord, and his wonders in the deep.]

[25] *Dixit, et stetit spiritus procellae, et exaltati sunt fluctus ejus.*

[He said the word, and there arose a storm of wind: and the waves thereof were lifted up.]

[26] *Ascendunt usque ad caelos, et descendunt usque ad abyssos; anima eorum in malis tabescebat.*

[They mount up to the heavens, and they go down to the depths: their soul pined away with evils.]

[27] *Turbati sunt et moti sunt sicut ebrius; et omnis sapientia eorum devorata est.*

[They were troubled and reeled like a drunken man; and all their wisdom was swallowed up.]

[28] *Et clamaverunt ad Dominum cum tribularentur; et de necessitatibus eorum eduxit eos.*

[And they cried to the Lord in their affliction: and he brought them out of their distresses.]

[29] *Et statuit procellam ejus in auram, et siluerunt fluctus ejus.*

[And he turned the storm into a breeze: and its waves were still.]

---

1. *Ps cviii*: Lewis is mistaken in numbering the psalm – it is Psalm 106 in the Septuagint and the Vulgate, and 107 in the Hebrew Old Testament. Verse numbers and translation have been added in [ ].

[30] *Et laetati sunt quia siluerunt; et deduxit eos in portum voluntatis eorum.*

[And they rejoiced because they were still: and he brought them to the haven which they wished for.]

[31] *Confiteantur Domino misericordiae ejus; et mirabilia ejus filiis hominum.*

[Let the mercies of the Lord give glory to him, and his wonderful works to the children of men.]

[32] *Et extollent eum in ecclesia plebis, et in cathedra seniorum laudent eum*

[And let them exalt him in the assembly of the people: and praise him in the chair of the ancients.]

Pares et nos referre gratias Deo aequum est.[2]

[It is right for us equally to give thanks to God.]

[2]

Journal
kept on board Ship
Ratcliff
from Sydney to London
round Cape Horn.
Duration from 16th February
1846
to 25th of June
1846
by J. Lewis Harding
St Mary's Sydney
15th Feb. 1846

2. This final verse is not found in the psalm.

[3] *Cloister Gardens – St Mary's Seminary*[3] *– Eve of departure*

15 February 1846

15th Feb. 'Well Lewis,' said Paul[4], 'Where will you be tomorrow evening at this hour?' Thus said Paul as we were all quietly walking together in the garden attached to the Cloisters of St Mary's, the eve of departure. The Novices meanwhile were busying to and fro preparing the Chapel of St Felician for the 8 o'clock Office.[5]

From this spot we have a beautiful view commanding the country in the direction of the sea. The declining sun mingles its yet warm rays with the mellow colouring of the evening sky. It sheds a mild radiance on the pinnacles of the Cathedral, it is reflected on the stained glass of the Library and Novitiate, it gilds the neighbouring promontory of Darlinghurst with its castellated mansions and range of high houses. The waters of the harbour are still. The little Bay of Woolloomooloo expands its lovely shores beneath the Palace of the Archbishop.[6] The verdant foliage of its shores overhangs its waters and the pathways along its banks reminds us of the pleasant excursions we had taken in the labyrinths and groves of this flowery and perfumed Eden.

---

3. *Seminary*: in contemporary usage the word was not restricted to a place for the formation of priests. St Mary's Seminary was a school for boys, very few of whom were intended for ordination.
4. James/John Paul Roche, born in Kilkenny circa 1810, arrived in Sydney with Polding, March 1843. Professed as a choir monk at St Mary's in April 1845; ordained priest in January 1846. He was stationed at Campbelltown from 1847 to 1877. He retired to his sister's home at Binnalong in 1877 and died there in November 1880. He was buried at Yass. Details about the Sydney monks here and throughout have been sourced in T. Kavenagh, 'Polding's Monks', *Tjurunga* 8(1974), Appendix pp i-xviii)
5. The chapel of St Felician was located on the left side of the northern transept of the cathedral. It was the conventual chapel of the Benedictine community and housed the relics of the third century Roman martyr Felician, which had been brought to Sydney by Ullathorne. (See Patrick O'Farrell [ed], *St Mary's Cathedral Sydney, 1821–1971*, Sydney 1971, 13.)
6. In 1835 Vicar-General Ullathorne leased the Woolloomooloo estate, established in 1793, and its house, embellished over four decades, for the bishop's residence. It was situated on a bay east of and within walking distance St Mary's. Polding established it as a house of formation for his novices, among whom was Lewis Harding. The tenancy ended in 1848.

[4] *Cloister Gardens – Eve of departure*

Dan[7] – 'Ah L[ewis] – when once you are gone you will soon forget these and yr companions, but we in the meanwhile, as you are tossed on the boisterous ocean, retired in our cloister shall offer our daily prayers for the Archbishop and you that restored to health of mind and body you may soon return.'

'Oh that we will', says Ignatius[8], 'besides it has been settled that our Mass is to be offered daily from this to the 6th of June as the Archbishop has directed.'[9]

How beautiful and consolatory the reflection that, however separated in body, by prayer we may still be as united as if we lived together in one social circle; may this close union between ourselves and God continue forever.

But here are preparations for the voyage – goods and boxes being brought in. They are the gifts of friends; here are cases of preserves of fruit, and clothing and what-not – all to be packed and sent on board without loss of time.

Not these, but the kindness and thoughtfulness that procured them are qualities that endear more and more and awaken as gratitude never fading among friends.

But one little lovely child steps forward from the seminary and says, 'Oh make haste and come, Mama is waiting for you,

---

7. *Dan*: perhaps Daniel Maurus Connell OSB (1825–1901), born in Hobart, educated at St Mary's Seminary, professed April 1845, ordained priest 1848 (first Australian-born priest).
8. John Ignatius McLennan (1821–1857), ordained deacon 31 January 1846. He arrived in Sydney with Polding, March 1843, and joined monastery; professed as 1846; ordained priest in January 1848.
9. The estimated arrival date was not realised, the Ratcliff not reaching London until 25 June. Bernard Ullathorne, who was consecrated bishop at Coventry four days before the delayed arrival of the *Ratcliff* in England, records that Archbishop Polding expessed his 'great regret at having arrived too late', since his 'principal object in coming to Europe was to solicit the Holy See to appoint me to be his Coadjutor' (*Autobiography* 242; Birt II.121).

[5] *Cloister Gardens – Eve of departure*

and we are going immediately. They are now with the Archbishop and these things are to be packed up; come and help. As for you, you are a bad fellow for going where you are all gone. I'll not come again. Mr Fynes has given us up.'[10]

And here are the things sent and they are from one and the other. Here are Mrs Plunket's; there Mrs Milford's and there the Harnetts', and all others besides.[11]

'Well', says Paul, 'we shall go and see you off tomorrow. Almost all the priests from the country are come up and will accompany the procession of the Archbishop to the King's Wharf and go on board with you as far as the Heads.'[12]

'We all go too' says Dan 'Meanwhile here is a note which you need give to the Archbishop after you are at sea. The Archbishop on reaching Rome is not to forget us while on the tomb of the Apostles, to let no despondency creep in under any circumstances.'

10. Henry Thomas Fynes was born in London in 1822. He matriculated at London University, shortly afterwards joining the Catholic Church, and on coming out to New South Wales, he studied in theology at St Mary's, Sydney, at the invitation of Archbishop Polding, and in 1845 was ordained priest for the Archdiocese of Sydney by Bishop Epalle, Vicar-Apostolic of Melanesia. Father Fynes exercised his ministry in New South Wales from 1845 to 1849, when he transferred to Auckland. Perhaps 'giving us up' refers to a schoolboys regret that Fynes had left teaching in the seminary, as Harding was now doing.
11. *Mrs. Plunket*: Maria Charlotte, wife of John Hubert Plunkett (1802–1869), Attorney General.
    Mrs. Milford: Eliza, Catholic wife of Samuel Frederick Milford (1797–1865), who arrived at Sydney with family in September 1843; Judge of Supreme Court 1856.
    The Harnetts: the family of Margaret Louisa, widow of Dr Patrick Harnett, who arrived at Sydney in July, 1832; deputy-surgeon based at Norfolk Island 1837–1839; in February 1839 appointed Colonial Surgeon with practice in Macquarie Street; died on 13th September, 1844.
12. The King's Wharf, built in 1813, was at the western shore of Sydney Cove, adjacent to the Government Stores in George Street (*Sydney Gazette*, 18 December 1813).

[St Mary's Cathedral]

[6] *Departure – Sydney Harbour*

16 February at 2 o'clock: Watson's Bay; breeze beginning to spring up; some few of the Company preparing to return; Doctor Gregory becoming anxious.[13] First two lads, two young gents in a tiny boat take leave with the Archbishop's blessing; a moment of fear and anxiety as they descend from the huge ship in their frail skiff which is being towed with great rapidity through the agitated waters. When the Archbishop called the Captain's attention, whose order was prompt, to 'see that young gent safe in the boat', given to a half dozen strapping sailors, which set all things right. Here were brought into palpable evidence the effect of well-directed orders, scientific or technical knowledge, prompt execution in overcoming an imminent danger. A few seconds comprised the entire act, and to a feeling of terror for their fate succeeded admiration and confidence as they were now under the care of two Brothers safely making for the shore.

How often before had we sailed together on these crystal waters of Darlinghurst and Garden Island, visited alternately

13. Henry Gregory Gregory OSB (1813–1877) was educated at St Edmund's, Douay, and Downside. He accompanied Polding to Australia in 1835. Ordained priest in 1837, he was sent to Norfolk Island with Fr John McEncroe in October 1838. He was granted an honorary Roman doctoral degree in 1841 and was appointed abbot of St Mary's monastery in 1848. He was controversially recalled to England in 1861, much to Polding's distress. They remained in regular correspondence.

[7] *Departure – Sydney Harbour – taking leave*

Sydney's hundred coves, landed at home at night after having taken possession of some Island or headland point which had served for our head-quarters during the day, whence we had explored inland, or coasted in fishing and clambered rocks, and admired all the day the various beauties of a fairy scenery.

Oh, what an affecting scene is that of parting from friends; it leaves the heart in a lacerated state for a long period, which no present distractions or consolations can assuage. Thus one after the other we seemed deserted as one after the other knelt to receive the Archbishop's blessing. His clergy that filled his cabin a little while ago, friends anxious for a parting shake of the hands, a last look have now left a void. The cabins appear empty, the decks hateful from the solitude that reigns and my cheek is still warm from their last embraces and my heart sorely wounded with its tumultuous and heavy emotions.

[8] *Departure – Off Sydney Heads*

The three steamers continued with us accompanying us out at least 8 miles. They were crowded with Ladies as well as Gents, and occasionally, as they wheeled around the ship, they cheered and waved their handkerchiefs and hats, a salute that was returned by us and our sailors. The sight was most exhilarating when, as the vast expanse seemed glittering in the golden light of a fine unclouded sunshine, brilliant as the colours of an oriel on the pavement of a Temple. The Archbishop imparted to the whole assemblage his parting Benedictions amid their repeated cheers and adieus.

The passengers and crew astonished remarked that more life or gayety in this scene afloat could not have been presented even if the Colonists had wished to *fêter* their most popular Governor.

And now Joseph,[14] being invited to a banquet, it was with no great relish, I assure you, that we saw spread before us all that the season afforded and fruits, all of the choicest productions of the Hunter.[15] Yet after all the fatigue

14. *Joseph*: perhaps Thomas Joseph Murray OSB (1785–1853): former soldier and monk, who came to Sydney with Polding in 1843 and was ordained in 1846 at the age of 60; chaplain at Norfolk Island 1846–1850.
15. *The Hunter*: the Hunter River valley is a fertile area north of Sydney.

[9] *Departure – Off Sydney Heads*

of excitement and watching we fell now proportionably depressed and could scarcely partake of the sparkling wines or join in the engaging conversation. And although all appeared calm without, it was not quite so in the organic system within, its derangement becoming more sensible as we receded from land.

Yet one little incident that would have amused you I cannot omit. Tell it not to Brothers Michael or Vincent;[16] it would have been too great a trial for them to have witnessed Templar falling overboard.[17] They would say that having made the voyage before he ought to have known better, but his nature was always to go about reconnoitering and poking his nose in every hole and corner. He endeavoured to step from the Poop into the boat that hangs alongside but he stepped a little too far and tipped over.

Facile descensus Averni[18]

16. Brother Michael Keenan OSB (1789–1852): professed as lay-brother April 1845; died at St Mary's Monastery, Lyndhurst.
    Brother Vincent O'Brien OSB (1803–1875): professed as lay-brother April 1845; died at Lyndhurst.
17. *Templar*: Polding's pet terrier, given the name 'Templar' after the ship that carried him and his master back to Sydney in March 1843.
    In 2009 Stella Maris College, established in 1873 by Polding's Good Samaritan Sisters at Wollongong, New South Wales, commissioned a statue of the Bishop with Templar.
18. *Facilis descensus Averni* 'The descent to hell is easy; it is easy to take the downward path.' Vergil, *Aeneid*, 6:126

Once overboard he made for the boat astern which indeed was the best proof he ever gave of sense and shewed a sagacity peculiarly his own; here he was rescued. In his tumble overboard he realised the old proverb many a slip between the cup and the lip – with this modification, that the same may be said of a slip between the ship and the boat.

[10] *Departure – Off Sydney Heads – Night*

There was a call of 'a dog overboard' and in his rescue he got sundry cuffs and kicks but at last got safely embarked again and was brought up and reinstated in the dignity of the Poop, for which his master had to pay 5s. The dog did not seem much troubled with sea sickness.

8 o'clock. Here then Paul are we at sea. I am seated in the Archbishop's cabin while His Grace reclines in his sopha exceeding tired and overcome by the day's transactions; 20 or 30 miles SE from the Sydney Heads. The *Ratcliff*'s pondrous bows press on the billows with a speed of but 4 kts an hour, and as the shades of night spread their canopy over us, His Grace begins to compose himself to rest enveloped head and shoulders in May's red cape.

The night is dark – 'Joseph is it you making that noise?' I perceive we are sailing although he said it was an ancient and sage rule, that of the old Dutch navigators to take in sail at night. 'Joseph, who's that?' L. Nikerbocker, who affirms that they always took in sail [at] night, put the helm to port and

[11] *Strange prospect – sick – Archbishop's cot broken*

turned in, by which precaution they had a good night's rest and were sure of knowing where they were the next morning and stood but little chance of running down a continent in the dark.[19]

19. Diedrich Knickerbocker, the fictional Dutch historian, created by author Washington Irving (1783–1859), reported 'that sage rule of the Dutch navigators' regarding the taking in of sail at night, as cited here by Harding (*History of New-York from the Beginning of the World to the End of the Dutch Dynasty by Diedrich Knickerbocker*, New York, 1880, 91).

17 February: Awake and behold – nil nisi prontus et aer.[20]

Latitude at noon 33°38' S. Lighthouse bearing SW distant 20 miles – Calm in the morning; evening W.S.W. moderate breeze; very sick all day; employed the carpenter in our cabins. The hook holding up the Archbishop's cot gave way under a very slight pressure.

Tell Lenehan that iron is better than brass and beaten iron is to be preferred to cast – no cast hooks.[21] It may be a matter of life and death; one might come down by the run in the middle of a dark and stormy night.

18th Feb. Wed.
The Archbishop somewhat better this morning. The calm continues but a slight rolling appears great rolling to us. One of the passengers mentions the case of a 120-gun ship having had her mainmast unshipped by the rolling during a calm. Our course is S.E. and at noon we are 120 miles only from Sydney. The temperature is much changed – clear weather and a gentle breeze springs up in the afternoon. The sailors are stowing away the anchor.

---

20. *Nihil est, nisi pontus et aer*: 'There is nothing but Pontus (sea) and sky' (Ovid's *Tristia*, 1.2.23–4).
21. *Lenehan*: perhaps Andrew Lenehan proprietor of '*LENEHAN*'S Upholstery Ware Rooms, 271 Castlereagh-street, between King and Market Streets'. It may have been he who supplied the Archbishop's faulty cot.

[12] *Animals sick*

Lewis got a roaring for not having brought sundry boxes of plants, birds engaged and other such, but manages to lay the blame on the absent *Prior Cathedralis*, who had nothing else to do and had not procured them.[22] It was quite tantalizing to see the abundance of plants and vegetable specimens brought by the Doctor – indeed the poop presents more the appearance of a zoological garden than a stage for Neptune.

The sheep and cattle begin to look sickly and quite out of their element. The once fierce horned beasts sink languidly on their knees; the sprightly goat is heard to groan at the crib out of which it has not strength to tear his food through the netting; Jimmy Ducks wonders at the general fainting that seizes on his various flocks. The wool-bearing herd complain in sickly bleatings. A distemper rages in the coops, ducks quacking as they roll their eyes and stretch their feeble necks to the sky. Hens breathe their last spontaneously. Grunters run wild and drop on the slippery deck as if struck by the plague which makes great havoc among such tender life.

We sit for dinner – the passengers besides the Archbishop and Lewis, as their names occur in the Newspaper: Arthur editor Way, Hicks, Major Elrington, Doctor Dobie, the chief mate Macintosh and 2d Mr Ward and the Captain.[23] Captain Gilbert seems to profess that maturity of experience which age imparts – mild and kindhearted. He has

22. *Prior Cathedralis*: Dr Henry Gregory Gregory OSB.

23. Major John Henry Elrington (died 1857) was a wealthy landholder in the Braidwood district of NSW from 1828; he was appointed Chief Magistrate of the district, resigning in controversy in 1839. He was described as a 'tall, redhaired, blue-eyed, soldierly man, with a sabre-cut across his forehead', a wound received in the Peninsular War (*Sunday Times*, 16 December 1923, page 30).
Dr Dobie: Robert Dobie (1793–1873) was born in Scotland; became a navy surgeon in 1814 and a surgeon-superintendent on the convict ships; in 1845 he was appointed to the *Ratcliffe* sailing to Hobart; e kept a medical journal on this voyage from 7 April to 4th September 1845; he died in 1873 at his residence in London.
Arthur Edwin Way – Magistrate and Clerk of the Course at the Homebush racecourse.
James Gilbert former captain of ships transporting convicts from Ireland, 1829–1834. See 'Convicts Ship Captains Index' at *Free Settler or Felon* database, https://jenwilletts.com/index.htm (accessed 21/12/2018).

been 20 years and more at sea. I'll not say that the conversation is characteristic however:

Major: 'I'll trouble you Doctor for some ham.'
Doctor: 'What again?'
Major: 'Again! Yes again. Why you would not

[13] *Conversation – 'By their tongue you shall . . .'*

ask me that question in your own house, at your own table. If you did I would never call on you again. Thank you (on receiving back his plate) and now I'll trouble the captain for some rice for the 3rd time.'

W. carries on the conversation about Louis Philip and of his own parentage.[24] He takes champagne although he says: 'The doctor is looking at him'; not that the doctor is abstemious himself, oh not at all – more anxiety about [f***s] health of others.

The Doctor instructs us how to select a good ship; a ship's age may be readily known, although painted afresh, by the ware and tear of her gangway and steps. He then attempts (in vain alas!) to brow beat Hicks on his mixture of sauces and returning to be helped so often, which will occasion him a headache. Hicks excuses himself that he gives half his mess to Templar, and besides he will not be controlled by the faculty or anyone else and wonders what is the good of living if good cheer is denied. A person might as well die at once.

The conversation then turns on the voyage and the four seasons we are to experience, Summer at present, winter round the Horn, and summer again along our homeward tract.

H[icks]: 'Mr McIntosh: I'll trouble you for some of that fowl, a little of the breast, aye, that very cut; no stuffing, thank you; and that bit of

24. Louis Philippe, Duke of Orleans and King of the French from 1830 to 1848, was allegedly a changeling. The story was that the previous Duke and his wife were travelling incognito during 1773 in Tuscany, when the Duchess gave birth to a daughter. The duke, desiring a son, bribed a local family to substitute their newborn male child for his newborn daughter. In 1830, the year of Louis Philippe's accession to the throne, the reputedly discarded daughter published her 'proofs': *Maria Stella ou un échange d'une demoiselle du plus haut rang contre un garçon de plus vile condition* (reprinted in 1839). King Louis Philippe was deposed during the revolution of 1848

the back you have just cut off. And I'll not trouble you again. Captain G. take a glass of wine with you. Shall it be Champagne or Sherry?'

'There is coal in every part of N.S.W.' says Hicks, 'on the Darling Downs, and wherever you will dig for it, even in Sydney – a part of the city is on a bed of coal.' Which is confirmed by the Archbishop: 'We have dug a well near St Patrick's and traversed through a bed of coke. Marble is also very plentiful – specimens in Government House, in many houses; marble from V[an] D[ieman's] Land for the altar of St Mary's. It would be

[14] *Conversation – Rev Mr Hanley*

expensive to have it worked and there it must remain.'

'Oh My Lord, you can soon do that', says Hicks addressing the Archbishop. 'It is only to make it known, anything you may want in that way among the Catholics, and you have it. Your church is much more liberal than ours. It is astonishing how eagerly your people contribute at public subscriptions. One would think that their very heart is set on the business.'

After some conversation on minerals and gold, a favourite topic, that of horses, was introduced, Way, Hicks and Major Elrington being squatters and having dealt in the same. Hicks relates how someone having lent a horse to the Revd. Mr Hanley at Moreton Bay on condition of taking another with him to Brisbane, after proceeding a considerable distance he mounted this young one which was very wild, which he [Hicks] would dissuade him from. However, as the one he had been riding had travelled a great way, he mounted the young one and stuck to it, not withstanding all the bucking of the untamed animal, greatly to his [Hicks'] admiration, who remarks that the Catholic clergy are generally considered as the best riders in the Colony.[25] Mr

25. The Bishop himself became an excellent horseman, as attested by the journalist and author Frank Fowler (1833–1863): 'He stands six feet two in his stockings, and sits his cob better than any other man in Sydney.' (Frank Fowler, *Southern Lights and Shadows: Being Brief Notes of Three Years' Experience of Social, Literary, and Political Life*, London, 1859). Fowler commented in an introductory note concerning his 'sea-sanctified MS.': 'the following pages were put together at sea, having been written in my bunk during a three-days' stiffish gale off the Falklands.'

Hanley is a hale and hearty, robust young man.[26] 'I met him occasionally; he was once riding off to some sick person and did not start till late. I warned him of the dangers of travelling in the bush so late. The following morning, I had many miles to ride and did not expect to reach the Ipswich Inn till late in the evening. Mr Hanley was there leading another horse and he would take it to drink at some water hole that I knew to be dangerous. He persisted nevertheless and fell over his horse's head

[15] *19th feb – Sea sickness – Archbishop – sugar*

into the mud, and thus all over mud and wet he had to continue his journey as far as Ipswich and to pass through the town in that plight.'

After dinner a breeze sprung up, which advanced us, although a little out of our course, with a celerity of about 6 kts, when in the evening it rose to a semi gale.

The Archbishop with a slight attack of the prickly heat.

19th Feb: cloudy, threatening strong breezes, tacking ship – reef topsails – lat. 37°S; long 151°E at noon; very sea sick.

The Archbishop alludes to Neil Arnott's theory on sea sickness, who attributes this to derangement of the peristaltic action first, hence a sympathetic affection of the stomach, and lastly that of the brain from its close affinity with the former organ.[27] The remedy to regulate the motions of the first and lie down flat on the back with eyes shut; use light and nutritious diet and aerated lemonade.

20th Feb The Archbishop remarks that by some mistake Mr Slattery's presentation to the Treasury for travelling expenses have been put on

---

26. James Hanley, born in County Tipperary in 1815, was educated for the priesthood at St John's College, Waterford. He arrived in Sydney in 1843 with Archbishop Polding and was ordained at St Mary's Cathedral in September. He was the first priest sent north to the Moreton Bay district. He spent 14 years at that mission.
27. The 1827 edition of Arnott's *Elements of Physics or Natural Philosophy General and Medical* was held in the Benedictine Library at St Mary's, which was transferred to Lyndhurst College in 1852. Bearing the Lyndhurst stamp, it is now held in the Benedictine Collection at the Veech Library. See also, Robert A. Bayliss and C. William Ellis, 'Neil Arnott, F.R.S., Reformer, Innovator and Populariser of Science, 1788–1874', *Notes and Records of the Royal Society of London*, Volume 36, Number 1 (1981), pp.103–123.

board and adds the hope that this is not by way of compensation for other more appropriate papers, with which His Grace ought to have been furnished on his own account from the Treasury.[28]

A stiff breeze set in during the night propelling us at the rate of 8 kts; prickly heat disappearing. Someone (blush not, who read this) who packed up the coffee and forgot the sugar. Here we are then without it. Saw an albatross (the first) and also a bird of new plumage –

Admiring some of Way's views about Sydney done in sepia.

[16] *Thunder storm – Divine Service*

21 Feb – Awoke in a thunder storm; latitude 40°13' S, longitude 154°32' E.

Tantis tonitruis and fulgetris ingravescere ut horrorem mortalibus incuteret –

Mare erat aestuosissimum et inter horrendos tonitruum fragores crebri micare ignes, aer incendi fulgoribus. &c &c[29]

The report of the thunder was of strange spluttering kind, like a hoarse cough of Eolus as if produced by some sudden irritation of the larynx.[30]

The wind continues variable all day and it is feared that after hanging so long to the southward we should be driven northward before clearing N. Zealand.

His Grace looks himself again and recovered.

22 Feb Sunday – fine morning – rate 8 kts.

The captain says we may sight N. Zealand next Wednesday. The Captain requested that either myself or the Archbishop should give

---

28. Father Thomas Slattery (1807–1882): ordained at Maynooth in 1837, he sailed to Sydney that year. After serving at Hartley and Bathurst, in 1848 he joined Bishop Gould in the new diocese of Melbourne.
29. *With such thunders and lightning-flashes it grew worse so that terror for mortals it struck. The sea was seething very greatly and between the terrible crashings of thunders, frequent lightnings flashed the air with flashes of fire.* (after Livy, *History of Rome,* 21.58.5).
30. *Aeolus*: keeper of the winds in Greek mythology.

Divine Service at a convenient time on the quarter deck, as we might prefer. The Archbishop acceded to the request: service at 11 o'clock. The passengers and all the crew that could be spared attended.

Sermon on the Gospel of the day, St Luke 18 ch. v. 31ff.[31] His Grace sat on chair and his audience were before him on chairs and benches stretched across the deck outside the cuddy, the weather being fine.[32] The prayers were read in the 'Garden of the Soul', the 'Come let us adore', the Scriptural Litany, the Lesson, Gospel and Epistle of the day, an instruction on the passion of Christ, reflections on the evil of sin; the time now afforded for reflection – all wonderfully

[17] *Templar – Cockatoo*

appropriate and persuasive, considering the mixed sort of congregation. After the sermon the *Miserere* and universal prayer were read.[33]

Our latitude is 42°23' S; longitude 157°7' E; our course S.E.; and wind N.W. and strong breezes – which with the divine service is all that is entered on the ship's log for the day.

We search for the Calender which ought to have been packed up, please yr rev Dr G, in the writing desk – it was not there.

The cockatoo and monkey play together. Templar now and then joins in the game, and the cat follows, and then the two goats. The monkey caresses and pats the cockatoo and paws him on the head. This the cockatoo resists and thinks it a great presumption that the monkey should stroke him as his own master would. Templar looks on most gravely as much as to say – 'If I had the least encouragement, I'd put you both through your pacings in less than no time.[34] I care not the cracking of chicken bones for you all.'

31. Luke 18.31ff : Jesus' third prediction of the Passion.
32. *Cuddy*: a saloon cabin at the stern of ships, where wealthy passengers could gather in greater comfort than those in steerage below.
33. *Miserere* (Psalm 100); *Universal Prayer*, attributed to Pope Clement XI, begins: 'Lord, I believe in you: increase my faith. I trust in you: strengthen my trust. I love you: let me love you more and more. I am sorry for my sins: deepen my sorrow.'
34. 'Putting through pacings': forcing one to demonstrate skill in a particular area.

Mrs. Harnett's ginger bread nuts taste well and seem to acquire additional relish in this latitude of cold and damp.

23 Feb We both passed a bad night. The Archbishop did not sleep. The sea was rough and the ship rolled disagreeably, yet going on rapidly in our course. A squall came on at 2 o'clock in the morning; all hands were piped on deck to trim the sails. It was all over at breakfast time.

Said Office for the first time together.[35] Weather becomes foggy, our S.E. course being changed for an E.S.E. one, that will bring us round the Southern Point of New Zealand; it will

[18] *Squalls – incidents – Magellanic clouds*[36]

then be eastward until we reach near the Horn.

24th Feb A very rough night, squalls came on thicker and faster every hour. The wind and rain and waves beat horribly against the poop. This is called New Zealand weather – very sick with something of the sensation of English weather. We make coffee with our patent apparatus and use a change of clothes to walk on the poop and sit in doors. Hicks complains of being unwell and submits to fast and abstinence for the time but proposes grog in the evenings.

Read the *Adventures of a Younger Son*, the novel, and also about the younger son 15th of St Luke[37].

25th Feb Ash Wednesday. The Archbishop slept not the whole night with the noise and confusion occasioned by altering the sails during a succession of squalls. The flapping of the ropes and blocks, the tramps overhead and the wild uproar of the elements were incessant.

---

35. *Office*: Divine Office, the obligatory daily prayers of clerics and religious, consisting principally of psalms, sung or recited at specified times throughout the day.

36. *Magellanic Clouds:* two irregular dwarf galaxies visible in the Southern Hemisphere, named after Ferdinand Magellan (1480–1521), Portuguese explorer who led a Spanish expedition to the East Indies from 1519 to 1522, resulting in the first circumnavigation of the Earth.

37. *Adventures of a Younger Son*: Edward John Trelawny's semi-autobiographical novel (1831).

Our lat is 47°42' S, long 163°9' E; continued rain and heavy squalls from the North. Our position appears to be not above 100 m. from the South Cape, our course lying between 30 or 40 m. of the rocks called the Snares.[38] God grant we may not be drawn into them by some current.

The wind hereabouts generally appears to die away about 4 o'clock in the morning and to resume its strength again at 8.

Albatrosses and cape pigeons seem to take a higher flight this evening – what do such unusual signs portend? On retiring to rest we observed a fine starry firmament. By the observing of the two congeries of stars, called the Magellanic Clouds, we discover the hour of the evening or night, as the one

[19] *The Snares – His Grace and the French*

mounts gradually over the other, so our friends at home by observing the N Pole Star.

26 Feb Discovered a treasure beyond all price – 'The World' – a small map of the world.

Our course is now E. until we reach the Horn. We have passed the Snares and the Antipodes are on our intended time. We calculate that from this point we have yet 180 degrees of Easting and 100° of latitude to travel. We have traversed so far only 22° – thus by degrees it is observed we shall at last reach our destination. Interested in the accounts of Borneo and places not generally known, described in the *Adventure of Younger Son*. The passengers spend their time in reading novels.

The dinner conversation on tumblers that hold a gallon used in the W. Indies. One naturally asks what is drunk in such tumblers? Why, Sangaria, a common West India drink, made of wine, water, sugar etc. etc – Way tells of tankards used at Oxford 18 inches high, and nothing but eating and drinking there from morning till night. If such is their caracteristic feature, doctor, you ought to be there to reform it.

---

38. *The Snares*: rocks 200 km to the south of the South Island of New Zealand.

From English to the French universities, and from them to the French in Sydney was a natural transition. The French consul with his £1200 a year[39]; the French whalers; the French man-of-war, Captain Berard, the frigate 'Le Rhin'[40] – Doctor Arnoux[41] – smart fellows – they were going shortly to New Zealand thence to France – Doctor Arnoux would spend a year at Paris and 2 in London – Doctor Pompallier on board 'Le Rhin'. The Archbishop had contributed to their increase (of the French) in Sydney from a patriotic feeling, to increase by their means the trade and commerce of the city. He had met in on one or two instances with feelings of jealousy, a petty jealousy at the increase of French missionaries, whom His Grace had caused to establish themselves in Sydney and form

[20] *Conversation on Jealousy about the French in Sydney*[42]

a House of Procure,[43] whence the South Sea Islands and the various missions to the Savages might be supplied from the Sydney markets with cotton clothing, flour and implements of agriculture and so forth – which formed no mean item in the trade accounting to at least 6 or £7,000 annually, benefitting by so much the Sydney market,

39. Monsieur Jean Antoine Marie Faramond was French Consul in Sydney from 1842–1853. He died during his passage home.
40. The French corvette, *Le Rhin*, after major repairs at Port Jackson, sailed for New Zealand with the French missionary bishops Pompallier and Viard on 12 January 1846. In the summer of 1843, Captain Auguste Berard of *Le Rhin*, had sailed into the land-locked harbour of Akaroa to protect the interests of his countrymen in the infant settlement. Three years before, they had left France in the *Comte de Paris* to found a colony, but their claims were forestalled by Captain Hobson, who sent a vessel from the Bay of Islands to proclaim British sovereignty. However, the original sixty immigrants were allowed to remain as settlers.
41. Dr Louis Arnoux was the surgeon onboard *Le Rhin*. In 1846 he presented the skull of a new species of beaked-whale to the Paris Museum of Natural History. The species was named after Arnoux and his captain: *Berardius Arnuxii*.
42. Suspicion of the French presence in Sydney extended beyond commercial matters. There was anxiety about French activity in the Pacific, especially in New Zealand. In a letter to Propaganda Fide, in December 1845, Polding commented: '... English and French politics seem to be incurring rivalry in their projects for Oceania.' (Polding to Cardinal Fransoni, 14 December 1845 [*Letters* II.49]).
43. *House of Procure*: In July 1845 Polding accepted the request of the Superior General of the Marist Fathers, Père Jean-Claude Colin, to establish a Procurate in Sydney, but with restrictions on the activities of the French Marists to be assigned there – 'no more than a simple Procurate' (Polding to Père Colin SM, 11 July 1845 [Polding Letters II.36]).

which otherwise would continue in the hands of the merchants at Valparaiso.

And now the passengers expressed their indignation at such a feeling of mean petty jealousy or bigotry and reprobated the conduct of one Campbell.[44]

Doctor Dobie: 'It is a great shame that such a feeling should prevail. Did old Campbell, the patriarch of the wharf, fear the French would come and seize his whaleboats? In time of peace especially a feeling of concord and amity should mark all our dealings with them, if it was but for the interest of civilization.'

From the trade with the French the conversation turned to that with China and the exportation of tea to the London market, one contending that all the best tea went to Russia, which was disproved.

And we were on this and the wool of N.S.W., when Hicks discovered on feeding his birds and petting them as he did from the table, in a small case of birds food a nest of insects and a centipede, which made him nervous from a dread of a bite from this insect, and the remedies it would require, for which the doctor's panacea was spirits of ammonia, a powerful alkali, that would neutralise any poison instantly. It would be

[21] *Ammonia – the Archbishop*

proper for anyone to carry a small vial of this, by which the bite of a mad dog, of a snake or any other venomous insect would be infallibly cured. For this it would be sufficient to dip a feather in the liquid and drop a quantity of it in the wound, rubbing it for a little while.

The Archbishop agreed to the remedy from experience of its success in the case of a bite from a snake at the orphan school. One of these children could not be persuaded to walk about with shoes; one day, going in the bush, she felt something cold about her foot – it was a snake and she felt the bite. A servant who lived there told her not to be

44. Robert Campbell (1769–1846), a Sydney merchant, pastoralist, politician and philanthropist. See Margaret Steven, 'Campbell, Robert (1769–1846)', *Australian Dictionary of Biography*, National Centre of Biography, Australian National University, http://adb.anu.edu.au/biography/campbell-robert-1876/text2197, published first in hardcopy 1966 (accessed online 6 August 2018).

alarmed. He cut the wound and sucked it for ½ an hour. Meanwhile the Archbishop and doctor being sent for, Doctor Harnett scarified the wound and washed it with spirits of ammonia. The child continued stupefied for some time, but slowly recovered.

In the evening in our cabin the Archbishop laughs and plays with Templar; remarks that we had the same weather in his last voyage this way round the Horn – no violent weather, and but one storm on the coast of Brazil.[45] His Grace alludes to the Mass said every morning for us, the difference of time between the Sydney and ours being about 20 minutes. Already we know when to unite with it in prayer – a great comfort in the bond of prayer, no matter how far removed; no sooner have we entered its magic circle than we are one.

[St Mary's monastery] From the top of the campanile[46]

[22] *Morning news – Hicks – Templar – Prayer*

27th Feb Hicks as usual after promenading about the poop and decks from 4 o'clock till breakfast time at 8 or 9, comes in, and if there is no one to address himself to as he prepares for breakfast, he talks aloud and relates all the news, so as to be heard by everyone in their cabins. The Archbishop laughs, and it amuses him to hear all the news Hicks thus contrives to collect from all quarters.

Templar, who has been sick of late, has taken to growl at everybody and shews of the pepper and mustard bread; nor is he so sick, but that he can eat well. Aye, Joseph, and be dainty too; behold how he leaps mast-high for a bone his Master has fixed there. This morning having fixed himself at Hick's door as at a Badger's hole. Oh, for Vincent to give him a chastisement – ! He sat with his nose to the ground and barked at any attempt to pass by him.

45. In November 1840 Polding sailed to England via Cape Horn in the brig *Orion*.

46. The campanile was separated by about 20 yards to the north from the east-west oriented cathedral. Its eight bells were first rung on New Years day 1844.

Templar leaping up for a bone

This evening life of St Leander, 18th Ch. St John and rosary as usual.[47] His Grace finds the benefit of Mrs Milford's cloak and extols her in his praises. I echo indeed with all my heart for my own also, which is very acceptable in this wintery weather, and we join our prayers for her and benefactors.

28th Feb Fine breezes, bracing weather, wind from the south cold and dry. The ship glides over the smooth water at the easy rate of 5 kts. A laugh at the Major, who had twice fallen from his cot during the night. He thoroughly awoke at the 2nd fall only and slept not the whole night after. It seems understood that everyone

[23] *Food – black swans – Stern Cabins – Templar*

is to enquire of the Major's health, particularly in which Hicks never fails. The Major on issuing from his cabin every morning at about 8 is heard to call George, the stuard's mate, and the name of George, George! is re-echoed, for some time in authoritive accent.[48] George

47. St Leander, bishop of Seville (feast day - 27 February), was the first to introduce the Nicene Creed at Mass. He died about the year 600.
48. *stuard*: Harding' spelling of 'steward'

arrives and completes his Master's toilet and puts on his shoes and attends him as obsequiously as ever the magistrate was attended at his seat of Mount Elrington on the Shoalhaven.[49]

The black swans are let run about the deck for air and exercise. The cow calves but does not afford much milk. The fowls die in threes and fours at a time from the effects of the too sudden changes in the temperature. The goats are doing well; one yields plenty of milk daily and, astonishing!, habitually sucks its own breasts; having become a favourite, it is fed with cake and fruit.

The Archbishop remarks about his stern cabin that he would advise no one to take that cabin from experience. His Grace says it is the most uncomfortable part of the ship, being the furthest removed from the centre of motion, it consequently rises up and down through the greatest space; the noise of the chains at the wheel is incessant. Its advantages are the stern window, its additional light and ventilation, and the great degree of comfort enjoyed there while passing through the Tropics. The larger accommodation etc.

Templar took a cruise in search of privateering rats and other pirates on the top of the hay stack. We expect to reach the Horn this day month; the average rate of 7 kts an hour is required for that purpose.

[24] *Antipodes – description*

1st March

Sunday. We were all called on deck early this morning with the exciting sound of 'Land ahead, land ahoy!' This is the island of Antipodes regarding which sung Lucretius:

'Illi cum videant solem, nos sidera noctis cernere et alternis nobiscum tempora caeli dividere et noctes parilis agitare diebus. sed vanus stolidis hoc omnia parturit error.'[50]

49. See 'ROMANCE OF A PIONEER FAMILY: MAJOR ELRINGTON AT BRAIDWOOD 100 YEARS AGO' (*Sunday Times*, 16 December 1923, page 30).
50. 'When those see the sun, we behold the stars of night; and that they share with us time about the seasons of heaven and pass nights equal in length to our days. But groundless error has devised such dreams for fools.' (Lucretius, *De rerum natura*, Liber I, line 1065.)

The island of Antipodes presents an aspect of dreary desolation. Its rocky shore almost everywhere rises perpendicularly to a height of perhaps from 60 to 100 feet; abrupt and hilly ridges offer an ascent in some parts to the more rugged and craggy peaks, which are interspersed here and there on narrow ledges of table land. A central cone of smooth surface and obtuse angle reaches a height of probably 1500 feet. At the western extremity of the island is perforated rock forming a natural archway of great dimensions, into which the waves appeared to roll with an unbroken billow. Its south and eastern boundaries and mural cliffs were lashed by the turbulent swell and a high surf. The interior appeared totally devoid of trees and bushes – here and there a patch of rusty verdure appeared

[25] *Antipodes – situation*

over an uncultivable surface.

The outline of the various masses and to judge from appearance at a distance one might take it to be of volcanic production – rocks of trass formation.[51] Here and there terraced cliffs inclined at an angle of 20 degrees resemble the limestone stratification in some of the neighbouring islands. Its circumference might be about 20 miles. It is the resort of thousands of birds, some came hovering about the ship for a while and returned again to the island. It has possibly not been visited since its first discovery, which was either by Captain Bristow in the *Sarah* in 1806, or by H. M. Ship *Cornwallis* in 1807, when were discovered also the Lord Auckland and Bounty Islands.[52] Myriads of birds resort on these rocks.

51. *trass*: light-colored porous volcanic rock.
52. The island group was first charted in 1800 by Captain Henry Waterhouse in HMS *Reliance*. The Lord Auckland Islands were discovered by Captain Abraham Bristow in the whaler *Ocean* in 1806. In 1807, HMS *Cornwallis* was ordered to Australia and after visiting Port Jackson, she sailed to New Zealand and crossed the Pacific Ocean to the Juan Fernández Islands searching for enemy (French) shipping.

The Boobie (apud Herbert)[53]

The day being favourable Captain Gilbert took various sets of observations for the purpose of ascertaining with all possible exactitude the true position of Antipodes Island, and having worked out their various results it would appear, according to these calculations, that the centre of the Island is 53 miles more to the westward than marked in Horsburgh's *India Directory*.[54] Thus, therefore, instead of being considered in Long. 179°30' E., it would be 178°38', and as a degree of longitude in these latitudes measures about 38 miles, the difference amounts to about a degree. It is also within

[26] *Antipodes*

about 30? miles of the spot which may be said to be the true antipodes of London.

The day was particularly favourable for taking the observations, the atmosphere being clear and the moon, though young, distinctly vis-

53. *Boobie*: the name 'booby' was applied to this sea bird because of its habit of landing on sailing ships, where it was easily captured and eaten.
54. The Scottish hydrographer, James Horsburgh (1762–1836), was the author of *Directions for Sailing to and from the East Indies, China, New Holland, Cape of Good Hope, and the interjacent Ports, compiled chiefly from original Journals and Observations made during 21 years' experience in navigating those Seas*, also known as the 'India Directory', published in 1811.

ible. The ship under easy sail about 4 kts, and the Island lying during the whole day about S.E. 5 or 6 miles distant.

In the evening, as we saw the sun shining on its summits before setting, the thought of its lighting at the same moment the summits of our native hills, rising with them as it now sets with us, could but inspire us with sentiments of admiration and hope.

Island of Antipodes

Our passage from Sydney to Antipodes Island has been of 14 days, and it is consoling to reflect that nothing disagreeable has occurred on board as yet – on the contrary, each day seems to bring us nearer to the comforts of a family. And as to the fare of the ship, if it lasts as it has commenced, the *Ratcliff* will be the Phoenix of ships, for not only is the food that is served

[27] *Sermon – our friends – Incidents*

at table fresh and wholesome and sufficient, but likewise there prevails a taste of elegance and a cleanliness about the stuard and waiters quite praiseworthy.

'Divine Service' at 11 o'clock in the same order as observed last Sunday. The sermon on the Gospel of the day – God as our Father – motives of repentance for offences against so good a Father, whose providence watches over his children on whatever part of the globe they may be situated; motives for a diligent observance of His commands – 'If I am Father and Lord where is my honor?' *In fine* His Grace impressed on his audience the nature of their responsibility as rational creatures, and the work of their salvation must be work of their own hands with the grace of God.[55]

55. *in fine* (Latin): 'altogether'.

We thought on the happiness of our friends in Sydney in being present at the Holy Sacrifice. We joined them in spirit at St Patrick's and at St Benedict's and at their meeting for the propagation of the faith.

In the evening, after night prayers and rosary, read the life of St David, Archbishop of Wales and ch. 7 Ecclus.[56]

2nd March The Archbishop spent a bad and sleepless night owing, as he says laughing, to the absence of the usual noise during the night of sailors reefing, and dancing corrobory as they do in the gale and squalls. But all was calm as if we had been drifting in a current, perhaps towards the island! Templar was not the better either for, for some cause, his master had to get up and give him a beating.

3rd March Major Elrington has a bad cold and cough; it is feared he may not live out the voyage. At his age (near 70) the least cold or damp affects him materially. We saw a whale spouting about 1 mile on our starboard bow. Archbishop read 4 pages of *Manuale Eccl.*[57] We opened Mrs Plunkett's box and it contained gingerbread, nuts and a variety of good things. What a virtue is filial affection and solicitude! 'No thanks, however,' says the Archbishop, 'to the "gentleman" who directed

[28] *Ship in sight*

to be written on the said box – "parcels for Ireland"'. If an extreme desire to obtain some sugar had not suggested the possibility of it being contained by a higglety pigglety mistake in the said box, the probability is that its contents would have made the voyage undisturbed.

The poop was painted with 3 coats of paint and varnished with oil and wax. The Captain now applauds his invention. It is surprising indeed to see the glossy appearance, which the poop presents notwithstanding the continued tramp and wear and tear. Some of the boards on

56. The Book of Ecclesiasticus, also known as *The Wisdom of Sirach* is an Old Testament collection of ethical teachings. It was Lewis' daily spiritual reading during most of the voyage.

57. *Manuale Eccl.*: perhaps *Manuale ecclesiasticorum, seu Collectio decretorum authenticorum Sacrae Rituum Congregationis*, Roma, Typis Sacrae Congregationis de Propaganda Fide, 1841.

the main deck opened owing to the lightness with which the wood has been compressed and screwed down under weather, but the ship is quite new and strong, this being her 2nd voyage only.

Spiritual reading: Ecclus. ch 7; St Cunegunda, Empress.[58]

4 March Two days in one. Awoke this morning with the cry of 'Ship ahead'. The monotony of shipboard life somewhat broken by interesting enquiries as to all about the ship – whence comes she, where is she going? The signals not being at hand, we did not communicate with her, though sufficiently near to do so. The meeting, however, of this vessel is attended with one good effect, the signal colours are now hooked up and in readiness for any other occasion that may require their use. The next may be of far greater consequence than this, if, for instance, we meet a man-of-war and do not hoist the colour, it may be deemed an act of contumacy and be followed by an admonitory shot.

This affair of the ship was succeeded by another of a more domestic character, but not less interesting – a number of marauders had

[29] *Albatross*

been following and hanging about us for a number of days. Being becalmed they deemed the opportunity too good to be lost; accordingly, they came to close quarters. We threw out a couple of grappling lines and brought them to. In very simple language, we put out two lines and caught a couple of albatrosses, one of which no doubt the *Diomedea exulans*, the other perhaps a *fuliginosa* , not being so large and having a dusky hue on the breast and on the wing.[59] The former measured 9 feet 9 inches from tip to tip of wings; the weight 18 lbs and ½. We requested the butcher to kill them, which he did by running a needle in the back of the head. Some of the sailors tore out the quill feathers so that our birds were rendered useless as species. By way of practice, however, the doctor skinned one and cleaned it, and I clipt and cleaned the entire wing of the other, which, however, is

58. *St Cunegundes* (975–1040): Patron saint of Lithuania – feast day 3 March.
59. *Diomedea exulans*: wandering albatross; the name of the genus *Diomedea* comes from the Greek hero Diomedes, who, according to legend, was driven by a storm to Italy and was stranded with his companions who were turned to birds. *Diomedea fuliginosa*: perhaps the 'sooty albatross'.

not likely to preserve as we have no preparation of arsenic soap and proper instruments. These birds are enormous. The down under the feathers is amazingly thick and beautiful.

Albatross – sketched on the spot

'Having entered upon our west longitude, we have disposed of the supernumerary day we have brought with us from Sydney and have accordingly, after keeping one Tuesday, keep this day another. The explanation of this phenomenon we refer to the Professor

[30] *A day gained travelling Eastward*

of Philosophy and request that he will give *viva voce* that explanation which it would take us too long to give. But another question arises: 'How is the Office to be kept? The Office of the 3rd was recited yesterday; the Office for the 4th can only be recited tomorrow and this day, in virtue of the permission of the Holy See, we have recited the rosary. Perhaps it would be quite as proper to have recited the ferial office.'

This day therefore is one day gained. The Spaniards came round Cape Horn to proceed to the Philippines Islands; in proceeding then westward and not having made allowance for the day lost, it is said that at some of their establishments they are yet a day behind, so that the Monday of Europe is their Sunday and so on, which the Archbishop thinks is as great an error as that of the Quarto Decimans and ought to be rectified.[60]

It is therefore plain that I have a day to dispose of and cannot do better, Mother, than to offer it to you. How many have desired at the hour of death for one hour, which is not however your case, for your piety

60. Christians of Asia Minor celebrated Easter on the 14th (quartodecimo) of the first month (Aviv), while the church of Rome celebrated it on the following Sunday.

makes you rather anxious to leave, I know, than to remain in this world – Oh, that your son resembled you. Nevertheless, I lay up this additional day and offer it you from whom, under God, I received life itself as a present unique, and what probably no other son has ever yet offered to his mother, you may boast of having received from yours. It is not a present I could offer anyone else, nay not even to my Pollylou, to whom I would get away pretty [?]; this is for a mother alone.

Spiritual read: Ecclus ch 3; St Werburga, Feb 3.[61]

Our latitude: 17°49' S; longitude: 173°35' W; wind S.S.E. tacked and wore ship.

[31] *Gale*

5 March

Last night it blew in squalls, which succeeded each other stronger and stronger and stronger until it reached to a violent gale from the Eastward, and this evening we are lying-to. But the ship is dry and high out of water.

4 ch Ecclus.; St Casimir, Prince of Poland.[62]

6 March A sleepless and uncomfortable night. Archbishop disturbed by the noises and myself by my complaint. The dead lights in the Archbishop's cabin were put up.[63] This is the weather for a ship being 'pooped'.[64] One night I imagine myself in a fort battered on all sides by the enemies' battering rams and balissters, that must end by crushing the building and sending us to the bottom. Then succeeds a lull – the ship seems stopped in her onward course. You know not what will follow. Then after a short while succeeds a lift-up slow and solemn and then a fall as awful into the yawning depth below. Then the melancholy cries of the sailors as they hawl at the ropes and the shrill sound of the word of command piercing amidst the hoarse howling of the winds 'all hands ahoy! Tumble aft; let go your top gallant halyards; main tack and sheet let go; claw him up, claw him up.'

61. *St Werburga* (650–699): Benedictine nun and patroness of Chester.
62. Casimir (1461–1484), Patron of Poland and Lithuania. Feast day – 4 March.
63. *deadlight*: a protective cover or shutter fitted over a porthole or window on a ship.
64. *pooped*: ship impacted by a wave breaking over the stern, sometimes causing it to capsize.

All which to the inexperienced in these matters occasions alarms and apprehensions the more distressing from not knowing what they will end in.

In the evening we find that we have drifted 35 miles out of our course, and the captain begins to be anxious about our slow progress, having a wife and family, who expect his return.

'May God grant', says the Archbishop, 'that this may be the last time that we may traverse this immense body of waters.'[65]

Spiritual reading: 5 ch Ecclus. on false friends; St Collette.[66]

Latitude 48°12' S; Longitude 172°19'; increasing gales and squally.

Procellaria Pelagica
Lin[naeus][67] –
Mother Carey's chickens[68]

65. It was indeed the last time that Polding sailed via cape Horn. His two subsequent voyages to Europe, in 1854 and 1865, were via the Red Sea.
66. *St Colette of Corbie* (1381–1447): French abbess and the foundress of the Colettine Poor Clares; feast date 6 March.
67. *Lin*[naeus]: Carl Linnaeus (1707–1778) was a Swedish botanist, physician and zoologist, who established the binomial nomenclature for organisms. He was one of Harding's authorities on bird names.
68. Stormy petrels were thought by sailors to be the souls of dead seamen and were called 'Mother Carey's Chickens'.

[32] *Meetings in Sydney*

7th March A fine day, nearly becalmed; fished unsuccessfully for an albatross; Mr Way unwell – taken an emetic complaining of constriction about the throat and pectoral muscles.

8th March – Sunday, but Monday in Sydney – 'The first – alas!' says His Grace, 'of the many distinct proofs that we have reached another hemisphere from that in which we have so happily passed these latter years.' While I write this, Doctor Gregory is probably at St Benedict's meeting and exclaiming: 'Why don't you give another clap, another cheer?' And addressing perhaps some little child, some little Catherine Duffy, or an Anne or Mary Walsh, or little Driscoll, or a Catherine Tinson.

'Look at Kate Tinson, she is not more than 12 years of age and she has brought more than 15/ – . Another clap for Catherine Tinson! Total amount for St Benedict's this evening £6/5/6.' Then in comes poor Bede tired and fogged from St Patrick's accompanied by Father John and triumphing in their £2 over St Benedict's.[69]

69. *Poor Bede*: perhaps this is Rev Bede Sumner OSB (1803–1871), sub-deacon of Downside, who joined Polding's band of missionaries in 1835. He was ordained priest in Sydney in May 1836. He ministered at St Patrick's 1845–1846. He died and was buried at 'Subiaco', the monastery of the Benedictine nuns on the Parramatta River.
Father John: Very Rev. Dean John McEncroe (1794–1868) was chaplain on Norfolk Island with Lewis Harding from October 1838 to September 1842, when he sailed back to Sydney with the dismissed catechist. He was priest-in-charge of St Patrick's, Church Hill, from 1844 until his death.

'May Sts B[enedict] and P[atrick]', says His Grace, 'pray for us and all those who collect for their respective churches.'

Having been becalmed all day, apprehend that we may be formidable rival to the ship *Everetta*, which, as Doctor Dobie says, was 73 days in reaching the Horn and 158 altogether reaching London, i.e. 5 months and more.[70]

Divine Service at 11 o'clock as usual hitherto. Spiritual reading in the evening from Peach.[71]

March 9: St Frances; the Archbishop was in her house.[72] Ecclus ch 7.

[33] *Albatross – Grey*

9th March Progressing at the rate of 8 kts which is quite delightful after yesterday's calms. A strong breeze sprang up at an early hour, which has been increasing hourly ever since and has caused the ocean to rise and the skies to wear something of the same appearance as on the day of the preceding gale. The Captain points to the clouds and the scud traversing the moon's disk at a great rate. Petrels and albatrosses on the wing playing about the ship. Grey describes them thus:[73] These seabirds he says hold their holiday in the stormy gale. The lordly and graceful albatross, whose motion is a very melody,

---

70. The *Eweretta*, often misspelt *Everetta*, a 365 ton barque built at Blackwall, was engaged in transporting emigrants to Australia. Dr Dobie was surgeon on *Eweretta* on its return voyage to England in April 1842 (*Sydney Herald*, 15 April 1842, 2).
71. 'Peach' could refer to one of two publcations:
    1. Rev. Edward Peach (1771–1839), *Sermons for every Sunday and Festival of the year, chiefly taken from the sermons of M. Massillon*, 3 vols., London, 1807–1808. Two copies of these volumes are held in the Benedictine Collection at the Veech Library, Sydney; one set is inscribed: 'The Archbishop's Library'.
    2. *Practical reflections for every day throughout the year* by the Rev. Robert Lane (1673–1710) (alias Bowes) enlarged and edited by Edward Peach, 3rd edition London, 1835. This text is also in the Benedictine Collection with the *ex libris*: Rev. J. Sumner, Sydney 1835.
72. *St Frances*: Santa Francesca di Roma (1384–1440); feast day 9 March.
    Her house: the 'casa santa', a religious community she established in 1433 at Tor de' Specchi, near the Campidoglio in Rome. Polding visited the 'casa' during his stay in Rome in 1842.
73. George Robert Gray, *A list of the genera of birds with an indication of the typical species of each genus*, London 1840.

swept screaming by upon the blast. The smaller cape pigeons followed us fast passing and repassing across the vessel's track. At last one of them spies a fragment on the waters which had been thrown overboard. A moment it hovers above then plunges down, but the other birds have seen it too and all pouncing on the spot move their wings confusedly and seem to run along the waters with a rapid and eager motion. Now is there discord wild among them – a screaming and diving, swimming and running, mingled with a chattering noise. No sooner does one gain the morsel than another tears it from him. Who will be the victor here? – the albatross, for he sweeps triumphantly over all, swoops down and with a scream scares off the timid little multitude, whilst high above his head he holds his arching wings and now in pride and beauty he sits upon the waters and drifting fast astern gradually fades in the twilight.

The Captain during the prevalence of these strong breezes has set two men at the wheel. It makes a great difference in the going of the ship if there is a good or careless helmsman. There is not any one circumstance perhaps after the attention of the Captain than the right management of the tiller and which tends more to the comfort of the passengers.

[34] *The Helmsman*

The ship in the hands of a careless helmsman bounds and leaps along unmanageably across the furrowed billows, something like a kangaroo rushing violently in the midst of his foes, or like a mad bull escaped from the herd and hunted over hill and ditch. He foams and tears up the earth in useless rage. A series of plunges marks the wayward tract of the struggling ship. Terrific seas are shipped, which deluge the decks and penetrate the hatchways in torrents not to be checked. The waves, as if irritated by the careless floundering of the bows are roused into battering her hollow flanks, until the she be subdued either into cautiousness or disabled by one ominous crash.

The careful and experienced helmsman, on the contrary, guides with a steady wheel the foaming bows of his obedient ship. He knows when to raise her head adorned with lofty figure and gracefully and smoothly to lift her over the yielding billow. Whether descending the intervening hollow or gradually emerging or racing up the opposite hill, he guides her with unerring peristaltic action peculiarly suited, avoiding the deeper trough and clearing the opposing wave obliquely, and thus disappoints the blow. He either puts her head onto, or eases her off the wind, just as the contending elements oppose or slacken their force. And in cross running waves he aims to luff for the one and bear up for another, acting ever in instinctive sympathy with the heaving billow and the action of the breeze on the taut sail.[74]

But the captain's experience, of course, is the main

[35] *St Gregory*

security. He watches the winds and weather and the ship's sails, and by his judicious management of furling unfurling, reefing and lying-to, each in proper time, the ship is always found to go an easy course and to carry on pretty steadily in all weathers.

We begin to play at cards and backgammon in the evenings from 7 till 8 o'clock. Major Elrington enjoys vastly his game of the latter with the Archbishop.

Spiritual reading – Ecclus. ch. 8; 40 Martyrs of Sebaste;[75] Peach, March 10.

Latitude: 46°50'; Longitude: 169°23' W

10th March Sea continues very high. The breeze strengthens and slackens alternately. Since yesterday we have run 5 degrees or 200 miles, nearly proceeding at the rate of about 7 kts. Our ship is not a quick going one, or with such a gale we should have run 9 kts at least.

The backgammon and whist proceed – the latter not so quietly as the former.

Spiritual reading – Ecclus. ch. 10; St Eulogius, priest and martyr of Cordova.[76]

74. *luff*: head to wind.

75. *Martyrs of Sebaste*: 40 soldiers martyred in 320AD; feast day: 10 March.

76. *St Eulogius*: died March 11, 857.

11 March Vigil of St Gregory the Great – feast of Doctor Polding, Doctor Gregory etc etc. and we wish My Lord Abbot a happy feast.[77]

The wind being more aft, we set our studding sails.[78]

Templar fell from the poop, a height of 8 feet – an omen that he is not to reach England as he could here have broken his neck had he not been doomed to be drowned.

12 March Latitude: 47°27' S; Longitude: 158°11' W

Full moon and steady breeze; 8 kts all day. Feast of St Gregory the Great, Pope, Confessor etc.

'Left Doway for Acton Burnell in 1803. Left my mother's house and went with my sisters to Woolton where now Mr. Philips resides.[79] There I remained and received the best part of my education under my excellent master, who in his way wished to bring me up after the manner

[36] *J.B.P* [John Bede Polding]

of young Cyrus.[80] I learned to ride without a saddle, to dig in the garden, when I wanted to play, to eat what was put before me, and be contented with what I got, to undervalue eat and drink – all these things with as much Greek as !!! 2 years there – and I am sure I don't know how I learned it but learned it and two books of Cyrussed – St Matthew, St Mark and part of the Acts of the Apostles in Latin from some cause or another – I don't know; I was a mere dunce; read *Selecta Vetera* part of Cornelius Nepos[81] and prospered in all they

77. *'Gregorians'*: the monks of St Gregory's, Downside.
78. *studding sails*: long and narrow sails used only in fine weather on the outside of the large square sails.
79. *Mr. Philips*: Samuel Maurus Philips OSB (1794–1855), classmate of Polding at Acton Burnell and Downside, ordained priest 1819, missioner at Woolton from 1822 until death.
80. *Young Cyrus*: the boyhood of Cyrus the Great is recounted in Book I of Herodotus' *Histories*.
81. *Cornelius Nepos* (110 BC-25 BC): a Roman biographer. His simple style of writing made him a popular choice in the teaching of Latin to beginners.

wished to teach me except in Lat. writing,[82] and that I never could learn, and that because probably no one ever taught me the mystery of it – gave me a reason why I was to hold my pen so and so.

In 1805, October, summoned out of bed at 4 o'clock in the morning to leave dear Wolton and all its innocent enjoyments. And a sad parting there was when I took leave of poor Peggy the housekeeper and Henry the butler and Mrs Porter. But I got out of her good graces by the last trick I played on her – cat going up in the garret and dirtying among the apples; played the cat a trick; reserved six large cockle shells; got pitch to fill them and caught cat and fastened cockle shells by means of pitch to the feet of this cat that mewed and complained sadly of such shoeing. The cat went to housekeeper's room &c &c; did not deny it when charged with it, a great complaint – Doctor Brewer my Uncle tasked me.[83]

In Oct 05, left them *tandem* 5 or 6 in the morning;[84] reached Chester for dinner, Elmsmire about 40 miles same evening.[85] Next morning proceeded to Shrewsbury, thence to Acton-Burnel, Shropshire, the seat of Sir Editor Smythe, which we reached for dinner next day.[86] The Rev Mr Sharrock, in rel[igion] Father Jerome – the uncle of Mr. Heptonstall – who was then prior of the house,

[37] *J.B.P* [John Bede Polding]

wore a Welsh wig under which it was gen[erally] said was contained as much Greek as might be found in the head of any man in Eng-

82. *Lat. writing*: perhaps Italic writing
83. *John Bede Brewer OSB* (1742–1822): Polding's uncle, monk of St Lawrence's Priory, Dieulouard in Lorraine; President-General of English Benedictines from 1799 till his death.
84. *tandem*: finally.
85. *Elmsmire*: Ellesmere, Shropshire.
86. Sir Edward Joseph Smythe, 6th Baronet (1787–1856). The English Benedictines at Douai in Flanders from 1607 were driven out in 1795 by the French Revolution. They went first to Acton Burnell in Shropshire, the home of Sir Edward, an Old Boy of the School, where they remained until the move to Downside in 1814. Polding completed his schooling at Acton and there received the Benedictine habit and the name 'Bede' in 1811.

land.[87] A tradition handed down is that the preface of Pastorini's *Ch. Hist.* is from his pen.[88]

It may be asked why I went to Acton Burnel. There may have been many reasons. One, I imagine, that influenced Doctor Brewer, President of the Congreg[ation], to show his impartiality towards the several houses belonging to it. His older nephew Doctor Slater was sent to Dolland, the house of his own profession; his great-nephew, H. Brewer, the present provincial of the North Province, was sent to Lamspring.[89]

87. *Welsh Wig*: a simple head hugging cap adorned with a row of 'curls' at the nape of the neck, which prevents draughts or rain getting into the collar. It was a popular nineteenth century choice with working men.
88. *Signor Pastorini*: the pseudonym of Charles Walmesley OSB (1722–1797), a monk of St Edmund's, Paris, and Vicar Apostolic of the Western District of England. His principal work was: *General History of the Christian Church from her birth to her Final Triumphant States in Heaven chiefly deduced from the Apocalypse of St John the Apostle*, Dublin 1771. The book prophesied the end of Protestantism by 1825. Later editions contained a preface by an anonymous editor.
89. *Edward Bede Slater OSB* (1774–1832): cousin of Polding; his monastery of profession was Dieulouard in Lorraine, from where, following the French revolution, the community relocated to Ampleforth. In 1819 he was appointed Vicar Apostolic of Vicariate of Mauritius, which included New Holland; following criticisms of his administration, he abandoned his vicariate in 1831 and died and was buried at sea on his voyage back to England.
Henry Anselm Brewer O.S.B (1792–1849), cousin of Polding, educated at Lambspinge and Ampleforth, ordained priest 1816, died at Liverpool.
The Abbey of Saints Adrian and Dionysius at Lambspringe in Lower Saxony was occupied by the English Benedictine Congregation from 1644 until suppression in 1802.

I was sent to St Gregories[90] – the inmates had found an hospitable asylum after being banished from Doway in the hospitable roof of Sir Ed Smythe, who had received his education with them and had a particular veneration for Prior Sharrock, the Community at this time consisting of Prior Sharrock, Dom Levos monk of the Congregation of St Maur, Dom Leveque a monk of the Monastery of Arras – [to] this monastery the Benedictines were indebted for their establishment at Doway – Father Joseph Rowdon, who died about the year 1807, Father Raudoff Ratcliff, who died at Acton Burnel circa 60–70 years old.'[91]

I could not procure any more of this manuscript.

We made our coffee this morning for the first time, having reserved it for the celebration of the feast of St Gregory; drank to Doctor Gregory's health and the nuns who had sent the coffee.[92] The spirits of wine prepared by Mr Bray for our first voyage in the *Oriental* in March'35,

90. The patronage of St Gregory the Great, who had sent the monk Augustine as head of the papal mission to England in 597, was carried by the Douai community to their foundations in England..
91. *James Jerome Sharrock O.S.B.* (1750–1808), was educated St Gregory's at Douay in France, becoming prior there in 1781 and continuing in that office at Acton Burnell. In 1806 he declined episcopal ordination as Coadjutor to his brother Gregory, the Vicar Apostolic of the Western District.
Dom Levos (phonetic spelling of Leveaux): Joseph Martin Leveaux OSB (1745–1828), a monk of the Maurist Congregation who was aggregated to the English Benedictines during the French Revolution. He was Novice Master at Acton Burnell and Downside, returning to France in 1816.
Arras: in 1611 the abbot of St Vaast Abbey at Arras, Philip de Caverel (1555–1636) built and endowed a monastery for the English Benedictines at Douai in the Spanish Netherlands.
Joseph Rowden OSB: perhaps John Joseph Burden (1777–1807) clothed at Acton Burnell 1796; ordained 1803.
Raudoff Ratcliff: Ralph Radcliffe OSB (1772–1842) was educated at Douay in France and ordained at Acton Burnell in 1803, where he remained as missioner until death. He was famous in the Congregation for his schoolboy escape from Douay during the French Revolution. *Raudoff*: Harding's attempt at spelling *Radulf*, the Old English version of *Ralph*.
92. The only nuns in Sydney in 1846 were the Irish Sisters of Charity who had arrived with Bernard Ullathorne on the last day of 1839. At the time of the sailing of the Ratcliff, the community of nuns was still located at Parramatta, where they began their ministry to female convicts and orphans. Two English Benedictine nuns would return with Polding in 1848.

11 years ago, since corked up, were today opened.[93] The lower part of the cork had

[38] *Nymph Coffeeanea*[94]

suffered a sort of decay, so that it crumbled instead of obeying the cork screw. Father Therry's little apparatus was brought up for heating the coffee or liquid by means of spirits of wine. A portion of coffee was poured in by way of experiment; the little measure of spirits of wine was duly filled and poured into the stand prepared for its reception with hand not less bold than the one who thrust a spear in the Trojan horse. We drew from Wartman's armoury (match maker) which with cunning skill having tipped with fire we plunged into the spirits eager to drink the flame – beneath, around, the fire claims the sway, now fiercely does it play around and with the eagerness of female curiosity would it peer within, but with a shield not less broad or bright than that of bold Tytides' son a jar protected the precious liquid which holy hand (the nuns') had prepared.[95] With wondering eyes we gazed astonished, we heard a voice of complaint from within; listening attentively we could distinguish the doleful accent of the nymph *Coffeenea*: 'The fire has caught hold of my feet. It has heated all the sides of the pot. I can find nowhere a place for – Oh, in what a terrible plight have I got',

93. Possibly the poet Rev Edward Atkyns Bray (1778–1857), vicar of Tavistock. He and his author wife, Anna Eliza (1790–1883), became friends of the Trelawny family, following their visit to Trelawne House in 1833.
94. *Coffeenea*: Harding's invented name for a coffee-nymph;*-nea* from *Naiads* the nymphs presiding over fountains, wells, springs, streams, brooks and other bodies of fresh water.
95. *Tytides*: perhaps the sea-nymph Thetis, mother of Achilles, who, in his battle with Hector, was provided with a shield forged by the god of fire at the request of Thetis.

when, like a pair of brave knights, we came immediately to the rescue and delivered the Nymph from

[39] *Mem[ory] Of Religious – (Dan)*

her perilous situation – in other words sea.'

The Archbishop was fairly driven out and obliged to the coffee having sung, we poured it into glasses, purloined some sugar from the Stuard, for which Doctor Gregory must answer, and with many thanks and many sweet remembrances for those who had prepared the beverage we enjoyed our innocent festivity.

13 March The night spent in trimming sail and reefing and by us in acts of patience to the tune of 'Ye Gent[lemen] of Sydney, who sleep at home at ease, little do ye think of the turmoils of the sea.' The Archbishop was obliged to make his bed on the floor, wrapped in blankets and cloaks. But the gents of Sydney, the hooded gents at least, did think of us, and the moment being opportune, I read my address, that also of my confreres, who had written it and placed it in my hands as we left Sydney.[96] It ran thus:

'If you will, my Lord and Father, be so condescending as to attend to the three following requests of one of your poor children, it will afford him much consolation in your absence

1. That when you arrive at the Tomb of the Apostles to beg their intercession in behalf of your children
2. That you must not be sad under any circumstances
3. That you will hasten back to gladden their hearts, who will follow you in spirit throughout your voyage unceasingly praying to God to attend and protect you.

Monday morning Feb 11 1846.'

Spiritual reading: Ecclus. ch 13; St Maud.[97]
Lat 46°58' S; Long 154°17' W; full moon, steady breeze at night.

Looking out of my cabin window during the silence of midnight, I contemplated the appearance of the sea and sky, both seeming dissolved in soft repose. Thought on the friends left and those about to

96. *Hooded gents*: the cowled monks of St Mary's.
97. *St Maud*: wife of German King Henry the Fowler; patron saint of misbehaving children; died in 968; feast day 14 March.

meet in another hemisphere and of a lad, a friend of ours, who had gone to England and had written

[40] *Herman*[?]

home lately to say he hoped to see his mother and brothers and sisters again in two years, when he hoped they would go over to England, but that meanwhile he could only look up at the moon and vainly seek the impress of the reflection of their features there daguerrotyped.[98]

Here we were now cradled on the waters which heaved and rolled in their onward course. The broad expanse, this terracqueous globe stretched before me. The moon shone with a pale light through a range of dense cumulous clouds, which cast their shadows here and there when shadows assumed the appearance of land, while the sparkling stars seemed the fires of the blacks in the bush and among the hills. Straight forward the light of the moon on the waters formed a luminous and glittering tract, which extended to the horizon unbroken, not unlike some noble estuary opening and expanding amidst romantic hills overhung with woods and foliage.

Dark albatross and petrels, now on the wing it appears, flitted across this silvery tract of Cinthia's creation, and now and then alighted on the crest of the swelling wave;[99] others would follow, screeching and tossing about their nimble bodies, attacking and attacked, they fought with their horny bills.

Revolving Phoebe meanwhile discarded the western horizon and was about to illuminate other seas and shores we had recently left.[100] Oh, thou Phoebe, called the Triple Hecate, prayed I, propitious deity, on leaving this Hellish sphere, where thou now reignest, give no unfavourable message to the lad who looks up to thee.[101] Shall his desire

98. Perhaps the lad was George Canning Therry, who in 1841 had been sent to Downside, where he continued his education over the next seven years, opting finally for a military rather than an ecclesiastical career.
99. *Cynthia*: Selene, the Greek personification of the moon, and the Roman Diana were sometimes called Cynthia.
100. *Phoebe*: another synonym for Selene.
101. Hecate, often represented in triple form, was a granddaughter of Phoebe. Harding identifies 'Triple Hecate' with Phoebe and the moon.

of again seeing his daddy and household gods within two years be granted? To his longing wish, say!

[41] *A prophecy – Mr. Ward*[102]

Whereupon to my astonishment Hecate with gracious smile made answer, 'be it so', understandably, perhaps, said she 'and inform him of it. Two years he must wait – and as a sign of my favour be it known and observe when you shall have noticed that twice I have by [*****] decrease unravelled, and twice again filled up my silver horns into a perfect orb then on that night you shall cross Earth's central line and you shall then behold me with delight shining with a full and complete disk surveying with my vertical rays your wall girt castle' – Having thus spoken she vanished behind the wavy horizon leaving all around dark. Immediately I prepared a morsel of the weed, rolling the tender leaf around snowy white paper which I kindled at a flame – Tell it not to Joseph – and puffed now and then yielded a perfumed smoke that ascended to the skies in path of the departed goddess, a ceremony to be repeated again only when on her reappearance as foretold.

14 March Before daylight we were caught in a squall which taking the sails aback puzzled our 3rd mate – but a tyro in the practice of seamanship – hence much confusion and noise arose, much rolling and pitching and a storm of anger burst from the Captain's cloudy brow, which darted as streaks of forked lightning on the devoted head and brains of Mr Ward. After a time all was again restored to order. It was said to have been the tail of a gale that had blown over from the north. Grand and majestic waves rolled in regular succession, covered with a swelling froth which without much wind

[42] *cold – chilblains – currents and swell*

continued all the day. In the evening the sun was noticed setting in a bank, indication of a change of weather. By a bank is understood a horizontal stratum of cloud in which the sun sinks at least ½ an hour before sun setting.

Doctor Dobie's hands are covered with chilblains. The Archbishop gives him sprits of wine to rub over them.

102. *Mr. Ward*: 2nd Mate.

Spiritual reading: Ecclus.; St Abraham and niece.[103]

15th March Sunday – No service, the weather being unsettled, at which contretemps a few of the passengers express their regret. This is the coldest day we have yet. The Therm stands at 58, in Lat 48°56' S, Long 146°35' W. The wind from the N.N.W. – fresh breeze, squally weather. The swell of the sea seems to produce curious phenomena – flowing from the West North and North East at one and the same time, while the wind is N. by E., and the ship can scarcely keep her course. The rationale of the above phenomenon has not probably been yet explained. Captain Cook and Forster describe many such.[104] Last week we noticed the swell after a calm to set in from the S.W. during the same afternoon and in the course of the night. The wind sprang up from the W. by N. It might have been supposed that the swell being harbinger of the wind would have been followed by it in due course. Yet this can scarcely be the case as the atmosphere being more easily put in motion than the ocean ought to proceed with greater velocity.

Spiritual reading: Ecclus 14; St Julian of Cilicia *apud* Peach.[105]

[43] *Fogs – St Patrick – Father McEncroe – H.G.* **[His Grace]** *writes*

16th March The wind having moderated during the night, the ship pitched greatly. We wished for a ceiling in the cabins to deaden the sound of the tramping on deck. We appear to be entering the region of fogs, so often referred to by Cook and Forster in their passage round the Horn, where they met with nothing but fog, sleet and snow – sleet, snow and fog. The mist dissolves itself into rain and we have but fog and rain alternately. And this moist state of the atmosphere, rather than the cold, affects the system injuriously, and it is much colder to the sensation than the degree of the Therm[ometer]

103. St Abraham the Hermit and his niece St Mary the Harlot: forth century saints of Mesopotamia.

104. Johann Reinhold Forster and his son Georg were the scientists who accompanied James Cook's second expedition, which returned to England via Cape Horn (1772–75).

105. Julian was a forth century martyr.

would lead one to suppose, for it stands at 56 degrees. However, under the influence of the rain the swell subsides.

Being the vigil of St Patrick, we wish Father McEncroe a happy feast. Spiritual reading: Ecclus. ch 14; St Patrick.

17th March St Patrick's Day – Lat 50°24' S; Long 131°3' W – Thick cloudy and squally with strong breezes, which afforded us but a restless night. The swell was from the N.E. but being met by another from the N.W. a cross sea ensued. Towards evening both these subsided and were succeeded by a long heavy swell from the westward. We see few birds owing to their scarcity and to the prevailing fogs. Yet a bird of a new plumage visits us in the afternoon, not so large as the albatross, but larger than the cape pigeon, remarkably swift on the wing, white underneath and brown above.

One month having expired, the Archbishop begins to write and thinks it high time to buckle on, but a passenger will always find a great difficulty, nay the impractibility of long continued efforts at study on board. The organs of body through which the mind acts being clogged and in an abnormal state refuse their wonted and required pliancy to the mandates of the spirit and are not to be imprudently urged or a victory here might prove in the end to have been a dear-bought one or rather a permanent loss to both the victor and vanquished. The exercise of patience, distraction and amusement in that case would appear to have been a gain rather than a loss of time.

Spiritual reading: Ecclus 15; St Cyril, Presbyter and Confessor.[106]

[44] *Sickness – weather – birds – porpoises caught*

18 March Passed a restless night, the ship pitching deeply and violently by reason of the cross swell. There was none of the latter during the day, but its effects remained and the violent headache most of us endured were a warning to seek for repose if obtainable, as significantly as the heat of boiling water would warn you to withdraw the hand out of the kettle, provided it were not tied there.

Towards evening the S.W. swell was met by another from the N.W., whilst in spite of both, a long and heavy one forced its way from the

106. *St Cyril*: a forth century bishop of Jerusalem.

west. The misty state of the horizon not unfrequently takes the appearance of land, and it is not unreasonable to suppose that distressed ships working through the fog incidental to these latitudes have been deceived by similar appearances, perhaps to their destruction.

We notice that this is the 10th day that the wind has been blowing from the N. and is called in jest the N. Trade by the Captain, who is surprised that the sea should be so little agitated considering the strength of this wind. Could we but go free before it, our progress would be greater, but it behoves us not to be driven to the leeward of our course, as we have yet considerable progress to make in our eastings. We therefore sail close to the wind and proceed at an average rate of about 6 kts, whereas to take full advantage of the wind it would drive us on at the rate of 9 kts or more.

One bird only, an albatross, was seen today. One of the black swans died from cold and exposure. The cockatoo seems also in a precarious state.

Ecclus, ch. 15; St Joseph; Archbishop – prickly heat still.

19 March This morning the sun shone out, though with wintry brightness. The monotony of sea life was somewhat broken by the cheering exclamations proceeding from the forecastle and occasioned by s shoal of porpoises. Contrary to all analogical proceedings in this weather, they continued in their playful gambols about the ship, even after 3 had been struck and partly drawn up. On every preceeding occasion

[45] *Porpoises – and birds –*

with the first blow which drew blood, the fish had disappeared. The exception may be accounted for by the supposition that we were visited by 4 distinct shoals succeeding each other.

As circumstance worthy of remark is in the numerous flocks of albatrosses and other birds, which visited us very shortly after the capture of a porpoise, undoubtedly attracted by the scent of blood, which indeed was perceptible to those who stood on the forecastle when the reeking bowels protruded under the knife, not a bird was visible; before 20 minutes they hovered about the ship. Whence came they? From this we may conclude that the following of the ship by the albatrosses is a mere accidental circumstance, for that they are spread over every part of the latitudes in which they are generally observed, fulfilling the duties of scavengers in clearing the surface of the ocean of dangerous substances which would otherwise putrify, and fulfilling on the sea the office of the vulture on land. Thus travellers in S. America traversing the pampas, having killed a bullock for their use and eat of what they wanted, although there was no vulture in sight at the time, in no less than an hour after killing the animal at least 50 vultures were observed hovering around the prey, patiently waiting for coming in for their feast.

On returning to the poop we were much amused by the eagerness of the birds to pick up their portion, which the sailors threw over to them with their usual humanity. Whilst the grave albatross cautiously descended to scoop up the morsels from the surface, an envious wave would come most provokingly in the way. In the meanwhile a little brisk looking bird, somewhat smaller than a Cape pigeon, regardless of ceremony, dived beneath and triumphantly bore away the prize. Then again, there would be an amazing clatter of wings among the small winged tribe as down a whole covey of these dashed upon a piece

[46] *Anniversary*

seen by many at the same time – a portion of the bowels about 3 yards in length had attracted the notice of an alderman-like albatross. He took up some two feet or more of this at one swoop, seemingly at a loss of what to do with the remainder, when the difficulty was solved by one of his kindred performing a similar operation at the other end. Thus in a twinkling, giving a resemblance of the Siamese twins, or to the heroic progeny of Leda (Castor and Pollux)[107] or to descend from heroics, bearing a strong resemblance to two storks strangling a serpent so often met with as the emblematic device of the old painters.

This is the anniversary (St Joseph) of the Archbishop saying 1st Mass in the year 1819, his Grace being ordained priest on the 4th of March

107. *Castor and Pollux*: half-twin brothers in Greek and Roman mythology, known together as the Dioscuri. Their mother was Leda, but they had different fathers-Castor was the mortal son of Tyndareus, the king of Sparta; Pollux was the divine son of Zeus, who seduced Leda in the guise of a swan.

by Bishop Poynter, or on the Saturday of the Easter week occurring on the 1st of March of Lent in that year. Brother Maurice Philips, who was professed at the same time, was ordained with His Grace. We had our devotions this day. We had no picture of St Joseph however, and no crucifix except the cross the Archbishop is doomed to wear and bear. In default of these to animate our devotions, our small token of our respect with lighted candle and fumes of incense we recited the Vespers of the saint. May he receive this small offering of our grateful affection. May the light of his example illumine our steps and the fragrance of his virtues pervade every power of our souls.

Our Lat. is 51°50' S; Long 128°45' W.; squally and reefing.

Ecclus – ch 17 – St Cuthbert, Bishop of Lindisfarne.[108]

[47] *St Cuthbert*

20th March Another porpoise was taken about 8 o'clock this morning.

South Sea Porpoise – Delphinapterus leucoramphus-Peron[109]

It was cooked and said to be as good as beef. The skin or blubber was cut up and will yield, it is thought, about 4 or 5 gallons of oil, which is more valuable than sperm. The whaler, with whom the Archbishop returned to Europe 3 yrs ago, assured him that this oil fetched as high a price as salad or olive oil.

108. St Cuthbert (c. 634–687): a monk, bishop and hermit of the early Northumbrian church in the Celtic tradition.
109. *Peron*: François Auguste Péron (1775–1810) was a French naturalist and explorer; in 1800 he joined Nicolas Baudin's expedition to Australia, during which he observed the South Sea porpoise near Van Diemen's land.

The sun shone out this morning, yet it felt very cold – Therm 58 degrees. The wind still from the N.E.; numerous birds about. The ocean is remarkably smooth; the swell is from the N.E.

We celebrated the festival or 1st Vespers of St Benedict with all due honour, having lit a candle and burned a fumigating pastile, which emitted a fragrant odour. Spiritual reading as usual: Ecclus ch. 17; life of St Cuthbert. This reminds His Grace of Prior Sharrock, who on his death bed directed a play day to be given to the students on St Cuthbert's day. (Recollect this, Ye, my dear lads of St Mary's seminary, and exercise your right of petition every 20th of March.)

This great Benedictine saint has the city of Durham for his monument, the city having grown up about the church built about the year 1080 to receive his remains. Though Mr. Raine, one of the present Canons of Durham has written a long disputation to prove that the body of St Cuthbert was exhumed about the year 1827, yet his labour has been in vain.[110] This body still remained in repose. The exact spot is known only to 3 individuals, monks of the English Congregation of the Order of St Benedict. The secret has been for very many years, His Grace believes, since the reformation in the congregation and has never been divulged, except when on the death of one of the three, the secret has been communicated, the two surviving imparting it to some 3rd party and thus is the secret kept and handed down

[48] *Icebergs*

until the Lord in his mercy shall again cause true faith to be established in England and the Cathedral of Durham, swept clean from its present abomination, shall witness processions of holy monks as silent and slow they proceed along its solemn aisles to sing the praises of the Lord in this sanctuary, wherein for so many ages their forefathers worshipped.

---

110. James Raine, *Saint Cuthbert: with an account of the state in which his remains were found upon the opening of his tomb in Durham in the year 1827*, London, 1828. The remains were reported to be skeletal and Raine concluded that the claim of incorruptibility, 'the tale of centuries', was disproved. On the tradition of the removal of the incorrupt body of St Cuthbert to a secret location in Durham cathedral see Conor O'Brien, 'Attitudes to St Cuthbert's Body during the Nineteenth Century', *Northern History*, 53(2016) 236–248.

21 March Called up early this morning to see an iceberg. It passed within a mile or more of ship. At that distance it appeared about ¼ of a mile in length and about 100 feet in hight – guess work.

Iceberg – March 21, 1846 – in Lat 52°50' S; Long 121°40' W

It formed a bright object contrasted with the grey sea and sky. Its summit appeared as if covered with snow, which again was set off by tints of light blue and green that bordered its lowermost outline and gradually faded in light streaks descending without reaching, however, the water line. It was accompanied by another smaller iceberg not more than 30 feet in hight. Two more icebergs were seen during the day, but at a greater distance, and resembled distant towers or spires.

The hight of an iceberg being estimated at 300 feet, and the specific gravity of ice compared with sea water being given as 8 to 9, the depth of the iceberg below the surface was reckoned to be 2,400 feet, or not far from ½ a mile, what was the depth of the Ice Island above, under the surface?

Our icebergs are said to have brought a difference of 3 degrees in the temperature, which would have been much greater had we passed to leeward of them.

[49] *St Benedict – The conveying albatrosses home – Albatrosses*

Captain Cook frequently provided his ships with fresh water from icebergs. But one advantage we derived from them was the erection of a stove in the cuddy, and we had the enjoyment of a fire.

This being the feast of St Benedict was kept of course: Vespers was recited in his honour with lighted candles and burning pastils; we enjoyed with grateful remembrance of our Sydney friends some of the good things prepared for us – excellent coffee, the little spirits of wine, prepared ginger etc etc, the gifts of Mrs. Plunkett and Mrs. Milford. Our repast was truly classical. The ship biscuit serving us as plates, at its conclusion we could say with young Ascanius: 'Eheu! com[m]edimus et mensas.'[111]

22 March Sunday a delightful day for a landman – a calm, picturesque sky and clear horizon; numerous birds; we caught 3 albatrosses. The day passed with the usual quiet and cheerful way – divine service in the cuddy; sermon on the salvation of the soul being the only truly important business of each one.

23rd March We all had a desire to convey one of the albatrosses we had caught yesterday to England, but having witnessed its reluctance to take food even when forced into its mouth even after being without sustenance for 28 hours and having heard this testimony of McEnzie, who has been 36 years on the salt water, to the effect that many birds of the kind within his knowledge had been brought or induced to take food, but all invariably perished under the influence of tropical heat, we came reluctantly to the conclusion that the attempt to convey it alive to England would be only a continuation of misery to the bird. Hence, therefore, the decision was to be made between the value of the life of the bird to itself and the value of the bird deprived of life to the sailors, who, condemned to salt meat for 4 months, had a right to exercise the dominion given to man over the beasts of the field and the birds of the air.

Spiritual reading Ecclus. ch. 19; St Ireneus, bishop.[112]

The albatross belongs to the family of *Longipennes* or great tails, and *Palmipedes*[113], the most massive of all aquatic birds &c – Cuv[ier][114]

---

111. *Heus! etiam mensas consumimus* (Aeneid VII.116): 'Hey! We are even eating our tables!'
Ascanius: one of the founders of the Roman race, a major character in Virgil's *Aeneid*.
112. *St Irenaeus* (140–202): bishop of Lyons.
113. *palmipedis*: broad-footed.
114. *Cuv*[ier]: Baron Cuvier (1769–1832), French naturalist and zoologist. Harding refers to Cuvier's *Le Règne Animal* (1817) regarding birds and fish. His 11-volume *Histoire naturelle des poissons* began to be published in 1828.

the diomedea melanophis – Cuv[ier].

Besides this the *Diom. spadicca, d. Brachyma, D. Chlororhynchus, D. Fuliginosa*, and others more or less brown or blackish, but whether they form varieties of the *Exulans*, or are distinct species has not yet been ascertained.[115]

[50] *damp – cold – a fall on deck – contrary weather*

24 March Stormy uncomfortable day, nothing done except the recitation of Office and spiritual duties. We also commenced a little devotion for a favourable wind – 5 *Paters* and *Aves* with the *Memorare*.[116]

The albatross that we had kept these three days past was thrown overboard. It appeared weakened from cold and want of food.

The humidity impairing the non-conducting powers of the clothing, the cold therefore is more sensible and penetrating, than one would feel in fine weather with the mercury ranging much lower on the scale than it does at present.

---

115. *Exulans*: wandering.
116. *Pater*: the Lord's Prayer.
Ave: the Hail Mary.
Memorare: 'Remember, O Most Gracious Virgin Mary'-a popular prayer seeking the intercession of the Blessed Virgin Mary.

25 March The Annunciation. Lat 56°18' S; Long 113°53' W; wind N.E. by N. squally; reefing sails; a gloomy day; the ship uneasy and making one very uneasy too.

The Archbishop had a tumble on the deck. The hip bone suffered – mem[o]: very dangerous to walk either with thick or new shoes on the slippery deck. The thinner and older the soles, says the Captain, the better. Moreover, in making the turn at either end of your walk, turn to leeward – *experto crede Ioanne.*[117] We understood that the passage round Cape Horn was one of constant westerly winds and prevailing smooth seas from its name of pacific. It is just the contrary with us – N. and N.E. winds and seas as high and constant gales can make them.

Spiritual reading: Ecclus. 21 – caution against sin; St Ludger.[118]

26th March The same cold and damp scarcely counteracted in the Cuddy even by a good fire in the stove. Add to this the pitching and rolling and the continuance now for the 14th day of the same N. E. wind induces the Captain to wish he had taken the route of Cape Lewen.[119] A sailor called Newman having made this route by Cape Horn 6 times already, this being the 7th, says he never was in so slow going a ship. His passage in the *General Hewit* from Sydney to the Horn was of 32 days only, they then took a course more to the south, where they met with N.W. winds.[120] The average passage is 6 weeks.

Spiritual reading: Ecclus. ch. 22; S[ain]t lives book fell behind the box and so we could not read it this evening.

S. Lat 57°; Long 112° W.

---

117. *Experto crede*: 'trust in the expert';
Ioannes: perhaps Harding's young brother Jonathan.

118. *St Ludger*: founding bishop of Munster in 804.

119. Cape Leeuwin is the most south-westerly mainland point of the Australian continent. The cape is named after a Dutch vessel, the *Leeuwin* ('Lioness'), that charted the nearby coastline in 1622.

120. *General Hewett*: three-deck sailing ship launched at Calcutta in 1811 and named after General Sir George Hewett (1750–1840), Commander-in-Chief in India, 1809–1813), Commander-in-Chief in Ireland (1813–1816). On her first voyage from England, 1813–1814, she transported convicts to Australia, after which she was engaged by the East India Company; refitted in 1842, she left London with immigrants in July 1843, arriving at Port Jackson in December. She departed Sydney for London via Cape Horn in April 1844; perhaps this was the voyage on which the sailor Newman sailed.

[51] *Cooper – furthest South: 61° – birds*

27th March Reading Cooper's *Benedictines*[121] – outrage on common sense; with difficulty waded through it – perceive the author is not a Protestant, not even a Deist. If he wrote like Walter Scott he might do much mischief, but he is so inconsistent and improbable, even mean – his characters full of expedients, listen through key-holes. Compare him to Walter Scott! – like comparing a murky star to the moon in her brightness. He cannot carry out a character. In the 'Red Rover' he makes his sprig of English nobility speak such vulgarity – quite a caricature; and his ladies, as ladies never spoke. He certainly never heard two English Gents or ladies conversing. His sea pieces alone are good; there he is in his element.

After sunset the sky became somewhat clearer overhead. Large quantities of heavy scud were driven or edging off in an easterly direction settled down in a heavy black bank, which gradually touched the West by rounding to the South and S.W. Another bank apparently arose from the N.W., and in the course of ½ an hour the entire sky became obscured as usual. Very nearly the same appearances might have been observed a fortnight ago, when this N.E. wind set in and they are now noted to see what will follow.

No albatrosses, but plenty of small birds called by the sailors Cape Hens.

Templar has taken the habit of waking the Archbishop every morning by licking his face as much as to say, 'good morning, how do you do'.

28 March Latitude 60°30' S; Long 105°W; Therm 52.

The same weather continues; a thick haze pervades every quarter, attended with this advantage of keeping down the sea, which, considering the heavy wind, is extraordinarily smooth. Birds called Molly Mauks appear.[122] They dart in the water from a great hight, dive and on rising run on the surface of the wave before rising on the wing.

121. James Fenimore Cooper (1789–1851) a prolific American writer. In 1832 he published the novel *The Heidenmauer or the Benedictines – A Story of the Rhine*.
122. *Mollymawks*: a species of medium-sized albatrosses.

29 March Sunday – We have reached the Latitude 61°20' S, which has been and will be, says the Captain, our furthest south.[123] Our Longitude is 104° and the Therm is at 51°. Our N.E. wind has at last left us, or we it.

[52] *[Whale]'s & birds & Royals. Snow*

The men's clothes being wet from the state of the weather, there was no Divine Service.

30th March This morning a whale was seen close to the ship. He spouted and made a turn or two round the vessel. Fog and fine weather now alternate; the wind is S.S.E. The swell from the N.E. has not yet entirely subsided; it has been met by a broken surface swell from the S.S.E., from which circumstance it is augured that the wind will continue for some time from that quarter.

It has been remarked that the birds during a calm leave us. The first bird since Saturday made its appearance at two o'clock, since which time the vessel has gradually progressed from 2 to 7 kts. It would appear from this circumstance that a certain agitation of the water is subservient to their finding their food. Hence it is not rash to conclude that when the birds leave the ship, we shall have a calm of some duration, which is a fact worth ascertaining and observing further.

The Royals were this morning set and drew full, whilst on the deck the wind was powerless to move the dogvane.[124] It is in fact only when

123. 61°20' S was the southernmost latitude reached by the *Ratcliff*. During the 1835 voyage on the *Oriental* the southernmost latitude recorded by Lewis was 40°45' S on 7 July. He left latitude blank on the following days as the ship approached Hobart Town at latitude 42°52' S (see *1835 Journal*, 102–104).

124. *Royals*: the sails attached to the royal mast, which is above the topgallant mast. *Dogvane*-a small weather vane mounted within sight of the helmsman.

the wind is very light that the royals are of any use. They serve however to convey to the ship a quantity of motion which enables the wind to act with more power, light as it may be, on the lower sails. Hence, as Bazil Hall remarks, the royals are of very little use except in light airs such as prevail in the tropics.[125] And if you see the royals hoisted in a good wind, he says a legitimate inference may be drawn that the officer in command is a puppy in his way. Such puppyism, however, is pardonable on approaching a port and on occasions of a gala character.[126]

31 March A beautiful morning. Those only who have been enveloped in rain and raw fogs for many days can appreciate the beauty and cheeriness of a fine morning.

Towards 11 o'clock the sky became over-clouded and snow fell with a raw wintery feel, which continued throughout the day. About 2 o'clock birds appeared – Cape hens. The swell from North E. has entirely disappeared; one from the S and S.W. has set in, not in long and continuous but broken rifflingly. Towards evening the wind, which in the morning carried us at the rate of 8 kts, has subsided almost to a calm.

[53] *Various swells – intense cold – rough sailing*

1st April Lat 60°45'; Long 95° W. Therm 46°

Towards the close of the evening the wind from the E. gradually subsided; it veered towards W., dying away from 5 kts to 2 or 3. It thus continued until about 3 this morning. It then set in steadily from the N.W., from which point, with some variation towards the west, it has blown all day at the rate of from 7 to 9 kts. About 8 hours after the wind had reached us the swell set in westerly. It may be inferred perhaps that the wind will blow for some time in this direction from this following swell. At all events, it merits remark.

Cape pigeons and whale birds in great numbers – the latter a slate coloured bird is so-called, says the Captain, from the circumstances of their hovering about the whale while the sailors cut it up.

125. *Basil Hall* (1788–1844): British naval officer, author and Fellow of the Royal Society; he published the journals of his voyages from 1822 to 1841.

126. *puppyism*: displaying affectation, conceit or impudence, like a puppy.

The smoothness of the water is remarkable considering the violence of the wind. This doubtless increases the speed of our sluggish vessel.

Ecclus. ch. 28.

2 April Lat 61°20' S; Long 92° W; Therm 44°

Last night the wind continued to blow with considerable violence from the N.W. accompanied by rain and sleet. The vessel drove along through a heavy sea at the rate of 8 kts, pitching and rolling most disagreeably. Towards morning the wind veered to the S.S.W. and took up permanently in the S., from which quarter it has continued to blow all day. The cold has been intense; showers of snow have fallen from time to time.

Opened the nuns' box and with gratitude partook of the French plums; the lemon syrup of Mrs. Milford carefully packed up again for the Tropics.

An immense swell following us from the westward, which a swell from the S. seems not to influence. The confusion and roughness of last night caused frightful dreams and imaginings, awakening every 10 minutes not knowing what might next happen. No sleep till daylight – an impression not yet effaced.

3 April Lat 60°56' S; Long 84°W; Therm 41° in cabin, 36° on the Poop. The air today is intensely cold; awakening during the night a peculiar [****ness] is felt in the eyes; dense clouds on the horizon which it would seem no wind could penetrate. The wind shifted from point to point as if it could not please itself; it certainly did not please us,

[54] *Cold – a current from the Pacific into the Atlantic*

for we are becoming very impatient under the influence of this excessively cold weather that so benumbs the bodily organs that the spirit within must be content to sleep as the torpid dormouse.[127] We sit where we can get a place near a melancholy looking stove. Oh for the bright sun, gay mornings and real substantial heat of Australia. I wonder whether we shall ever be warm again. Is not there such a word as perspiration in the language, what does it mean. If the Eng-

127. A nocturnal animal, the dormouse is particularly known for its long periods of hibernation.

lish language be spoken in these latitudes, that word has no use in it. It is quite fitting that we should pass through the Tropics in order to become warm before again entering into civilised society, for otherwise most assuredly we should be much in the same state as two Egyptian mummies entombed since a thousand years ago.

4 April Lat 60°16' S; Long 78°12' W. Strong breezes, thick weather, hail, snow and squally. Hens freezing; fling snow balls at each other. The hen coops are covered with sheets of ice. A large heavy swell follows us from the west[war]d.

It appears evident that a strong current from the N. sets in towards the S., of which it behoves all navigators to be aware, though this is not mentioned in chart or publication. Indeed, there has been great remissness on the part of Government in this matter. The passage from N.S. Wales and the Australian Colonies in general to England is made by Cape Horn. The distance to the Cape from Sydney has been accomplished by a very slow sailing vessel, the *Achilles*, from Hobart Town in 28 days, by the *General Huet* from Sydney in 32 days, whilst the *Everetta* was employed 73 days in accomplishing the same distance.[128] We shall probably be more than 50 days, and this I conceive to be about the average. If the direction of the winds at various periods of the year were ascertained, the currents with their sets-in and rate, it is presumed that much good would result. At present each Master of a vessel has only his own particular experience to guide him aided by the casual remarks with

[55] *Wild aspect of sea sky and birds in a storm – Palm Sunday – Two contrasts*

which his nautical friends may favour him. If their observations ever could be gathered and entered into the registers of office and published for general utility, it would be one step to improvement.

'Mais revenons à nos moutons.'[129] It is not possible for one only conversant with the calm waters of Sydney Cove, which the heaviest

128. *The Achilles*: migrant ship. In July 1844 it returned 49 of the emancipated French-Canadian rebels to London.
129. Idiomatic French expression meaning 'let's get back to the subject at hand'.

storm can only move to a small bustle (à la Stallard)[130] to conceive the dark deep shadows cast by these snow squalls over the water, by which we are surrounded. Pacific in name, they present a fearful aspect as we gaze upon them from the poop. The wild bird itself appears shunningly to float above them at a greater distance and even to dread, lest its instinctive desire of prey should compel it to come in contact with these deeply dark and gloomy waters. As the Cape pigeon flies in the distance in a line with the distant horizon, [it] may be easily imagined to be some lone bark containing some wretched few saved from shipwreck. And in the howling of the blast we may fancy that we hear cries of distress. As its white breast glistens in an instant of partial sunshine, we may imagine some white flag hung out to attract our notice. The approach of the bird dissolves the painful allusion.

April 5

Sunday – Palm Sunday. Two contrasts – snow squalls continuing to pass over with considerable rapidity affording us a continuation of westerly gales, which drive us on at a rate varying from 6 to 8 kts. Gleams of bright sunshine in the intervals become more precious after the gloom of the past days, if we may use this word. The skies take an appearance which denote our proximity to land, i.e. a more speedy clearance of the atmosphere overhead and rapid settling down of the clouds in the land quarter. Such an appearance we had after having traversed the vast abyss between the Cape of Good Hope and Cape Lewin, as we approached the latter promontory on our way out. But to advert to another contrast. How lonely are we here – no trace of verdure, nothing which might bear a semblance to the vegetable productions of nature which, receiving the blessing of the Church, we might bear in hand in affectionate commemoration of the only triumph of our meek Saviour. Here are we two lonely travellers over the wild waste of waters equally removed from those endeared to us by nature and by habits long continued of most affectionate intercourse,

130. Stallard: perhaps Philip Martin Stallard, prominent Sydney Catholic and secretary of the St Patrick's Society and member of the inaugural committee of the Catholic Committee (*Australasian Chronicle*, 14 October 1841). In 1850 he was found guilty of forging a promissory note in the name of Rev Sumner, Vicar-general, to whom he had been secretary. He was sentenced to three years with hard labour.

[56] *Palm Sunday*

not permitted even to participate in those rites of religion, which on Earth serve to unite, tho' after a manner perhaps imperfect, the members of Christ's mystical body. Oh, that we had already entered the society of the Blessed, where neither place nor space, but grace alone becomes the link uniting one to one and all to God.

Because the weather is somewhat uncertain, the cold uncomfortable, even our awkward disjointed service, such as it is, must be omitted, whilst the rain may pour in torrents and the winds blow in furious emulation from each quarter of the heavens. Yet St Mary's is thronged to over flow – rich and poor, priest and people all so comely in their simplicity, receiving from him who represents the head of the church with devout faith and holy joy the branches, over which the blessing of our affectionate mother the church has been poured, determined to enjoy in its passing a glance of comfort, as they accompany their Saviour in his humble triumph of which we are reminded as we face the dark, under the influence of the beams of his most beautiful emblem, the sun, which seems to hasten away as the snow storm approaches – and so, the faithful enjoy their Saviour's welcome into Jerusalem so soon to be over-clouded by the sorrow of Gethsemanie, by the atrocities of Pilate's Court, till the tempest burst in all its fury upon Calvary's mount. And probably another year, not to say two, must elapse before we can have part in the mysterious observances of this blessed week. May we feel even as our first parents, when banished from the Paradise, which the Lord God had given unto them, over the sinfulness, which has brought upon us this heavy infliction.

6th April Awoke this morning by sudden violent squalls from the Eastward. The noise and confusion of aprising the Captain and calling all hands, and then reefing and furling sail, was more than we had experienced. We were sorry to hear the wind was dead ahead and, not having been able to take a sight or observation of longitude during these few weeks back, our apprehensions now turned on the probabilities of further delays, either by being compelled to lie-to or being driven to the northward before we could well

[57] *Cape Horn – New birds – sublime ocean scene*

double this Cape. We were, however, relieved at noon from our uncertainty by having it in our power the take the requisite observations, as the sun shone brightly at intervals through the squally clouds and horizon was clear. Our longitude thus ascertained places us, to our astonishment and also to the agreeable surprise of the Captain, in 67° long., which is the longitude of Cape Horn, and Lat 28°25' [sic], which is a degree or 120 miles to the southward of it.[131]

Cape Horn from a Spanish Chart

We therefore now enter the South Atlantic. We are greeted by its numerous birds, and among others by some of new plumage - some of sooty brown, others about the size of Cape pigeons, but entirely white. To this latter our cockatoo made signs of recognition and seemed to claim a sort of kinship, for he eyed them eagerly and gave tokens of wishing to fly up to them but heeded they him not. The sailors call them the natives of the Faulkland Isles, and Cape Horn pilots. The ship rides over mountainous waves with the instinctive tact of a duck, basking in its own element. Nevertheless, as we are lying to under a single reefed maintop sail and fore top stay sails, the gale is powerful enough to drive us at the rate of 2 kts per hour in a N.N.W. direction against the current of the Pacific into the Atlantic. The appearance to windward is that of continuous lofty ridges crowned with surf, which resemble avalanches of snow as they roll down the declivities of an alpine scenery.

8 April - Lat 57°5' S; Long 66°24' W. Strong breezes still and heavy squalls; sea running high; lying to, close reefed. Weather moderated in the forenoon, when we proceeded on our easterly course with a disagreeable and uneasy motion caused by a cross swell.

131. Lat 28°25': the latitude was later corrected in pencil by another hand writing 58 under 28. Latitude of Cape Horn is 55.9833 S; latitude 58 is thus 2 degrees south of Cape Horn, or 120 nautical miles (one degree of latitude = 60 nautical miles)

9 April Maundy Thursday – our conversation brings us back to Sydney and to the affecting ceremonies which take place during this holy time. Will Bishop Pompallier be there to bless the Holy Oils in the absence of the Archbishop, and whose

[58] *Maundy Thursday – Good Friday – large waves – picturesque fog – birds – body floating*

consecrated hands will become still more sanctified by bearing the body of the Lord amidst the homage of a people bending down in adoration, and the chancels prepared with studious decorations and studied ostentation of church wealth, be it rich or poor, emblem of the faithful heart in which, notwithstanding the ignominities of Calvary, necessarily required for man's salvation, Jesus loves to repose. And where is that sepulchre formed? Will the chapel of St Felician be rendered more dear to us by its being selected for this holy purpose?[132] And then all this livelong night the members of the community of the Holy Guild [and] the faithful at large will emulously strive, who shall most abundantly pour out the sacred ointment of their tears and burn most profusely the incense of holy prayer, prematurely perhaps, but yet most lovingly over the body of their saviour now pale and inanimate. Oh, may he, who receiving the homage from his beloved mother and the devout St Joseph of Arimathea and from Mary Magdalen, yet still thought of the distant souls confined in Limbo and visited them in his love imparting to them much consolation. May he also visit us separated wandering children deprived of all participation in religious rites with our brethren on earth, not yet worthy to be admitted amidst the blessed in heaven. May he give to us to rejoice in the glories of the resurrection animated by the hope of being united 'ere long to our brethren in the hemisphere of the west.

10 April Good Friday – Lat 57°8' S, Long 60°44' W; wind N.W., fresh gales, squally, continued rains, reefing and unreefing – in fact, the wind seemed to blow as if exhausting its strength and bending the ship and masts to a fearful degree, while the sea runs high; yet the ship bears it well. Towards noon it moderated and a heavy sluggish fog settled on the swell unmoved by the wind. The ocean presented a picturesque effect, opening here and there through the fog, which let

132. The chapel of St Felician was used as the 'chapel of repose' during Holy Week.

one perceive one or two large undulations, a gentle sweep of hill and dale, and on the declivities of these water vallies birds innumerable floating, running, congregating, pursuing and pursued. Divers also, probably penguins, were also distinguished about.

Penguin

The mate told us of the body of man seen floating

[59] *Black swan died – unusual rainbow – Fast*

past the ship with arms and legs crumped up, his clothing that of a sailor, of a blue colour with light facings. The Archbishop had dreamed of the man [*****] being dead at Coventry and the bells tolled as he entered the city.

Our 2nd and last black swan died.

We are about 300 miles from the Falkland Islands and we have seen a small land bird about the size of a lark. His Grace says that passing the Canaries about 200 miles distant in the *Templar*, small birds flew about the ship, His Grace having caught one; it was a green linnet, which he and Doctor Markham brought to Sydney.[133] His Grace says he will bring some birds back with him.

133. *Green linnet*: European greenfinch.
Dr John Markham came to Australia as surgeon of the *Templar*, arriving in March 1843.

We continued still enveloped in fogs, when towards evening a peculiar clearing away of the W. and S. seemed to intimate that an agent was there at work, whose influence did not immediately reach us. The sky overhead became beautifully clear for a while still toward the horizon in every other quarter besides the one mentioned. The mist was gathering thicker and darker where immediately opposite the sun the atmosphere, overcharged with moisture, took the arched appearance of a rainbow colourless and dead – the difference between a rainbow reflected by rain and another by mist only. Presently detachments of clouds of fog broke away assuming the form of 'mares tails', as the sailors call it.[134] At 4 o'clock our ship having been put about was given a N.W. course.

Doctor Dobie stiffly attacking me on the fast, remarking how easy we took it. He acknowledges he is ordered to fast by his Book of Common Prayer and to keep these days as well as us, but he thinks, he says, temperance alone was intended by that law and that he pleases God by his temperance. He acknowledges that fast to be of divine precept and makes out, I can't tell how, that we should obey it, as if a divine precept did not bind him and his. It was not easy to make him understand that tho' the fast was of divine precept, the times and days of fasting were of the churches appointment, who might exchange them, commute or suspend where there was a reason for it. The more one sees of this Protestantism, the more one becomes convinced how much it substitutes man for God – anyone must be convinced of this who notices how everything is made subservient to serve public opinion and appearances.

11 April Easter Sunday. We awoke this morning with the sanguine expectation of hearing the cheerful voice of Hicks proclaiming that we were proceeding

[60] *Easter Sunday – sudden squall at dinner – Barometer – The Captain*

cheerily along towards the north with a 7 kt breeze. Alas a gloomy silence prepared us for the worst. The faint hopes of last evening had disappeared. During the night the N. wind sternly refuses further progress.

---

134. *mare's-tail* (Hippuris vulgaris): a common aquatic plant

Owing to the state of the weather the continued employment of the men in cold and wet, prayers were not publicly said. We retired to perform our usual exercises of devotion, after which we enjoyed a little repast prepared for us by the kind hand of the Sisters of Charity. We talked about the beautiful service of St Mary's, about the probable progress made in the erection of the new monastery, in the church of St Benedict, and the recreation which the young would enjoy after the retirement and exercises of Holy Week, and how the Vicar Gen[eral] and Mr. McEncroe and Mr. Sumner will pass these two next days.

At dinner we met in no better spirits than might have been expected considering the raging weather outside, apprehending an increase in the violence of the gale. The Captain took his usual precautions, but as he issued his orders sitting at dinner, people were rather surprised at their extent. The Mizen and Mizen topsails to be taken in; mainsail furled; topsail close reefed. It was the barometer that had given this timely warning. The fury of the squall was great and for some time did the cloudy N. wind top our ship with its dreadful hurricane to the confusion of the mate and sailors, who little expected so sudden an irruption. They remark that their passage here alone was as good an apprenticeship in the manouvering of reefing and unreefing, as any two of their former voyages.

Indeed it is a great comfort to sail under the care of a man such as Captain Gilbert, to whom 20 years experience has given the maturity of prudence untainted by timidity. He just does at his leisure that which the inexperienced and injudicious generally direct to be done in a bustle.

The Archbishop praises little May and her cape which he wears, this tippet having saved him from the cold and rhumatism, for which His Grace says he will send her a little present as a remembrance.

Lat 56°36'; Long 59°40' W.

[61] *last efforts of north trade wind – our old enemy – The bottle of whiskey*

12 April During the night the weather moderated and the wind becoming more westerly, we were enabled to take our proper course Nth. This, however, did not last; the wind became again due N. Once more we were enveloped in fogs. At last a vast quantity of vapour scudding across seemed to settle to the westward and promises a clearance. Again the skies became overspread, a calm took place, after which the long wished-for breeze became perceptible from the W. and pushed us on gradually from 2 to 7 kts per hour against a heavy swell, which the North continued to send and over which the ship plunged and rebounded desperately. It was in one of these savage *rencontres* that the Archbishop's tray broke and fell. The ring by which it was suspended had fairly worn through. Rings subject to perpetual friction should be bound round with cord.

The sun went down in unusual beauty and the Eastern sky itself coquettishly exhibited such a blending of blue, pink and violet colours as was much admired.

13 April Had we not been driven far to the eastward, we might have enjoyed the pleasure of soon obtaining a sight of the N.E. coast of the Falkland Isles. We are now likely to be driven still further eastward, the wind having resumed its old quarter from the N.W. A mist, the usual concomitant of the wind here has again settled densely around us. Later in the day it lulled and in the evening broke forth again from the desired quarter; we were at dinner, the Captain and the mate immediately left the table to make the preparations to take advantage of the change. The head sea is not so great as yesterday and to commemorate our present fair prospects the Captain brought at the dinner table a bottle of whiskey.

14 April Lat 54°43' S; Long 54°45' W; heavy head swell, wind N. by E., reef and unreef. Taking notes from Horsburg-Forster on the best times for sailing in these latitudes, from Captain Cook and

Pringle[135] – and the Archbishop remarks on the provisions and sundry necessaries required on such voyages, and general remarks on ships and crews.

[62] *a Tornado – a sail in sight – the 'Mary Dare'*

15 April We may well commence our log this day in the words of the song: 'Oh! Pilot we have passed a fearful night! There was danger on the deep'[136] – never more applicable. The wind which had commenced to blow from the westward gradually but rapidly increased to a gale and from that to a hurricane, intermitting but at rapid intervals. The sea arose to a prodigious hight; the vessel, at one time lifted up on the mighty billow, was gliding down the next minute into a trough, deep and dark; again struck on the side by some immense swell, whose progress it checked, ship was, as it were, a place the least to be desired by any landsman. The sails were all taken in; the ship made snug, still sleep was impossible. The Captain himself slept not this night. In the morning waves in long continuous ridges, others lofty and pyramidal; our course, though not exactly what we wish, yet rather favourable, being exactly between the Falkland Island and the Aurora Isles;[137] driven 152 m N.E. since yesterday noon.

16 April Lat 50°46' S; Long 50°3' W.

This morning was beautiful, and a long time had seemed elapsed since we were invited to early rising by the bright beauty of the sun penetrating into our cabins through the cuddy windows. They diffused cheerfulness around our watery world.

To add to the interest, 'a sail in sight' was announced as we proceeded. She appeared following on the same track as ourselves; we gained upon her and about 12 o'clock were within 3 miles of her. Here we hoisted signals, which from some circumstance or other were not duly responded to. On this Captain Gilbert signalised that he would bear down and

135. Sir John Pringle, President of the Royal Society 1772–1778.

136. The hymn 'Oh, Pilot! 'tis a Fearful Night' was written by Thomas Haynes Bayly (1797–1839) an English poet, songwriter and dramatist.

137. The Aurora Islands were three phantom islands first reported in 1762 by the Spanish merchant ship *Auroral*, halfway between the Falkland Islands and South Georgia. The islands were last reportedly sighted in 1856, but continued to appear on maps of the South Atlantic until the 1870s.

speak. This was understood and preparation made accordingly. After a time we came up. She proved to be the brig *Mary Dare* – 200 tons – laden with ore, 52 days from Callao and bound to Swansea.[138]

[63] *Discrepancy in dates – a Lunar – birds*

After a few interrogatories, as usual with the speaking trumpet, we separated, leaving her behind. At sunset she appeared 8 miles astern. The sea today was remarkably smooth and the air nippingly cold.

17 April Lat 49°25' S; Long 47°15' W.

On the ship log the 17th is the day on which the speaking to the *Mary Dare* occurs. This difference of a day, [which] occurs now and then shewing a little discrepancy between that log and my own, is accounted for by my having omitted a day lost in our Eastings, the ship's log on the contrary, keeping up the same day and date as they occur in voyaging from one spot to the other on the globe. But in some remarkable instances I have adopted their date.

This day was remarkable from the circumstance of the Captain and his mates being engaged in taking a lunar in a series of observations on the sun and moon.[139] The morning was particularly favourable, the sky being cloudless and the horizon distinct and the edges of the moon's limb well defined, which gave our latitude and longitude as above.[140]

138. Callao – a port city of Peru.

139. 'Taking a lunar' sighting is part of navigating procedure on a sailing voyage. In celestial navigation, lunar distance is the angle between the Moon and another celestial body. A navigator can use a lunar distance and a nautical almanac to calculate Greenwich time. Longitude can then be determined without the use of a marine chronometer.

140. The 'lunar limb' is the edge of the visible surface of the moon as viewed from earth.

The air was piercing and cold; the wind was unfavourable and drives us too much to the eastward. Towards the middle of the day a strong head swell had set in, by which our progress has been greatly retarded. It increased towards evening so as to render the deck and cuddy equally unpleasant. The Captain observed that there had been or would be a gale here. For the present it is difficult to imagine anything more tiresome, more sickening, more at variance with the comfort of sitting at one's own table at home in a quiet room.

Vast numbers of birds hover around us, probably from the vicinity of a whale, one having been seen in the morning.

Sterna hirundo.
The common tern or Sea Swallow

Our little friend the *Mary Dare* was again seen this evening at about 10 miles astern and to windward. A sad disaster was well nigh befalling Templar, who by the by is a great favourite on board.

[64] *Templar – an adage – sea voyage no time for intellectual improvement*

Though frequently chastised for going into the boat which hangs alongside, he still retained a grievous propensity to pop therein to pick his bones or to hide them as he may fancy. This day he jumped intending to reach the boat which is at a certain distance from the edge; he missed his aim and hung pitiously by his forepaws from the side of the boat and over the sea, swinging to and fro, when our good friend Major Elrington, observing his perilous situation, kindly rescued him and still more kindly made him feel the [vis***] of a rope's end in the hope of curing him of his folly.[141]

18 April Lat 48°24' S; Long 43°43' W.

During the night the wind veered round to the N., dead ahead, driving us in an easterly course. Moreover, a heavy swell ahead and large masses of clouds now gather to windward, denoting an increase of wind. Soon after, in fact, it became a gale and we had to close reef. Our hope is that with the discontinuance of the rain, the gale may cease according to the old remark that if rain begins and wind succeeds you may expect a strong and long continued gale. But if the

141. In 1847, Polding's pet dog *Vin* was not so fortunate. As recounted by Edmund Moore OSB in his journal kept during the voyage to Australia, Vin was lost overboard in the Southern Ocean on 20 December: 'Dr P's poor dog Vin (called after the ship *St Vincent*) fell overboard. It soon disappeared as we were going pretty fast. The albatrosses, molly-mawks etc. soon began to attack it.' ('Journal 1847–48', *Tjiunga* 7[1974], 88). See also entry for the same day in the diary of Sister Scholastica Gregory OSB ('Fragment of a Diary', *Tjiunga* 26[1984], 60).

wind commences and rain follows, you may expect the gale to subside, which the Archbishop rendered thus in rhyme for the use of our 1st mate McIntosh: 'If wind begin and rain prevail, true may you expect to cease the gale.'

We have reason to remark that whoever imagines that a sea voyage will afford a season for mental exertion, for literary acquirement for a making up of past deficiencies or for preparing the means for more successful efforts for the future, has only to experience the cold, contrary winds, fogs, gales with the delightful never-failing accompaniment of sea sickness, which such a voyage as ours has abounded with, and he will be radically cured of the sweet delusion.

[65] *Storm – pyramidal waves*

19 April Sunday Lat 48°7' S; Long 41°58' W.

No service, too wet and stormy; too excited and too ill to write.

20 April No log written yesterday, weather too bad, great tossing. Our jib sail was carried away, our starboard bulwarks lashed the water, and for a few seconds we thought the ship on her beam-ends; all was made snug once more. Though under close reefed topsails only, we were driven the entire night at a rate of 8 or 9 kts. The blast at times was quite appalling; one mountain wave after another threatened to engulf the ship. It was a dizzy sight and the roar of artillery seemed nothing to that of the breaking of the waves on the flanks and bows of the resounding fabric. Each successive tolling of the bell made us rejoice that another hour of the night had passed. With the morning dawn the wind, but not the sea, moderated. We were glad, however, to perceive that the cross sea had been succeeded by a regular, though monster ocean swell. The water also had assumed its natural colour, which on the previous day had led us to think from its appearance that we were either near land or passing over the mountains of some submarine archipelago. The decks were wet and still strewed with sand and cinders cast over for the purpose of enabling the men to work with more security and with better footing. May the Almighty be praised for having preserved us from so many dangers.

The Captain remarked that in the cross seas, from some cause not apparent, the concussion and meeting of the waters would dash them against each other in the pyramidal form, which appeared so remarkable. It was not only here and there a solitary one but extended over the whole field of vision. These watery pyramids arose in every direction. I need not say that we did not close our eyes this night.

Lat 45°32' S; Long 40°35' W.

[66] *Contrary weather – boisterous seas*

21 April Lat 43°28' S; Long 38°11' W. Wind N.W., reefed still, mizen topsail torn.

22 April Lat 41°40' S; Long 35°58' W. Fresh breeze and gale, heavy cross sea, reefed still rain and lightening from the S.E. Continue unwell.

23 April We now have a broad and lengthened swell following aft, while our course is to the N.N.E. The swell seems to sink under the ship and to rise again ahead of us, leaving us as it were in the pit of such an amphitheatre of the Colloseum, whose slope intersects the horizon for half a ½ mile or more and is enlivened with birds innumerable of various sorts – white and spotted, and striped and brown, and sooty and black, and of all sizes from the swan-like albatross to the swallow that skims the surface of our ponds. Thus we mount over the heaving waters thus piled up above us, and plunge again headlong down the watery steep. Soon after, this swell was met by another from the N.W. occasioning a jumble of seas over which it was most unpleasant to pass and then the scene which met the eye became gloomy – a turbulent sea overarched by a most dismal atmosphere, rain driven along by the howling wind, and that contrary. Our gallant ship, like a poor bird whose wings were clipped and pelted by rude boys, under shortened sail, patiently awaited the issue.

Towards evening the wind lost its violence and veered round to the westward. The sails were again set and we proceeded on our course. The stars at night shone bright and cheerily, here the Dorado, there Xiphias, on one side the Bird of Paradise and the Phoenix, on the other, nearer still, the Pica Brazilica and Indus Sagittiferus.[142]

Lat 39°43' S; Long 36°48' W.

---

142. Names of various constellations.

[67] *Currents of Cape Horn and Rio de la Plata – Entering a milder climate*

24 April Towards morning the ship again fell off in consequence of the wind becoming northerly. These extraordinary cross seas through which we have literally laboured, we suppose to be occasioned by the confluence of the current round Cape Horn setting in as it does from the S.W. and the current from the N.W. occasioned by the discharge of the vast waters of the Rio de la Plata. Owing to the former we have been more than once agreeably surprised by finding ourselves carried to the northward even though the wind was almost dead against us. The latter has caused us, from whatever quarter the wind blew to experience a powerful swell from the N.W. Sometimes in fact it was impossible to say which was the prevailing swell, the sea was so chopped up by currents and winds adverse.

Whatever may be the season of the year, I am convinced the passage round Cape Horn must be necessarily boisterous in these latitudes. December, however, should be the month of departure from Sydney, not later. We are probably experiencing the equinoxial gales of the equator come down this way.

As regards the day, it has been moist, misty, gloomy, squally, sickening to the last degree and worse than all, we had no soup for dinner.

These latitudes are called the roaring forties – Squallshire, capital Borington. When shall we be in the thirties and the Tropics.

Our comfort is that the weather is become considerably warmer and we expect the Sydney feel again in a few days, provided we be thawed again.

25 April We perceive that the late heavy weather has damaged some portions of our light works, both astern and on the bows. The figure head itself has been injured. The dead lights are now removed from the Archbishop's cabin windows. The weather at present, although rather squally still at times, is generally fine. The sun now and then shines out gaily. The ship shoots along merrily and we are glad to exchange the solemn booming swell of the ordinary ocean for the pettish wayward chopping seas, through which we have had to toil for so many days. This [was]

[68] *stove removed – retrospect – food – phosphorescence*

scarcely within our remembrance, when we passed 24 hours so comfortably as the last. We believe it was somewhere about the antipodes a long 6 weeks since. The interval has been filled with cold, sleet, snow, hail, gales, squalls and contrary winds. The altar of the god Vulcan – *vulgo*[143] – a stove, at which shoes have been burned and stockings singed during the last month, was now removed from its standing place in the cuddy. We are now proceeding at the rate of 6½ kts without a perceptible motion of the vessel. So much justice obliges us to say in praise of the good ship *Ratcliff*, and in grateful acknowledgment of the Sydnean climate into which she has brought us.

Today we had for dinner a pair of ducks with a small piece of pork served for nine of us, fine as regards size, fatness, flavour. Indeed all the poultry have come to table in a creditable state, a proof of what may be effected by due attention and care. They form a pleasing contrast to the miserable skeletons, which with ludicrous solemnity, about once a week, used to appear on the table of the *Oriental*, when Captain Allen used to ask, 'What will you have Mr. Curtoise? What part?' And the cleverest falcon that ever pounced on a bird could not have picked an ounce of meat even from the carcase of a gigantic turkey, and that ounce, how hard and tough – my teeth ache at the remembrance even now.

We have noticed of late a much larger quantity of phosphorescent matter in the water. Indeed the quantity of diamond like scintillations elicited by the friction or movement of the rudder in the water renders the view of the water from the stern cabin window not less beautiful than interesting.

Lat 35°19' S; Long 35°30' W.

26 April

Sunday – The breeze still continues; our canvas is stretched to the utmost and we are going on gloriously. In consequence of the rain that fell during the night and the men's clothes being wet, we had not public prayers. We did not forget, however, that having passed the latitude of Sydney, that by reason of the circumstance, slender as it was in connection

143. *Vulgo*: in plain speech.

[69] *Sunday – Lat. of Sydney – Sea clouds – 210 miles from noon to noon*

with our friends there, we prayed not with the less fervour and with a sort of pain. Also did we contemplate that each successive degree would now remove us further and yet further from those latitudes, in which had been so long concentrated our feelings. May that Almighty Power, whose shield of mercy extends throughout space, protect the Pastor and the flock now so far separated.

We took a goodly repast from the stores which formed our feast, which brought to our minds the affection of those our friends who had laid them in.

As usual we walked on the poop, for on Sundays everyone is dressed and must show himself on parade. So far is this feeling carried that it would appear as if the dress on this day formed an essential part of the Service or worship. 'Thence we surveyed the wild waves of the ocean now swelling as it were into large heaps of water resembling truncated Hills, now forming vallies of stupendous width and depth, over which the birds seemed to fly in mid-air, a bright sun shining above, throwing a cheerfulness over the scene, which otherwise would be fearful. We could not but admire how Providence in the physical world, as in the moral, subdues all things to its own gracious purpose. One of these mountains of water, one of those valleys seemed to be sufficient to bring destruction on our ship, which still gaily held on its way, for almost was audibly heard a voice saying to the waves as it approached – "thus far etc" – so gently did it fall away by the ship's side.'

Lat 32°48' S; Long 34°37' W.

27 April Our breeze from the S.E. still continues, tho' it is not the Trade, but very like it. At noon we found we had made the longest run in the 24 hours since we had left Sydney, having progressed 210 miles since yesterday at noon. We have now been 10 weeks on the voyage and expect to be 7 more. The day has passed in the monotony usual at sea. The sun shone bright and fleecy clouds becoming more bright as they approached the zenith, gave as they approached an impulse to our breeze.

Lat 29°43' S; Long 33°16' W.

28 April Not a bird around; the sea has subsided almost to a calm; a current helps us imperceptibly on our course with a force of 1½ kts, which added to that

[70] *Preparations against the heat – Conversation – steam to Sydney*

of the breeze makes our rate varying from 3 to 5 kts per hour over a smooth unrippled swell such as a Spaniard would call 'mar de la damas' or 'ladies sea'.[144] The sky overhead is of a deeper blue. The sun's altitude at noon is said to be 70° and the weather as warm as a warm summer day in Sydney. Preparations are making to draw out the awning which fits over the poop and quarterdeck during the Tropical heats. Templar lies in the shade already with his tongue out. The passengers get their hair cut by the Stuard and are dressed in light clothing. Our wine at dinner was changed from sherry to casse, which change, however, was not so much approved of; no more champagne served, but honey is helped at the breakfast table.[145] The fresh meat is not so abundant and what is served of mutton is tainted.

30th April Lat 26°3' S; Long 32°23' W.

Light winds and cloud which made the day cool and agreeable in the cuddy, although on the poop the heat began to be very sensibly felt. Towards evening heavy banks of clouds arose to receive the sun in the west, and soon after sunset the breeze from that quarter became much brisker and we proceed now at a rate of 8 kts. If it continue 36 hours, we may hope to be within the full influence of the Trade wind, about which so much has been said. The Archbishop's razor and penknife sharpened by the carpenter. The conversation on steam to Sydney and the line likely to be adopted by the E. India Company, whereby Sydney will doubtless be brought within 60 or 65 days of London, and within less than 30 of India-via Port Essington 2,340 miles, 12 days; Singapore 2,060 miles more, 12 days; Ceylon etc.[146]

144. Lewis' Spanish seems to let him down: 'mar de las senoras'(?).
145. *casse*: a disorder that occurs in wine making it turn from red to brown, or white to yellow, on exposure to air.
146. *Port Essington*: small settlement established in the vicinity of present-day Darwin in 1831, in the hope of using it as a stopping point for ships; it was rarely used and abandoned in 1849.

The coal stations are convenient; excellent coals from the pits at Newcastle, N.S.Wales, can be put on board there at 7/- to 7/6 per ton and the freight to Port Essington about 20/- to 22/- per ton. A coal depôt would thus be formed at a rising British Settlement at a cost of 27/- to 30/- per ton. Lombock or Batavia, which would be the route from Port Essington to Singapore, can be supplied with coals from our new settlements of Labuan in Borneo or from Calcutta.[147]

[71] *S.E. Trade winds commencement described – Tropic of Capricorn – latitude calculated – anniversary – Trinity Isle May*

1st May This day we fall in with the S.E. wind, Trade wind, as they call it, at the same time that we crossed the Tropic of Capricorn in longitude 29°57' W. Tropic of Capricorn is the utmost limit of Apollo's progress towards the Antarctic. He stops here also from *trapo* [Greek letters] to turn – the sun turning within the two constellations of Capricorn and Cancer – never depassing either.[148]

At the dawn of day a vast bank of cloud was observed in the East and it was naturally supposed that after the lull in the wind, that just then took place, the breeze would set in from that quarter. The sails were set accordingly. However, the wind resumed in the N.W., from which point it had blown all night. During the entire day heavy matters of clouds with rain came up from the W. and S. The wind still persevering, however, it gave way at last under these repeated attacks. By and by the whole heavens became over-clouded; rain from the S. and S. by W. fell and cooled the air considerably. Then followed a lull and just about sunset the wind shifting from the S to S.E. opened in glorious style, driving us along at a rate which from 4 to 5 kts increased to 8, a rate which we are now going.

---

147. *Lombok*: island east of Bali.
Batavia: capital city of the Dutch East Indies, present-day Jakarta.
Labuan: late in 1845 there was speculation reported in Sydney newspapers that Labuan, an island at the tip of Borneo, would be settled by the British as an intermediate station between Singapore and Hong Kong. In December 1846 the Treaty of Labuan with the Sultan of Brunei formalised the British acquisition. It became a coaling station.

148. In Greek mythology, one of Apollo's more important daily tasks was to harness his chariot with four horses and drive the sun across the sky.

We have been more particular in describing this commencement of the S.E. wind, which from its regularity in these latitudes is called the Trade Wind, because we flatter ourselves few have had as good an opportunity for observation.

The altitude of the sun is 50°49' at noon; its declination 15°4'. Subtracting the above 50°49' or 50 from 90 for zenith distance and again subtracting the 15°14', the sun's declination being north and adding 11 for hight of eye and corrections leaves: 23°56' our present latitude.

2nd May Anniversary day of the Archbishop's election to the Episcopacy with the title of Hiero-Caesarea *in partibus infidelium.*[149]

We are now approaching the Island of Trinity, marked in several manuscript charts, and the Martin Vasquez rocks, but a few miles on our lee bow.[150]

[72] *C. Fisher – atmospheric changes*

Horsburgh describes this Island as one of about 6 miles in circumference. It is high and uneven and just discernible from a large ship's poop at 18 leagues distance – as rocky and barren but with some productive spots; as of unsafe anchorage owing to the N. winds and S.W. gales frequently experienced in its neighbourhood where the trade winds are not regular.

At the S.E. end of the island is a conical rock of 1160 feet in hight, having trees on its summit and a waterfall at above 700 feet in hight

149. *Anniversary day*: the Brief of Pope Gregory XVI electing Polding to the See of Hiero-Caesarea, when he was named Apostolic Vicar of Madras, was dated 3 July 1832, not May 2 (see Pope Gregory XVI to J. B. Polding, 3 July 1832 [Adjutor Deus I.3–4]). Polding at first accepted and then declined the election. The Brief remained in force and was the basis of his consecration on 29 June 1834 and appointment as Vicar Apostolic of New Holland and Van Diemen's Land.
in partibus infidelium: 'in the lands of the unbelievers'. Bishops who did not exercise full episcopal jurisdiction, auxiliary bishops and vicars-apostolic, were given the title of a suppressed ancient diocese, usually in areas overrun by Muslims. Hierocaesarea was a town and bishopric in the Roman province of Lydia in western Anatolia. Polding chaffed under the 'foreign title', of which he was relieved on appointment as Archbishop of Sydney in 1842.
150. Trindade and Martin Vaz is an archipelago located in the Southern Atlantic Ocean about 1,100 kilometres east of the coast of Espírito Santo, Brazil.

is projected from it. Captain Ch. Leahy makes mention of a church with a cross on it standing at the upper part of the bay, where ships may anchor at the S. and S.W. sides of the island. The watering place he describes as near the church. Not far from here Revd. C. Fisher was lowered in the deep by us.[151]

A troop of flying fish were seen for the first time by the Captain. All our birds have left us, except the Mother Careys.

Though we are now in the Tropics the temperature is comparatively cool. The Therm. stands at 76°. Heavy clouds pass over us discharging showers of rain. At one time the heavens are most serene and in a few minutes clouds hang over in every direction. A vacuum is thus created and a breeze proportionable to the intensity of the shower succeeds. Thus from a calm, in a surprizingly short time, we proceed on a course of 7 or 8 kts. We are not to be surprised at this, as it is the winter of these latitudes or rather the rainy season, for the sun in its progress is now gone to the north.

At present we glide on at the rate of 9 kts with not much wind owing to the smoothness of the water. There succeeds a lull and we advance not more than 2 or 3 kts and soon walking and racing alternately.

3 May

Sunday Lat 18°49' S; Long 29°43' W

25 days (says the Captain at breakfast) from the Horn, 15 of which were spent working up 40 degrees of latitude (a considerable quantity of Easting, however, was made) the remaining 10 days we have

[73] *fine clouds – Sothern Cross – Service and Sermon*

made 22 degrees of Northing and some Easting. This day has not been precisely a calm. We progressed slowly at an average of 3 kts. Sufficient breeze was abroad to take away the sultriness of these latitudes; without it the heat would indeed have been oppressive. The clouds begin to assume those fantastic hues and shapes which the imagina-

151. Rev. Mr. Clement Fisher was one of the priests who embarked with Bishop Polding on the *Oriental* in 1835. He was priest-in-charge of St Anthony's Church, Scotland Road, Liverpool, which was built in 1833. He died at sea on 28 May, at longitude 23°37' west and latitude 22°54' south.

tion readily gives to beasts and birds and monstrous things of its own creation. This evening a black cloud soon after sunset assumed the shape of a wide-mouthed dragon of horrid form with tail coiled over its back, most unlike indeed to that form which we would fain suppose the genius of these favoured latitudes would assume.

The Southern Cross still appears at a considerable altitude and reminds us of that sweet spot where we resided so many years and almost directly over which it might usually be discerned.

The weather being fine we had divine service on the quarter deck. The Archbishop preached on the immortality of the soul proved from reason and from scripture, the resurrection of the body from the fact of our Saviour's resurrection, and in the spirit of the argument used by St Paul in the Corinthians ch. 15, 1° Epistle.

The sermon was well calculated to work a change in the minds of untaught sailors, to give them a love for religion and to inspire them with a desire of loving God and of addressing him in prayer. It taught them of their responsibility to their creator, of their superiority over the brute creation which blindly follow their instincts. It opened to them an easy path to virtue and showed that of vice as base and to be shunned. *In fine*, it inspired them and everyone with lively sentiment of hope of salvation and of a blessed immortality in a region of happiness where they who seem now lost on the wide world would be again united to their friends – a son to the father and a brother to a sister; the children to their parents and all in God.

[74] *Early voyagers employment on board – heat, its effects – an anecdote*

The performance of divine service on board reminds one of the accounts left by the early voyagers and discoverers of the Indies, where chaplains were usually appointed to ships and that they conveyed missionaries to the newly discovered countries, to China and Japan and the Islands. It appears from them that Office was still said on board in common, conferences held and studies carried on among these religious, almost in the same way as in their colleges and schools at home. At appropriate hours one of them instructed a class of sailors in the catechism; another met his class to recite the rosary or litanies of the Blessed Virgin, while another group further on received various instructions. The Holy Sacrifice was offered almost daily, if the weather permitted, and morning and night prayers were said in common. The Captain and most distinguished passengers frequently giving the example and edyfying the more ignorant by their regularity and frequent reception of the Sacraments.

4th May Lat 17°50' S; Long 28°35' W

Day passed in the usual monotony of a calm at sea. It is chiefly during a calm in these latitudes that the heat is felt to be too oppressive for mental or for bodily exertion. The attempt particularly of the former brings on extensive lassitude. It appears therefore advisable to take advantage of these occasions to allow the faculties to be in a state of repose, preparatory to future exertion; an apparent loss of time will thus be found in reality a gain.

We all took cold water baths this morning; it is found to be very refreshing and invigorating. One of the sailors threw himself overboard to enjoy a swim. The Captain asked him why he went overboard as he exposed himself to the danger of losing his life from sharks.

[75] *The Archbishop on board the 'Duke d'Orleans'*

The man replied that he had been in the coal hole and wished to wash himself. Then said the Captain: 'Go to the coal hole again and learn to wash yourself as a man ought to do without risking his life.'

It was on this day 1840 that His Grace reached Havre, having left Talauano, then the port of Conception in Chile in latitude 36° on the 2nd of February, and rounded the Horn the 8th March and about our present position.[152] His Grace remarks on Easter Sunday that year they had a High Mass on board their French whaler, the *Duke d'Orleans* of 500 tons. The men had prepared for their Easter duties a long time previously by gen[eral] confessions etc, some of them not having complied for 30 or 40 years previously, some wept bitterly on the occasion and approached truly penitent. A stop was put to sin, at least for some period, which was so much gained. The officers here had set the example, yet some of these had an excuse. For instance, that they never went oftener than once a year at the return from the voyage and that then they must go to their curé, who otherwise would be displeased with them. The conduct of the men was truly edifying. During High Mass and at the elevation they bent their foreheads down to touch the deck. They sang hymns composed in their own language. It was astonishing what intelligence they showed on board such a ship, a whaler. The 'chef de cuisine' for some time previously collected scraps of these hymns and putting them together attuned them to airs and drilled the rest to sing them with some degree of taste. This 'chef de cuisine' afterwards had some nice *plats* and preparations by way of refreshment when the service had ended. In the evening they had vespers. The doctor was a clever fellow, who kept an account of the voyage. It was put in the papers on arrival and afterwards copied in the 'Ami de la Religion' and then into other papers.[153] One circumstance

[76] *Southern and Northern Constellations – The Cross, the Great Bear – St Helena – Irregularity of the Trade*

in particular: the men all came to service with their vials to be filled with holy water and to receive a portion of the breads as is customary in the French churches, partaking of a portion of it and reserving the

152. Harding recorded the wrong year for Polding's arrival in Europe at the end of his first return voyage. He sailed from Sydney on 11 November 1840 on board the Chilean brig *Orion*, accompanied by Ullathorne and Gregory, arriving in Europe early in May 1841 on board a French whaling vessel.
Talauano: Harding's attempt at spelling *Talcahuano*, port of the city of Concepcion, Chile.

153. The story eventually found its way into the *Bengal Catholic Herald*, in which a translation of the doctor's account in the *Havre Journal* of 11 May 1841, was published on 19 March 1842.

remainder to show to their mothers and to their curé. One of them stated that his portion presented thus to his mother in token of his having fulfilled his Easter duties would give her more pleasure than if he presented her with a pocket full of gold.

This evening besides the Southern Cross at an altitude of about 30° we perceive also the Great Bear at an altitude of 12°. This is the first time we have noticed the Great Bear (although the Captain says it was visible some 4 or 5 days ago) owing to the clearness of the sky. We are now about abreast of St Helena. The most remarkable constellations of both Hemispheres appear: the Peacock, the Apis Indica, the Chameleon, Nubicula Major and Minor.

5th May Lat 16°49' S; Long 30°15' W

A strong head swell from the north that McIntosh cannot account for unless by supposing that a strong breeze from the north had prevailed here. Our wind too is N.E., very different from the S.E. Trade, which is also unaccountable and we seem to have very little of S.E. Trade. At the same time the heat is very oppressive during the day. This it appears is the same throughout the Tropics, calms, clouds and breezes making the difference in the actual heat experienced.

We have been rather singular in not meeting with birds or flying fish or signs of life around and which abound in the accounts of voyagers in the Tropics. For the waters themselves

[77] *Ocean pregnant with life – very ill – Bolivia – Fr Barber*

are teeming with life in these torrid zones. The Archbishop in his last passage hereabouts made a little excursion in the boat with the Captain of the 'Duke d'Orleans'. They noticed myriads of animalcula floating about on the surface and at some depth under the calm surface[154]. His Grace picked up a piece of wood of a few inches in length and breadth which had evidently been floating about for months and on it a little crab that seemed to have attached his fortunes to it.

Mr. Way's health seems worse, the climate acting injuriously on his constitution. The food also, of which he can partake but little, goes

154. *Animalcule* ('little animal', from Latin) is an older term for microscopic animals or protozoan.

much against him. The cocoa we have in the morning is too rich and oily, and we have no black tea. And most of his sources of amusement seem to be exhausted, the entertaining books he reads as he reclines on his bed being all read and finished. And having no resources left, he appears quite unhappy.

We are not far from being abreast of Bahia, described so lately in Grey's entertaining work. Bahia, the Bay, from which the city now takes its name, was called by its discoverers 'Bahia de todos los Santos', the Bay of All Saints. It was described as one of the finest harbours in the world. The proper name of the city is St Salvador, next to Rio the largest and most flourishing city in Brazil and is the more ancient capital. The population is upwards of 100,000, more than 2/3rd of whom are slaves or freemen of colour. It is on an eminence or on the summit of an acclivity of 600 feet in hight – *vide* Conder's *Geography.*[155]

We keep this day as the anniversary of the profession of the Very Reverend Doctor Barber and of the Revd. Mssr. Rolling and Wassal, the first the president of the English Benedictine Congregation at Sandbrook [Stanbrook] near Worcester.[156] They were professed in the yr 1808. Mr. Hebdin took the habit with them; he is since dead.

[78] *Heat – food – amusements – meteorological phenomena*

6 May Lat 13°20' S; Long 31°20' W

Our progress has been greater than we anticipated, the wind having shifted nearly due east. The heat continues to increase; its effects are very relaxing.

This day month we reached the Horn and today are we a long way northward of Bahia.

155. Josiah Conder (1827–1830), compiler of the thirty-volume geographical tome *The Modern Traveller*.

156. Luke Bernard Barber OSB (1790–1850) was educated at Acton Burnell and ordained priest at Downside in 1815. He was president of the English Benedictine Congregation and vicar of the nuns at Stanbrook from 1842 until death.
Thomas Austin Rolling OSB (1790–1864) was educated at Acton Burnell and ordained priest at Downside in 1815.
Thomas Benedict Wassall OSB (1791–1871) was educated at Acton Burnell and ordained priest at Downside in 1816.

The want of fresh meat begins to be badly felt, our supply of sheep and pigs having failed from desease. Our sole resource is in our poultry, which is served every 2nd or 3rd day

A flock of flying fish was seen. Some lines are put out to catch albacores and bonitos.[157] The bait used an *eau de cologne* bottle or a candle, on which are fastened a few feathers.

Thunnus alalunga (Cuv[ier]) albacore
Auxis vulgaris (Cuv[ier]) bonito

The sailors have their musical party forward; a couple of flutes on which they play to direct the dance.

The Archbishop writing a calendar.

7th May Lat 10°45' S; Long 31°16' W

A fair breeze and cloudless sky; 7 kts an hour. Since yesterday we have sailed 155 miles and drifted west 3 miles with a current. This current is caused, it is said, by the bending of the land westward, where it goes to form the Gulph of Mexico.

Doctor Dobie, from his journal on board the *Everetta* 2 yrs since, informs us that they were 5 days making the Equator from this spot and 56 days in reaching London.

157. *Albacore*: long-fin tuna; *bonito*: schooling fish of the tuna and mackerel family.

We appear now only to be under the full influence of the trade wind. A succession of dense and heavy clouds are observed to rise in the N.E., but instead of coming on directly overhead, they skirt the horizon until they reach the S. of East, when apparently under the influence of the wind prevailing there, they come over, not unfrequently discharging rain. It may be remarked that the more regular and heavy these clouds are in succession, the more

[79] *Promises at starting our voyage of an adequate supply of food being furnished – deceptive! – Mr Wilson*[158]

steady and strong is the breeze. At the same time that the S.E. wind is observed to prevail in the lower regions of the air, a current in the directly opposite direction of considerable rapidity may be seen

A few flying fish were seen today; a line was put out without effect, which is the more provoking as it is not only a disappointment to our anticipated amusement, but a positive loss in our present dearth of fresh food. We must therefore be resigned if we are no better off than most other voyagers and submit like them to deprivations ever incident on the latter half of a voyage, in spite of the promising prospects at starting.

8th May Lat 8°2' S; Long 30°18' W

This day has been in every respect similar to the preceeding. The heat, except when exposed to the full power of the breeze, is oppressive. In or out of the sun we are in a state of profuse perspiration owing in part to the large proportion of salt meat that forms our diet at breakfast and dinner. The Therm. ranges in the cabin from 84° upwards. Mental application is very difficult; a great lassitude is felt. Our stock of fish, hard and dry as it was, is now exhausted. His Grace rejoices now that Doctor Gregory did not come home on board this ship, as our present food would have ill agreed indeed with his complaint.

We dined on boiled potatoes partly to avoid the great scandal of certain parties very watchful of our words and actions and partly that the authority on board might feel their gross negligence in not procuring

158. Robert William Willson (1794–1866) was the first bishop of Hobart Town from 1842. His episcopacy was dogged by an ongoing dispute with the pioneer priest, John Joseph Therry, over church property and debts.

proper food for us on Friday, after their attention had been expressly called to the necessity of making such provision both by Mr. Wilson and by Dr Gregory himself.

Our stock of live provisions amounts now to about 5 dozen poultry – ducks and hens

[80] *Lewis unwell – a Nautilus – a boat*

chiefly. Supposing our voyage to be 7 weeks additional, we being 9 at table, the average is about one per week for each person – a small provision this to be divided into 7 days of the week.

9th May Lat 5°25' S

The Doctor, on his passage homewards in the *Everetta* in'34; says he was 5 weeks and two days making the western Islands, and 2 weeks from thence home, from this place making 7 weeks that we shall in all probability be on the voyage yet, a voyage that is becoming irksome in the extreme. The heat and food and altogether seems to have so far disagreed with me also, as to bring on again the attacks of my complaint, which I had some slight hope the voyage would have removed. The Archbishop now tells me the doctor thinks 7 years may not bring an end to this my purgatory. It will require that time at least to effect a sensible recovery with proper care and precautions. Meanwhile my weakness prevents me standing on my legs with sufficient firmness to walk or to counteract the motion of the ship when the breeze blows and metics and pills and this prospect of 7 more weeks here make me feel indeed not too sure of reaching home yet. The number 7 must be a fatal one. We were told that having once passed the Horn, the remainder of the voyage would be nothing worth speaking of, but what say we now?

We observed a nautilus of a beautiful purple colour. This and a white bird somewhat larger than a pigeon are the first of the kind we have seen since entering the Tropics.

Towards evening a boat drifted past us. The sailors however could not make out the name astern as it floated deep and full of water. It was painted yellow inside and striped with red outside.

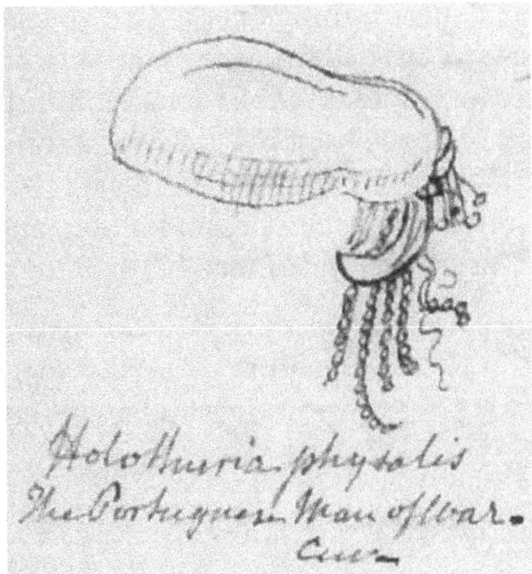

Holothuria physalis.
The Portuguese Man of War (Cuv[ier])

10th May Sunday. Lat 2°51' S. Much too unwell to write. The last event this evening was a ship in sight. It was discerned by the aid of the moon that shone brightly in the clear heavens.

[81] *Cross the Line in Long 29° W – remarkable coincidence*

It appeared to be about 4 or 5 miles away to the eastward, a brig, perhaps a Portuguese on her way to Rio, perhaps a vessel to Sydney, this being also the tract of our outward-bound ships.

11 May We crossed the line today, a little before sitting down to dinner. The sun's observed altitude at noon was 71°33', its declination 17°52' North. We crossed the line in Longitude 29°20' W.

We are still drifting to the westward at a rate of 2 kts an hour in a current. Although we have had the wind favourable and these few days back have progressed at a rate of about 8 kts per hour, still owing to this current we have scarcely made any Easting. Our magnetic course is now altered to N.E. we expect to pass a little rock (St Paul's) at about midnight, which is placed in some charts at 1° north and in line with our present altered course.[159]

159. The Saint Peter and Saint Paul Archipelago is a group of 15 small islets and rocks in the central equatorial Atlantic Ocean.

By a strange coincidence, turning over a former log, I perceive that on this day 11 years we crossed the Line in the ship *Oriental* (Captain Allen) on our way to Sydney. We then crossed it in Longitude 20°8', far to the eastward of our present position. By a coincidence not less remarkable, we find that the same number of days (84) has been spent in sailing from Sydney here, that we required to take us from the Line to Hobart Town (via Cape Good Hope).

This evening a flying fish was caught; it flew on board attracted apparently by the light. It is something like a herring and 7 or 8 inches in length; its wings are 4 or 5. The moon is full and bright.

12th May Too unwell to write and confined to bed.

Lat 1°16' North; Long 28°15' W; wind the south-east, variable; cloudy; passing showers.

[82] *Average rate between the Trades – Lemonades – birds – fishes – tea on the Poop*

13 May Incidents few and unworthy of record or rather there are none. As regards our progress it is necessarily slow since yesterday morning having lost the S.E. Trade and not having reached the N.E. one, which during the months of March, April and May commence about 6° north. Our latitude today is 2°5' North, which gives a progress of 45 miles. The Captain says that the average going between the Trades is 30 miles a day; so we have been favoured.

We have seen no fish as yet in the northern hemisphere, except a few skip-jacks, and no birds but a sort of gull, which is supposed to be a land bird, or a *photon athereus*, the Tropicbird.[160]

Photon Athereus. Lin[naeus]. The common tropic bird

160. *Phaethon aethereus*-red-billed tropicbird.

14th May Lat 3°2' N; Long 28°4' W

His Grace awoke about 2 o'clock and taking it to be 6 in the morning looked out of the stern windows and beheld the moon shining brightly midway up the heavens. The Archbishop these few days has left off cocoa in the morning for water and lemonade.

The Southern Cross appears no more than 16° above the horizon.

The heat of the weather is very oppressive and induces sleep and the slightest exertion is followed by profuse perspiration.

Numerous shoals of fish were seen near the ship and also in the distance disporting on the waters. Medusae also, some of a brown colour and shaped like mushrooms, are seen continually floating past the ship.[161]

The water is so smooth that we glide through it most imperceptibly. Large clouds sail along with an equally gentle advance, while towards the west the setting sun seems to delight in decorating them with a profuse variety of gorgeous colours, which appear to be still more

[83] *Night in the Tropics*

set off by the bright and uniform silvery hue of the western wave upheaving slowly and majestically the line of the horizon.

Incited by the prospect and the quietness around, we had the tea served up on the Poop, where the company sat enjoying the cool and the sailors forward enlivened the watch with their airs. The conversation on American manners – one remarked that it's common for the householders and ladies to go to market themselves accompanied by a servant; that they purchased fish and meat, which they then sent home by the servant that had accompanied them. Another speaks in the abstract of human pursuits generally and the acquisition of gold, the idol of the majority.

The night was remarkably calm and fine as they generally are in the Tropics. Between 10 and 11 o'clock, the pleasantest time to be out, the full orbed moon enlightens and gilds the eastern sky. Its light, while I write, pours through one of many detached clouds of vast dimen-

161. *Medusozoa* – a form of jellyfish.

sions, which float high in the atmosphere on our starboard beam and hence by insensible gradations spread over the radiant horizon. It fringes every detached mass with a border of harmoniously blended colours, where the rose and silvery white and amber predominate in various degrees of tint and hue. The bold relief of their forms adds to their effect. In one quarter of the heavens they appear to rest on a dark bank; in another they form a series of strata broken and rugged resembling islands or floating icebergs, as we had seen them borne along in their brightness over the dark wave of the gloomy antarctic regions.

But that portion of the skies illumined by the direct and bright rays of Phoebe's placid countenance seemed to present as many successive changes or dissolving views as Geologists can point out of successive revolutions or creations at the founding of the globe. At one time the tract which extends from the ship to the eastern sky resembles a broad and glistening highway

[84] *Night in the Tropics*

leading to some fairy land, while the shadows cast by the ambient clouds combine with the light reflected from the calm ocean in producing on its surface the appearance or mirage [of] spires and towers and fortifications and cities, over which the grey smoke of evening fires appears to be swept in wreaths, until you fancy you are near enough to some harbour and hear the sounds of life and distinguish the motions of stirring fleets and shipping and of towns and something of the active bustle of a busy population. Then again and as distinctly as one's vision can make it, the scene changes into another one of a calm lake lighted by the moon, whose retired banks shaded by the umbrageous foliage of a forest, where stately trees, whose graceful and transparent branches are gently waved by the transient air.

Later it is park or tract of pastoral land with its trees and boundless slopes of verdure, then soon, as if emblematic of the country that is thus exhibited, a cloud assumes the form and appearance of some New Zealand chief or N.S.Wales inhabitant of the bush, long shinned, kangaroo-rumped, and with shaggy head of hair. You distinctly trace the track of the natives over the hills by the appearance of the forest here and there on fire. You distinguish their separate fires, the smoke which arises around in tiny streaks over a hundred different specks of light. So correct is the perspective, so gradual the transitions of tints and shades from the foreground to the furthest distance or remotest speck of cloud illumed by the moon's rays, so far is the whole picture with its countless details and various scenery on the most perfect keeping and harmony.

None but could have admired these works of nature; it was as if she herself were lecturing the beholder on her works and raising his thoughts from them to their author inculcating: *Pulchrum coelum, pulchra terra, sed pulchrior qui fecit ista,*[162]

[85] *a Meteor – domestic miseries*

when suddenly another revelation in the scenery took place. A meteor of unusual size and brilliancy was seen to cross all that part of the heavens described from east to north. The appearance lasted about 10 seconds. Its size was that of the full orbed moon, with a dazzling tail like that of a comet and of about 20 times the length of its diameter. Its course was momentarily behind a dense mass of cloud of a few miles distant and about 20° above the horizon and it comprised in all about 40° or 50° of the heavens. While it lasted it was beautiful and resplendent. The moon itself appearing to fade before it, as it startled us by its sudden glare similar – *parvulis componere magna* – to a Congreve rocket or blue light.[163] But its colours were infinitely more variegated, with a nucleus of red and amber chiefly; its streamer blended these with the most dazzling yellow, blue and green.

It burst at last into several portions, each in its fall bearing a streamer of light – *finis coronat opus.*[164] Whence this visitor? Was it projected from the moon? Or revolving as a satellite round our earth, disturbed in its motion by having penetrated our atmosphere, did it ignite? Or did it belong to the Nebular Theory as one of its myriads of bodies of

162. 'Beautiful the sky, beautiful the earth, but more beautiful He who made them.'
163. *parvulis componere magna*: 'compare great things to small'.
Congreve rocket: rocket invented in 1804 by Sir William Congreve (1772–1828).
164. *finis coronat opus*: 'the end crowns the work' (attributed to Ovid).

nebular matter heated through space, and suddenly condensed being brought within the earth's attraction?[165]

15th May Lat 3°40' N; calm , cloudy, occasional showers.

At Breakfast time the Major asked the Stuard to hand him over some dish. The stuard instead of readily complying when asked, served 1st one, then another and then attended to the Major, who tasked him roughly and added: 'I won't have it, Sir, take it away' And presenting his plate: 'Here, take this away also.' Way makes a remark on the Doctor taking soup twice at dinner. It is only because such remarks appear to me extraordinary and remarkable that I have entered them here. Why one passenger should remark thus on another, I can't account for,

[86] *employment of the sailors – atmospheric changes*

and why the Stuard should show a preference when all pay equally.

An albacore was seen and lots of Moluscae; no birds.

His Grace has completed 20 sermons written on board, 32 remaining to be written, being one for every Sunday of the year.

The sailors, who have little ship duty to perform in these fine days, employ themselves in picking pieces of old rope, splicing and twisting them into spun yarn. They use the needle and thread and various frames and wheels and spindles, some of these worked by the revolving windlass. They work mats of their spun yarn, which they employ to cover portions of ironwork and bolt rings and in protecting the shrouds from the friction of the running rigging.[166] These mats are of various patterns and neatly woven. The carpenter makes his lumber yard of the quarterdeck and is employed in cutting out spars and making repairs in the boats and painting them. While the cooper plies his trade also; and all of them under the superintendence of the Captain, who understands the business of each department.

165. *Nebular Theory*: this theory of the formation of the universe contends that clouds (nebulae) slowly rotate, gradually collapse due to gravity, eventually forming stars and planets. Names associated with the emergence of the theory are Emanuel Swedenborg, Immanuel Kant and Pierre-Simon Laplace.

166. *Shrouds*: standing rigging running from a mast to the sides of the ship to support the mast sideways.

The horizon is occasionally screened by a curtain of blue clouds concealed in which Eolus and Vulcan seem to be at work also.[167] Now and then they send us specimens of their art. The rain falls in torrents and the ocean underneath rises and spreads in long and sharp ridges. You expect a squall of wind and rain, and having prepared for it, the appearance vanishes 'ere it has reached within a mile of the ship. At other times and without the usual warning we find ourselves suddenly envelopped in one of these Tropical showers, which in a few minutes fills your casks and sails with such a provision of fresh water that will last for days.

During one of these showers the ocean assumes

[87] *Appearance of ocean intermediate of the Trades – Fishes – Patience on a Monument*

a variegated appearance and is intersected in all directions with light streaks of smoother water imitating pathways and roads and lines, canals and river courses in a populated district.

At night we perceived the north pole star for the first time only a few degrees above the horizon.[168]

16 May Still anxiously looking for the N.E. Trade, which however it is said does not set in at this time of the year until where [it] crosses the 6th degree of N. latitude, and as yet our latitude is but 4°6' N.

The weather is sultry and the sea calmer, and albacores and bonettos or porpoises are seen disporting on its surface in various directions, while we are reckoning the time it would take us to cross over from one trade wind to the other, from 6° S, say, and 6° N. At our present rate of progressing I find that at 1 knot an hour it would not take us more than 5 months: at 672 hours in a month and at one knot per hour 21 weeks only to cross, and it is said that we are fortunate to go even at this rate here in this Intertrades climate.

Way remarks well that the man who can stand on his legs (his complaint is the *tic douloureux*)[169] and says he is free from pain is in the

167. *Aeolus*: the keeper of the winds; *Vulcan*: the god of fire.
168. *Pole star*: stars close to the north and south celestial poles of the Earth.
169. *Tic douloureux*: a severe, stabbing pain to one side of the face.

state of enjoyment as great as a man need wish to be, in which I am fully tempted to agree with him, as here I sit bandaged with blisters and fomentations and with the doctor's implements lying on the table before me – while the Archbishop comes in and smiling says: 'Have you ever seen Patience sitting on a monument?[170] Were Thompson here and to see you sitting in that position quiet and thoughtful and these things before you, he might take an i–d–.'[171]

Paley somewhere remarks that pain and pleasure are balanced and that many pleasures become positive from previous pain, thus the man who has just been suffering from toothache or amputation, on recovering feels it a positive pleasure to be without pain.[172]

[88] *Birds of N.S.Wales – how conveyed*

17th May

Sunday. It having rained and the sailors jackets being wet, there was no Divine Service. We join in saying the Rosary and part of the Office and read the life of St John Nepomucene of Bohemia.[173]

The weather alternates in squalls and calms; one moment we are driven at 7 or 8 kts, the next one only. As I am a good deal in my bed, I have an opportunity of hearing the songs of the birds we have brought from N.S.Wales. The bell sound of the Lory reminds me of the delight their song-like chiming of bells afforded to Captain Cook while at anchor in Botany Bay. In fact, their music is like the notes of small bells exquisitely tuned.

The parrots and paroquetes bear the voyage well. They are distinguished by the length of the tail, parrots having short tails. Those feeding on sweet things, sugar etc are not so hardy and would not

170. *fomentation*: archaic word for *poultice*.

171. *an i–d–* : medical procedure involving incision and drainage.

172. William Paley (1743–1805) was an English clergyman, Christian apologist and philosopher. In his *Principles of Moral and Political Philosophy,* first published in 1785, Paley argued that man's basic instinct was to seek pleasure and to avoid pain.

173. St John Nepomuk (1345–1393) was the confessor of the queen of Bohemia and refused to divulge to the king the secrets of her confession; he is considered the first priest martyred for maintaining the Seal of the Confessional. His feast is celebrated on 16 May.

bear the voyage. We lost 3 Blue Mountain parrots that died of cold round the Horn. All these birds require great attention; they must be fed every day and watered regularly. Our birds are a large white Cockatoo, a king Parrot, all green, 3 Blue Mountains, two small cockatoo parrots, 3 Golars or rose–breasted Cockatoos, a few Budgereego – birds, about the size of a canary – the Lory, the rosella. They are fed on corn, canarie seed, Hemp seed and millet seed and canisters of sand are procured for cleanliness to strew their cages with.

Lat 5°9' N; Long 27°40' W. We are drifting to westward.

18th May His Grace not very well and complains of lassitude. He remarks that if Dr Gregory had been here we should have both been laid up together – a pretty pair. Way advises me to get rid of my cough before leaving the Tropics, or else I never shall, England being no place to go to

[89] *N.E. Trade – conversation on time required to cross it – population of Australia*

to be cured of such. Way gives up playing at whist in the evenings. He is too unwell for the attention it demands. The conversation is prolonged and is about emigration. Way prefers America on the borders of Canada as being much better without comparison. Another proposes as good speculation for a tradesman in N.S. Wales to export the roots and stumps of old cedar trees for cabinet makers at home.

19th May Lat 6°6' N

And we had not in the morning caught the Trade winds, but in the course of the afternoon we entered them very gradually however, and it was not till evening that we were confirmed in this our hope, both by its steadiness and by the swell. which appeared coming in steadily from the N.E. quarter. The air also became sensibly cooler. Having caught the Trade wind, we tack the ship to N.W.

As we sat looking out for the expected change, the Captain first perceived from the poop, as a little speck on the horizon, a sail. 'I said we should see one hereabouts', he remarked as he triumphantly pointed it out. It was taken to be a brig or a schooner or a slaver or a pirate.

From the journal of our voyage outward we find that we entered this Trade in N. Lat 27°54'. It follows that it embraces 22°, nearly 1320 miles. MacIntosh says we shall run across it in 15 days. In the Oriental we were 13 days crossing it, viz from Easter Sunday to the 2nd of May at the rate of 2° a day.

We now advert in conversation to the Scilly Isles. These are in 49 N. We have therefore 42 of northing, supposing we travel 1½ degrees a day. 30 days will take us to the channel; if 2 a day, which is more probable, then 21 days more takes us to the entrance of the Channel. We next advert to Sydney and the population of Australian Colonies amounting to 300,000 thus:

New South Wales and Port Philip – 182,000
South Australia – 25,000
V.D.Land – 58,000
Western Australia – 4,700
New Zealand – 17,000
and their respective annual

[90] *N.E. Trade – Horsburg – Constellations*

revenues: £438,000; 36,000; 136,000; 10,000; 25,000; and their total amount trade annually near 5 millions.

20th May Lat 7°28' N; Long 28°3' W

We are driven fairly before the Trade at the rate of 7 kts; saw a few flying fish and a shoal of bottlenoses, a sort of whale, in our wake.

21 May Ascension Day; too unwell to move out of my cabin for service or prayers.

Here a steady wind blows all the year round, except perhaps during two months, September and October, the hurricane months hereabouts.

Horseburg remarks that Homeward bound ships should here be kept good full, that their velocity may be increased in order to get speedily to the northward. But we find that we get driven as much westward as northward and scarcely make 80 miles a day of good northing. But he makes no mention of storms here, which in the Trade indeed are not likely.

22 May Lat 10°40' N; Long 31°34' W. The sun's alt. at noon was observed to be 80°7'.

The Archbishop gives a pot of French plums to Fergusson, who has a bad cough and recommends him to take no meat for a day or two. The poor boy is now sent below to sleep instead of out on deck. Otherwise they seem careless enough aboard ship about their prentice's health.

At night the N. Pole star began to appear much more distinctly, while the Southern Cross is proportionably depressed.

23rd May Lat 12°33' N; Long 33°19' W

The 2nd mate lounging more idly than became his duty, the Captain walked up to him and seized the book out of his hand as he was reading, and flung it overboard, and moreover a note against him on the log.

His Grace visits me night and day; at present feel getting somewhat better.

This evening Way congratulates himself on having once more beheld the N. Pole star,

[91] *Order of Divine Service*

which, when he left Sydney, he never expected to see again.

We admire here the most brilliant constellations of both Hemispheres. The North pole star, which owing to the cloudiness of the weather generally in the tropics, has yet been scarcely visible, appeared very bright this evening and at an altitude of about 13°. This altitude is the same as indeed in any latitude, and it represents, with a very trifling correction, the latitude of the place whence observed. It appears now about the same elevation over the N Horizon as the lowermost star of the Southern Cross is above the southern horizon, while the Great Bear is approaching more and more our zenith and the two bright pointers to the Southern Cross are yet remarkably conspicuous.

24 May

Sunday Lat 14°38' N

The order of Divine Service, which we have not had for some time now, was as follows: the men were seated in two rows across the quarter deck; the officers and passengers in the cuddy; the celebrant at the entrance so as to be heard by both parties, being seated and wearing a violet cassock and black cap and gold cross.

Commences by an extemp. prayer and then the 'O incomprehensible', followed by the prayers before Mass from the 'Garden of the Soul', the 'Come oh Holy Spirit', and 'O Lord open thou our lips', and 'Let us adore the Lord of Glory'. Then followed the Acts of Faith, Hope and Charity and the scriptural Litany, the Gospel and Epistle of the day, and some portion of the Scripture.[174] The instruction lasted for about ½ an hour and was concluded by an appropriated prayer and another for a safe voyage, psalm 69 for the

[92] *Sermon*

Divine assistance, a prayer for the Queen, and the conclusion 'accept this our service'. The men were remarkably orderly and attentive. Some of them followed in their own books the reading of the Script[ure]. They were all cleanly dressed and cheerful, and the weather delightfully fine. The sun nearly vertical and the sky cloudless, yet it was not too warm owing to the breeze.

Without attempting to reproduce the sermon merely on the ground of the admiration, which good speech always elicits in an intellectual audience, yet a few words on the topic treated will serve to remind the reader, who was present, of the pleasure and profit he derived at the time, while actually listening as the words fell from His Grace's lips.

174. *Garden of the Soul*: this manual of Catholic devotion, first published in 1751, was composed by Bishop Richard Challoner (1691–1781), Vicar Apostolic of the London District.

It was on the text, 'I am not come to call the just, but sinner to repentance.' His Grace here dilated on the grounds of hope to the sinner afforded by the character of our saviour J.C, as exhibited in his life and conduct. That much as they might have desired to have lived at the same time with, and to have enjoyed the company of our Saviour on earth, that they were to remember that He is not less powerful nor less merciful, nor less solicitous for the sinner's welfare. He continually calls upon us by his ministers to come to him and even as He healed bodily deseases whilst on earth, so is he now prepared to cure the ailments of the soul, of which corporal infirmities may be considered the type. We are never therefore to despair, but in all confidence to present ourselves before Him. Why should we despair? Do we not

[93] *Cape Verde – currents*

believe in Him to be God that is infinite in his power, in his goodness, in his love? Have we not his sacred word that He came on earth to save us? Cannot He, who burst asunder the barriers of the grave, break the bonds of sin, though they may have worn into our very frame? Did he not change Saul a persecutor into Paul an apostle by a single word? Do we fear the power of our spiritual enemies? That power He has destroyed by his triumph on the cross. Let us pray therefore to Him. His Grace insisted much, in this place, on prayer, fervent amendment of life and the dispositions of a true penitence, on which conditions alone pardon could be hoped for.

We are now passing abreast of the cape Verd Islands, a 'cluster belonging to Portugal and about 80 miles west of Cape Verd. Three of these islands are considerable, rising in lofty mountains. The Portuguese settlers are now few and poor. The Negro and Mulato natives become comparatively independent' (Conder).

25 May Lat 16°35' N; Long 35°40' W

Our longitude shews how fast we are declining to the westward. This Trade wind will indeed take us as far as the latitude 30, but by that time our longitude west will have increased many degrees, and if we harken to Horsburg we may find ourselves at this rate at a point somewhere midway between the Bank of Newfoundland and the Azores, and then we shall have to steer perhaps far to the northward. And who knows but that we may there again be drifting among the floating icebergs of the N. Sea,

[94] *Heat – vertical sun's effects*

as we were lately in the South.

The breeze also has much slackened and in consequence, with the sun vertical at noon, the air between decks feels vitiated and confined for want of any ventilating apparatus. And the smell of the poultry, even on the poop in the open air, is most offensive.

The appearance of the sea and sky also changes where the sun is vertical, for there is no longer that path of reflected light which always extends from the spectator to the horizon in the direction of the sun when in its declination, but the surface of the ocean on all sides presents more a reflected circle of bronze and of golden hue, whose boundary is a broad horizontal line or belt of light indigo blue. The sky also presents an analogous appearance.

Another change also from Sol being in our zenith, he has rendered us *Ascii* or shadowless.[175] Thus in turn we have now been *amphiscii*, or tropical inhabitants with our shadows falling both ways according to the sun's declension; *Heteroscii* while in the temperate zones with the shadows at noon never turning but one way only all the year. Neither were we far from being made *Periscii*, had we gone a few degrees further south, where our shadows would have circulated during half the year, whilst the other half we should have frozen in polar darkness.

Our sunset today at half past 6 and there followed 1 hour's twilight and it is a comfort to think our twilight is daily increasing and that long twilights will attend us up the Channel.

[95] *Our progress – papers right – Levee – Ferguson*

26 May Lat 18°3' S; Long 36°28' W

The Azores are now half way as to distance between ourselves and home. The weather could not be more beautiful, and we are as ever almost in these latitudes sheltered from the sun under a canopy of bold cumulostr. clouds.

175. *Ascii*: plural of Latin *ascius*, from Greek *askios*, meaning 'shadowless'. The word referred to the inhabitants of the tropics, where at some time of the year, the sun is directly overhead at noon, so that people don't cast shadows.

We overhaul our papers and the Archbishop finds all those he wanted, some of which he thought had been forgotten. There is a great deal to look over and write, and letters to prepare etc. etc., and scarcely anything has been done as yet.

Hicks thinks that we all ought to attend a Levee at St James on arrival – Gentlemen come from N.S.Wales! – but natural to call on the queen; indeed perhaps it will be expected. I don't suppose we shall be thought rude if we don't.

The poor boy Ferguson is in a sad plight with a cough that has been trying him for weeks. And yet is he made to sleep on deck; during his watch he wears no jacket or shoes. Way says that sooner than send a boy on a merchant ship, he would see him to Old Nick.[176] Indeed his food appears of a poor and wretched description. Ferguson never eats salt meat and gets what he can catch from the stuard. He is now unknowingly contracting a nucleus of desease on the lungs, which will begin to tell in 8 or 9 years time. At 8 and 20 he will die of consumption. The lad is now only 13 years of age and nothing but skin and bone.

[96] *Unhappy character – squatters*

27th May Lat 19°25' N; clear overhead and cumulous clouds border the horizon.

We are almost becalmed, but when a breeze rises we fall away to westward and with every effort fail in making a brisk northern course.

The Archbishop's feast – St Bede never kept so poorly before.[177]

One of the passengers gives up card playing entirely, which he had neglected of late. He says he feels no interest in it. He is a queer and quite unapproachable character. He complains of being unhappy, yet one fears to talk of religion to him, which he might hereafter make a subject of ridicule and conversation. Religion affords him no comfort within and he is disgusted with everything on board – food, mental occupation and books; there are no more to sooth the appetite.

176. *Old Nick*: a jocular name for Satan.

177. Lewis expresses nostalgia for the exuberant celebration of the Archbishop's name-day at St Mary's, Sydney beginning with pre-dawn ringing of the bells. See C. F. Fowler, 'Invoking the patronage of St Bede in New South Wales', *Australasian Catholic Record*, 94(2017), 294–304.

The conversation on squatters and squatting – really the more one hears of the life of the great squatters in N.S.W. the more one becomes disgusted with human nature. The selfishness of most of them is beyond all, as their worldliness is unconquerable. Woe to the poor man or squatter without capital or of small capital; if he were even the most virtuous and industrious, were he to attempt to settle in their neighbourhood, the dog's life he would lead of it. The land regulations they have constructed to serve themselves, and the vast grants of land they have obtained or seized upon, they may transmit to their offspring, while the poorer and the middle classes of colonists are precluded from purchasing. Thus none of the latter need emigrate nor the labourer, unless indeed he is satisfied to live his whole life a slave to a master with the nominal wages of a hut and rations 30£ a year.

[97] *Gulph weed – Gulph stream*

28th May Lat 20°56' N; Gulph weed seen.

The Archbishop very busy at writing yet feels a heaviness and giddiness and takes medicine.

Reading Playfair on the Gulph Stream and Osbeck on the sargasso or gulph weed and its contained animals.[178] It appears from these that from the mouth of the Red Sea a current of about 50 leagues

178. John Playfair (1748–1819) was Church of Scotland minister and professor of natural philosophy at the University of Edinburgh, best known for his book *Illustrations of the Huttonian Theory of the Earth* (1802). His comments on the Gulf Stream are found in Note XIX 'Transformation of Materials by the Sea' (pp 413–437).
Pehr Osbeck (1723–1805) was a Swedish Lutheran minister, explorer, naturalist and one of the 'Apostles of Linnaeus'. In 1750 he sailed as chaplain on a Swedish East India Company ship to China. It was on the return voyage in 1852 that he observed and studied the 'Grass-Sea' or 'Sargasso Sea', a part of the Atlantic adjacent to Florida. His published journal and observations of 1765 was translated into English in two volumes in 1771: Peter Osbeck, *A voyage to China and the East Indies*. Harding drew closely from the 'Grass-Sea' section in the second volume (pages 107–119), to which he either had access onboard or consulted afterwards.
sargasso: brownish seaweed with rounded air bladders floating on the surface; sailor legends claimed it covered the whole of the area of the Sargasso Sea, making navigation impossible, but in fact it only occurs not as one mass, but in large drifts.

in breadth sets continually to the SW. Doubling the Cape of Good Hope it assumes a N.W. direction, and on the parallel of St Helena its breadth exceeds 1000 miles. Then taking a direction nearly east it meets, on the parallel of 3°N. along the Northern Coast of Africa with a current from the N. Here joining they enter the gulph of Florida and, being reflected, form this 'Gulph Stream', which passing along the coast of N. America, stretches across the Atlantic to the British Isles. At the parallel of 38°, nearly 1000 miles from the straights of Bahama, the water of the stream is 10° warmer than the air. The course of the Gulph Stream is so fixed and regular that nuts and plants from the W. Indies are annually drifted to the western Island of Scotland. The mast of a Man-of-War burned at Jamaica was drifted ashore several months afterwards on the Hebrides, after performing a voyage of more than 4000 miles under the direction of a current, which in the midst of the ocean maintains its course as steadily as a river upon land and at the same time transports water of the temperature of the tropics into the climates of the north.

In this stream we now frequently see patches of seaweed varying in extent from a few roods to whole acres, and it is remarked that this weed or sargasso contains various fishes and the deposit of their spawn, which when conveyed to warmer latitudes comes to life.

Osbeck has noticed that the stalk of this ramose plant is scarcely distinguishable in

[98] *Gulph weed – animals life it encloses*

thickness from the branches, and is without all appearance of roots, yet it was able to push out new leaves.[179]

The globose parts of fructification were, like some of the leaves, stalks and branches, harder than usual, occasioned it seems by the slime which sometimes fastens itself there. In this some very small blackish grains or rather eggs of crabs and insects are inclosed. Sometimes a slime like the whites of eggs sticks to the leaves in which are innumerable quantity of snails' eggs joined together make a white or yellow chain like a Taenia, so wound backward and forward that one can

179. *ramose*: from the Latin *ramosus*, 'branched'.

neither find beginning or end.[180] Osbeck could distinguish no life in them with the microscope; being put into water it dissolved. The sargasso in stormy weather still keeps on the surface. It emits a green light, although its colour is yellow. Prepared with vinegar it eats like samphire.

Observing in this weed further, he discovered in it the following fish:

1. *Sophicus Histrio*: the American frog fish, with cirrus or beard and first dorsal fin bristly, but scarcely observable in the water, as it lies so close to the body. The mouth is large and feeds on crabs or young shellfish. Probably Providence has clothed this fish with fulcra resembling leaves, that the fishes of prey might mistake it for seaweed.
2. *Cyprinus pelagicus*: the body is narrow – whitish.[181]
3. *Syngnathus pelagicus*, whose length is about a span and is as thick as a goose quill.[182]
4. The *Scyllaea pelagicus*, or the Sea hare, whose body is like a jelly oblong, narrow and of a yellow–

[99] *Sails in sight – the 'Donna Maria'*

grey colour; it is 2 inches long and scarce an inch broad.[183]

5. The *cancer pelagicus*: the pinchers bend out very little; it is of a brownish colour.[184]
6. The *cancer minutus* is the most numerous of all insects here; it feeds upon sepias and little crabs. It skips about on the surface of the water, from one heap of seaweed to another. When it catches a worm it tears it with its chely and claws it into its mouth bit by bit.[185]

---

180. *Taenia*: a genus of tapeworms.
181. *Pelagicus*: species of fish living in the pelagic zone, the open ocean, neither close to the bottom nor near the shore.
182. *Syngnathus pelagicus*: pipefish found in floating rafts of sargassum weed.
183. *Scyllaea pelagicus*: a gastropod mollusc;
sea *hare*: a direct translation from Latin *lepus marinus*; the name derives from their rounded shape and from the two long projections from their heads and that somewhat resemble the ears of a hare.
184. *Cancer pelagicus*: ocean crab, from Greek 'cancer'.
185. *Chely*: chela, a claw or pincer.

Osbeck enters into a long and minute description of all the above animals. These notes are merely to assist in recognising them.

29th May Lat 23°10' N; Long 37°51' W; sargasso still.

A number of large Medusae were seen of a purple and yellow colour. The breeze brisk but varied from E. to N. Towards 10 o'clock a sail appeared in sight. The Captain remarked that they had had a very different wind from the one we have. At about 2 o'clock the strange ship passed close to us. We had hoisted the British flag, but she hoisted none until under our bow, and then the Spanish flag, a yellow striped, appeared halfway up her main masts. With a speaking trumpet we hailed and understood her to be the *Donna Maria*, brig bound for Porto Rico. She had all her sail and sluice sails set. She spoke also and asked by means of the trumpet 'Unde Voy'. There being no interpreter on board, no answer was returned, and, besides the interest, the appearance had awakened even to the preparing of landing a boat. It vanished as we perceived another and then another sail making towards us from the same quarter. On our further progress, however, they both took a different course.

We now crossed the Tropic of Cancer, so

[100] *Leave the Tropics and Trade – bid adieu to our friends – change in appearances of Sydney*

called, I suppose, from Apollo's crab like retrogradation as he moves back in June from that sign in the zodiac.

30th May: Lat 20°9' A great leap, it appears, since yesterday noon, one of 180 miles of northing, and already the character of the ocean and atmosphere is very different from that of the tropics, where we voyaged as across a lake, attended by an equal breeze and waves all running in the same direction, and without any necessity for once altering the sails. And now once more, we bid our Sydney friends farewell, but in the words of Lucan – 10 lb. [book X]: 'Those whom the turning you divides from us, their shadows ever be southward, as ours we northward ever see.'[186]

186. *Lucan*: Marcus Annaeus Lucanus (39 AD –65) was a Roman poet.

The motion of the sea is altered here, a motion very different from the easy gliding of heretofore, one of a cross waved and short tumbling sea.

The clouds likewise are no longer of that bold and detached outline and brilliancy of colour but resemble the *limborum strata* of meteorologists which effectually screen the sun altogether. However, as the Captain remarks, as long as it keeps cloudy we are likely to keep the breeze.

A brig was seen this morning, which, however passed, was to southward without notice. Ships, it appears, don't like to be put out of their way by curiosity, rarely even to get themselves reported. Yet our Captain wishes to procure provisions from the first who will sell us any, and should we

[101] *St Austin's oak tree – Complaints – Eau de Cologne*

meet none, then to call at the Azores. In fact, we are all earnestly looking out for something and find the voyage a tedious one, although all our available time has been fully employed.

His Grace is again poorly and languid, and we think that, if Dr Gregory had been, here he would not have known exactly what to have done with us, or to have managed for himself.

A white bird was seen of lofty and rapid flight resembling a hawk.

31 May

Sunday Lat 29°6' N; Long 36°36' W.

Pentecost Day. Owing to the wetness of the weather and the last night's blowing and rain, there was no public service. We had prayers together, however, as usual among ourselves in His Grace's cabin. Inter alia, the Sts lives – St Augustine of England and St Aldhelm.[187] It is remarked by Peach, who from his long residence in the vicinity of Worcestershire, had opportunities of learning local traditions, that the oak tree under which St Austin held his celebrated conference with the British Bishops is still in existence and about 6 miles from Worcester on the road of Hartelbury, an object, observes His Grace, worthy of being visited by a missionary.

187. The feasts of these saints occur on 25 and 27 May.

The Archbishop still poorly. This easterly wind gives him rheumatism, which is somewhat alleviated by the application of *Eau de Cologne* well rubbed into the affected parts.

The Major has the same complaint and suffers dreadfully between the shoulders, which a similar application relieves, but cannot cure effectively, he says, until a changed wind assists. The dampness of the weather, which becomes now again sensible since leaving the tropics and imbibed in the clothing, doubtless renders the body predisposed to cold and rheumatisms.

[102] *European sky – aqueous vapours condensing causing change of wind*

We look up at the sky and clouds with a degree of curiosity, as they wear an appearance, says the captain, quite European. The greatest difference appears to me in their altitude. which in Australia is apparently far greater.

The lengthened streaks or strata of watery clouds here appear to blend their own with the brighter azure of the sky and to combine both hues with that of the ocean, over which they cast a shadow of grey which is altogether peculiar and hightens the more soft and delicate tint of indigo, where in N.S.Wales the deficiency of vapour renders the atmosphere less blue, although its brighter sun reflects more gorgeous colours; more brilliant there but more diversified here are the heavens.

Hence also one cause of the partial and accidental winds called variables, where they are not overruled by the great current of the Trades; experiment teaching that one inch of water when evaporated will fill more than 2000 inches of space. 'And thus water falling in drops of rain possessed more than 2000 times the space when it floated in the atmosphere in vapours. This condensation occasioning vacuities causing winds of different kind and degrees.'

[103] *Madeiras – change from wet to dry – Portuguese Brig*

June

1st June Our Lat 31°12' N places us nearly abreast of the Madeiras, which extend from 30 to 32 N. Heavy showers of rain during which we are propelled at the rate of 7 kts and then lulled to 1 kt alternately, the wind veering to S.W. to W., and to S.W. again. When the thick masses of clouds broke and allowing the sun's rays to penetrate, under whose influence evaporation was sensibly accelerated, they soon became reduced to a fleecy, feathery cirrus foretelling a permanency of clear weather. The heavy rain had served to beat down the waves.

2nd June Lat 33°N; Long 34°W.

The early dawn brought to sight a sail, which bearing down came within hail at 9 o'clock, about breakfast time. She was desirous of comparing her longitude. Her name as well as we could make out was the 'Fidelio' from Brazil to Portugal, a fine built brig and of the tonnage of about 250T. It had no poop, but what is called a round house served the same purpose. They exposed a blackboard on which was figured their longitude; we did the same. The difference was but of a few miles. On withdrawing their board as a signal that they understood us, they proceeded on their course, the Senhoras in the brig no doubt wishing themselves in such a ship as ours that must have appeared to them as a castle on the waters, while their own pitched and rolled in a very unenviable style.

Scarcely had this one disappeared on the eastern horizon when another sail was perceived on the weather bow.

[104] *The Captain's dream – writing – H.G. [Henry Gregory] unwell*

It is remarkable that as we were walking the poop this morning, the Captain having related to us his dream of last night, it should now appear to turn out true. He had seen two vessels in his dream, one small and the other a very large one. Having now spoken the brig, should this other turn out a large ship or approach us, the Captain will no doubt profess himself a staunch believer in dreams, and that with some show of plausibility or experimental truth.

Engaged the whole day writing. completing the papers of the Synod, the order of the Synod, as per *Chronicle*, translated to Latin[188] – a general account of the Mission and exposition of its wants; letters to some bishops in Belgium &c &c; Archbishop finished his 'Status' about Hobart Town[189]; and a variety of other work.

The Captain and mates occupied in taking a Lunar in 59 sets of observations. The calculations completed gave for our present longitude 34°15' W.

As we sat down to dinner the ship we had seen proved indeed to be a large ship sailing from N.W towards S.E. She disappeared on the weather quarter and the Captain of course alluded again to his dream.

His Grace again unwell; was obliged to leave the dinner table as I sat with him and speaking of Dr Gregory. His Grace remarked how in a letter to Mr Heptonstall he had said (long after having apprised him of his sending Dr Gregory to England) that now 'somebody will go by the Ratcliff in place of somebody', meaning himself instead of Dr G.

[105] *Porpoises – birds*

3rd June Lat 36°8' N; Long 32°41' W

Ward, the 2nd mate, gets a second rating in the Log for 'skylarking'.

---

188. The First Provincial Council and Synod of Australasia was held at Sydney during September 1844. Archbishop Polding, in announcing to Cardinal Fransoni his imminent departure for Rome, stated that he would be bringing with him 'the Canons, Acts, Decrees, Admonitions of the Council of the First Synod of this our Province of Australia' to be 'placed at the feet of the Most Holy Father'. (Polding to Fransoni, 29 January 1846 [*Polding Letters* II.51]).
See *Morning Chronicle*, 28 September 1845.

189. Polding composed a letter to Bishop Willson of Hobart Town, written 'on board ship Ratcliffe near the Azores', apologising for the tone of earlier letters regarding the Therry controversy. He commented on the voyage: 'Our voyage, which we hoped to be short, has already exceeded the term expected. We are now becalmed 5 days near the Azores. I enjoy my leisure exceedingly and feel not the lassitude and tedium of which my fellow passengers continually complain' (Polding to Wilson, n.d. circa June 1846 [Polding Letters II.53–54]). The date of 2 June can now be confidently assigned to the letter. Mail was transferred from the *Ratcliff* to a pilot boat in the Channel on 22 June (see 121 infra).

We were amused by the sight of a shoal of about 40 or 50 porpoises, who disported on the billows for some time. They were joined by some stragglers, who came up cutting their way through the water with the celerity of race horses. Some occasionally leaped fairly out of water apparently 2 or 3 feet above the surface, when the form and colour of the *delphinus phocoena* was distinguishable with its horizontal tail and lacerated dorsal.[190] Their length was about 6 feet and colour dark brown or ferruginous.[191] They roll and plunge head foremost in the deep. A single wave or watery hill appeared of sufficient extent to contain them all without crowding, as emus and kangaroos are seen feeding in a herd on the declivity of a mamalordal hill on some sequestered and undulating opening in the bush.[192] The sailors endeavour to spear one and for that purpose station themselves with a harpoon on the bows and bowsprit. The fried liver well cleaned of fat is esteemed.

Two birds were seen about the size of pigeons, probably the *Upupa Epops* (Lina[eus]) if so the *coccis* in Spanish, so called on account of the note peculiar to it – their colour of a yellowish brown underneath tail feathers white and black.[193] It is described by Osbeck, who was surprized to see them out here; they being a common gull in Sweden.

4th June Lat 37°14' N; Long 32°30' W

Our progress is towards the southernmost of the Azores; uncertain yet whether we may touch thither or not, meanwhile

[106] *rolling – storm flood and inundations*

we advance at the rate of 3 kts; from that down to zero as we lay becalmed now and then.

The ship rolls heavily and with a sickening and unequal motion. This effect is owing to the want of a breeze to steady her and to the hight

190. *Delphinus phocoena*: a North Atlantic species of porpoise.
191. *Ferruginous*: reddish brown or rust-coloured.
192. *mamalordal*: perhaps nonce word for 'breast shaped'.
193. *Upupa Epops:* the Eurasian hoopoe.
Coccis: Spanish for coccyx from the Greek word for the cuckoo bird. It has been speculated that the name was applied to the tail-bone because of its fancied resemblance to the beak of this bird.

of the waves also, though no longer indeed the quick and bounding waves with rugged crests of a mile in length and lined throughout with a thick frothing and angry spray. They seemed yet just as full but more languidly expanded and more tardily formed and hence this sluggish rise and fall and alternate roll and pitch, slow and heavy, of the ship.

But what few have witnessed, we had the opportunity of contemplating now – a violent squall of wind and rain and at a short distance off only, without feeling its effects or coming any more in contact with it than a spectator looking on at an ordinary water spout. At first dark masses were seen that hung in various points. They shortly united and formed an impenetrable darkness relieved at one moment by the glare of lightning and the next by the vivid colours of a double rainbow. Then from the effects of the winds or rain or agitation of the waters individually or altogether, the sound of the rain on the surface and of the breaking of the waters into lines of foam was distinctly audible and at the distance of not more than a half or quarter of a mile broad travels of froth and spray like the windings of many rivers of unequal breadths were seen

[107] *Becalmed – the 'Jolly Robins' – Send a boat*

to extend and to lengthen to the right and to the left and all flowing in channels leading in various directions, like a country inundated by the overflowing of rivers and lakes of their muddy contents or as streams of lava pouring fast in all directions from the ignited crater of a volcano. And as the storm approached so these floods of agitated or effervescing froth increased in magnitude and roar, vying in fury with the rage of the storm above, which resembled a devastating typhoon from which we were separated but by a narrow belt of comparatively quiet and blue sea. It passed over and soon after at sunset. The electric clouds appeared far to windward and on our stern, but in activity still. Mother Carey's chickens were plentiful.

5th June Lat 37°14' N; Long 31°42' W

Early this morning a vessel appeared in sight standing the same tack with us. As the weather was calm, the Captain sent the boat in charge with the chief mate, the doctor accompanying and four men, together with the latest Sydney papers and a request to send us some black tea and fresh provisions to be paid for ready cash by the Captain' s own desire. The boat was 20 minutes reaching the ship and on its way seemed but a mere speck at times concealed by the large swell. On its return it was reported that the ship's name was the *Jolly Robins* Number 4526, Captain Beverly, 371 tons and 125 days from Calcutta.[194] They sent us half their provisions, 5½ pounds of black tea, with two bottles of cognac, and requested in return some green tea and some tins of flour. Captain Beverly had been all that time at sea without having sighted or spoken one vessel and was quite impatient and eager to reach home or speak with someone and get some news.

[108] *Write home by Jolly Robins – Her successful voyage*

Our latest news which we gave him was about New Zealand, the arrival of Gov[erno]r Grey there and the quelling of the disturbances between the colonists and natives.[195] And the news we received in return was that the British had taken Lahore and the territory of the Punjab; that the Govr. General with 50,000 troops occupied the frontier; the death of General Sale and as related in the 'Englishman' and

194. The *Jolly Robin* was still plying the Plymouth-Calcutta route in 1848 (*Morning Chronicle* [London], 3 March 1848, 8).

195. Sir George Grey (1812–1898) was a British soldier, explorer, colonial administrator. He was Governor of South Australia, from 1841 to 1845, when he was appointed Governor of New Zealand, serving from 1845 to 1853, and from 1861 to 1868.

Military Chronicle of last January.[196] The Sydney shipment of horses had failed, being ill provided with provisions.[197]

At noon the boat was ordered on a 2nd trip and the provisions requested were forwarded. Meanwhile we wrote letters – His Grace to Mr. Heptonstall and I to my friends. On the return of the boat we were informed that should the calm continue we might expect captain Beverly for dinner. The stores brought consisted of a ham, a bag of chalotts, some preserved fish, a bottle of pickle and some rice, all which was very acceptable.

The price of freight being very high at the time Captain Beverly left Calcutta, he has made an excellent return voyage. His vessel is registered 371 tons, but he has taken on board 500 at the rate of £6.10 per ton, which gives the sum of upwards £3,000. Our vessel of upwards of 600 tons will not receive, though fully laden, a larger sum, freight being much lower in Sydney. Indeed, Captains generally find it to their advantage to proceed even in ballast from Sydney to India to take in cargo when homeward bound.

6th June Out lat. and long. nearly the same as yesterday having advanced only 6 miles in the 24 hours. Towards noon the wind sprang up but contrary, being N.N.E. The weather, however,

[109] *a water spout – The Sunday Sermon*

is fine and promises to bring breezes. In the course of the day we saw the forming of a water spout. A long strip of white cloud hung downwards floating in a wavy line like a streamer of a man-of-war;

---

196. Field Marshal Henry Hardinge (1785–1856) was Governor-General of India from 1844 to 1848. In 1844 in the First Sikh War he waived his right to the supreme command, offering to serve as second in command under Sir Hugh Gough. He concluded the campaign with the Treaty of Lahore in March 1846. The following month he was created Viscount Hardinge of Lahore.
Major-General Sir Robert Henry Sale (1782–1845) was killed in action during the Anglo-Sikh War in December 1845. The town of Sale in Gippsland, Victoria, was named after him.
197. The exportation of horses from Australia to India began as early as 1835. It received a boost in 1845 following a visit of officers of the East India Company in search of mounts for the army (*Morning Chronicle*, 1 February 1845). In January 1846, there was a set-back following a significant loss of horses in transit on four vessels (*The Star*, 24 January 1846).

a somewhat similar process was carried on the surface of the ocean. A cloud-like substance appeared coiling itself encircling a vast extent and occasionally raising its head, until it seemed to uprear half its body, which reached midway to the cloud, as huge a creature as the celestial dragon that separates the two bears. It was the spirit of the deep and it realised all those ancient fables of sea snakes and dragons. Already you imagined the air filled with its dreadful hissings, and that you saw it brandishing from its mouth its forky tongue. With reason it was dreaded that by an immense leap it would shortly entangle the ship in its winding folds.

7th June

Sunday Lat 38°32' N; Long 32°50' W

Trinity Sunday. Divine Service at the usual time and place; the sermon on Christian holiness. The principles from which His Grace drew the general conclusion, that the life of every Christian ought to be holy, were briefly laid down and supported by passages from St Paul. The pretexts or excuses for not leading a holy life, arising from the false notion of the nature of holiness from the state and condition of life, from the difficulty of leading a holy life, were each and all exposed and confuted. After this a general exhortation to aspire after holiness by reason of the facilities given

[110] *floating timber – birds – railroads in Australia – and steam to Sydney*

of the certainty of success if the same earnestness be given as it is in temporal pursuits – the happiness prepared as a reward and from the present consolation which never fails to accompany a life of piety.

A piece of timber was observed as we were walking on the Poop, supposed to be the mast of some ship from the hoops and other indications about it. It is observed that we have now seen all that constitutes a shipwreck – the body of a dead man floating, a boat filled with water and a large spar or mast.

Some birds were seen called by the sailors 'Boatswains'.[198] They made the circuit of the ship and afterwards disappeared.

198. *Boatswain bird*: white-tailed tropic-bird so called as it makes a call similar to that of sailors.

Hicks lost one of his Australian birds, the Rosella. Its cage being left open, it flew up mast high when the flaps of the sail brought it down on the ocean.

The conversation on railroads talked of in Australia shown that they could not be successful when the population did not amount to 200,000; steam to Sydney a better speculation, as already shown.

8th June Lat 39°6' N; Long 33°47' W.

Calms and light winds. A calm at sea is proverbially tedious. Those however who had leisure did not experience a feeling of that kind as the entire morning might have been passed in observing the wonders of the deep. Soon after breakfast, apparently attracted by the offal of a pig thrown overboard, six or seven fish of a large kind supposed to be dolphins gamboled close astern. The attention was next directed to the appearance at a considerable depth of an animal vermiform judged to be from 12 to 15 feet in length and in diameter about 5 inches. This was presumed

[111] *a calm – Fish – Snakes – Sea worms – reach the Azores*

to be a sea snake. Its colour was opaque, dark blue on the back with yellow stripes and stars on the sides. After this, many were seen of various sizes. The [*****] snakes seldom reach a length of 5 feet. Their bite, it is said, is mortal, but we do not hear of snakes in these latitudes, although Arisotle indeed says 'serpentes marinos in terra aliquando degere posses', as if they were common in his time.[199]

We observed likewise innumerable worms, leech-like in form and of all sizes, transparent, opaque, of a light-grey and tipped with red at the extremities,

Vast numbers of Medusae were constantly floating past near the ship.

Small fish also about 18 inches in length with fins large and long, besides smaller fry in shoals. A piece of wood floated by loaded with barnacles was attended by a large troop of these small fish seemingly on the look out to catch a barnacle that might loose its hold. While the sly dogfish was seen lying in wait under the wood to seize the first

199. 'you are able sometimes <to find> marine serpents dwelling on land.'

of the latter that would appear off his guard.[200] Soon after midday a breeze sprung up.

9th June Lat 40°48' N; Long 30°50' W.

A steady breeze now took us at the rate of 8 kts in a N.E. course. Through a sea of deep blue, whose waves were crowned with a snow-white froth, a swell appears travelling from the east and another from the direction of the Western Islands. These, says Condor, form 3 separate clusters and are of volcanic formation about 800 miles from the western shore of Portugal, to which country they belong, and were called by them a*zor*, *azor* signifying a falcon from the number of Goshawks found on them.[201]

We have now rounded these islands and expect to reach the Downs in 10 days. And our tract is laid across a few rocks and islands said to exist and marked as doubtful on the charts, but whose existence Captain Gilbert denies.

10th June Lat 42°18' N; Long 30°20' W; a dull, damp and dreary day.

Our breeze of yesterday continued in unabated vigour till about 2 o'clock a.m.

[112] *painting of ship – Festival – Remembrance of our friends in Sydney – sighted two ships*

When the wind suddenly headed us and a great bustle ensued, all hands were summoned. The chief mate being ill, the Captain went on deck. A calm succeeded and what little air was stirring was put in motion from all points of the compass. No observation could be taken. Towards evening the breeze freshened, but not favourably. Many of our passengers seem much depressed by reason of the delay and annoyed by the perishing of the ship, another ingredient in the compound of villainous smells. A ship is seen on the larboard bow N.W. tract.[202]

200. *Dogfish*: small bottom-dwelling sharks that often appear in schools and prey chiefly on fish and invertebrates.

201. Josiah Conder (1789–1855), though never having travelled outside Britain, compiled the thirty volumes of *The Modern Traveller: a description, geographical historical and topographical of the various countries of the globe in thirty volumes* (London, 1834) and in the same year the single volume *Dictionary of Geography, Ancient and Modern*.

202. *larboard*: archaic term for port.

11 June Lat 43°11' N; Long 27°54' W Corpus Christi.

Wind favourable; the day damp and dreary and we would have been on land to celebrate this great festival. We united ourselves in spirit with our more happy brethren and heard Mass in union with the inhabitants of the Azores, whose longitude we have not yet passed.

The last of Mrs. Plunket's pastilles was consumed whilst we recited Vespers and Compline. We had also our little agape, wherein we partook almost for the last time of the bounty of our good friends. The nuns provided us with coffee, which even now may be called good, though its flavour has somewhat altered – the rasberry jam also provided by them-Mrs Plunkett's excellent ginger and our little feast concluded with Mrs. Harnett's gingerbreads and Mrs. Milford's wine, which is excellent.

We came up this day about 2 o'clock p.m. with a brig. She proved to be the 'Milman' of Belfast bound to Liverpool from Arica 68 days. Arica, whose situation somewhat puzzled us, is found to be on the western coast of America, latitude 19°S., but there must be some other part of that name nearer home.[203]

[113] *porpoises gamboling—A Calm – sea worms again – their variety*

Another ship was seen also on our starboard bow, following the same course E.N.E, as ourselves and is supposed to be our friend the *Jolly Robins.*

12th June Lat 44°20' N; Long 25°25' W

The day has been beautiful in every sense, a vast number of porpoises about the same hour 5 p.m. as yesterday; again they gamboled about the vessel. These animals appear the happiest in the creation. One would think they could not contain the exuberance of their spirits. They troop along sometimes in and other times half out of the water, sometimes in a body, then broken up into detachments like well mounted cavalry on a field day. This evening they were attended by a vast flight of birds, at which, as these skimmed over the crests of the waves, they leaped playfully or for a more serious purpose. They sprung but ineffectually if they intended to catch them.

203. *Arica*: a port city on the northern coat of Chile.

[204]

Our course yesterday lay directly over the rocks distinguished in the charts as Greave's Rocks, thus proving their non-existence, yet from the numbers of birds of short flight, which we have seen yesterday and today, the existence of some resting place in the vicinity may be rationally surmised.

13th June Lat 45°33' N; Long 23°30' W.

To the sad discovery of our impatient passengers the breeze died away into a calm about 2 o'clock am. Since then we have scarcely proceeded through the water at the easy rate of 2 kts per hour. We again amused ourselves looking on as the various fish and gelatinous substances floated slowly past. Their multitude and variety as they passed at different depths was astonishing – some small and pellucid with coloured snouts, others soft, smooth and slimy, creeping and clasping and contracting,

[114] *Divine Service*

their bodies – others emitting a purple colour, others of a rounded form with convex back and transparent, with fangs or tentacles, some of no colour but of the purest crystal jelly and others again ornamented with rays and divises in the form of a purple cross, probably varieties of the Medusa and Holothurian kinds.[205]

---

204. In ancient art Cupid, the god of desire, is often found riding a dolphin, an image that may represent the soul's journey.

205. Varieties of jellyfish and sea-cucumbers.

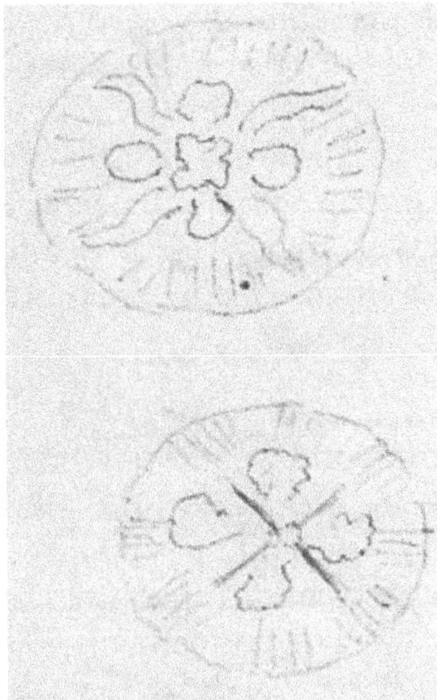

[jellyfish markings]

Towards evening the wind veered round to the south and gradually increased to a 5 knot breeze.

His Grace has written four letters on the voyage and passage out for the use of Missionaries.

14th June Lat 46°53' N; Long 21°51'

Sunday – Divine Service: the sermon on the Gospel of the day and 'There is a way that seems the good one'. Two great truths were familiarly explained of the mercy of God and of man's rejection of it under various pretexts. The mercy of God in his solicitude for man's salvation shown in the apostrophe our saviour makes to the impenitent Jerusalem,[206] in the parables of the prodigal son, of the good Shepherd, of the woman who searches her house for the lost coin, and how then it is that so many are lost from many presuming so far on that mercy, God at last withdraws his mercy, lest additional favours increasing responsibility, increase also damnation by the neglect made of them, and also by the delusion many fall into by a falsely formed conscience, there being a way that seemeth to man right, which leadeth unto death.

206. *apostrophe*: a form of direct address to a personified object.

These latter adopt false maxims, they take not the Gospel but self–love for their guide and seeing so many about them acting under a similar influence they consider themselves safe. Yet the example of the world is in itself a most grievous delusion of that world for which Christ prayed not, which we have promissed to renounce for it is seated in wickedness. This we are told to belong not to; this we are told not to love, yet Christians exhort each other to love their world

[115] *Substance of Sermon*

and say if we are in the world we must live like the world, and thus many are deluded into the life of the world, a life of idleness and sensuality, the life of the senses, unfit indeed for the disciples of a crucified God, and [**]ffling which with effect did His Grace apostrophise his audience: 'Thus may there not be many among you, many who have already determined to make up, as they call it, the restraints of a ship's life by indulgences on shore, and have not those better disposed been laughed out of their good purpose by the remarks of their companions.'

Thus enlarging one after the other on the various excuses offered by worldlings not to comply with the invitation of Heaven and showing how these excuses in many instances were made to appear plausible and even justifiable in themselves according to the text, that there is [a] way which appears to men to be good, but which leads unto death. It was next shown how even the most important affairs of life dwindle into insignificance and are mere child's play compared to the securing of one's salvation and to which all the rest should be only subordinate, not however, as he had remarked to them before, that the duties of life were to be neglected. On the contrary, as on their fulfilment likewise, as duties of one's state of life, salvation depended. His Grace concluded the 1st part almost in the words of St Chrisostom to St Austin when he enquired of him concerning the customs of the ancient Britons[207] – 'Enjoy yourselves ashore, but let it be after an innocent and godly sort in sobriety and in peace, in the bosom of your families or amongst your real friends. But do not plunge your immortal souls, created to enjoy happiness more pure and holy, into the excesses of

207. It was Pope St Gregory who advised St Augustine of Canterbury how to deal with the customs of the British Christians.

brutal drunkeness and in the low filthiness of impure cravings. Throw not away your hard-earned wages. If you have money to spare, have you not aged parents to whose comfort even a very little would add; younger brothers and sisters whom you might enable to commence a career, which might lead to independence? At all events lay up something for old age and the days of ill health and infirmity – surely better do so than to give up your money to those who have no care for you and who, when you have been sufficiently cheated, would kick you out of doors.' With regard to the delusion

[116] *Conversation – advantages of a sea voyage*

of false repentance, which was briefly and forcibly exposed, the nature of true repentance was elucidated and shown to be something more than a mere form of words, and in conclusion, all were exhorted to trust in God, but not to allow rash confidence to generate the three general causes of the condemnation of man: groundless presumption, the illusions of a falsely formed conscience and insincere repentance.

The advantages of a sea voyage are made the matter of conversation that people nowadays have little reason to exaggerate the discomforts of the sea, seeing the modern improvements, which make the travel of ocean as safe and pleasant to those who traverse it as the terrors of Neptune have lost their dark mystery by a more familiar acquaintance with them, and it has been proved that a voyage now a days is conducive to health and to the invigoration of the man mentally and physically. It was very well in days of old when ships could scarcely withstand one storm without being compelled to put into port for repairs. Thus Barré gives us an account of passengers and crew having started for America in 1557, and being obliged to put into port after a few days rough weather in the Channel. He saw most of them make off and abandon their design. They had experienced a bad day's storm and illustrated the proverb 'mare vidit et fugit' – they saw and took to their heals. In those days and as far back as the times of Anarcharis[208] it was doubted indeed whether they were to be reputed living or dead who committed their lives to the winds and seas, for such was the opinion of that philosopher – and Juvenal differed not from him when he says:

208. *Anacharsis*: sixth century BC Scythian philosopher.

> 'I nune et ventis animam committe,
> dolato confisus ligno, digitis a morte
> remotus quatuor aut septem.'[209]

The same timorous sentiments the world, says Macaulay, had wanted such spirits as Columbus, Cortesus or Drake and others who brought one hemisphere to some

[117] *The passengers their education*

acquaintance with the other.[210]

One great advantage in our case, it was remarked, was being conveyed in a 4 or 5 monthly voyage to see once more our native land and friends. One remarks how pleasant to meet again with a father and mother after years. Another alludes to the indulgence of his mother, and that mothers generally are over-indulgent to their boys as fathers are with their daughters. The Doctor thinks that Hick's mother allowed him always his own way, adding that he had a mother who had always kept him in high order. The Major quotes some saying to the effect of bringing up children the way they should walk etc. He had unfortunately lost his mother at the age of 13 and was sent in the army – a pretty provision indeed to be there without money or interest to obtain promotion. The Doctor is of a different opinion and says it is sufficient to give a child a good education and to have right principles instilled into him, that he should then be sent adrift to make his way in the world for himself. Another, without going so far, thought that any situation or employment suited to the time of life of the candidate presented its difficulties and hardships, that moral principles alone could help to overcome. 'It is quite true'. says the Major, 'and it agrees also with what the Archbishop presented to us this morning, that it was not so easy, even with regard to our salvation, that we require to be taught and to be instilled right principles to learn self-denial. For that, if we did not, after repentance came so late, it was not so easy then, after a bad life; for that it was not sufficient to say merely that one repented or to repeat a few prayers, but that much

209. 'Go now, and commit thy life to the winds, trusting to a hewn plank, four or seven fingers thick.' (Juvenal, *Satires*, xii, 57.)

210. Thomas Babington Macaulay (1800–1859), British historian and politician.

more was required, or that it would not be true, that "narrow is the path and difficult is the way, and few there are that find it".

The boy Fergusson got the strapado and being sent to the mast head for the day for obstinacy and disobedience of orders.

15 June Lat 48°14' N; Long 18°59' W; the day cold; our advance at 5 kts only.

A current sets in from the E.N.E of 1 mile per hour.

Five sails appear in sight, so numerous indeed are they beginning

[118] *(boy strapado'ed) – sails in sight – picturesque sky – a shark*

now to appear that we shall by and by take no more notice of them.

Our sunset was admired. The sea, the clouds, the colours which tinted them and the sky above was as soft and charming as the prettiest steel engraved vignette could have represented them.

In looking over our Sydney papers and some Irish and English ones we find that our latest English news is 9 months back. Captain Cook relates that he was over 2 years without hearing from home.

16th June Lat 48°58' N; Long 16°13' W.

We are gliding almost imperceptibly through the water. The raw air from the easterly quarter has yielded to the bland south-west and under its influence we are apparently settling into a calm. Three vessels in sight. One of these supposed to be the 'St George', which was to have left Sydney 3 days after us.[211] Tomorrow perhaps will decide the problem. One Mother Carey's chicken visited us today – *hoc rara inter maria avis.*[212]

17th June Lat 49°25' N; Long 13°56' W; a dull gloomy day.

A dense fog accompanied us and shifted the wind; to be feared it may last some days and that then the weather may be fine and no wind. The dullness of the day towards evening was somewhat enlivened by

211. The *St George* sailed from Sydney on 22 February 1846 with 24 passengers and colonial produce.

212. *Hoc rara inter maria avis*: 'this <a> rare bird <to be> found at sea'.

the report of a shark cruizing about the vessel. It was of a dark colour, about 7 feet long; a hook was thrown over with a half–pound of pork attached, but without success. He was seen several times during 3 hours.

18th June Lat 49°23' N; Long 13°50' W.

This morning it was found that we had been moved out of our calm by a foul wind. Our course was sometime south. About 11 a.m. the wind worked round to the N.W. Since

[119] *Fish – sails in sight – hailed by a Scillonian*[213] *– outer soundings*

then we have a 3 or 4 knot breeze. About 2 p.m. we spoke an American ship of magnificent size, supposed to be a Liner. We see on each side of us many vessels apparently homeward bound. The sight of these vessels is very pleasing. We all, however, long to reach the end of our passage, hence it grows very tedious, too much so indeed. The shark that was playing about the ship yesterday evening was seen again this morning. Porpoises also are very numerous, feeding on medusae that appear to be floating very thick and in great variety. A slight change in the colour of the water is perceptible, tho' we are in the 13° of longitude. This must be attributed to our high northern latitude, as sounding extends considerably more to the westward on the northern side of the approach to the Channel.

19th June Lat 49°16' N; Long 11°38' W

Feast of the Sacred Heart which we fondly hoped to celebrate on shore. We have entered soundings; numerous vessels are seen around us all day; at this moment 11 are in sight. The sun set magnificently in colours of rose and amber. Five ships on the horizon appear black from the contrast of the light behind; they float in calm repose. We were apprehensive in the morning that our breeze, as light as it was, would either have left us or yielded to a N.E., judging from the heavy bank of cloud in that direction. However, after breakfast our breeze freshened and has carried us along briskly. The current from the N. was very perceptible this morning. Our longitude, reported to be

213. *Scillonian*: inhabitant of the Scilly Isles.

11°30' by chronometer and 11°6' by lunar, places us as far west as the western coast of Ireland, with a difference of 40 minutes in time between ourselves and London. We are hailed by a small craft, cutter rigged, about the size of the Plymouth trawlers. They come out thus far to accost the homeward bound ships and perhaps to traffic and smuggle their news and vegetables for tobacco and other things. This one was a pilot or fisherman from Scilly. Toward evening we were hailed by

[120] *Sails – Steamers – Man–of–war – Templar*

another of the craft, who cryed out 'Stop her! Stop her!' to the infinite amusement of the Mate, Mr. McIntosh, at this good Scillonian's hail.

20th June Lat 49°26' N; Long 8°40' W

We sailed almost side by side ½ mile apart of another ship for some hours, yet with telescopes, owing to the obliquity of the visual angle, the name was not to be made out. Some read 'L'Acceuil', others 'Blanche', others 'Punch'. And it was not worthwhile signalizing. She was a bark of about 300 tons that at last got ahead of us. The passengers on board were easily distinguishable. Next appeared a steamer. Though the appearance of the clouds told a flattering tale about the continuance of our breeze, yet the experienced eye saw indications that it was on the decline. This became perceptible soon after noon and we are now just moving through the waters. We shall deem ourselves fortunate to reach the Scilly Islands tomorrow instead of the Lizard, as we expected. The heat is apparently as great as that ordinarily experienced in N.S. Wales.

Let this day be marked, says His Grace, for Aye in the calendar, inasmuch as a Templar bold on a hapless rat, a tale has told fitting a valiant cat – in plain prose Templar, to the great edification of the ship's crew, who were spectators of the feat, killed a rat which started unexpectedly from a heap of rubbish in the forecastle.

Commenced a novena for the Archbishop's intention.

21st June Lat 49°10' N; Long 8°5' W

Sunday. At daylight, a ship which had been observed in the distance last night came up with us. It proved to be a Man-of-War carrying 28 or 36 guns. She approached as near as about 40 yards and exchanged flags. She had no name, Men-of-War only hanging their names astern in port. Owing to the variableness of the winds in these latitudes or rather to the bad humour of the Captain on account of the calms, we had no public service, and the remainder of the day we had foul wind in punishment.

[121] *Seaweed – a Pilot – The Lizard*[214]

There is a strong head sea, very unpleasant, bringing on us all premonitory symptoms of sea sickness. We are now sailing abreast of the French coast, a [****ss] for the Tower of Kreskere and the inhabitants of the chateau.[215] The Lizard may be about 100 miles ahead and the Scilly Islands in our neighbourhood. We notice seaweed drifting from the shores.

22 June Lat 49°40' N; Long 6°54' W

214. *The Lizard*: the most southerly promontory of England; the first land seen by ships on entering the English Channel.

215. As the *Ratcliff* approached the Channel, it passed between two coastlines familiar to Lewis, Brittany and Cornwall.

The morning opened gloomily enough; heavy dark clouds hung over the ocean, which heaved and heaved as if its last power of motion was about to expire. As the day advanced a little vessel might be observed here and there, and gradually the air once more took the form of wind. It was calculated at noon, though no observation could be taken, that we were 50 miles from the Lizard. When a glorious breeze sprung up which rapidly increased to 6,7 and 8 kts. Towards evening the dense clouds favoured us with heavy rain, which continued for some hours. About 7 o'clock a Cowes boat approached in the view of landing passengers and of taking the mail. Of the former none were disposed to accept his offer, and the vessel hove to for the purpose of delivering the latter. But the fellow most awkwardly dropped astern, not before however he had imparted the most satisfactory intelligence that we were just 13 miles E.N.E. of the Lizard, the revolving lights of which, we had the happiness to discern some few minutes afterwards.[216]

Lizard N. by W. 4 Leagues; 22 June, Monday at sun down

And like mariners of the olden time might well on first sight of land, after such a voyage, give thanks to God in strains of the *Salve Regina*, which seamen used in times of distress and joy alike, we were now about to embrace our friends.

[122] *The Channel*

The Captain now called out to turn her head to south east.

23 June The first dawn of light afforded us a glimpse of the coast. At 4 o'clock a.m. we were abreast of Plymouth, sailing over a short chopping green wave at the rate of 8 kts. Abreast of the Portland Bill at 4

216. The light of the Lizard lighthouse, built in 1751, on a clear night, could be seen 100 miles away.

o'clock, we could admire the appearance of the coast as far as Albans Head.[217] We continued favoured with the same breeze until beyond it, when at 1 o'clock p.m. the wind increased to a perfect gale. Its first effect was to tear away our stunsails. We were in sight of the Isle of White [Wight], part of which and the Needles we perceived more distinctly. A pilot attempted to arrive at us but had to put back.

At 9 O'clock p.m. Beachy Head came in sight and as the night set in the sea appeared more turbulent and the wild appearance of the sky and clouds foretold a blowing night.[218] Whoever approached the land after 4 months voyage without feeling figetty and sickly – *quis est hic et laudabimus eum*.[219] At all events we have moved from Cabin to Poop and from Poop to Cabin at least tenfold more frequently than is our usual wont. We have packed up and picked up and made some little progress in such matters, but as for the rest it must be acknowledged it has been a *dies non*.[220] In this humble acknowledgement we conclude our notion of it.

24 June A Happy feast to you.[221] At 5 o'clock this morning we came in view of Dungeness. Its low coast and sandy beach extended miles; its light house seems built of red brick.[222] The weather was somewhat moderated.

[123] *The Pilot*

In the morning and boats that appeared to have sought shelter during the night were seen making away from the land and making their course in all directions. One of these, the Pilot boat, reached us about 6 o'clock, and the Pilot, towing his boat, informed us of Sir Rob Peel's

217. *Portland Bill*: a narrow promontory at the southern end of the Isle of Portland, on which were located two lighthouses.
St Alban's Head: the most southerly part of the Purbeck peninsula.
218. *Beachy Head*: a chalk headland in East Sussex.
219. 'Who is he, and we may praise him?' (*Ecclesiasticus* 31, 9–11)
220. '*dies non*': day on which no business is conducted.
221. *June 24*: feast of John the Baptist.
222. *Dungeness*: a headland on the coast of Kent, England, formed largely of a shingle beach. Its lighthouse was built in 1792 and replaced in 1902.

quitting the Ministry.[223] The same Pilot boat conveyed ashore one of our passengers, Mr. Way.

No sooner had the pilot stepped on board than with the self-sufficiency of a Parker he issued his orders of: 'Set the jib there! Eh! Good morning Captain Gilbert. Why! Where did you get that set of lubbers you have there!' 'Surely', whispers the mate, 'these are the fellows that do know their business. But who that does not know that Pilots are the proudest, most tyrannical and self-sufficient set imaginable. They would be great in the eyes of a paltry boat's crew.' 'Put your helm to port!' was the next imperious mandate. 'Hey – Stuard bring me a glass of brandy and water. Here boy, fetch up that will you.' Unable to stand any longer the airs of this new personage, Templar, who had eyed my man for a few seconds, now ran at him and gave him a bite on the knee, which did not fail to bring down this puppyism-personified to something of the level of common man. The rebel dog, however, in the scuffle got imprisoned in a hen coop, while proud bouncing took the lesson quietly, lowered his pretensions, and tried what putting on civility would do.

I must add that a part only of the above took place. It was something, as we had fancied, must happen at the appearance of such a lordly person as a Pilot generally is. But ours was a different character – an elderly, mild and unassuming man, who led us on in good style, pointing out as we passed this and that interesting object on the shore.

We now steered in view successively of the 'Cinque Ports', Fokestone, Rye, Dover, Deal and Sandwich. But not to anticipate, here at Dungeness we were on the spot where

[124] *The Channel*

the flood, which enters the Channel from westward, comes in contact with the flood from the North Sea through the Straits of Dover and called the 'Meeting of the Tides'.

223. Sir Robert Peel (1788–1850) was a British statesman and Conservative Party politician who served twice as Prime Minister (1834–35 and 1841–46). After the outbreak of the Great Irish Potato Famine in 1845, his decision to join with Whigs and Radicals to repeal the Corn Laws led to his resignation as Prime Minister in June 1846.

At Dover we find ourselves back as it were in our east longitude again, i.e. on the Sydney side of Greenwich, and which we had left as we passed in sight of Antipodes Island, 115 days since. We breakfasted today in sight of Dover, looking on its castle, its railway trains, its new ranges of expensive houses, the pier, the steamers, the green fields and white chalk cliffs. A steamer is just starting for Calais.

An hour after breakfast we were near Deal; instead of high cliffs here is a long wavey sweep of lowland. We distinguish the flag floating, at all events, on Walmer Castle partially conceiled among trees. The town extends along the shore – presents as busy a scene as that afloat in countless boats and sails of every size. Here a boat from the shore brought letters to the Captain, who signalised his ship, whence by electric telegraph the arrival of the *Ratcliff* will be reported in London in one minute of time.

At 10 we approached the Goodwin Sands and South Foreland, and as we are informed an hour too late to take advantage of the tide; nevertheless, we push on.[224] It is broad daylight. What if we had been driven here by the gale in the dead of the night. Monstrous rollers are breaking into foam as they travel over the all-deceiving sands covering a tract of miles apparently ahead of us. Here we are told that the *St George* from Sydney has just passed before us.

Off Ramsgate and Broadstairs two steamers were racing who should come first. On one being hailed the other immediately left the field. The one engaged took us in tow; his charge was £25. Here the coast terminates again in chalky cliffs but of less

[125] *Up the Channel – Mouth of the Thames*

elevation than the cliffs of Dover. These towns are sheltered by trees and the high ground about them. But Deal and Sandwich seem spots more picturesque and the country around more fertile.

224. *Goodwin Sands*: a 16 km long sandbank lying 10 km off the Deal coast in Kent. Lying close to the major shipping lanes through the Straits of Dover, the Sands were the cause of many shipwrecks.
South Foreland: a chalk headland on the Kent coast; it presents a bold cliff to the sea and commands views over the Straits of Dover.

Holland Bay appears crowded with churches and steeples and towers, and gentlemen's seats. There are a few green buoys with the word 'wreck' printed on them in large characters to warn the passer-by to keep a good lookout.

At 1 o'clock p.m. we coast along the isle of Thanet – have a good view of Margate with its ancient church and new buildings rising around it. To the eastward the coast is low and inland the country appears diversified by patches of woodland, villages and steeples.

At 3 o'clock we reached Herne Bay having passed the Reculvers. Its church and hamlet, Herne Bay now a watering place, ages ago was covered by the ocean which formed once an estuary separating Thanet from the mainland. Corn now grows where then ships floated and citizens have here country houses. Our course is here over what is termed the 'Flats'. The captain overruling the hesitation of the pilot, who thought the tide too low to admit of our ship to pass over, determined to proceed, although other ships have dropped their anchors patiently awaiting another tide. We triumphantly rode over them and were now within 50 miles of Greenwich, towed on at the rate of 7 kts through squalls and heavy rains, when at 5 o'clock we reached the mouths of the Thames and Medway. Here vessels in countless numbers ply about in every direction on waters smooth and placid. The land appears low and well wooded. And now leaving the open sea we make towards this fairy lake, lined with woods and ships and towns and country villas, and watering places. Here is the 'Sea Reach'; nearer in the foreground appears Southend on the Essex side, the Isle of Sheppy, Shearness, the Nore – Sheppy is said to be rapidly encroached on by the sea, houses and property being

[126] *Anchor at Gravesend*

carried away by each successive storm. With the wind and tide against us we advance nevertheless at the rate of 5 kts, expecting to reach Gravesend by same night, from which we are yet 30 miles distant.

Some pilot boats here fasten themselves to our stern for the sake of a lift. We enter into conversation with them; they speak of the fine weather and season, the dearness of life, the fear for the potato crops.[225] His Grace tells that in N S Wales there is plenty of work for them and for every industrious man; that had they been there they would not now be complaining of want of employment and food there was cheap – meat a penny a pound, a quarter loaf 3d . They were surprised at our quick passage from the Lizard, and they pointed to a brig that had been 3 weeks working its way from Guernsey only.

As we advance we can but admire the gentle undulations of the land, the green hills, once more, and the woody valleys and sandy beaches and we listened to the sounds and busy hum of life wafted by the breeze from shore.

At 10 o'clock p.m. the landsman took his station on the larboard chains;[226] he swings out his line and calls by 'Mark five!', in his peculiar nautical accent. Night comes on with a sky overcast – dark and cold.

25 June At 1 o'clock a.m. dead of night, Ratcliff hailed by various parties. The paddle wheels of the towing steamer ceased their noise and the sounds of the anchor chain, as notch after notch it clanked against its iron stay, told us that we now at last lay anchored at Gravesend. But we were not left to sleep, for now arrived customs officers and other officers and functionaries, little respecting the sacredness of the hour consecrated to Morpheus and the God Selene.[227] They roused the Captain and startled him with earnest questions regarding desease on board: 'Did you communicate with any of the Mediterranean ships? You landed an invalid at Folkstone. It is reported you have sickness on board. How many invalids?' The quarantine regulations were talked of, but the captain soon pacified the whole troop, which departed at last.

At 8 o'clock we beheld the sun shining blithely on the buildings of Gravesend, the winding river, the

[127] *Up the Thames – Archbishop leaves ship*

trees and meadows and terraces and churches.

For breakfast was served fresh meat and fish, butter, eggs, milk and baskets of ripe red cherries, while a messenger from the *St George* came in to settle a bet with one of our passengers as to which of the

225. 1846, the second year of the potato famine, was the year when the crop blight became total in Ireland.
226. 'Landsman'-a sailor with less than a year's experience at sea.
227. *Morpheus*: a god associated with sleep and dreams

ships, the *St George* or the *Ratcliff* would first reach home.[228] It must be a drawn bet, for if they entered the river first we must reach London before them, as we have now two steamers at our service and they have none as yet. The wind blows with the strength of a gale and is on the increase, though the weather is clear and the tide is against us. Yet is curious of remark that we should have parted from the *St George* in the Sydney Harbour 130 days ago and travelled 16,000 miles, and this day have met at the rendezvous within one hour of time of each other.

At 9 o'clock the anchor was raised to the tune of 'Cheerily Oh! My hearties!', lustily sung with the stentorian voices, just as the Antwerp steamer passed by and as the Rochester and Chatham trains were making their appearance, arriving thence a distance of 30 miles in 20 minutes. Our progress was slow at first, even with the help of two steamers, but the *St George* we left astern.

Each bend of the river offered new beauties to the sight. Here were jetties lined with steamers and a busy population, buildings of great dimensions and country seats upon lovely banks sheltered by noble trees, where art had successfully combined with all the advantages of each, populous marts and quiet rural scenery side by side.

At 11 o'clock, while passing one of these jetties it was made among the passengers and Captain that they would take the first steamer plying upwards and make their way to Tower, leaving the ship in charge of her present pilots. No sooner thought than done, and it was with a tear of regret I saw them depart and assisted the Archbishop over the side of the ship. Not being so active and to avoid the hurry, I resolved to remain quietly on board until in the docks, when I should hear from His Grace and know whether to direct my steps quietly in a cab to our intended temporary residence in Manchester Square.[229] Thus bidding them adieu I waved my handkerchief to the Archbishop now on the steamer's deck.

At 2 o'clock reach Woolwich; here the river

228. The *St George* sailed from Sydney on 21 February, two days after the *Ratcliff*. Among the 73 passengers onboard the *St George* was Francois Xavier Prieur, one of the French-Canadian convicts returning home via England. In 1840 Polding had intervened with Governor Gipps to prevent the Archadians being sent to Norfolk Island.

229. *Manchester Square*: an elegant eighteenth century garden square in the Marylebone area of London.

[128] *Up the Thames – Greenwich*

is about ¾ of a mile in breadth, and we are about halfway between Gravesend and London. The country on the right bank extends in grassy plains as far as the eye can reach and dotted over with flocks of sheep and herds of cattle. On the left Woolwich, backed by hills, is diversified with country seats, green banks neatly trimmed and woody screens. The dock yard, a mile in length, is peopled with busy artificers. The arsenal and Foundry and The Laboratory, the Military academy, the Artillery barracks, Military hospitals, Marine barracks – buildings forming a magnificent range – present such a scene of busy employment as would bewilder the unhabituated. We proved a great annoyance to numberless small craft as working in short tacks by reason of the violence of the gale, and by reason of the great length of space we occupied. Two steamers, one before the other, connected with long hawsers and towing this unwieldy wool-laden Sydney ship. Here the 'Hirt' steamer among countless others passed us by with the rapidity of an arrow. An inscription on her side, 'From London bridge to Blackwall for 3d', distinguished her from others.

On our approach to Greenwich, steamers passed and repassed thicker than ever; their rate 10kts. The masts of vessels appeared to thicken like trees in a forest lining the river *a parte de vere.*

We pass 'Bow Creek', 'Shooters Hill' with its exercises of archery, 'The Mast House', a lofty tower used for the purpose of masting and demasting large ships, 'The East India Docks', the Blackwall railway, and come in sight of 'Greenwich Hospital', a palace occupying an extent of terrace of many hundred feet. A lofty dome covers what is called the painted hall completed by Christopher Wren. It provides, it is said, 3,000 inmates and supports a school of 500 children, and distributes besides annual sums to a great number of out-pensioners. Just behind the hospital is Greenwich Park and the Royal Observatory, from whence we reckon our meridian. Beautiful trees shade these abodes and the whole country indeed bears a park-like appearance.

Contending still with a hard gale, adverse tide and a feel of piercing cold, we urge on fire and steam, pass the Isle of Dogs, range along miles of wharfs

[129] *Up the Thames – London*

and warehouses, crowded with the busy scene of industry. It appears now but one continued line of life and activity and business increasing as the approach of the grand Emporium of the world – So as His Grace often remarked – here may be seen the difference of life and manners in this age and the ages of faith. In the latter were eminent minds far removed from darkness and superstition, who conceived the buildings of York Minster and of our ancient cathedrals – minds that exerted their influence around in elevating the thoughts of their fellow men to higher destinies. In the former current of thought and ambition runs horizontal in seeking ways and means of rapid communication with fellow creatures, all their pursuits alike horizontal and seeking the Earth for ultimate object and the means of sensual or external gratification and self-forgetfulness.

We now get a glimpse for the first time of 'St Pauls' from spot called 'The Pool'.[230] Here was pointed out to us the 'Bangalore', ship in which Governor Fitzroy performed his voyage to New Zealand, and now undergoing repairs.[231] Now the river, from the infinite number of the vessels of all description with their tapering spars and yards, resembles well those seas and bays in southern climates where you have to cut your intricate way through forests of mangroves trees that mantle the coast and extend into the waters and growing out of the muddy tide and shallow estuaries.

Thus appeared the City Canal, the West India Docks; over the Thames Tunnel, Rotherhithe, Wapping, and lastly London Docks, a scene of unequalled trade activity, amidst which at 3 o'clock p.m.

[130] *London – Archbishop – Dr Murphy – Mr H. – Farewell*

the Ratcliff gliding slowly through the entrance of the 'London Dock' was greeted from its quays by its anxious owners and a crowd of spectators and officials who soon found means of gently binding in a snug berth our wave-tossed weary ship.

230. 'The Pool' was the stretch of the Thames from Rotherhithe upriver to London Bridge, the farthest reach that could be navigated by a tall-masted vessel.
231. Robert Fitzroy, Governor of New Zealand (1843–45), was half-brother of Charles Augustus Fitzroy, Governor of NSW (1846–1855).

And where think you, Paul, were we two days after this? Why, in company with Dr Murphy himself, Bishop of Adelaide, to our surprize arrived in London the same week with ourselves;[232] we dined together – His Grace, Dr Murphy, Mr Heptonstall and some friends.

On the 29th of June, His Grace with myself called on Dr Griffiths, the Bishop of London, where his Grace went to say Mass for the Anniversary day (the 13th) of his consecration as Bishop of Hiero-Caesarea.[233] We prayed for you all (Archbishop and clergy of St Mary's and the Monastery) and trust that in return you will not omit to remember me in your daily prayers for your friends, that accomplishing God's holy will I may be again united to you, if not here for the present, in heaven.

And I remain, My Lord Archbishop, my dear Mr McEncroe, Dr Gregory [and Dr Gregory], Prior, and Subprior, President, Infirmarian, Antiphonarian,[234] Sacristan, Professed and Novices and Friends – Most respectfully and devotedly yours

J. Lewis Harding
London 29th June 1846

The End

---

232. Bishop Francis Murphy had sailed from Adelaide via the Cape of Good Hope on 9 February, a week before the Radcliff sailed via Cape Horn: 'CLEARED OUT: Monday, February 9th—The barque *John Heyes*, 370 tons, Woodward, master, for London. Passengers: Right Rev. Dr Murphy . . .' (*Adelaide Observer*, 14 February 1846, 6). The *John Heyes* arrived at London on 28 June.

233. Thomas Griffiths (1791–1847), a convert at the age of 14, had been Vicar Apostolic of the London district since 1836.
It was actually the 12th anniversary of Polding's episcopal consecration on 29 June 1834.

234. The Antiphonarian had a specific role in the monastic recitation of the Divine Office.

Appendix I
Documents and Correspondence relating to the 1835 Voyage

15 February 1834 Right Hon. E. G. Stanley to Governor Bourke[1]

(HRA XVII.371)

Downing Street
15 Feb. 1834

Sir,

I have received your Despatch Number 68 of the 21st August last, in which you state that you have submitted to the Legislative Council of New South Wales the inadequacy of the means at the disposal of the Government for affording Religious Instruction and Education to the Catholic Population in the Colony, and that the Council have, in consequence, voted the sum of £900 for the Salaries of Six Roman Catholic Chaplains, and a further sum of £600 towards the maintenance of Schools for Children of that religion. I entirely concur with you in opinion that the addition of four Chaplains to the number already employed is not greater than is required by the necessity of the case. Agreeing also with you in the extreme importance attached to the selection of Clergymen to be appointed, I have communicated

1. Right Hon. E. G. Stanley: Edward George Stanley (1799–1869), Secretary of State for War and the Colonies from April 1833 to June 1834. As Earl of Derby he served as Prime Minister - 1852, 1858–185, 1866–1868.
Governor Bourke: Dublin-born Major-General Sir Richard Bourke (1777–1855) was appointed Governor of New South Wales in March 1831 under the Whig administration of Earl Grey, November 1830 to July 1834. Bourke resigned in January 1837.

upon the subject with Dr Bramston, and I hope that no long time will elapse before they proceed to the Colony.[2]

I have etc.,
E. G. Stanley

6 March 1834 Right Hon. E. G. Stanley to Governor Bourke

(HRA XVII.389)

Downing Street
6 March 1834

Dear Sir,
With reference to my Despatch of the 15th Ultimo upon the subject of the additional Roman Catholic Chaplains, for whom provision has been made by the Legislative Council, I think it right to inform you that I have communicated a Copy of your Despatch (with certain omissions in the concluding part of it, as marked Extract) to Mr. Edward Blount, who has warmly interested himself in favour of the Catholic Community in the Colony[3] . . .

I remain etc.,
E. G. Stanley

26 April 1834 Bishop Bramston to Cardinal Pedicini[4]

(*Adjutor Deus* I. 7–8)

London
26 April 1834

Most Eminent Lord,

It is with great sorrow that I have been informed that there are in New Holland and in the island generally referred to as Van Diemen's Land more than twenty thousand Catholics the majority of whom

2. James Yorke Bramston (1763–1836), Vicar Apostolic of London District 1827–1836.
3. Edward Blount (1769–1843), from an old Catholic gentry family, was a Whig member of the House of Commons active in the cause of civil rights for Catholics. He played a conspicuous part in the campaign leading to the passing of the Catholic Emancipation Act in 1829.
4. Carlo Maria Pedicini (1769–1843) was Cardinal Prefect of Propaganda Fide from 1831 to 1834.

have been expelled from England for their crimes and who are now dispersed throughout the region and are longing greatly for the ministry of the Church. This will be clearer to your Eminence when you learn that throughout that entire region there are no more than four Catholic priests, only two of whom hold official status and enjoy a stipend granted by the respective governments. How great the need is for an increase in the number of priests became so clearly apparent to Sir Richard Bourke, the Governor of the Province, and also to those who constitute the Councils there, that the former earnestly appealed to the Minister of the Crown for the Colonies in England that another four Catholic clergymen be sent out to these regions without delay. On the suggestion of the Reverend Father Ullathorne, Vicar General of that Province, the Governor insisted to the Minister of the Crown in England that no one should be sent out who had not – to my surprise! – received my approval. It was also positively suggested to me that the clergymen to be sent should be Englishmen and the Minister for Colonies in accordance with this proposal asked me to choose four clergymen born in England.

Alerted by this petition, as I had no more among my own subjects whom I could send, I discussed this matter of such importance with John Birdsall, the very Reverend President of the English Benedictine monks, since I judged that, among the clergy of the Order, four could easily be found possessed of high qualifications and suitable for this ministry.

On account of the difficulty, or rather the impossibility, sufficiently proved from experience, of any adequate communication between the Island of Mauritius and New Holland, the President of the English Benedictine monks and the Superiors of that Order in England are led to the point of concluding, just as I do, that nothing can be arranged for the Spiritual ministry in New Holland unless a Vicar Apostolic is appointed, honoured with Episcopal character, who would live in that province, and preside over all ecclesiastical matters. I have put this suggestion to the Minister for the Colonies and I remain convinced that no objection could arise from any aspect of it. I have therefore taken it upon myself to write about this to your Eminence, asking, in all humility but not less earnestly, that the sacred Congregation for the Propagation of the faith might give this same advice to His Holiness. In order that this matter be better decided,

I indeed, both humbly and at the same time earnestly, recommend that the first Vicar Apostolic be John Polding, a monk of the Benedictine community in England. Perhaps your Eminence will not be too greatly surprised when you remember how he conducted himself when recommended by me as the best prepared of all and then destined for Madras. However, I was persuaded of this by the opinion stated by the President of the monks and the other Superiors of his Order, and by the reputation for learning, zeal and devotion he enjoyed among the monks, and also by my own acquaintance with him. All these qualities persuade me, even apart from the unfortunate business of the Vicariate of Madras (this business others think, and I am heartily in agreement, should be attributed indeed to the desire which he cherished for many years of dedicating himself to the salvation of souls in New Holland and so he was reluctant to have his life diverted into any other channel) that he has been trained in everything which would be wished for in Vicar Apostolic with episcopal character in Nee Holland. I am convinced that this would be found very acceptable to the Ministers of the Crown.

The spiritual need which in New Holland sadly prevails everywhere does not permit of any delay. The worthy President has now informed me that there would be little hope of gaining the consent of his subjects to leave their homeland for New Holland unless a new Vicariate is set up there, and all those who are prepared to undertake the work desire to have the Reverend John Polding as their ecclesiastical superior in those regions. Therefore I most humbly and most assiduously solicit that, as soon as possible, through Your Eminence's efforts, the Reverend John Polding be appointed Vicar with episcopal character in New Holland.

I am holding the brief by which this worthy priest was to be raised to the see of Hiero-Caesarea which I received when it was Your Eminence's intention of sending him to Madras. If the sacred Congregation agrees, it is possible for me to apply the Brief by which he was to be named Bishop of Hiero-Caesarea to his consecration and then I could deliver it to him with all the Faculties which would be granted to him from the sacred Congregation for the Apostolic government of new Holland and the island generally known as Van Diemen's Land.

I pray God to keep Your Eminence safe and well for long years.
+James Bishop of Ursulo and Vicar Apostolic in the District of London.

17 May 1834 Cardinal Pedicini to Bishop Bramston

(*Adjutor Deus* I. 6–7)

Rome
17 May 1834

Most Illustrious and Most Reverend Lord,

With great joy we received your Lordship's letter of 26 April in which you stated that a great opportunity was being offered to establish an Apostolic Vicariate in New Holland and Van Diemen's Land. Thus will be accomplished just what was so long desired, namely that the many thousands of Catholics living in that vast region may be reinvigorated by the presence of a Pastor and by the increased number of priests he will be able to bring with him and so they will find more easily and more abundantly the means of salvation. Their spiritual needs could not be justly met by the Apostolic Vicar in the Island of Mauritius on account of the extremely great distance and the great lack of ministers with whom he is working. It was most gratifying to hear from you that Reverend Father John Polding, a monk of the Benedictine Congregation who has so earnestly refused the Apostolic Vicariate of Madras to which he was already elected, has for long years ardently desired to devote himself to the salvation of souls in New Holland and so has been equipped with all that is needed for the erection in that region of an Apostolic Vicariate with episcopal character. Without any delay petition has been made to His Holiness that he would graciously entrust to the worthy monk the Office of Apostolic Vicar in New Holland and in the Island generally known as Van Diemen's Land. His Holiness after rightly reviewing this request, has graciously consented to the prayers of the Sacred Congregation and to your petitions and has ordered the Apostolic Letter to be dispatched. The Brief by which the worthy priest was at that time elected to the See of Hiero-Caesarea when he was named Apostolic Vicar of Madras is in your hands. By force of that Apostolic Brief you will be able in the meantime to consecrate him Bishop of Hiero-Caesarea and make the arrangements necessary for the Prelate and his fellow-workers to embark for New Holland. I hope shortly to send you the Apostolic Letter for the said Vicariate together with the granting of the faculties required for the New Vicar Apostolic and I pray God to keep Your Lordship safe and happy for long years.

Amplitudinis Tuae Uti Frater Studiosissimus,
C. M. Cardinalis Pedicini, Prefectus.
A. Maius, Secretarius.

May 1834 Bernard Ullathorne OSB[5]

(Ullathorne, *Autobiography*, pp 88–89)

In May, 1834, my old Novice-master, Father Polding, was appointed first Bishop of Sydney by Gregory XVI. He undertook to provide the other three priests applied for, and the four received the usual passage and outfit provided by Government. Meanwhile Lord Stanley had replied to my letter, not only approving my application, but adding that, should our wants increase, he would be happy to attend to any further recommendation supported by the Governor of the Colony. Not long after, Sir Richard Bourke received a letter from Lord Stanley announcing the appointment of the four priests, one of whom, Dr Polding, was invested with the dignity of a bishop. He then expressed his regret at my being superseded, and proposed that I should go to Hobart Town with the same stipend.[6] When Sir Richard read the letter to me, I laughed, and said: 'Your Excellency will understand our ways better than Lord Stanley. I should be of material use to the Bishop in the beginning. Let him take the stipend of £400 a year which you recommended for the Vicar-General, and let me take the ordinary stipend of a priest.' 'Well,' he said, 'there is no other man in the Colony who would have made such an offer.' So I remained in my old position, and the Bishop received the £400 a year. My next point was to secure a proper residence for the Bishop before his arrival, a residence that would suitably represent his dignity as the head of the Catholics of Australia. I succeeded in renting a large and stately house, built for the first Protestant Archdeacon, and which at that time alone occupied the Vale of Woolomooloo, with an extensive domain attached to it. It joined the Sydney Park, in which stood his Cathedral.[7]

---

5. William Bernard Ullathorne OSB (1806–1889): clothed at Downside 1824 and professed 1825; ordained priest 1831; in 1833 sent to Australia as Vicar-General of Bishop Morris of Mauritius; returned to England in 1840; first bishop of Birmingham in 1850.
6. Ullathorne mistook the source of the proposal that he proceed to van Diemen's Land. It came in a letter to Bourke from Lord Aberdeen in February 1835 (see below).
7. The incomplete St Mary's stood on the eastern side of Hyde Park.

3 June 1834 Pope Gregory XVI to John Bede Polding OSB[8]

(*Adjutor Deus* I.8)

3 June 1834

Venerable Brother,

Greeting and Apostolic Blessing! The office of Pastoral ministry entrusted to Us demands especially this one duty, that with total devotedness and effort, we are solicitous for the spiritual good of the Faithful in order to direct them in the way of God's commandments and by fitting supports to help them to seek their eternal salvation. Therefore, because experience has revealed the enormous difficulty of communication in a useful way between New Holland and the Island of Mauritius, since our Venerable Brother, the Bishop and Apostolic Vicar in the Island of Mauritius has the spiritual care of New Holland also laid upon him, it would seem to be impossible for the needs of the greater number of Catholics living in the said New Holland and neighbouring Island of Van Diemen to be properly cared for unless a Vicar Apostolic with the rank of Bishop be appointed to live in that vast region and preside over ecclesiastical affairs. Therefore, on the advice of our Venerable Brothers, the Cardinals of the Holy Roman Church, who are in charge of matters concerning the Propagation of Faith, We have decided that this office should be entrusted to you, Venerable Brother, with complete confidence in the Lord that, by your outstanding learning, devotion and zeal for Catholic religion, you will adequately discharge all the duties committed to you. Therefore, by virtue of this letter absolving you and ordaining that you be absolved from every sentence, censure and penalty of any kind whatsoever of excommunication, suspension, interdict inflicted for any reason, if by chance these have been incurred, We have chosen, appointed and deputed you Vicar Apostolic of New Holland and of the neighbour-

8. Pope Gregory XVI (1765–1846), born Bartolomeo Alberto Cappellari, he was elected pope on 2 February 1831; he had been a monk of the Camaldolese order. John Bede Polding OSB (1794–1877), born in Liverpool; educated by Benedictines at Acton Burnell, 1805–1810; clothed at Downside 1810 and professed 1811; ordained priest 1819; Novice Master 1819–1834 and Subprior 1826–1834; appointed Vicar Apostolic of Madras, but declined the honour; appointed Vicar Apostolic of New Holland and consecrated bishop, 29 June 1834; sailed for Sydney, February 1835.

ing Island of Van Diemen with all powers and faculties in accordance with Our good pleasure and that of this Apostolic See . . .

Given at Rome under the seal of the Fisherman's Ring on the Third day of June in the Fourth Year of Our Pontificate.

For the Lord Cardinal Albano.[9]
A. Picchioni, Substitute.

4 June 1834 Dom Birdsall OSB to Dom Barber OSB[10]

(Birt I.231)

Vialta[11]
Broadway, Worcestershire
4th June 1834.

Dear Mr Barber,

Last night's packet brought two Roman letters; one mediate to Dr Bramston, the other immediate to me. By the former all we advised about the New Vicariate is granted by Rome, and granted gladly. As the letters were expedited from London on Saturday, you perhaps have heard from Downside that Mr Polding is to be consecrated Bishop Hiero-Caesarensis, *vigore* the former Brief (pro Madras) and, in a few days he is to expect the regular faculties and provisions from Rome, constituting the New District and independent Vicariate, and him the Vic. Ap.

9. Lord Cardinal Albano: Gianfrancesco Falzacappa (1767–1840).was created Cardinal-Priest in 1823 and Cardinal-Bishop of Albano in 1830.
10. Luke Bernard Barber OSB (1790–1850), monk of Downside, Prior 1818–1830; Vicar of nuns and resident chaplain at Salford 1830–1838 and at Stanbrook 1838 to 1850; President-General of the English Benedictine Congregation 1842–1850. John Austin Birdsall OSB (1775–1837) was a monk of Lamspringe Monastery in Germany, ordained priest 1801; founded mission at Cheltenham, Gloucestershire, and based there 1809–1834; President-General from 1826 to 1837; died at Broadway, Worcestershire, where he had founded a monastery to replace Lamspringe.
11. *Vialta* (via alta): the name Birdsall gave to his monastery at Broadway

6 June 1834 Dom Barber OSB to Dom Deday OSB[12]

(Birt I.232)

Salford Convent.
6th June, 1834.

... Polding has received his appointment as Vic. Ap. of New South Wales, and is to be consecrated Bishop of Hiero-Caesarea *in partibus*. It is not unlikely that you will be receiving an application from Duck to go out with him.[13] Do me the favour to agree with me and put a decided veto upon it. We are weakening ourselves at home to serve missions abroad. And this to oblige Dr Bramston who wants to rid himself of the solicitude which these foreign missions bring to him-a Bishop, too, who would disdainfully refuse to give one of our subjects an appointment to a chapel in London! Downside is in great trouble about this appointment. Mr Brown is much hurt and justly, for he never knew of the negotiation until it was brought to a termination.[14] It was no secret here, but I troubled my head very little about it, as I never conceived that Rome would have offered a Bishopric again to such a vacillating mind.[15] There will be, or I am much mistaken, something to do in his mind, before he gets on board a vessel. When he begins to think that perchance he may meet with a watery grave before he gets among the Bushmen, he will wish his head from under his mitre.

12. James Benedict Deday OSB (1773–1845), Downside monk, ordained priest 1800; Provincial of Canterbury 1826–1834.
13. James Ambrose Duck OSB (1797–1848), Downside monk, ordained priest 1824; at Cheltenham with President Birdsall OSB 1831–1835.
14. Thomas Joseph Brown OSB (1796–1880) was a monk of Downside where he was Prior from 1834 to 1840. He became bishop of Newport and Menevia in 1850.
15. In 1832 Polding had vacillated concerning his appointment as Vicar Apostolic of Madras, first consenting and then declining. He reported that the only one advising him against had been Mr. Barber, 'who knew me well'. (Polding to T.J.Brown OSB, 12/10/1832 [*Polding Letters* I.27–28]).

29 June 1834 Testimonial of Ecclesiastical Status

(*Adjutor Deus* I.9)

London
29 June 1834

On the 29th day of June, 1834, on the Feast of the Most Holy Apostles, Peter and Paul, in our private chapel in London, the Apostolic Letter written in form of a Brief having been read out, and his profession of faith made according to the articles now for a long time established by the Holy Apostolic See, and after he had sworn the oath prescribed for Bishops and Vicars Apostolic by the Holy see, the Assistant Bishops being his most Illustrious and Most Lordship Thomas, Bishop of Olena and Coadjutor Vicar Apostolic of London, and his Most Illustrious and Most Reverend Lordship Stephen, Bishop of Nilopolis and Vicar Apostolic of Eastern Oceania, during Solemn Mass we conferred ritually and canonically the rite of episcopal consecration on his Most Illustrious and Most Reverend Lordship John Polding, Bishop-Elect of Hiero-Caesaea.

+ James, Bishop of Ursulo, Vicar Apostolic of London
+ Thomas, Bishop of Olena and Coadjutor Vicar Apostolic of London
+ Stephen, Bishop of Nilopolis and Vicar Apostolic of Eastern Oceania[16]

Mid-June 1834 Prior George Turner OSB[17] to Pope Gregory XV

(*Birt* I.242)

The Community at Downside did not allow Dr Polding to be taken from them without making an effort to retain his services. The Prior forwarded a petition to the Pope, Gregory XVI, asking that the appointment might be re-considered, and that he should be left to carry on the great good he was effecting at St Gregory's. In this

16. James Yorke Bramston (1763–1836), Vicar Apostolic of London District 1827–1836.
Thomas Griffiths (1791–1847), Coadjutor Vicar Apostolic of London District 1833–1836, Vicar Apostolic 1836–1847.
Étienne Rouchouze (1798–1843), priest of the Congregation of the Sacred Hearts of Jesus and Mary (Picpus Fathers), Vicar Apostolic of Eastern Oceania 1833–1843.
17. George Turner OSB (1770–1854), monk of Douai, ordained priest 1800, Prior of Downside 1830–1834.

petition it was pointed out how Downside had, within a very few years sent four of her sons to Colonial missions, that is, Dr Morris, and Fathers Spain, de Colyar and Ullathorne; and with strength so reduced it was well-nigh impossible to meet this new call. It added that Dr Polding was 'the column and the mainstay of the establishment', and concluded with an earnest appeal to the Holy Father to 'leave him on whom the entire studies of the College depend, and who fills so admirably so many of the offices of the house.'

[29 June 1834] Polding to J. A. Birdsall OSB

(*Polding Letters* I.32–33)

35 Golden Square[18]
London
[29 June 1834]

Dear Rev Father President,

To you, ever dear Father President, I feel impelled by a sense of dutiful subjection which dignity cannot extinguish, and by affection which present and approaching events render more intense, to address the first announcement that I am now numbered among the successors of the Apostles! Numbered among them to do the work of the Apostles; and may that divine Spirit which proved his power in the weakness and innate unworthiness of those first selected to receive it, even now manifest that Power in one far more weak and worthless. Thanks be given to God, my fears are dissipated; and armed with the strength which comes from above, I hope to press forward to do the work of God. Oh! Continue your fervent prayers for me – co-operate by all means in the sacred cause; let me be considered only as a Deputy of our Congregation, extending the wing of its care over a land far distant and very wicked. I do hope I shall leave my native shore in the consolation of realising in my own regard the words of the Prophet: *Pro patribus tuis nati sunt tibi filii*;[19] and that in a few years the Benedictine Province of N.S.Wales shall be deemed no inconsiderable or uninteresting part of our Holy Institute . . .

18. 35 Golden Square, the residence of Bishop Branston and the location of his private chapel, where Polding was consecrated bishop.
19. Psalm 44, v. 16: 'Your sons will succeed your fathers.'

I must write a line to Downside by this Post; and as Dr Bramston wishes me to accompany him, I must conclude with the renewed expression of my sincere and affectionate attachment, and believe me to be ever, ever dear Father President,

Your dutiful son in J.C.
+John Bede Polding.

I reside at Pagliano's Leicester Square till Thursday or Friday.[20]

22 July 1834 Cardinal Weld to Prior Brown OSB

[see petition of mid-June above] (*Birt* I.242–243)

Cardinal Weld, who ever showed himself the sincere friend of St Gregory's and of the Benedictines in England, and through whom the petition had been presented wrote in reply that it was too late for the Holy See to reconsider the matter. His letter concluded by reminding the community that the truth of the Gospel saying, "Date et dabitur vobis" [Give and it will be given to you], is never better exemplified than in the case of those religious Orders who generously and their members to the Foreign Missions.'

20. Pagliano's Sablonière Hotel in Leicester Square was owned by Charles Joseph Pagliano and his wife Mary (Floris), a prominent London Catholic couple. It was in this hotel that the inaugural meeting of the St Vincent de Paul Society took place in England with Pagliano as its first president in 1844. Leicester Square is a short distance from Golden Square. A Miss Floris, possibly Elizabeth, older sister of Mary Pagliano, of the family famous for their Jermyn Street perfumery established in 1730, was benefactor of Polding's mission (see Birt I.261).

24 July 1834 Charles Henry Davis OSB to Edwin Davis[21]

(Birt I.241–242)

St Gregory's College
Downside
24 July 1834

. . . I suppose you have heard of the Right Rev. Dr Polding's consecration. His loss will be felt greatly by our community, but perhaps no individual member of the college will feel it more than myself. He has ever been my spiritual Director and my best of friends; I have always looked up to him as to a tender and affectionate parent, and as such he has ever proved himself to me. I assure you that were it the will of my superiors, I would with pleasure accompany him to New Holland. One of my fellow novices, formerly a student at Douay, is going with him.[22] I almost envy him.

6 August 1834 Polding to Secretary of State for the Colonies

(*Polding Letters* I.38–39)

London
6 August 1834

The Memorial of John Bede Polding D.D., Catholic Bishop and Vicar Apostolic in New Holland and Van Diemen's Land

Your Memorialist most respectfully represents that, in consequence of a communication on the part of His Excellency General Bourke, the Governor of New South Wales, stating the great good which had

21. Charles Henry Davis (1815–1854), Downside monk, professed 24 June 1834, the day on which this letter was written. He was ordained priest 1840 and consecrated Bishop of Maitland and Coadjutor to Dr Polding in February 1848 by Bishop Ullathorne at Bath. He arrived at Sydney in November 1848. He was a foundation member of the Senate of the university of Sydney, 1850–1854, and first president of St Mary's College, Lyndhurst, 1852–1854. He did not ever travel to his diocese of Maitland, which was regarded as a titular diocese.
Edwin Davis (1819–1880) a student of St Edmund's College at Douay, France, was a brother of Charles. He became a novice at Downside in 1838, receiving the name Oswald and was ordained priest by his brother in March 1848. Another Davis brother, Richard Francis (1805–1889) had also joined the Benedictines.
22. Dom Henry Gregory Gregory OSB, professed on the same day as Henry Davis, was a member of Polding's missionary band.

resulted to the colony from the labors of the Catholic Clergy, and that the Colonial Government had consented to provide Salaries for four additional Clergymen, Dr Bramston consented to procure them, but thought it right to state to the Secretary for the Colonies that the appointment of an Ecclesiastical Superior with Episcopal Authority was considered by Himself and others in Authority in the Catholic Church, an object of absolute necessity not only for the Administration of those Rites of Religion it is the peculiar province of a Bishop in the Catholic Church to administer, but also to establish discipline.[23] In this proposal the Secretary for the Colonies acquiesced and concurred . . .

Your Memorialist is now employed in seeking the necessary number of Clergy to accompany him, which imposes upon him considerable expense in Travelling. In addition to this there are other expenses incidental to the Situation he fills, which he has not means to defray. Your Memorialist begs leave respectfully to submit that his Salary as Bishop of New South Wales and Van Diemen's Land only amounts to £150 a Year, and that from that Sum he is unable to defray the Expense he now incurs, and therefore prays that the Right Honorable Secretary of State for the Colonies will direct such advances be made to him as will enable him to effect the objects he has in view in the shortest possible period.

And Your Memorialist will ever Pray etc.
+John Polding D.D.
Catholic Bishop and Vicar Apostolic in New Holland and Van Diemen's Land

[August] 1834 Polding to J.A.Birdsall

(*Polding Letters* I.42)

76 Upper Berkeley St

Dear Rev. F. President,
You will be surprised to see the above. I am here for a few minutes, and must write to save the Post. Card[inal]Weld has presented me

23. The establishment of discipline was particularly sought by the civil authorities in the case of the Rev. John Joseph Therry, who had been suspended from his public ministry by Governor Darling in 1825.

with all his Episcopal ornaments left in London, and has directed me to come here in search of them.[24] . . .

I have still no satisfaction from the Colonial Office. I saw Mr. S. Le Fevre yesterday.[25] He could do nothing; but promised to speak to Mr. Rice and to request him to hasten an answer to my Memorial. Shaw Le Fevre is about to leave the Colonial Office, being appointed Commissioner of the Poor Laws. For this I am extremely sorry, succeeded as he is by a Saint, Sir George Gray, to whom he will introduce me next Tuesday.[26] This, you observe, dear Fr President, may be of some advantage to me and of course I shall return from Norwich thro town.

Seeing the uncertainty in which this Colonial Office keeps me, I think it would be hazardous to engage myself to preach at Cheltenham on Sunday following.[27]. . .

The Bell rings – pray for me – I am ever affectionately

Yours
+ J.B.Polding

I asked Shaw Le Fevre what he advised me to do. He told me to remain quiet; not to think of engaging a ship or leaving for country till my memorial was answered.

---

24. Thomas Weld 1773–1837, member of recusant Weld family of Lulworth Castle, Dorset. Upon the death of his wife [in he renounced his wife] in 1815, he renounced the family property to his next brother and prepared for the priesthood. He was created a cardinal by Pope Pius VIII in 1830.
25. Sir John George Shaw-Lefevre(1797–1879) was a barrister, Whig politician and civil servant. He briefly served as Under Secretary of State for War and Colonies in the final months of the Grey ministry.
26. Sir George Grey (1799–1882), nephew of Earl Grey. He was appointed Under-Secretary of State for War and the Colonies, when Lord Melbourne succeeded Earl Grey as Prime Minister in July 1834.
27. Birdsall combined his role as President of the English Benedictines with his ministry at Cheltenham.

August 1834 Polding's Appeal for Help

(*Birmingham Catholic Magazine*, August 1834; Birt I.244–246)

Downside College, Bath.

Aware of the many appeals, annually made to the generous and charitable feelings of the public, we have long hesitated whether we ought to add another to the number

The pressing wants, however, of the Catholic population of New Holland, and the Island of Van Diemen, committed to our care, who are as little ones crying for bread, even the bread of eternal life, whilst there is no one to break unto them, compel us to cast aside every consideration, except that of exerting ourselves to relieve their spiritual distress . . .

Thousands of wretched creatures will, through the charity now solicited, have reason to bless the heart that compassionates, and the hand that assists them . . .

Contributions for the spiritual relief of the Catholics of New Holland and Van Diemen's Land may be transmitted through Messrs. Wrights, Henrietta Street, Covent Garden, London.[28]

Books, vestments and other articles for the church or seminary may be addressed to the Rt. Rev. Dr Polding, 63 Paternoster Row, London.

+ John Bede Polding, Bishop of Hiero-Caesarea and V.A. New Holland and V.D. Land.

14 August 1834 Polding to J. A. Birdsall OSB

(*Polding Letters* I.40)

London
14 August 1834

Dear Rev. Father President,
I have been in London nearly a fortnight and have effected very little. My object in coming was to ascertain clearly what the Govern-

28. In 1759 Anthony Wright appeared on a list of London bankers. In 1775 he took his son Thomas into partnership. In 1813 the firm became known as Wrights & Co. It failed in 1840.

ment intended or was disposed to advance, to enable me to provide instruction, present or future, for the Catholics of New S. Wales, and also to obtain what I could in the way of assistance from individuals; and thirdly, to make some preparations for my voyage. Thrown as it were into the Sea of difficulties, I am left to exert myself, for tho Dr Branston is all kindness to me personally, yet he will not interfere at the Colonial Office in my favour. I must rely entirely upon my own exertions. I prepared a Memorial, a copy of which I shall have gratification in shewing you when we meet, detailing the state of the Catholics of New S.W. and suggesting the means of relief. This I presented in the sixth; and after three days spoiled by one circumstance after another, I had an interview yesterday, 13th, with the Secy. for Colonies, Mr. Spring Rice, accompanied by Mr. More O'Ferrall.[29] We were received very courteously, and in reference to my Memorial he pledged himself to promote all recommendations of Gen. Bourke, the Governor of N.S.W., favourable to any objects proposed by me, and in general to protect the Caths against any interference on the part of officials, of which I find here have been instances. He approved highly of the plan of educating Clergy in the Colony itself, and in the view of promoting this plan, will consider favourably the application I have made for a sum of £400, to take out two Catechists in addition to the four priests . . .

If you would find a convenience in having the young professed ordained earlier, I could defer my visit to Ireland to a later period . . . The Vessel I first intended to take, the *Augusta Jessie*, has been hired to convicts, and I have not selected another as yet . . .

Ever most truly yrs.,
+J.B.Polding

16 August 1834 *Freeman's Journal* (Dublin)

The Right Rev. Dr Bolding(sic) is appointed Roman Catholic Bishop of New Holland and Van Dieman's (sic) Land. He goes out accompanied by the Rev. Mr. Corcoran, an Irish priest.

29. Thomas Spring Rice (1790–1866) was Secretary of State for War and the Colonies from June to November 1834.
Richard More O'Ferrall (1797–1880) was an Irish member of the House of Commons and later Governor of Malta (1847–1851).

18 August 1834 Polding to Sir Herbert Taylor[30]

(*Polding Letters* I.41)

33 Golden Square,
London
18 August 1834

Sir,

Having been recently appointed with the sanction and concurrence of His Majesty's Government Ecclesiastical Superior of the Catholics in New South Wales and Van Diemen's Land, it has been to me a most painful subject of anxiety, to find they are most destitute of means of Instruction and Moral improvement. Reluctant to embarrass His Majesty's Minister by a direct application for pecuniary assistance, I have opened a Subscription in the hope or raising, by the donation of the charitably disposed, a sum which may enable me to provide the means of Instruction and Moral Improvement for the people under my spiritual care. It is truly gratifying to me that His Majesty's Secretary of State for the Colonies has expressed to me his most earnest desire that suitable instruction should be provided for them. Permit me to entreat you to lay before His Most Gracious Majesty[31] the case of my wretched flock. His tender solicitude for the welfare of his people reaches even to the distant clime to which I am about to proceed. I offer an humble petition in the name and on the part of nearly thirty thousand – that is, of one third of the population of those Colonies.

May I indulge the hope that His Majesty will cause me and them to rejoice in being considered deserving objects of His Royal Bounty. I ask this great favour to be extended to us, not only to be enabled by this means to render essential service to the cause of Morality, but also that I may urge as a most powerful argument in the event of disturbance (which may God in his mercy prevent) for loyalty and peaceable bearing-the positive proof of the wise beneficence of our Sovereign in the relief He will vouchsafe to grant us.

30. Lieutenant-General Sir Herbert Taylor GCB GCH (1775–1839) was from 1805 the first Private Secretary to Kings George III, George IV and William IV.
31. His Most Gracious Majesty: William IV (1765–1837) King of the United Kingdom of Great Britain and Ireland and King of Hanover from 26 June 1830 until his death on 20 June 1837.

Confident that a claim so just and so urgent will excite your sympathy, I have preferred addressing myself personally to you, instead of writing a formal memorial to His Majesty, and earnestly entreating your attention to the accompanying statement, with the greatest respect, I have the honour to remain,

Sir
Your most obedient humble servant,
+J.B.Polding

24 August 1834 Polding Sermon at Norwich

(*Norfolk Chronicle*, Saturday, 6 Sept, p 2)

The Catholic Chapel, in Willow-lane, which has been closed for some weeks for repair, was opened last Sunday last, with High Mass.[32] Dr Polding, Catholic Bishop of New South Wales, officiated . . .

The sermon in the morning was plain, sensible, and unpolemical; and that in the evening was a powerful appeal in behalf of the benighted flock of the Right Rev. Pastor of New South Wales. On both occasions the chapel was filled with persons of the best ranks of provincial society.

10 September 1834 Polding to T. Spring Rice

(*Polding Letters* I.43)

Dublin
10 September 1834

Dr Polding presents his best respects to Mr. Spring Rice and as he could not have the pleasure of waiting upon him at the Colonial Office previously to his departure from London, he takes an early opportunity to testify his gratitude, and to express the great gratification he has derived from the kind reply to his Memorial, which he has had the honour to receive from Sir George Grey-so satisfactory as regards the young Candidates for the Ecclesiastical State Dr Polding proposed to take with him to N.S.Wales. Dr Polding trusts that 'four' may be included in the 'limited number' mentioned by Sir George Grey.

32. Holy Apostles chapel was established in Willow Lane in 1786 and was served by the Jesuits.

From the kind and liberal feeling evinced in the letter of Sir George Grey to meet Dr Polding's wishes, and to enable him to carry into effect his intentions respecting the moral improvements of the large portion of the population of N.S.Wales professing the Catholic Religion, he is relieved from the anxiety which arose from his want of means to sustain his present expenses, fully convinced that he may rely with perfect confidence in this case, indeed in every other respect, in the liberality of His Majesty's Government.

[Unsigned]

15 September 1834 (Monday) *Freeman's Journal* (Dublin)

Yesterday, the Right Rev. Dr Powlding (sic), (late of Downside College) and recently consecrated a Bishop for New South Wales, sang Pontifical High Mass in the Church of the Conception, Marlborough Street, Dublin.

26 October 1834 Polding Charity Sermon at Liverpool

(*Liverpool Mercury*, Friday, 31/19/1834, p 6)

On Sunday last, at Seel-street chapel, the Right Rev. Dr Polding, R.C. Bishop of New Holland and Van Dieman's (sic) Land, preached an eloquent and impressive discourse in aid of a fund for erecting chapels and schools, and purchasing books for Catholic inhabitants of those countries, to which he is about to proceed.[33] The collection made after the sermon amounted to £60.10s.8d. in addition to which, Charles Blundell, Esq. of Ince, has contributed the munificent sum of £100.[34]

33. St Peter's Chapel, Seel Street, was built in 1788 by Rev Archibald Benedict MacDonald OSB (1739–1814). Bishop Polding stayed at the Chapel House awaiting his embarkation; Dom Michael Placid Sinnottt (1803–1896) was missioner at that time. Benedictines served the parish until 1976. The parish was closed in 1978 and the church deconsecrated in 2003.
34. Charles Blundell: the Blundell family was granted land at Ince in Lancashire by William the Conqueror following the invasion of 1066. The family name was later added to the village – Ince Blundell. The Blundells were a recusant family, faithful to the Catholic church since the reformation. Charles' grandfather, Robert, built the family mansion in 1750 and it was extended and embellished by Charles' father, Henry, a prolific art collector. Charles inherited the estate in 1810; upon the death of the bachelor Charles in 1837, with no direct male heirs, the Ince Blundell estate was transferred to his distant cousin Thomas Weld of Lulworth on condition that he add Blundell to his surname.

(*Freeman's Journal* [Dublin], Saturday, 8/11/1834 [extracted from *Falmouth Packet*])

On Sunday week a charity sermon was preached in Seel-street Chapel by the Right Rev. Dr Polding, Catholic Bishop of New South Wales and Van Diemen's Land, in aid of the funds for building chapels in these colonies. The Right Rev. Prelate represented the Catholics in those parts, amounting already to nearly thirty thousand, to be in the greatest want of religious aid, being nearly destitute of pastors, of places of worship, and of books of religious instruction. He compared his poor flock to the strayed sheep in the desert, which the good pastor, leaving the ninety-nine, went forth to seek, and after an eloquent appeal, which drew tears from his auditory, a collection was made, amounting to upwards of sixty pounds, and which was afterwards increased by many handsome donations.

8 November 1834 Extract of a private letter

(*Australian*, 17 March 1835, page 3)

London
8th November

A Catholic Bishop has been consecrated for your Colony and you may expect him over very shortly. He is a Monk of the Benedictine Order, the best and most rational of all the Catholic Orders. He is namesake of the Venerable Monk of Jarrow, and bears the honored name of John Bede. I hear he is now collecting funds for the erection of a Cathedral and a College. I heartily wish him success, for I do not know any more effectual mode of exciting spirit and imitation in our Church dormant.

14 November 1834 Advertisement

(*Liverpool Mercury*, Friday 14/11/1834, p 1)

On Sunday next, the 16th instant, a Sermon will be preached in the Catholic Chapel of St Mary's, Edmund street, by the Right Rev. Dr Polding, Bishop of Hiero-Caesarea, and Vicar Apostolic of New South Wales and Van Diemen's Land. After the sermon a Collection will be made for the Promotion of the Religious Instruction of the numerous Catholics in those Colonies.

16 November 1834 Bishop Morris OSB to Miss Catherine Wheble[35]

(Birt I.239)

Mauritius
16 November 1834

. . . So my friend Polding has got his mitre. He was inclined to play the coquette; for after he had refused the first to go to Madras, he then turned round, was mighty sorry, and wished he had not been so hasty; for he wrote me last year a long letter upon the subject. However, I am glad he las has been raised; he deserves it for all he has done; and I am satisfied he will do much good – must – wherever he goes. He has a good head, a better heart, and an overflowing of zeal. Thirty years have gone over our heads since we first became the friend the one of the other. We were novices together, made our vows at the same Altar and the same hour, and went hand in hand together, till I was sent into the wide world to commence my missionary career, he remaining at home to prepare others for the same task. Neither he, nor I, certainly had any reason to indulge, even in our most soaring moments, the idea of being placed among the Princes of the Church; but so it has pleased God to ordain; may we be ever worthy of the high honour.

[December 1834] Letter of Bishop Polding to Sydney

(cited in the *Tasmanian*, 22/5/1835)

A private letter has been received at Sydney, and extracts from it sent here, from Dr Polding, the Right Reverend the Catholic Bishop of Austral-Asia. His Lordship states that he is to embark in the first prison ship which is to sail for New South Wales in the month of January.

35. William Placid Morris OSB (1794–1872), monk of Downside, ordained priest 1818, consecrated Apostolic Visitor of Island of Mauritius 1830, a Vicariate that included New Holland and Van Diemen's Land, where Bernard Ullathorne OSB had been Morris' Vicar General from 1833 until Polding's appointment. Morris was recalled in 1840 and replaced by another English Benedictine, Dom Bernard Collier (1803–1890).
Lucy Catherine Wheble (1809–1886): the Whebles were a Catholic family, resident since 1801 at Woodley Lodge, Woodley, Berkshire; there was a chapel associated with their house.

8 December 1834 Letter to the Editor of the London *Standard*[36]
(*The Standard*, 10/12/1834, p 3; extracted in *The Tasmanian* 8/5/1835, p 5)

London
Dec. 8, 1834

Sir – I beg leave to request you to insert the following letter in your truly valuable and talented paper. Mr. Spring Rice and several other members of the late administration have lately made a government grant to a certain Dr Polding (lately made by the Pope a Catholic bishop, and ordered by the Pope to go to Australia to re-establish a Catholic mission in that colony), of one thousand pounds per annum; moreover the grant has been increased by an additional grant of a thousand acres of land in any part of New South Wales, in order that Dr Polding may found a Catholic College there; further, Mr. Spring Rice has agreed to pay the passage or outfit of Dr Polding, and of the Catholic Priests who are intended to accompany him. The question, therefore, must be considered in two points. – 1st, whether the King of England or the Pope of Rome is to manage the spiritual affairs of the British Colonies. Secondly-Whether or not the people of England are to be taxed in order to pay for the maintenance, &c., of a Catholic Bishop in New South Wales? It is intended that this Dr Polding should sail for Australia in the first week of January next; he may be heard of at Dr Branston's, a Catholic Bishop, living at 35, Golden-square. I trust that you will call the attention of the public to these facts.

I have the honour to be, sir,
Your most obedient humble servant,
A Supporter of Church and State.

14 December 1834 From *John Bull* newspaper[37]

(extracted in *Sydney Herald* 21 May 1835, p 2)

We have a high regard for the talents, the amenity, and the activity of Mr. Spring Rice. He was a most popular and efficient Secretary of the Treasury, and we dare say would have been in time, if fate had

36. *The Standard* newspaper was founded in May 1827.
37. *John Bull* was a Sunday newspaper established in London in 1820.

permitted, a very excellent Colonial Secretary. Tapps, the Twickenham coachman, says he thinks the Right Honorable Gentleman would look better if he did not let his hair grow so long over his collar behind; but that is a mere matter of taste. What we are now going to say is of a graver cast of accusation-not against Mr. Rice personally, but against the late Government, while he was at the head of the Colonial Department. We are told that the late Ministers have granted to a Dr Polding, Roman Catholic Bishop of Hiero Caesarea, a sum of one thousand pounds sterling per annum, and one thousand acres of land, for the establishment of a Popish College in New South Wales, together with the expenses of the outfit of the said most eminent Hiera Piera, and his suit, We shall be too happy to contradict this statement if we have been misled; and as the said Bishop of Hiera Piera or whatever it is, is living at Number 33, Golden-square, at the Right Reverend Dr Bramston, there can be no great difficulty in putting us down, if we are wrong.

22 December 1834 Earl of Aberdeen to Governor Bourke[38]

(*HRA* XVII.610)

Downing Street
22 December 1834

Sir,

. . . In consequence of the further provision, which has been made by the Legislative Council for the maintenance of the Catholic Clergy, four additional Priests will shortly proceed to the Colony, one of whom will be invested with Episcopal Authority with the view of giving to the Roman Catholic Population the benefit of certain Rites of the Roman catholic Church, which it is understood to be peculiar to the province of a Vicar Apostolic or Bishop to perform . . .

I am etc.,
Aberdeen.

38. Lord Aberdeen: George Hamilton-Gordon (1784–1860), 4th Earl of Aberdeen, held the office of Secretary of State for War and the Colonies from December 1834 to April 1835 in the first ministry of Lord Melbourne.

Late 1834 Committee of St Mary's Church, Sydney, to Governor R. Bourke

(*Adjutor Deus* I.13–14)

The Memorial of the lay members of the committee of St Mary's Church, Sydney, in the name of the Roman Catholics of New South Wales, respectfully sheweth: . . .

That the Roman Catholics of New South Wales feel it their duty, whilst it is their pleasure, to acknowledge, and they do acknowledge with heartful gratitude, that, under the paternal government of your Excellency, their moral and religious wants, have not been neglected, nor their calls for assistance disregarded.

Catholic schools had increased in number. Assistance towards the erection of places of worship has been afforded, and we are now made happy with the intelligence that a Bishop of our Church, of whose paternal character, piety, zeal and attainments we hear the greatest praises, may be hourly expected to preside over and regulate the affairs of our Church, and to provide for its necessities in this colony, and that he is accompanied by a number of clergymen, not adequate certainly to the demands of the colony, but who will continue very much to relieve our hitherto bereaved condition . . ..

And your memorialists in the name of their Roman Catholic brethren, respectfully solicit, and pray, that your Excellency and the Honourable Legislative Council would be pleased to take into consideration the expediency and justice of providing the Right Reverend Dr Polding with such salary as may be deemed adequate to the respectability of his station and due fulfilment of its functions.

30 January 1835 Bishop Polding to Mr. R. W. Hay[39]

(*Polding Letters* I.48)

33 Golden Square
London
30 January 1835

Dr Polding presents his Compliments to Mr. Hay and has great pleasure in forwarding to him the enclosed Certificate received from the Owner of the *Oriental*, by which Ship Dr Polding and party have agreed to sail to New South Wales.

[no signature]

February-March, 1835 Polding in London

(Polding Letters I.119)

John Gorman, when I was in London in Feb-March 1835, lived during the day as an errand Boy with the Rev. Mr. Jones, an intimate friend of mine. The Boy expressed a wish to accompany me to N. S. Wales. I desired him to pause before he undertook to do it. He became more ardent in his request. I referred him to his Father and Friends, and especially to Mr. Jones, who was most interested in his welfare. They most cheerfully conceded, and when I finally left London, the Father and Mother and Uncle placed him in the carriage with me and most confidently and unreservedly placed [him] in my care, happy to have him thus provided for.

39. Robert William Hay ((1786–1861) was Permanent Under-Secretary of State for the Colonies from 1825 to 1836

20 February 1835 Earl of Aberdeen to Sir Richard Bourke[40]
(*HRA* XVII.682–683)

Downing Street
20 February 1835

Sir,

With reference to my Despatch Number 4 of 22nd Decr., 1834, apprising you of the intention of the Government to appoint four additional Chaplains to the Establishment of the Roman Catholic Clergy at New South Wales, I have the honor to acquaint you that the following Priests have been selected, and will shortly take their departure for the Colony, viz:-Revd Dr Polding; Revd Mr Cotham; Revd Mr Corcoran; Revd Mr Sumner.

To each of the above persons an allowance of £150 has been issued by the Colonial Agent, in aid of the expense of their passage to the Colony; and you will understand that they will respectively be entitled to receive, from the date of their arrival, a stipend of £150 per annum.

There is one point connected with the position of the first named Clergyman to which I beg to call your attention. Dr Polding, when first selected, was intended only to officiate as Chaplain; but, as it was subsequently considered advisable by the Church to which he belongs that, with a view to giving him greater influence over the Clergy of the Colony, he should be permitted to exercise Episcopal authority, the sanction of the Government was given to the arrangement. The powers and authority thus proposed to be vested in Dr Polding are superior to those conferred on the Revd Mr Ullathorne as Vicar General, whilst the salary of the latter is higher than that assigned to the former. I am not prepared to sanction the augmentation of Dr Polding's Allowance, so long as there is another Roman Catholic Clergyman in the Colony entitled to the same amount; but on the other hand, it appears

40. Regarding this despatch of Lord Aberdeen, Polding commented in a letter to Dom Thomas Brown at Downside: 'It was most unfortunate for me that Lord Aberdeen was Minister at the time of my leaving England. His despatch is so precise that the Governor here has his hands tied up. He can neither give me an acre of ground or anything else till the state of things be altered by the Home Government.' In the same letter he referred to Bourke as 'a most excellent Liberal Governor – a man of enlightened and affectionate heart, with cold self-calculating Scotch Tory Officials' (Polding to Brown, 1 November 1835 [*Letters* I. 58]).

desirable to avoid the possibility of any unpleasant feelings existing between them. I, therefore, propose that Mr Ullathorne should be removed to Van Diemen's Land upon the same rate of pay as he now receives, when, if you deem it advisable, Dr Polding's Salary might be augmented to £200 per annum. As I do not anticipate any objection on the part of Mr Ullathorne, to this arrangement, the necessary communication on the subject of it will be made to Colonel Arthur;[41] but as the transfer of that Clergyman's services to another Colony may, if too early pressed, be attended with personal inconvenience to him, you will of course give him every reasonable latitude in this respect which he shall require; and upon his removal to Van Diemen's Land, you will furnish him with a letter of introduction to Colonel Arthur, defraying at the same time, the expenses of his Passage thither.

Dr Polding will be accompanied by three Students, Messrs. Gregory, Spencer and Kenny, who are in course of preparation for Holy Orders, but who are intended to act for the present as Catechists. The Colonial Agent has issued to each of them the sum of £100, in aid of the expenses of their passage to the Colony; but no expectation has been held out to any of them by this Department, that they will receive any salary or allowance whatever from the Government.

As it is very desirable that Dr Polding should be enabled to exercise a salutary influence over the conduct of the Roman Catholic Chaplains, I beg to suggest the propriety of your adopting some arrangement with a view to ensure the object.

I am, etc.,
Aberdeen.

1 March 1835 Birdsall to Benedictines accompanying Polding

(*Adjutor Deus* I.15)

To the Brethren of the English Benedictine Congregation setting out for New Holland.

Let it be known to our Brethren, as far as it applies, that it has been decided by our Fathers assembled in General Chapter of the Congre-

41. Lieutenant-General Sir George Arthur (1784–1854) was Lieutenant Governor of Van Diemen's Land from1823 to 1837.

gation at Downside in the year 1834 that on all of our members who are joining the Most Reverend Lord Polding, Bishop of Hierocaesarea and Vicar Apostolic and will undertake missionary work in his vast new Vicariate, it is expressly imposed that they are to obey diligently the Most Reverend Vicar Apostolic and complying with the wishes of the same Most Reverend Vicar Apostolic, they are to perform assiduously whatever he asks of them.

Dom Augustine Birdsall,
President General.

3 March 1835 Meeting of Catholic Committee Hobart Town

(*Tasmanian*, Friday 6 March 1835, page 3)

Resolved—That we have heard with great delight that religious consolation is at last to be afforded to the much neglected Catholics of this Island, and that a Bishop has been appointed to this Colony, whose name is BEDE, and who, with FOUR other Catholic Clergymen, may be daily expected.

6 March 1835 Polding to Colonial Office

(*Polding Letters* I.49–50)

42 Seel Street
Liverpool
6 March 1835

Sir,

In the arrangements I had the honour to propose to His Majesty's Secretary of State for the Colonies, respecting the means of Instruction for the Catholic Population of New South Wales, in addition to the four Clergymen asked for by the Governor Gen. Bourke, I requested to be allowed to take four Ecclesiastical Students, who would hereafter when ordained, give their services as Clergymen to that country and in the meantime render material assistance in the capacity of School Master or Catechists.

This arrangement was approved by the Rt. Hon. T. Spring Rice, His Majesty's Secretary of State for the Colonial Department, in the month of October last and kindly acceded to by the rt. Hon. The Earl of Aberdeen.

In consequence, however, of the doubt I expressed to you respecting the fitness of one of the four I had selected to be hereafter ordained, I declined presenting more than three for the sum of one Hundred pounds each [is] allowed for the expenses of the voyage.

Since my arrival in Liverpool, application has been made to me by the Rev. Mr. Fisher, a Clergyman about 30 years of age, whom I have known for many years. His character stands deservedly very high amongst all who have witnessed the zeal, the mildness, firmness and assiduity with which he has fulfilled his arduous duties in this Town. Owing to the heavy labour he has had to endure, being naturally of a delicate frame, his health has caused him to desist from duty during the last three Months. He has been strongly advised to reside in a warmer climate by his Medical attendant, whose letter to me I take the liberty to enclose.

Mr. Fisher is very desirous to accompany me. The object of my present application is to request that he may be permitted to have the sum of one hundred pounds, as one of the four Catechists to defray the expenses of the voyage. I would not offer this request were I not under the sincere conviction that his conduct as a Christian Minister and a Gentleman etc. will be a most valuable acquisition to the Colony, to which on the 15th inst. I am about with my party to proceed.

I have the honor to remain, Sir, Your most obt. Sert.,

J.B.Polding.

22 March 1835 Polding to H.T.Heptonstall OSB[42]

(*Polding Letters* I.50–51)

Liverpool
22 March 1835

My dear Confrere,

I am now writing the last letter you will receive from me in England. In the first place I give you full authority to transact business in

42. Writing in May 1836, Polding encouraged Heptonstall him to join him in the Colony: 'My dear Hep. – do cut your stick, as Gregory says, and come out – the very place for you – Procurator of the District and Seminary, and Major Domo of the Episcopal Palace – there is a sesquipedalian title and no responsibility' (Polding to Heptonstall, 1 May 1835 [*Polding Letters* I.58]).

my name and on my behalf and shall never hold you responsible for errors of judgment in the exercise of the discretionary powers with which I now entrust you . . .

Mon[day]: I have not[hing] to add except to thank you, as I do most heartily, for your affectionate Solicitude about me. We are all in good Spirits. I do not expect we shall be out of the river before Friday, so that I may hear from you once more.

God bless you, my ever dear friend,
+ J.B.Polding

26 March 1835 Polding to J. A. Birdsall OSB

(*Polding Letters* I.51–52)

18 Steel Street
Liverpool
26 March 1835

Dear Rev. F. President,

The truly paternal kindness of your last letter would have been sooner acknowledged, had I not been kept in a state of uncertainty about the period of sailing, and I deemed it almost impossible to have a satisfactory answer in time. We shall certainly be in the river to-morrow and probably set out for our destination. Your good wishes attend us, your prayers ensure our safety. All that is of the period before Profession, in our breasts, feels sore and aggrieved – we are unworthy of the name we bear if in our sorrows we do not rejoice . . ..

Adieu, dear Rev. F. President. This last day of my *sejour* in England for many years has commenced. I consecrate its first moments to the expression of the earnest wish, I shall ever entertain, that our Congregation may continue in the hand of Providence to distribute largely the mercies of Heaven to the ignorant and depraved. I beg my kindest regard to all under yr roof, to Mr Barber and all my friends, and believe me ever to be, with the greatest respect and veneration,

Your truly attached affect. Son in J.C.,
+ J.B.Polding.

26 March 1835 Polding to T. J. Brown OSB

(*Polding Letters* I.52)

18 Steel Street
Liverpool
26 March 1835

My dear Confrere,

This, the last letter I shall write in England, conveys to you and my dear Confreres the deepest wishes of my heart. It is almost exhausted by these painful partings, yet whole and sound to its purpose. May God bless you, and may my dear Alma Mater ever rejoice in the holiness of her Children. Gentle, good and kind, may the Spirit of our Holy Father rest in joyfulness within her walls. Accept my blessing and dearest love.

Ever most affectionately yr Confrere,
+ J.B.Polding.

26 March 1835 Polding to I. Ph. Cardinal Fransoni[43]

(*Polding Letters* I.52–53)

18 Steel Street
Liverpool
26 March 1835

Most Eminent Cardinal,

Now at last I can tell you of our departure, perhaps tomorrow, for the Vicariate in New Holland, to which the favour of the Apostolic See has appointed me, unworthy as I am. Assuredly I would have departed long ago if I had not been detained by some changes in the Administration of the Government and by the furious storms prevailing this year far beyond my anticipation. But the recent months have not past without bearing some fruit. I have collected from the alms of the faithful very much to support the needs of the Mission about to begin in New Holland – for example, quite a large sum of money, church furnishings and a number of religious books for use

43. Giacomo Filippo (Iacobus Philippus) Fransoni (1775–1856) served from 1834 to 1856 as Cardinal Prefect of the Sacred Congregation for the Propagation of the Faith.

in the Seminary, the establishment of which was strongly urged upon me by His Eminence Cardinal Pedicini when he was laudably presiding over the Sacred Congregation for the Propagation of the faith.

Coming out with me are three priests and the same number of choir religious, two of whom are already in Orders, and also a young Scotsman desirous of embracing the clerical state, all of them having a good testimonial from their Ordinaries and regular Superiors, and who say they are burning with zeal for souls. Of the priests, the senior is a Secular, a former student of the English College in Rome, Father Clement Fisher, who when back in his Mother country was so afflicted with poor health that, after a short time on the English Mission, being unwell, he has left and his Bishop, on the advice of the doctors has granted him the permission to seek the healthier region of New Holland with me.

The second is Mr Corcoran, of the Irish branch of the Dominican Fathers, who was formerly attached to the community of St Clement in Rome.[44]

The third is Mr. Ambrose Cotham, a professed English Benedictine monk of the monastery of St Edmund at Douai. The names of the others are: Brother Bede Sumner, a subdeacon, Brother B. Spenser, both professed monks of the Benedictine monastery of St Gregory the Great at Downside, and Brother Gregory Gregory, a monk of Saints Denis and Adrian of the same Congregation, and John Kenny, the Scotsman.[45]

In addition to the faculties conceded to me in favour of that undeveloped Mission in New Holland by the Apostolic See already, there are still two which I am venturing to seek from His Holiness.

1. Because in England and Ireland, from which countries the majority of colonists have migrated, abstinence from flesh meat on a Saturday has been dispensed and besides, it will be difficult

44. Corcoran prepared for the priesthood in Rome, living at the Irish Convent of San Clemente, and was ordained in that city in 1825. He was assigned to Dominican convents in Perugia in 1827 and then Lucca in 1829 where he pursued further studies. In 1831 he returned to the British Isles and took up a private chaplaincy in the Trelawny household.

45. The English monks from the monastery of Saints Denis and Adrian at Lamspringe near Hildesheim in Germany, relocated briefly to Broadway, Worcestershire. Gregory was clothed at Downside as a member of the Broadway community.

if not impossible to recall them to the old regulations, I humbly beg that the same dispensations from abstinence and from some feasts conceded to England be granted to my Vicariate.

2. As it has been found from experience that the Benedictine spirituality has virtually from its beginning produced missionaries well adapted for the conversion of pagan peoples, and for many centuries in England the Fathers of the Anglo-Benedictine Congregation (on the registers of which I myself and the greatest number of my companions are enrolled) has been worthily and effectively making their presence felt in the Apostolic Mission, I plead with the Holy See to be permitted to establish in my Vicariate, if it seems reasonable, the same Rule of life as is now in England, with the same provisions.

As soon as possible after the end of the five months at sea and my investigation of the state of the Vicariate, I shall furnish Your Eminence in a long letter with all that the Sacred Congregation would be interested in knowing.[46]

Meanwhile, I request the blessing of the Sovereign Pontiff and of Your Eminence, and all in the Sacred Congregation I humbly pray every best wish.

Your Eminence's most humble servant,
+J.B.Polding, Bishop of Caesarea.

[26 March 1835] Polding to W. D. Scott OSB[47]

(*Polding Letters* I.53)

[Liverpool]
[26 March 1835]

My ever dear Mr. Scott,

After yourself nothing could be more welcome or more painful to me than your truly affectionate lines. You are indeed my true and

46. Polding's first report from Australia to Propaganda Fide was in a letter dated 10 February 1838, communicated via Dom Bernard Collier (1803–1890), Roman-based Abbot-Procurator of the English Benedictines and from 1840 to 1863 Vicar-Apostolic of Mauritius (Letters I. 96–98).

47. William Dunstan Scott OSB (1792–1872) monk of Downside, Procurator of Southern Province (1826–1842).

constant friend, one on whom my desponding spirit has often rested or obtained encouragement. May God be with you – pray for me. We are all ready to embark. The vessel will sail about 9 if possible. I think she will remain on the river till Friday. Remember me to Mary West.

Ever affectionately Yours,
+ J.B. Polding.

1 May 1835 CLERICAL APPOINTMENT

(*Tasmanian*, Friday 1 May 1835, p 7)

The highest Catholic Ecclesiastical Authority has appointed the Reverend Dr Paulding (sic) to the important station of Bishop of Austral-Asia. This Prelate, with six Clergymen, to be stationed by him as he may see necessary, embarked on board the *Sir Thomas Munro*, and may be daily expected. The brother of one of them, a highly respectable gentlemen, arrived in the *Bachelor*.[48]

3 May 1835 Polding to L. B. Barber OSB

(*Polding Letters* I.53–54)

Oriental (at sea)
3 May 1835

My dear Mr. Barber,

I had not time to write to you to mention the day of our departure from L'pool – to thank you and my dear Sisters at Salford for their many kindnesses to me. Of course you would hear of it in due Season. We have now commenced our 6th week and the time has passed quite as pleasantly as I could have anticipated, except as regards some circumstances of which you will hear at a later date. The weather is extremely hot – the thermometer stands at 85 in the shade. We enjoy

48. As soon as August 1834, Polding began enquiring about passage from London. Ships considered were the *Augusta Jessie*, the *Sir Thomas Munro*, which was wrecked at Cape Verde Islands in December 1834, and the *Enchantress*, which sank off Bruny Island in July 1835.
Lawrence Cotham, surgeon and later a publican, brother of Fr. Ambrose James Cotham, had arrived in Hobart Town on 18 April 1835 on the brig *Bachelor*, which sailed from Liverpool on 14 December 1834.

nevertheless a breeze which is very refreshing. I cannot say I am much incommoded by the heat, but poor Bede Sumner is quite a melting mood, and poor Mr. Cotham is not much better. We are all quite well and in excellent health, for which God be praised. Quite united amongst ourselves and on good terms with our fellow passengers. We live in some sense *Conventualiter.*[49] We meet three times each day for Office; have our meditation and Spiritual lecture together. I have commenced a course in Moral Theology with the young men, and the priests and myself hold a conference on the Sacraments three times each week. Tuesday and Thursday are half recreation days. Such is our present course of life, which we commenced as soon as we recovered from sea sickness and have never interrupted one day. We received the Holy Communion for the first time on Maundy Thursday, and again on Easter Sunday. I proposed saying Mass on that great Festival, but the water was so rough we could not meet except for Office. To my shame, I must say, I am as much inclined to laugh when I ought to be serious, by sea as by land: indeed, more so. Such queer things do sometimes happen. For instance, I was giving the blessing at Prime on Easter Sunday, and just as I said the word *disponat* the ship gave a lurch and seated me on the floor of my cabin.[50] Bede was thrown to the side opposite to that on which he was sitting, and no sooner there than another lurch sent him back to his first position.

Then we are so curiously habited. I, of course, am dressed *a la ordinaire* – but of the rest, one in jockey coat, another without or else panting like expiring oysters. I celebrated Mass last Sunday and again today assisted by the Priests. Thus assisted, there is small risk. I am sure you would enjoy the voyage extremely. The Captain is extremely civil and kind – our provisions hitherto as good as could be expected. The quantity of water is somewhat restricted – we have each half a pint for washing and by the time we reach Sydney I shall be enabled

---

49. *Conventualiter*: 'in community mode'.
50. Perhaps the Bishop was thrown to the floor while reciting this part of a long prayer: . . . *etiam abundantiam omnium bonorum spiritualium et corporalium et gratiam Spiritus Sancti qui me bene per omnia disponat* . . .: Obtain also an abundance of all good things, spiritual and bodily, and the grace of the Holy Spirit so He may set all things in good order for me. He wittily played on the meaning of disponat/set.

to wash in a thimbleful – I am slung up each night in a thing called a Cott. I swing about 2ft from the ceiling. How I would like to see you ride this most skittish horse. It goes to and fro like the pendulum of a Clock for a quarter of an hour after you are in, but the danger is on getting in or of either going over or tumbling out. I have had two accidents. At one time the ropes at the feet broke and another those at the head – down I cam and only hurt my toe. We have not had any stormy weather – the ocean generally presents a wild melancholy spread of water, monotonous as a whole, tho each individual part is in motion. We passed in sight of Antonio, one of the Cape Verd Islands, the only land we have seen ever since we bade adieu to Cape Clear. We have not observed many fish. Two or three whales, and some bonitos – one was speared two days since and we had it for dinner. Gregory, who lives in the same cabin with me, saw yesterday a Shark astern. We hope to catch one shortly. It is delightful to witness the Shoals of flying fish about the size of herring which sometimes take a course thro the air to avoid their enemies. One came into the Cabin of a Passenger. I hope all are quite well. Do write to me a long letter – direct Sydney, New S.W.

Something is paid with the letter – 8d. in London. How is the arbitration going on?[51] I do not think I will have time to write so fully to Downside as I could wish – please therefore to send this letter and also mention to the President with our united respects and love and wish all that is kind to our good Sisters. My hand is shaking with the heat and the motion of the vessel is so great I am afraid you will scarcely make out this.

Ever most affly yr Confrere,
+ J.B.Polding.

51. The 'arbitration' referred to the effort to resolve the longstanding conflict between the Downside Benedictines and their local bishop, Peter Augustine Baines (1786–1843), Vicar Apostolic of the Western District. Baines had been a Benedictine of Ampleforth. In 1829, following jurisdictional disputes, he withdrew the missionary faculties of the Downside monks, among whom was sub-prior Polding. This scandalous public dispute led Rome to establish a process of arbitration which finally resulted in resolution in August 1835, while Polding was in Hobart Town (see Pamela J. Gilbert, *This Restless Prelate: Bishop Peter Baines*, Gracewing, Leominster, 2003).

14 May Musical Festival

(*Sydney Herald*, 14 May 1835, p 2)

We understand that a grand Performance of Sacred Music, consisting of the Messiah, &c. is in course of preparation at the Catholic Chapel, which will be given on the arrival of the Roman Catholic Bishop, who is expected daily.

16 May 1835 Cardinal Fransoni to Polding

(*Adjutor Deus* I.18)

Rome
16 May 1835

Most Illustrious and Most Reverend Lord,

With great joy I learnt from Your Lordship's letter, dated 16 March that you would most likely sail from Liverpool early next day with your companions and your fellow workers in the Mission whose names you have given to me. But I was glad to hear that the delay, which owing to circumstances, forced you to stay in England, turned out fruitfully; for indeed from the large sum of money collected from the alms of the Faithful, you achieved a great advantage for the Mission in New Holland.

You have petitioned for two faculties besides those already granted you by the Holy See, namely, that the same dispensations from Saturday abstinence and on the Feast Days granted to England be extended to your Vicariate, and that you be given the Faculty of establishing in the same Vicariate and English Benedictine Congregation, such as now flourishes in England, with the necessary adaptations. His Holiness graciously assented to the first of your petitions, as you will gather from the attached documents, but the Holy father has decided that at least for the present the second faculty be withheld.

When your voyage has ended and you have examined the state of the Vicariate entrusted to your Pastoral care, I shall await your accurate report on specific matters.

Now I pray God to keep your Lordship safe and well for long years to come.

Your most devoted brother,
G.F.Cardinal Fransoni – Prefect.

18 May 1835 PAPAL RULE OF OUR COLONIES

(*Sydney Herald*,18 May 1835, p 4)

Surely the *Standard* must have been misinformed when it states that a Dr Poulding has lately been made a bishop by the Pope and commissioned to go to Australia to found a Roman Catholic. Church, &c, &c, there; that Mr. Spring Rice granted him £1,000 per annum, paid for the outfit of himself and his chaplains, and given him 1,000 acres of land wherewith to endow and support a Roman Catholic College! It is impossible and yet we know not how to disbelieve our contemporary's assertion any more than we know how to measure Mr. Spring Rice's affection for the Church of England. But this we ask, is the King of Great Britain or is he not, head of the Church throughout his dominions? and if he is, by what authority does Mr. Spring Rice set up the Pope's in his Majesty's Colonies? We are not quite clear but that Mr. Rice, if he has perpetrated so bare-faced an action, has subjected himself to the penalties of *praemunire* enacted against all who hold any intercourse with the Pope of Rome.[52] We will make further enquiries, and if we find the *Standard*'s report to be correct-let Mr. Spring Rice look to it!

21 May 1835 Colonel Christopher Bird to Bishop Morris[53]

(Birt I.257)

Liesbeck Cottage near Cape Town
21 May 1835

. . . The accounts I have of Dr Polding give me but small hopes he is touching here. I don't believe he was to leave England before April; he takes out 7 gentlemen besides himself, 4 of whom are priests, the others are in Orders, but go under the name of Catechists. Government

52. *Praemunire*: the offence of appealing to the authority of a foreign court, especially that of the pope, and thus questioning the supremacy of the English crown.
53. Christopher Chapman Bird (1769–1861), Lieutenant-Colonel and Colonial Secretary at the Cape. He was dismissed from office in 1824 for refusing, as a faithful Catholic, to take the unmodified oath of loyalty to the Crown containing elements offensive to Catholics. At his appointment in 1807 he had taken the modified oath of loyalty devised for the Catholics of Quebec. Bird lived in Cape Town until 1843 when he retired to Bruges in Belgium.
Bishop Morris exercised ecclesiastical jurisdiction over the Cape Colony, part of his Vicariate Apostolic.

allows these gentlemen £150 a year each, but not more to the Bishop than to the others; besides this, £50 a head is allowed in aid of their passage; but Dr Polding has been very successful in a quest which he has made in aid of his mission, and he has preached several sermons with the same view; at one of these at Bath, he collected £138. He is to establish a seminary at Sydney, and he has invited me to send my youngest son thither for the next 3 or 4 years, which I shall seriously consider of, when I hear of the success of his undertaking.

22 May 1835 By the bye

(*Australian* 22 May 1835, p 2)

By the bye, we are informed that the newly appointed Roman Catholic Bishop was one of the passengers to this place by the *Sir Thomas Munro* which was wrecked unfortunately, on one of the Cape De Verd Islands, and that he has gone back to England.

23 May 1835 Mrs. Sarah Neve to Dr Polding[54]

(Birt I.258–259)

Cheltenham,
23 May 1835

Right Rev. and Dear Sir,
I cannot let an opportunity pass without saying, How do you do? – where will this find you? . . .

It may be as proper now as at any other time to say that I mean after my death to bequeath to your Library (i.e., the Library of the Bishop of New South Wales) some books which may be very serviceable thereto, it being an Infant Library . . .

Adieu, my dear Rev. friend. Pray give me your blessing and good prayers. I say nothing for my neighbours as they will speak for themselves.

Ever remaining,
Your most respectful servant,
Sarah Neve

54. Sarah Neve (1767–1842), widow since 1828 of Anglican rector Rev. Charles Neve, was a benefactor of the Benedictines' Gloucestershire missions at Cheltenham and Sodbury.

28 May 1835 Death Notice

(*Liverpool Mercury*, September 4, 1835)

On the 28th of May last, on board the Oriental, the Rev. Clement Fisher, late of St Anthony's Chapel, in this town.

1 June Ship News

(*Sydney Herald*, 1 June 1835, p 3)

By a letter received in Sydney from one of the passengers of the *Sir Thomas Munroe*, it appears that the whole of her cargo was lost. The Roman Catholic Bishop coming out to this Colony was a passenger in this vessel, has it appears stopped at the Islands, in expectation of meeting with a passage by some vessel touching there.

Whig Colonial Misrule

(*Sydney Herald*, 1 June 1835, p 4)

Now the very latest act of Mr. Spring Rice, previous to his leaving office, was the appointment of a Popish Bishop to New South Wales, paid by the Protestant State of England at the rate of £1,000 per annum, to confess and administer spiritual consolation to the transported Irish rebels in that colony. There, reader, do you think I could conclude with a more choice morceau? Certainly not. And so ends my chapter of Whig Colonial Misdeeds.

7 August 1835 Ship News

(*True Colonist* [Hobart], Friday 7/8/1835, p 8)

AUG. 7.—Arrived the Oriental, from Liverpool, the 20th March, with the Right Rev. Dr Poulding, Catholic Bishop of Austral-Asia, Rev Mr Corcoran, Rev. Mr. Cothram, Rev. Mr. Gregory, Rev. Mr. Spencer, Mr Lamner [Sumner], Mr Kenny, Mr Rording [Harding], Mr Curloy, Mr Smith, and Mr Curloys, cabin passengers, and Mr Giles, Catherine M'Canbish, James Steward, M. Darcy and John Gorman, all for Sydney. Van Diemen's Land - Mr. Elliott and Mr. Roberts.

Bishop Paulding

(*True Colonist*, 7 August 1835, p 2)

We had the pleasure to-day of seeing this Gentleman visiting the unfortunate man, Dunn, in company with Mr. Connolly. We hope we will now hear no more Catholic dissensions here, and that the Bishop will set everything to rights.[55]

11 August 1835 Domestic Intelligence

(*Colonial Times*, Tuesday 11 August 1835, p 7)

By an advertisement, we find some of the Catholics have thanked His Excellency for being civil to their newly arrived Bishop. This is a high joke-what, thank His Excellency for common decent conduct towards the highest dignitary of the Church in the Colony! Why, forsooth, we shall hear some day of a vote of thanks being returned to him for eating his dinner with a knife and fork.

13 September 1835 Shipping Intelligence

(*Sydney Herald*, Monday 14/9/1835, p 2)

ARRIVALS. From Liverpool via Hobart Town, yesterday, having sailed form the former port in April, and the latter on the 5th instant, the ship Oriental, 507 tons, Captain Allen, with merchandise. Passengers, Rev. Dr Poulding (sic), Catholic Bishop, Rev. Mr. Cochrane (sic), Rev. Mr. Spencer, Rev. Mr. Gregory, Mr. J. Curteys, Mrs. Curteys, Mr. Flowers, Lieutenant Caswell, R. N., Mr. James Smith, Caroline McCaudlish, John Gorman, James Stewart, Edward Coffee, and Michael Davey.

---

55. Mr. Connolly: Philip Conolly (1786–1839), pioneer Catholic priest in Van Diemen's Land, arrived in Hobart in 1821.
The prisoner Dunn had been sentenced to death for a burglary. He was hanged on 11 August.

Arrival of the Bishop

(Ullathorne, *The autobiography*, p 110)

ON September 13th, 1835, the Right Rev. Father Bede Polding, Bishop of Hieroccesarea, Vicar-Apostolic of New Holland and Van Diemen's Land, arrived in Sydney, accompanied by three priests and four ecclesiastical students. He had stayed for a time in Hobart Town, where he was received by Governor Sir George Arthur with marked courtesy and hospitality. He found things in the same state in which I had found them; but left there a Benedictine priest, the Rev. Father Cottram (sic), and an ecclesiastical student, afterwards Dean Kenny, to open and teach a school for the people.

The Bishop's house was ready for his reception.[56] The Catholic population received him with great joy, and presented him with a handsome carriage and pair as expressive of their wish to maintain him in his dignity. He was well received by the Governor and the chief officials, to most of whom he was the bearer of letters. He received a stipend of £400 a year, and I retained mine and remained to assist him in my former office.

20 September 1835 Installation of Bishop Polding

(*Sydney Monitor*, Wednesday 23 September 1835, p 3)

The installation of the Right Rev. Dr Polding, Catholic Bishop of these Colonies, took place on Sunday last in the Catholic Church, Hyde Park. The Bishop was received at the great door at the west end of the building, by the Clergy dressed in their sacerdotal vestments, and having put on his Episcopal Robes, and assumed his Crosier and mitre, he and the Clergy moved in procession to the foot of the High Altar, chaunting the *Te Deum*, accompanied by the organ, at the conclusion of which, the bulls of consecration from the Holy See were read by the Rev. Mr. Ullathorne, after which his Lordship received the submission of the Clergy, according to their dignity in the Church. On introducing his Lordship to his flock, the Rev. Vicar General delivered

56. Ullathorne had leased the Woolloomooloo estate, established in 1793, and its house, embellished over four decades, for the bishop's residence. It was situated on a bay east of, and within walking distance of St Mary's. Polding established it as a house of formation for his novices, among whom was Lewis Harding. The tenancy ended in 1848.

an appropriate discourse, during the delivery of which, the Bishop appeared to be deeply affected; his Lordship then addressed the congregation in a most feeling and impressive manner, dwelling with considerable force upon the merits of the Rev. Gentleman who had filled for some time the office of Vicar in this Colony, and the excellent qualities of the Pastor, to whose zeal they were indebted for the noble structure in which they were then assembled, and whose absence on this occasion seemed to be much felt by the congregation.[57] The Bishop concluded by alluding to, and complimenting the gentlemen by whom he had been accompanied, and hoped that the Flock would abide by the instructions of those who had forsaken their Country and friends, in order to administer to their spiritual wants. High mass was next performed by his Lordship in a most edifying manner, at the end of which he gave his solemn blessing to a crowded congregation, in which we observed a great many Protestant ladies and gentlemen. Mr. Cavendish presided at the organ, and the music, which was most beautiful, was we understand executed by Mr. Rust and several of the clergymen. Mrs. Rust was in excellent voice, and her execution of some of the most difficult passages was delightful in the extreme, she certainly appears to much more advantage in sacred music than at concerts. From what we have heard of Dr Polding, we are led to anticipate the best results, both in a religious and moral point of view, and hail his arrival amongst us with the greatest satisfaction.

REMINISCENCES OF THE VOYAGE

Very Rev. Dean John Kenny[58]

(*History of the Commencement and Progress of Catholicity in Australia up to the Year 1840*, Sydney 1886, pp 67–69)

57. The absent pastor was John Joseph Therry.
58. John Kenny (1816–1886) was 19 when he sailed with Polding's missionary group to Australia. After six months as a catechist in Hobart Town, he sailed to Sydney and joined Polding's household of seminarians, studying and teaching catechism to incoming convicts. He was ordained priest in 1843 and served in country districts until 1867 when he was appointed to the mission of North Sydney. Polding honoured him with the title of dean in 1872. In 1875 he had brief interim charge of the diocese of Armidale and was said to have later declined an offer of the bishopric (see John Barrett, 'Kenny, John (1816–1886)', Australian Dictionary of Biography, National Centre of Biography, Australian National University, http://adb.anu.edu.au/biography/kenny-john-2298/text2969, published first in hardcopy 1967, accessed online 23 January 2019).

Full of zeal and fervour, the new and first bishop of Australia immediately began to select subjects for his distant and extensive vicariate. Many were the applicants to help him in his arduous mission; nine persons were chosen to accompany him, viz., three priest, Revs. Fisher, J. Corcoran, and A. Cotham, O.S.B.; Rev. J. B. Sumner, O.S.B., sub-deacon; catechists and ecclesiastical students, Rev. John Spencer, O.S.B., professed; Rev. H. Gregory, O.S.B., professed; and Messrs. Harding and Kenny. The bishop applied to the Home Government for pecuniary aid to assist in bringing out those missionaries to the colony. It was in February 1835, that Lord Aberdeen appointed four additional Roman Catholic chaplains for New South Wales, with an annual stipend of £150 to each, and in the number was included Dr Polding, the bishop; the catechists received £100 each. When all things were ready, the heroic party met in Liverpool at the Misses Slater, relatives of the bishop, and nieces of Bishop Slater of Mauritius.

It was in the month of April [sic], 1835, that the company, with the Right Reverend Dr Polding, sailed from Liverpool in the good old ship 'Oriental'; she was towed to Birkenhead by a steamer, on which were a great many of the bishop's friends and admirers, wishing him God speed and praying for the success of his glorious mission. When the 'Oriental' was leaving Liverpool and moving down the Mersey, the poor Irish labourers at the docks gave three hearty cheers for a prosperous voyage. Alas! Some of them had friends in that far distant land, to whom they hoped the bishop and clergy would give consolation. It was all well with us, (the writer was one of the party) till we reached the Bay of Biscay; then old ocean seemed to dispute our passage; we encountered a terrible sea, and were tossed to and fro by the winds and waves, and never shall I forget the last assault, when a towering wave, erect as a wall, fell over us, forced in the front of the cuddy and cabins; their contents and seats were floating in the saloon. But the old East Indiaman stood it bravely, and this was the first and last rude shock she received. After this we enjoyed fine weather and fair winds, with nothing to incommode us except *le mal de mer*. So soon as we were recovered from our sickness, and able to keep our equilibrium, by the directions of the bishop we were engaged in study – some studying theology; and there were frequent religious conferences, over which Dr Polding always presided; and others employed in preparatory studies, under the direction of a priest – so that the ship became like a small ecclesiastical seminary. When the vessel was steady we had mass every morning, and the bishop gave us a discourse every Sunday. We were becalmed at the line, and had only crossed it about a fortnight when a great affliction befell us in the loss of one of the priests, the Rev. Fisher. He was sickly when he came on board, but it was hoped that the sea voyage would restore to him his health. He died calmly and resigned to the will of God, having received the last rites of the church at the hands of the good bishop. Most serene was the afternoon, when wrapped in a canvas shroud his remains were lowered from the Archbishop's cabin into a watery grave;[59] both sea and sky in their solemn silence seemed to condole with us. The sacred mysteries had been celebrated that morning by every priest for the repose of his soul, and matins and lauds were said around his remains before he was committed to the deep. 'Requiescat in pace.'

The 'Oriental' had favourable winds and fine weather till we neared the Derwent River, in Tasmania, where we were prevented by contrary winds for some days from reaching Hobart Town. We cast anchor in the Derwent, some distance from the town, on the 6th August, 1835. There for the first time we enjoyed the delights of the Australian climate; smooth as glass were the waters of this majestic river, and not a leaf stirred on its thickly wooded banks, not a breath of wind to stir the sails. The brace old ship after the travel of 16,000 miles lay motionless on the bosom of the waters, with her image perfectly reflected from the glassy surface. We were soon surrounded by many boats, full of people curious to see the new arrivals and gather some new from home. Lieutenant Small was the first visitor. Some of us were rather disappointed at the civilised appearance of our visitors; for we expected to see canoes filled with sable strangers, the native blacks; we thought the former rather common place, not differing in face, clothing, or manners, from those we might have seen had we only reached as far as the Firth of Forth, in Scotland. Two of the bishop's party went to Hobart Town, the Reverends Corcoran and Sumner, and they brought us the news that the town was larger than they thought, and that an old priest, *viz.* Father Connelly, had been there for twelve years; that there were some respectable Catholics, but his flock was not numerous; but it gave us a good opinion of the land and climate when we saw in their hands a few apples which they brought from father Connelly's garden. His Excellency, Governor Arthur, sent his boat, well manned,

59. Polding did not become an Archbishop until 1842.

to take the bishop ashore. The day we left the ship we were introduced to Father Connelly, at his residence, by the bishop, and dined there . . ..

Bishop Polding left Hobart Town on 5th September for Sydney, in the same ship the 'Oriental', in which he came, accompanied by one priest, three religious who were professed monks of St Benedict and two ecclesiastical students viz: Messrs. Harding and Gorman. He left in Hobart Town Reverend A. Cotham and Mr. John Kenny.

Sizar Elliott[60]

(*Fifty years of colonial life*, Melbourne 1886, pp 20–26)

On the 27th of March, 1815, I left Brunswich Dock, Liverpool, in the ship Oriental, captain Allen, bound for New South Wales, calling at Hobart. There was a lot of friends to see us off. As soon as the passengers could show themselves, I found that the principal figure amongst them was the Right Rev. Dr John Polding, Bishop of Hiero Cœsarea and Vicar Apostolic of New South Wales. He with some clergymen were going to Sydney.

After the first day or so, we all mustered at table, eleven gentlemen and one lady, the wife of one of the passengers. The Rev. Mr. Cochran [sic], in giving his experience of his first night on board, said: 'As I laid on my back in bed, I found myself standing upright.' We took our departure from Cape Clear on the 31st March, Lat. 51°8' N, Long 11°12' W.[61]

60. Sizar Elliott (1814–1901) was born in England and taken to Canada as a child following the death of his father; he sailed from Liverpool for Hobart Town on the *Oriental* in February 1835. He soon moved to Sydney where he was an innovative merchant. When his business failed, he moved to Melbourne, where in 1858 he became a City Councillor; in 1859 he was appointed a magistrate (see E. A. Beever, 'Elliott, Sizar (1814–1901)', *Australian Dictionary of Biography*, National Centre of Biography, Australian National University, http://adb.anu.edu.au/biography/elliott-sizar-3478/text5325, published first in hardcopy 1972; accessed online 6 January 2019).
Cardinal Moran reproduced Elliott's reminiscences about the voyage as an 'Additional Note to Chapter VI' in his *History of the Catholic Church in Australasia*, Sydney, 1894. He described Elliott as 'one of those who sailed in that vessel for Tasmania, probably at present the only survivor of the expedition' (p. 1000).
61. Cape Clear Island lies south-west of County Cork.

I can't but say its an awkward sight
To see one's native land receding through
The growing waters – it unmans me quite,
Especially when life is rather new.

The ship I found to be an old East Indiaman, teak built. She had been in the China trade, making one trip a year. We carried four guns and a quantity of small arms, as there were still pirates investing high seas. The cabin allotted to me was large and comfortable, and with my hammock swinging in the centre I could read or sleep at ease. We soon settled down to business and enjoyment; and the ship being well formed, we were not long in becoming a happy family.

One part of our work was making ourselves into a defensive body against pirates. Each man and boy on the ship had his place in case of attack, and it may be interesting to young people of this safe age to see how we had to be prepared for battle fifty years ago.

VICTORY or DEATH
QUARTER BILL[62]

TO COMMAND
Captain Allen

HELM
Andrew Cheyne

COCK PIT
Dr Sampson, and Right Rev. Dr Polding to assist

GUARD COLOURS
Mr. Curtoys

QUARTER DECK
Mr. Henry

MAGAZINE
Joseph De Luza

PUMPS
Kirk Carpenter

62. *Quarter Bill*: a list specifying the stations to be taken by a ship's officers and crew in time of action.

TO PASS THE WORD, & c.
Andrew Harrison

FORECASTLE
Small arms men:

Wm. Slater, Capt., Mr. Spencer, A. MacLachlan (Boatswain), Mr. Kenny, Wm. Hughes, Jos. Steward.

1ST GUN.
Arthur Davis, 1st Capt.
Jas. Gaunson, 2nd do.
John Russell, sail trimmer.
Andw. Aukeron, firer and boarder.
Robt. Kirk., 2nd sail trimmer.
Boy Heath, carry powder.

2ND GUN.
Georges Nares, 1st Capt.
C. McGregor, 2nd do
H. Moran, sail trimmer.
J. Smith, firer and boarder.
Jas. Rossi, 2nd sail trimmer.
Boy Brocket, carry powder.

3rd GUN.
John Davies, 1st Capt.
Geo. Brown, 2nd do.
Rd. Newton, sail trimmer.
Js. Cowan, firer and boarder.
Edwd. Coffee, 2nd sail trimmer.
John Carman [Gorman], carry powder.

4th GUN.
Jas. Pugh, 1st Capt.
Edwd. Wilson, 2nd Captain.[63]
Edwd. Walker, sail trimmer.
Edwd. Cawlfon, firer and boarder.
Mick Daicy, 2nd sail trimmer.
Boy Veal, carry powder.

MAIN TOP
Mr. Smith and Boy Cockle

FORE TOP
Mr. Roberts and Boy Bently

MIZEN TOP
Mr. Elliott and Boy Fisher

Small arm men under direction of Mr. Lancaster (third mate):
Mr. Cocran [sic], Mr. Cotham, Mr. Gregory, Mr. Harding, Mr. Fisher.

63. While in Hobart, Wilson was charged with 'deserting from the *Oriental*. He was admonished and returned.' (*Colonial Times*, 18 August 1835, page 8).

Fortunately, there was no actual need for all these preparations; we never saw a pirate, and therefore never had to put to the test our motto 'Victory or Death', and perhaps that was well.

The second Sunday out, the Bishop gave us an invitation to attend divine service in his own room. I attended, and was much pleased. He gave us an excellent *extempore* sermon. The service was in English, except the hymn. The Rev. John Benedict Spencer presided at the piano. But the conducting of sermons was not the Bishop's only strong point. He was a most social and kindly man; he joined in whist parties, and invited us to his cabin once a week for a social evening, singing and music. He was fond of a bit of quiet fun and amusement. I remember on one occasion I made my appearance in his apartment; on entering, he said,' Pray, Mr. Elliott, what may be your pleasure tonight?'

'Why, my Lord, said I, is it not our social evening?'

'Yes', said the Bishop, 'but where is your tumbler?' The reason for this question was, that on a swinging tray in the cabin was a jorum of punch, and each one on entering had to fill his glass, and sit down where he could.

I was not much of a larrikin, but on one occasion Mr. Roberts and myself played a trick on the Bishop. Before going to his cabin, we made up our minds that we would have a song out of the Bishop; and this was the way we went about it. We all sung our songs in rotation, after which Mr. Roberts called on the Bishop for a song: 'It is your turn now, my Lord.'

'My turn for what?' said the Bishop.

'To sing a song; we have each had our turn.'

The Bishop was sitting in his easy chair, he cleared his throat, and sang nearly through one verse, but broke down, and finished by saying, 'Gentlemen, I cannot sing you a song, but I will preach you a sermon.' He had beaten us; we will not wait to hear the sermon.

Twelve or thirteen of us used to assemble on these social nights, and the kindly feeling that these evenings engendered helped us to pass the time more pleasantly and enjoy our voyage. The character that he then had he retained during the time he was in Sydney; he was always liked, was a most liberal-minded man, and during his residence in New South Wales (a period of twenty years) he so won upon the people that at his death thousands of persons of all denominations attended his funeral.[64]

We crossed the line on Saturday the 9th of May. We had had our usual exercise at the guns, part of Saturday's drill to be ready for pirates, and had gone to tea. After tea, Neptune's messenger made his appearance over the bows and was desired to walk aft, and a pretty fine messenger he made. He was painted black, and had on an old hat, the crown of which was cut into four quarters, and the points left sticking up. He asked a number of questions, and informed us that Neptune himself would make his appearance to welcome his children on Monday. Presently, word was brought that a ship was bearing down upon us. We all rushed out of our cabins to see her, when we were immediately drenched by water thrown upon us from the maintops and poop.

On Monday, great preparations were made for the proper reception of Neptune. At twelve o'clock, his train appeared. It was headed by a man on his hands and knees covered with a sheep-skin and made to represent a bear, he had a chain from his leg to Neptune's carriage. Then followed eight constables with clubs, painted all manner of colors, and commanded by a chief with a drawn sword. Following these were the men who had crossed the line before, dragging Neptune and Amphitrite seated on a gun-carriage with an awning over them formed by four hand-spikes attached to the carriage. Neptune had immense whiskers, breast and stomach naked and a sheep-skin over his loins, and a trident in his hands. Amphitrite was one of the apprentices painted. He had on gown, bonnet and curls.

When all was ready, Neptune hailed the *Oriental*, and was desired to come aft. A sail had been doubled and suspended by the corners and about a couple of hogsheads of water put into it. When Neptune came aft, the sailors were called one at a time, blindfolded, drenched with water, and drawn up in line and asked questions such as, 'Did you ever cross the line before? Will you eat brown bread when you can get white?' Anything to make them open their mouths, upon which a brush was thrust in full of soapsuds. They were next mounted on a ladder that reached to the rim of the bent sail, and seated there while

64. Polding died in Sydney in March 1877, 41½ years after his arrival.

the face was tarred and scraped with the half of a pair of sheep-shears, and finally dropped into the water and well ducked by the bear. The ministers were let off, which was by no means fair, while the rest of the passengers were kept below and called up one at a time. The Doctor was called up and had to go through the ceremony, except the tarring. He cut up rough, and attempted to throw a bottle overboard that was standing on the deck, but being a 'little in the wind' it struck the bulwarks, and the doctor and mate got to words, and from that to blows-or I should say, the doctor got the blows from the mate, and tried to show fight but could not, and so went down to his cabin crying.

When it came to my turn, I stepped out. They asked the usual questions, and tried to stop my mouth with soapsuds, and then let me into the water, and gave me a good soaking. The tar brush was close at hand, and one of the men gave me a rubbing, in spite of the captain's positive orders that passengers should not be thus treated. The captain seeing this, stopped proceedings, stopped the grog, and set all the men to work, and the day ended unsatisfactorily to all parties.

On the 13th of May, my twenty-first birthday, in the evening, while we were at tea, a large meteor rose from the larboard fore-yard-arm. It appeared like an immense ball of fire a foot-and-a-half in diameter, and with a blue tail three timed its length. It passed nearly over the poop; the second mate moved from his place, thinking it was coming on him, and it split in two and vanished, leaving everyone to conjecture what it was. It was as bright for the time as if the sun was out, such a splendid sight I have not seen. Lat. 37° S.

After a very interesting voyage of 133 days we arrived off Hobart, and saw Mount Wellington in the distance, with its top covered with snow. This was on the 7th day of August 1835. It did my eyes good to see snow once more. My next view of this Mountain, forty-three years afterwards, was under very different circumstances. The next day we all landed. That was in the old convict days. There were some eight or ten men to be hung next morning. The Bishop's first work was to visit the jail, to see if he could render spiritual assistance to any of the condemned men.

I stopped here a week, and the ship went on to Sydney, leaving Father Cotham behind.

Appendix II
Documents and Correspondence relating to the 1846 Voyage

27 January 1846 Polding to Sir George Gipps[1]

(*Polding Letters* II.50)

Sydney
27 January 1846

Sir,
On the 18th of December I had the honor to address a letter to the Government in reference to the proposed absence of the Vicar General, the Reverend Dr Gregory, from the Colony on public business requiring confidential agency in Europe.

On the 30th of the same month I received a communication conveying a favourable consideration of my application, which I very gratefully acknowledge.

Since that period, on a careful review of all the circumstances, with the advice of those it becomes me to consult, I have come most reluctantly to the conclusion, that I shall best promote the public interests in question by personally visiting Europe. My absence will not extend beyond eighteen months.

I have therefore most respectfully to solicit Your Excellency to transfer to my absence from the Colony that kind consent and concurrence you were pleased to express in reference to that of Dr Gregory.

I have etc.
+ J.B.Polding

1. Major Sir George Gipps (1791–1847) was Governor of New South Wales, arriving in February 1838 and departing in July 1846.

29 January 1846 Polding to G.F.Cardinal Fransoni

(*Polding Letters* II.50–51)

Sydney
29 January 1846

Most Eminent Cardinal,
I have already signified to Your Eminence that I had intended to send as deputy to Europe my Vicar General, on account of very grave causes pertaining to this mission – among the chief being that the deficiency of Missionaries could be made good . . .

However, a second reason, and indeed a very grave one, for visiting the Holy City is to ask from the Sacred Congregation that in its wisdom it would provide more amply for spiritual needs so that on behalf of these regions especially the number of Bishops be increased. At least it seems necessary, so that the infant Church on the death of the Pastor might not incur grave loss, that it should appoint a Coadjutor for me . . .

Taking advantage of this same opportunity, there are to be placed at the feet of the Most Holy Father, the canons, Acts, decrees, Admonitions of the Council and of the First Synod in this our Province of Australia in the name of the Archbishop, the Bishops and the Missionaries.[2]

I have informed Your Eminence that it was my intention to send Rev. Father Gregory Gregory to Rome. It is necessary to alter that intention . . . To speak the truth, many matters have made common knowledge, which I am unwilling to recount. Enough to call to mind the rumour that is being spread abroad about Dr Gregory's going to Rome to be made a Bishop; if suspicions, or rather assertions were turned into truths, no small scandal would prevail.[3] Wherefore Gregory himself,

2. Polding was Archbishop of Sydney, which covered the whole of the Colony of New South Wales, and Metropolitan of a Province covering the other Australian colonies, Van Diemen's Land, South Australia and Western Australia, in all of which bishops had been appointed by 1846.
3. Rumours about Gregory becoming a bishop could have been fuelled by the fact that in January 1846, in the absence of a third bishop, he participated with Polding and Bishop Pompallier, all three clad in 'splendid copes wrought in gold', in the episcopal consecration of Philippe-Joseph Viard at St Mary's Cathedral. (*Morning Chronicle*, 7 January 1846, page 2). See Appendix II: *The Sentinel*, 19 February 1846 and Lang's letter to *SMH*, 14 March 1846.

devoid of all ambition, is on account of those rumours much opposed to a journey to Europe.

In this state of affairs what is to be done? Together with our Missionaries we have offered many prayers, many Masses, to seek out the divine Will. Then when we consulted those whom we are accustomed to consult in our difficulties it seemed best that we ourselves should personally travel to Europe. I must also signify to Your Excellency what opinion the most skilled doctors have given viz. that it is much better for Gregory, whose health is not robust but quite uncertain, to remain in Australia rather than to be engaged in journeying through so many dangers of climate.

Besides, thanks to God the Giver of all gifts, all things are in peace; enterprises happily begun are progressing towards completion and directing those works is rather the duty of the Vicar general than of the Archbishop. Wherefore, against my will, and also reluctantly, now that I am growing old, I am again attacking the difficult and long journey. I am in a state of difficulty. The consolation is that while I have not thought of such a thing, it is allowed to me once again to kiss the feet of His Holiness, the Pastor of all the faithful and, as suppliant, to seek his paternal blessing for myself and my people.[4] There are many things in my heart pertaining to quite serious religious matters in this country which I do not deny I am anxious to reveal to Your Eminence. However, the ship will be sailing on 12th day of February.

From the city of London I shall again write to Your Eminence; and I shall send an account of the state of the Mission and of the Province and I shall explain in all simplicity and humility, what things in my opinion are to be done. Thus, without delay all being placed in the hands of Your Eminence, my absence from my jurisdiction may be made as brief as possible.

With the greatest veneration,
I am
Your Eminence's most humble servant,
John Bede, Archbishop of Sydney.

---

4. Polding had expected to be kissing the feet of the aged Pope Gregory XVI. However, Gregory died on 1 June 1846, aged 80. It would be the feet of the 54 year-old Pius IX, that Polding would stoop to kiss in June 1847.

31 January 1846 Sir George Gipps to Lord Stanley[5]

(HRA xxiv.748)

Government House[6]
Sydney
31 January 1846[7]

My Lord,
I have the honor to report to Your Lordship that the Most Reverend Dr Polding, the recognised head of the Roman Catholic community in this Colony, is about to proceed to England with my consent and concurrence.

By my Despatch Number 179 of the 20th November, 1840, it will be seen that Roman Catholic Clergymen, not being Officers of the Government, are not considered by the Executive Council to fall under the provisions of the 22d Geo. 3rd, ch. 75, in respect of leave of absence.[8]

In have informed Dr Polding that I do not feel I have authority to order payment of his Salary (£500 per annum) during his absence; but I beg to recommend it may be granted to him under Your Lordship's authority, and charged on Schedule C of the 5th and 6th Vict. ch. 76.[9]

There are funds in the hands of this Government amply sufficient for the purpose; and I shall pay into the Military Chest the sum of £750 (being the amount of his salary for a year and a half), as soon as I am informed that the payment of it is sanctioned by Your Lordship.

My Despatches dated and numbered as in the margin will shew that Dr Polding was absent from the Colony from the close of the year 1840

5. Edward George Geoffrey Smith-Stanley (1799–1869), Lord Stanley of Bickerstaffe, was Secretary of State for War and the Colonies from September 1841 to December 1845, in Peel's second ministry.
   At the time of Gipps letter, Lord Stanley had been succeeded by William Ewart Gladstone (1809–1898), then a Conservative.
6. Gipps occupied the newly completed Government House in Sydney in 1845. The dilapidated state of the original Sydney residence had led governors to prefer residing at Parramatta from 1821.
7. By this date, unbeknown to Gipps, Lord Stanley had been replaced at the Colonial Office.
8. Colonial Leave of Absence Act of 1782.
9. Australian Constitutions Act of 1842.

to some time early in 1843; but I have not on that account thought it necessary or right to object to his again proceeding to Europe.

I enclose a copy of Dr Polding's letter to me of the 27th instant.

I have &c.,
Geo. Gipps.

Sir George Gipps to Lord Stanley

(Despatch marked 'private' [HRA xxiv.748]) Government House

Sydney
31 January 1846

My Lord
Referring to my public Despatch Number 25 of this day's date, I beg leave to state that Dr Polding proceeds to England with my full concurrence, and that I am anxious he should be well received at the Colonial Office.

It may be right for me to state that, by this Government and myself, he is designated '*The Most Reverend Archbishop Polding*'.[10]

The circumstances under which he assumed the style of 'Archbishop of Sydney' are stated in my despatch Number 38 of 28th March, 1843. The title of Archbishop of Sydney is never given to him by this Government, nor the appellation of 'Your Grace', but they are very generally by the members of his own Church.

I am confidentially informed by Dr Polding that one of the objects of his visit to Europe is to procure the appointment of an Englishman as Coadjutor to the Roman Catholic Bishop of New Zealand; and that, if this can be effected, the present Bishop, Dr Pompallier, who is a *Frenchman*, will withdraw from the Island.[11]

10. Polding was named the Archbishop of the newly created Archdiocese of Sydney in 1842. He had chaffed under the 'foreign title' of Hiero-Caesarea, for which he was regularly mocked in Sydney.
11. The prospect of the departure of the French bishop from New Zealand would have been pleasing to the British Government. Britain had annexed New Zealand in 1840, but continued nervous about French intentions. This attitude found expression in sectarian newspapers in Sydney (see articles in *The Sentinel* and Rev. J. D. Lang's letter in Appendix II).

4 February 1846 Polding to Bishop R.W.Willson[12]

(*Polding Letters* II.52–53)

Sydney
4 February 1846

Mr dear Lord
In my last letter, I informed your Lordship that circumstances requiring a visit to Europe, I had resolved to send the Vicar General.

Since, on a careful review of all circumstances, I have concluded that a preferable arrangement will be to leave the V.G. here to conduct affairs in my absence and to proceed in person. I shall accordingly sail in the Ratcliffe which is put down for the 12th of this month. As she has been deferred more than once, I apprehend the day of sailing will not be beyond the 15th.

In the course of duty I shall have to visit the Holy City and lay before the Holy Father the state of the Archbishopric and Province.

Of course the affairs of the Church in Your Lordship's Diocese will be mentioned, and I think it but right to signify the same to you. In order that you may adopt such means as may seem required. Certainly I shall petition for a decision as regards the exercise of Archiepiscopal authority Your Lordship protested against. It is desirable that all documents and statements be in the hands of the Cardinal Prefect in or about the month of September.[13] . . .

It was odd of Polding to be proposing to advocate an English coadjutor for Pompallier, given that in January, at St Mary's Cathedral, he had consecrated Philippe-Joseph Viard as Pompallier's coadjutor. Pompallier was co-consecrator (*Morning Chronicle*, 7 January 1846). Perhaps the intricacies of Catholic hierarchy were beyond the comprehension of Governor Gipps.

12. Robert William Willson (1794–1866) was a Nottingham priest recommended by Polding to be first bishop of Hobart Town. Initially very reluctant, Willson was finally consecrated by Bishop Ullathorne and arrived in Van Diemen's Land in May 1844. He and Polding had been at odds over ecclesiastical administration, which resulted in an acrimonious exchange of letters. Willson resigned and returned to England in January 1866 and died four months later.
13. Cardinal Prefect of the Congregation *de Propaganda Fide*, the Papal agency responsible for pre-diocesan missionary jurisdictions.

11 February 1846 Monk of St Mary's to Polding

(Harding Journal, 13 March 1846, p. 39)

If you will, my Lord and Father, be so condescending as to attend to the three following requests of one of your poor children, it will afford him much consolation in your absence

1. That when you arrive at the Tomb of the Apostles to beg their intercession in behalf of your children
2. That you must not be sad under any circumstances
3. That you will hasten back to gladden their hearts, who will follow you in spirit throughout your voyage unceasingly praying to God to attend and protect you.

Monday morning Feb 11'46.

16 February 1846 DEPARTURE OF HIS GRACE THE ARCHBISHOP

(*Morning Chronicle*, 18 February 1846, page 2)[14]

MONDAY last being the day fixed upon for the departure of his Grace the Archbishop of Sydney for Europe by the *Ratcliff*, at an early hour in the morning a large concourse of persons assembled in the vicinity of the metropolitan church of St Mary.

Notwithstanding the gloomy appearance of the weather on Saturday and Sunday, and the indications of rain which the atmosphere presented, Monday morning opened with a cloudless sky, and the day throughout was as propitiously fine as could have been desired.

It had been previously decided upon that the Brethren of the Holy Catholic Guild of St Mary and St Joseph should accompany his Grace in procession from the Church to the Circular Wharf, the place of embarkation, and at about half past eight o'clock the Brethren began to assemble.

---

14. Sydney's first Catholic newspaper *The Australasian Chronicle* (1839–1843) underwent a controversial change from a Scottish to an Irish editor in October 1843, resulting in a change of name to *The Morning Chronicle*; it underwent another name change in July 1846, becoming *The Sydney Chronicle*, which survived until September 1848. After 21 months without a Catholic newspaper, the *Freeman's Journal* was founded in June 1850 and lasted until 1942.

Having robed themselves in the Guild uniform, the Brethren proceeded from St Mary's, which was crowded to excess by an affectionate flock, anxious once more to join their beloved chief pastor in the holy services of their Church.

About ten o'clock, his Grace preceded by the monks and clergy entered the church, and prayers were read by the Very Rev. the Vicar General, who was deeply affected on the solemn occasion. Tears were streaming from eyes, and sighs heaving from hearts in all parts of the sacred edifice at the thought of parting though only for a time, from so endeared a prelate, and many a fervent prayer was breathed to the God of all mercy that he would be graciously pleased to vouchsafe a speedy return to the father of his flock, whose mildness, and truly Christian spirit, has made him not only the beloved of all over whom he has the spiritual charge, but has gained for him the respect, the esteem, and the admiration of the whole community.

As soon as prayers were ended, during the reading of which his Grace was much affected, the Archbishop rose from his knees, and, having ascended the steps of the altar, gave his episcopal blessing to the congregation. The procession was then formed outside the church . . .

The procession proceeded from the church along Macquarie-street, down Bent-street, past the old Guard House to the Circular Wharf, where the *James Watt* steamer was in waiting to receive his Grace.

Thousands of persons attended the procession the whole of the way, and on its arrival at the Circular Wharf that place was crowded with persons anxious to obtain a sight of his Grace previous to his embarkation . . .

The procession having arrived at the Circular Wharf, his Grace went on board the *James Watt* attended by the clergy, the council of the Guild, a large number of the Brethren, and upwards of 300 persons, many of whom were members of other than the Catholic communion, but who were anxious to testify their respect for the Archbishop by accompanying him to the Heads.

Two other steamers were also in attendance, the *Cornubia* and *Comet*, each of which was crowded with passengers; a number of boats of various sizes, many of them filled with ladies, were also in attendance, and accompanied the *Ratcliff* for a considerable distance down the harbour.

His Grace and those persons who intended to accompany him having got on board the *James Watt*, she moved off the wharf, and steamed round to the *Ratcliff* which was lying in the stream. On the steamer coming alongside the ship, a gangway was rigged, and his Grace went on board the vessel destined to convey him from our shores, amidst the fervent prayers and good wishes of his people, to whom he again dispensed his blessing.

The steamer then took the ship in tow and proceeded slowly down the harbour, the shores of which down to below Fort Macquarie, were covered with spectators.

The other two steamers also accompanied her, one on either side. An excellent band was on board the *Comet*, which played several airs appropriate to the occasion, as the vessels slowly proceeded along. On nearing the Heads the *Cornubia* and *Comet* shot forward and went out a good distance to sea; they then returned and steamed several times round the *Ratcliff*, the band on board the *Comet*, each time she neared that vessel striking up an appropriate air, and the passengers on board greeting his Grace with hearty cheers.

The *James Watt* kept the *Ratcliff* in tow until she was about fifteen miles outside the Heads, when sail was made and the warps were cast off. The *James Watt* then steamed round the *Ratcliff*, his Grace appeared upon the poop, took off his hat, and waving his hand took a final adieu of his beloved and loving flock. Before leaving the *Ratcliff* to return to Sydney, the passengers on board the *James Watt* and the *Comet* gave three hearty cheers, as a farewell to his Grace, which was responded to by the seamen on board that vessel; she then got under way and having a fair wind, she very soon lengthened the distance between the two vessels.

The steamer after taking on board the pilot turned her head once more towards Sydney, about half-past four o'clock, to the great comfort of many not only of the ladies but also of the gentlemen on board, who for the last hour or two before had been suffering severely from sea sickness. She reached the Company's wharf about half-past six o'clock in the evening, when the numerous passengers she had on board all appeared to be very well pleased to set their foot once again on *terra firma* . . .

His Grace is accompanied on his voyage by the Rev. Mr. Harding, and it is expected that, should all things go well, his Grace's absence from the Colony will not exceed eighteen months. May God grant him a safe and speedy return to the bosom of that flock in whom his heart is centred

'DEPARTURE OF DR. POLDING FOR EUROPE'

(*The Sentinel*, Thursday 19 February 1846, p 2)[15]

And so the very reverend divine, John Bede Polding, his Grace the Archbishop of Australia, Metropolitan, Spiritual and Political Ruler, thus inducted into the Sydney See, by his Holiness the Pope of Rome, in defiance of our noble Protestant British Senate, has again left the shores of Australia Felix, (it must be so, under the benignant reign of Popery,) for another European spiritual and political tour.

Last Monday morning afforded indeed a sight of the multitudinous followers of the Holy Cross! St Mary's was all on the *qui vive*. Extra prayers and masses were offered and solemnised to all the saints, below and above, including the blessed Virgin, for their protection over his Grace, whilst on the stormy deep for foreign lands, in due form and ceremony, after which the papal cavalcade *en masse* to man, woman, and child, consisting of friars, capuchins, monks, confessors, catechists, in their several grades; holy men of the order of the Guild, clad in black surplices and white bands, with wands in band, emblems of the cross, dangling by their sides, intermixed with a body of non-descripts, clad in green and party colors, with banners of the same (hurrah-for *Ould* Ireland!!!) all headed by a Christian, bearing in a *christian like manner* HIS CROSS-(not the real one, for it was a *golden one*)-and a very numerous papal host, amongst whom were several of the bright ornaments of the city municipal clique, &c., &c., started from the holy convent at ten o'clock, to ship his reverence at the Circular Quay on board a steamer, and thence to the Ratcliff, captain Gilbert, which was safely done in due form. Three steamers

15. *The Sentinel*: Sydney newspaper in print from January 1845 to September 1848. The prospectus announcing its publication described it as: 'a weekly journal of religious, political, and commercial intelligence for the Colony of New South Wales. "I stand continually upon the watch-tower in the day-time, and I am set in my ward whole nights" (Isaiah xxi. 8).' (*Colonial Observer*, Thursday 26 December 1844, page 5). Its editorials and articles were aggressively anti-Catholic.

were in readiness to receive the Archbishop's friends, making excellent freights, to tow and accompany the ship as far as the Heads. After which, some fiddlers having been engaged and gastronometical preparations carried out, it was intended, not to commemorate the departure of the Papal pastor, 'sorrowing for one as though he were not,' but to land and do something in the bush of Australia by way of picknicking and tripping it on the light fantastic toe.

That Doctor Polding is a gentleman and scholar, and also courteous and a benevolent man in pecuniary matters, must be acknowledged by all to whom he is known; and the respect thus paid him by those of his papal see and followers, as justly due and open to admiration, but, like Eli of old, he has rebellious and ungodly children about and within the precincts of his holy church of St Mary, as exemplified at mob-meetings, and particularly in the late public meeting on education, where a ferocious and bigoted 'Father' led on a ruffian mob in opposition with such hideous yells, that Christendom appeared to have been taken possession of by demons. That these proceedings were sanctioned and abetted by the holy clique of St Mary there is no doubt whatever, and hence the Pope's legate in this colony, however noble his personal traits in political, and above all in religious matters, deteriorates from that character, which Christianity would bestow upon him, and places him in juxta-position, after all, of a true follower of the Lamb of God.

And wherefore the hasty and sudden departure of his Reverence to European lands, instead of Doctor Gregory, his secretary? We augur State Politics and Religion to be the moving causes-and perhaps secular motives. . .

With Papal France there is commotion-Popery is in a fix by the opposite parties of state education-Tahiti is still in arms against her ruffian Papal invaders, and France must succumb, and thus defeat the energies of St Mary's clique and their pious missions to the Pacific Isles . . . Pompallier and his minions cannot yet French papalise New Zealand, and get her lands from the Great Company and John Bull . . .

These may be the inducements for the Bishop's return to Europe. How will he take the *Bull* by the horns? Will he increase his Papal strength in this Colony by bringing out more of the priestcraft to shut the Bible up, to keep the ignorant in grossest darkness, and to rally on their cause by sword and by fire? Or will he rather, amidst the storm in Europe, accept of a *Cardinal's hat*, and use his policy in the Vatican, and induct Dr Gregory to the Papal Archbishopric of Australia?[16] . . .

10 March 1846 Rev John Dunmore Lang to the Editors of the *Sydney Morning Herald*[17]

(*Sydney Morning Herald* 14/3/1846)

'ORIGINAL CORRESPONDENCE: ROMISH TACTICS'

Sydney,
March 10

. . . Gentlemen, permit me to state in conclusion-for I have no wish to revert to such a subject again-that in my humble opinion the present is a crisis of transcendent importance to our common Protestantism, as well as to the future welfare and advancement of this colony. We are evidently crossing the Rubicon, and I fear we are crossing it towards Rome in more quarters than one. Any one must be blind not to perceive the extensive conspiracy on foot to Romanise this whole hemisphere. Look at what has been accomplished for this purpose already within the last ten years. The Rev. Dr Polding arrived here, I think, in the year 1836, as the first Romish bishop in these regions. He has since been in Europe-about five years ago-and was made an Archbishop. He is now on his way thither again, for a Cardinal's or 'scarlet coloured' hat, it is said, but certainly to strengthen and extend Romish influence with a view to Romish domination, in these uttermost parts of the earth, and thereby to secure for the Popedom a far more extensive domain than it is now losing in Germany. In the meantime there has been a Romish bishopric erected in New Zealand, to which a coadjutor-bishopric has been added within these few weeks; the former under the Rev. Dr Pompallier, and the other under a M. Viard, both Frenchmen. There has also been another Romish bishopric erected for the western isles of Polynesia, under M. Epalle, a third Frenchman, besides bishoprics in Van Diemen's Land, Southern Australia, and Swan River, all of them having their respective estab-

16. This is a version of the rumour circulating in Sydney: a red hat for Polding with residence in Rome and succession of Gregory to the See of Sydney.
17. John Dunmore Lang (1799–1878), Scottish Presbyterian clergyman, politician, journalist and scourge of Papists.

lishments of priests, schoolmasters bound to the Popedom by the Romish vow of celibacy, and sisters of charity; and we are presently to have one likewise in Port Phillip. Now, the real character of all this, as a regularly organised plan for the establishment of Romish domination in these regions, is evident from the case of Swan River, where the entire population does not exceed four or five thousand souls, of whom a large majority are Protestants. What the real object is of appointing a bishop, with a whole array of priests and sisters of charity, for such a mere handful of people as the Roman Catholics of that Lilliputian colony must necessarily be, it is not difficult to divine . . .

I am, gentlemen, your most obedient servant.
JOHN DUNMORE LANG.

25 March 1846 Polding draft sermon[18]

(Sydney Archdiocesan Archives [*Adjutor Deus* I.152–154])

5 June 1846[19] **Polding to Bishop R.W.Willson**

(*Polding Letters* II.53)

On board ship Ratcliffe
Near Azores
5 June 1846

My dear Lord
[During] the leisure hours of my voyage I have been enabled to devote [myself] in part to that self-recollection and self-examination, which

18. This sermon was written on board the *Ratcliff*. It is a draft of sermon 'on the need to correspond with present grace' (4 pages, double sided, 8 handwritten pages in total). It contains no reference to being at sea, but in contrast to Harding's even writing, that of Polding shows every sign of having been written on a rolling ship (see Introduction, Figure 6). Lewis recorded in his journal that 'His Grace has completed 20 sermons written on board, 32 remaining to be written, being one for every Sunday of the year.' (*Journal*, 15 May 1846, 86).

19. Harding's Journal mentions that on 5 June, when close to the Azores, they encountered a ship, the *Jolly Robins*', with which they exchanged goods. The heading on page 108 of the Journal reads: '*Write home by Jolly Robins*'. This gives some certainty to 5 June as the date of the letter, replacing the uncertainty expressed in *Polding Letters*.

to persons in my station are more especially requisite, but from which external duties on shore too generally withdraw me. I feel conscious that there have occurred expressions in my correspondence stronger than necessary or liable to convey a sense not by me intended, and thus to give pain to Your Lordship. I regret this circumstance, and beg you will accept my expression of sorrow for the same . . .

I long to be back in the scene of my labour, and hope not to be later than February before I re-embark. Our voyage, which we hoped to be short, has already exceeded the term expected. We are now becalmed 5 days near the Azores. I enjoy my leisure exceedingly and felt not the lassitude and tedium of which my fellow passengers continually complain.

Adieu, my dear Lord. Pray for me, that in Meekness and in patience, I may fulfil the responsible duties of my state. Be assured of my continued supplications, and in all sincerity believe me to be

Your affectionate Br[other] in J.C.,
+J.B.Polding, Sydnien[sis]

26 June 1846 Arrival in the Downs

(*Sydney Chronicle*, 7 November 1846, page 2)

We perceive amongst the English news recently received via Port Phillip, that the *Ratcliffe* (Captain Gilbert) which our readers will remember left this port on the 16th February last, having on board his Grace the Archbishop of Sydney, arrived all well in the Downs, on the 26th June, having made the passage in 130 days, being rather a lengthened voyage for so fast sailing a ship. We hope that we shall have the pleasure of communicating to our readers some intelligence from the Archbishop himself by the next packetship.

30 June 1846 Polding letter to Sydney

(*Sydney Chronicle*, 21 November 1846, page 2)

As we anticipated, a letter has been received by the *Thomas Lowry*, from his Grace the Archbishop. The letter is dated London, June 30th, and the following affecting extract from it, relative to his Grace's departure from the Colony will, we are sure, be most acceptable to our readers:

'How loving is that good people the Almighty has been pleased to call me to direct. To see them coming round and round the ship, following us out farther and yet farther, loath to separate from me. A heart must be of stone not to be sensible to such affection and respect-I long to be back; London, England have no charms for me; where my treasure is, there is my heart-my people are my joy and my crown. In February next, I hope to embark.'

The letter states that the Right Rev. Dr Murphy arrived in London, and met the Archbishop two days after his Grace's arrival.

30 June 1846 Polding to all the Faithful, Clergy and Laity, of the Archdiocese[20]

(*Pastoral Letters* 222–223)[21]

London
30 June 1846

Greetings,
The grief which the death of our Most Holy Father Gregory XVI caused us-grief such only as a son may experience under the bereavement of such a parent beloved for his affection and venerated for his virtue – has been greatly mitigated by the choice which divine Providence has directed to be made of his Successor . . .

We direct the *Te Deum* to be recited or sung in each Church on the Sunday after the receipt of this Pastoral. Moreover that the name 'Pius' be inserted in the canon of the Mass, and in prayers for the Head of the Church. It is our wish also that the Holy Sacrifice be celebrated by each Priest within our jurisdiction on three different days for His Holiness.

May the peace of God be with you all.

---

20. The letter was read at St Mary's Cathedral, Sydney, on Sunday 20 December, followed by the singing of the *Te Deum* 'in thanksgiving to the Almighty for the elevation of his present Holiness Pope Pius IX to the see of St Peter, as a worthy successor to the late venerated Gregory XVI'. (*Sydney Chronicle*, 23 December 1846, 2).
21. Gregory Haines et al (eds), *The Eye of Faith: the pastoral letters of John Bede Polding*, Lowden Publications, Kilmore, 1977.

3 July 1846 Polding and the 'Society of Oceania'

(*Morning Post* [London], Monday, 6 July 1846, p 8)

On Saturday, a public meeting was held at the Sabloniere Hotel, Leicester-square, the Right Rev. the Bishop of Ivry (sic)[22] presiding, to establish the 'Society of Oceania' in aid of missions to the Southern Pacific Ocean. Abbé de Fonvielle stated that the proposed society would be ancillary to the oeuvre of the propagation of the faith in France, the object of which was to forward Roman catholic missionaries to the Pacific and elsewhere, and to keep up a connection between those missionaries, their bishops, and their countries; he also stated that France had during the past year dedicated three ships to those purposes, and that ere another twelve month elapse, England would build one for the same mission. The Bishop of Sydney, F. Jerningham, Esq., Messrs. Scott, Murray, Barnewell, Pagliano and Lucas addressed the meeting, after which resolutions were passed establishing an English branch of the 'Oceania Society'.

(*Sydney Chronicle*, 9 December 1846, page 3 [from *The Tablet*, July 11])

A public meeting was held on Friday, the 3rd instant, at Nind's Sabloniere Hotel for the purpose of taking into consideration the propriety of establishing a branch of the 'Society of Oceania,' established in June 1845 in France. The Right Rev. Dr Morris, Bishop of Troy (sic), presided on the occasion . . .

His Grace the Archbishop of Sydney rose to propose the first resolution, and in an eloquent and able speech, which we regret we have not space to insert, confirmed all the views of the venerable Abbé from his own experience, and stated that he looked forward with feelings of unmixed delight, to the establishment of this society, the want of which none could so fully appreciate as those who were situated like himself. He concluded by hoping that the Catholics of the United Kingdom would come forward in support of this undertaking, particularly those who were contributors to the Society of the Propagation of the Faith, as it would materially save the funds of that Institution, and enable it to send out more and much wanted missionaries.

22. William Placid Morris OSB (1794–1872) titular Bishop of Troas, former Apostolic Visitor of Mauritius (1831–1840).

(*Sentinel*, 17 December 1846, page 2)

We earnestly direct the attention of our readers to the following extract from a communication of the Tahitian correspondent of the Polynesian & Sandwich Islands paper, of the 28th. September: 'We believe business has received a death blow here by the establishment of a commercial missionary store by the Jesuits of France. Their object is to disseminate the Romish faith throughout the islands in the Pacific, and their first step is to ingratiate themselves with the natives by selling them goods at costs and charges, undersell the merchants, and drive them off the island. The society is the most wealthy and influential in France. They are to have a house in Valparaiso, Tahiti, and Oahu, and branches at the Navigators, Wallis Island, New Caledonia, and the Ferjees.[23] They have twelve ships of the size of the *Arche d'Alliance*, two of which are here now, with some twenty or thirty Jesuits on board, and a number of small vessels. It is so arranged that one of them will leave France every month, to keep their establishment supplied with goods.'

The Society here alluded to is called the Society of Oceania, and has been recently instituted in France, for the avowed purpose of disseminating the principles of Popery in the South Sea Islands, by means of a sort of commercial mission. Large funds have been collected in France for the purchase of such goods as are required by the natives of the islands, and these are sold by the Jesuit traders at such a low cost as to neutralise all competition by honorable merchants, which cannot fail to purchase the confidence and good will of those simple people. A branch society has been established in London, to co-operate with the Parent Society, and an attempt will be made to establish a similar branch in Sydney under the patronage of the Popish emissary, who has assumed the title of Archbishop of Sydney, though that attempt will probably be deferred until the return of this usurping priest to the colony.

23. Navigators: Samoan Islands; the Ferjees: Fiji Islands.

8 July 1846 Polding to Earl Grey[24]

(*Polding Letters* II.54)

6 Leicester Place
Leicester square
London
8 July 1846

My Lord,
I have recently arrived from New South Wales on important public business connected with the Catholic Church in the Australian Colonies, and I shall feel greatly obliged if Your Lordship will permit me the honour of an interview on a day as early as may be convenient. Whatever information I can give on the state of the Colony of New South Wales, I need scarcely add, is placed unreservedly at your Lordship's service.

I have the honor to be,
My Lord,
Your Lordship's ob[edien]t h[um]ble ser[van]t.
+J.B.Polding

9 July 1846 Polding to Earl Grey

(*Polding Letters* II.55)

61 New Bond Street.
London
9 July 1846

My Lord,
I have the honor to report my arrival by the Ship Ratcliffe from New South Wales having sailed from Sydney on the 16th of February. As my voyage to Europe has been undertaken reluctantly on Ecclesiastical business entirely of a public character with the full sanction and concurrence of His Excellency the Governor Sir George Gipps, I have respectfully to request Your Lordship to authorise the payment of my

24. Henry George Grey, 3rd Earl Grey (1802–1894) was the eldest son of Prime Minister Charles Grey. He became Secretary of State for War and the Colonies on 6 July 1846 in Lord Russell's first ministry.

Stipend during the leave of absence granted me, that is for the space of Eighteen Months, commencing from the 16th of February last.

I have the honor to be,
My Lord,
Your Lordship's Obedient Servant.

15 July 1846 Polding to Cardinal Fransoni

(*Polding Letters* II.57)

Most Reverend Eminence,
After a long and painful voyage of nearly 129 days during which, as well as inevitable troubles of cold and heat, I had also to suffer rather severe privations, here I am by the Grace of Heaven, arrived within a short distance of London. Here I have already been given four new Missionaries ready to set out for Australia as soon as I have succeeded in increasing this number on account of the urgency of my mission.

But this is not the only object of my visit to the Metropolis. Some business related to the Mission needs to be transacted face to face with the Ministers of the Colonies, the Head of which I have found by good fortune to be now changed. And certainly, it was from the Minister, Lord Stanley, that there issued some laws rather hostile to out Missionaries who are assigned to the convict prisons . . .

And now I am heartily delighted to have had our grievances listened to by the new Minister, Earl Grey, the successor of Stanley . . .

I shall make haste to visit the honoured threshold of the Most Holy Apostles in order to cast myself down at the Feet of the new Sovereign Pontiff[25] and to confirm to Your Eminence the homage of my

25. Giovanni Maria Mastai-Ferretti (1792–1878), was elected Pope on 16 June 1846, taking the name Pius IX. He died in February 1878, one year after Polding's death. After meeting Pius in May 1847 Polding was full of admiration in letters to Sydney: 'The Archbishop describes His Holiness as the most English looking Italian he has ever met with. His appearance is said, by his Grace, to be that of a well-bred English gentleman, with a stature rather above the ordinary height, and a proportionate degree of stoutness. The countenance of the Pope is very susceptible of expression, and he does not appear to entertain the smallest particle of that worldly policy which deems the concealment of the feelings as the first accomplishment of a statesman.' (*Sydney Chronicle*, Wednesday 4 August 1847, page 2).

profound respect; meanwhile I hope to give you pleasure by enclosing a Pastoral letter which I have written from here to my clergy and people, and in expectation of your commands, I kiss the Sacred Purple and take the honour of signing myself,

Your Most Reverend Eminence's most devoted and obedient servant,
John Bede Polding
Archbishop of Sydney.

16 July 1846 Polding to English Clergy and Friends

(*Polding Letters* II.58–59)

England 16 July 1846
One of the causes which has impelled me to undertake the long voyage of sixteen thousand miles, with great grief to leave my flock, and at great inconvenience, to visit Europe, is the absolute necessity I am under in obtaining means to erect a Seminary for the Australian Missions . . .

Can any work tend more to the glory of God and the good of souls? We pray you, therefore, to assist us in erecting our Seminary – We earnestly solicit you not to refuse us aid.

I have the honor to be
Your very faithful servant in Jesus Christ
[+J.B.P.]

6 August Polding to Benjamin Hawes[26]

(*Polding Letters* II.61)

31 Seel Street
Liverpool
6 August 1846

Dear Sir,
I shall feel exceedingly obliged if you will have the goodness to expedite the documents preparatory to the issue of my stipend as I am somewhat inconvenienced by the delay . . .

26. Benjamin Hawes (1797–1862) was a British Whig politician. He was Under-Secretary of State for War and the Colonies in the Russell government from 1846 to 1851.

I have the honor to be, Dear Sir,
Your faithful ser[van]t.,
+J.B.Polding, Sydneien[sis]

24 August Polding to Bishop R.W.Willson

(*Polding Letters* II.61–62)

My dear Lord,
So soon as the present ministry was formed and installed in Office, I lost no time on obtaining an interview with Lord Grey, and having first orally explained to his Lordship the state of the case, and the infraction of Church Discipline involved in the present regulations for the Convict Department. . . [It] is of the greatest advantage to us that Lord Grey is in office and not Lord Stanley, for as these Regulations were devised by the latter and he is proverbially obstinate and has adopted as a maxim that whosoever is paid by the State is a servant of the State, under its control and to do its bidding, there can be no room for doubt as to the difficulties which would have been in our way.[27] Mr Hawes is a man equally liberal. He is a plain, straightforward man. I have seen no persons in the Colonial Office I like so well . . .

My kindest regards to all the Clergy and believe me to be my dear Lord,

Your affectionate Br[other] in J.C.,
+J.B.Polding, Sydneien[sis]

27. Willson and Polding, though at odds over ecclesiastical administration, were one in their opposition to Lord Stanley's Regulations for the Convict Department.

1 September Polding at Cheadle[28]

(*Morning Chronicle* [London] 3 September 1846, reprinted in *Sydney Chronicle* 3 February 1847, page 3)

DEDICATION OF THE NEW ROMAN CATHOLIC CHURCH AT CHEADLE . . .
The procession was headed by an incense-bearer, followed by a cross-bearer, and two attendants with lights next came ten acolytes in couples, followed by a choir of twenty-four, who chaunted the psalm *Laetatus sum*. Two other cross-bearers preceded sixty of the clergy, robed, who were followed by the Archbishop of Damascus, the Archbishop of Sydney, the Right Rev. Dr Morris, Bishop of the Mauritius, Dr Griffiths, Bishop of London, Dr Gillis, Roman Catholic Bishop of Edinburgh, Dr Brown, Roman Catholic Bishop of Wales, and the Right Rev. Drs. Wiseman, Wilson, Briggs, Sharples, Wareing, Ullathorne, and Riddell, the Roman Catholic Bishops or 'Vicars Apostolic' of the other districts in England.

(*The Pilot* [London], 14 September 1846, p 4)

A very wealthy and very superstitious nobleman devotes a portion of his revenue to the erection of a fancy Church – a splendid architectural gim-crack – and straightway, the votaries of Rome are fain to persuade themselves that the middle ages are coming back again.[29]

28. Polding, who had brought to Australia church designs and ecclesiastical furnishings and fabrics of Augustus Welby Pugin (1812–1852), was present at the opening of Pugin's splendid gothic-revival church of St Giles at Cheadle in Staffordshire. Polding, as an Archbishop, was regarded senior to all the bishops of England and Scotland. The Syriac Archbishop of Damascus was in Europe seeking assistance for 'the persecuted Christians in his diocese, who are completely at the mercy of the fanatic Druses' (*The Standard* [London], 14 April 1846, 2).

29. The nobleman was John Talbot, 16th Earl of Shrewsbury and 16th Earl of Waterford (1791–1852), who, having helped finance Pugin's St Chad Cathedral in Birmingham in 1842, in 1846 commissioned the architect to create at Cheadle a church that would have no rival.

24 September 1846 Polding in Dublin

(*The Tablet*, 26 September 1846, reprinted in *Sydney Chronicle*, 30 January 1847, p 3)

Association for the Propagation of the Faith. On Thursday the annual ceremonies of the High Mass, &c., offered up for the advancement of this glorious society, took place in the Metropolitan Church, Marlborough-street. The church was densely crowded long before the commencement of the ceremonies. The nave was thronged with much of the wealth and respectability of our city. The choir in front of the great altar was railed in for the clergy and dignitaries present not officiating. Archbishop Polding of Sydney, Bishop Murphy of Adelaide; Bishop Murphy (elect) of Hyderabad, and Bishop Briggs of York, were present.[30] . . .

The *Kilkenny Journal* says:-' His Grace the Most Rev. Dr Polding visited the Right Rev. Dr Walsh at St Kyran's College on Thursday last. His object was to represent the spiritual wants of his diocese, and to solicit priests for his destitute mission . . . For its vast extent of territory it is his Grace's anxious wish to provide zealous missionaries. At present he applies for twenty-four and he undertakes to furnish them with adequate means of support. In that colony the children of the Catholic parents are, in many instances, debarred from baptism till they are ten or twelve years old, because he has not a sufficient number of priests to place the reception of that so necessary a sacrament within their reach. Multitudes are several days' journey distant from a clergyman, and many have not beheld the face of one for several years.'

30. Francis Murphy (1795–1858), appointed Bishop of Adelaide in 1842.
Daniel Murphy (1815–1907), Vicar-Apostolic of Hyderabad 1846 to 1865, Bishop of Hobart 1865–1888, Archbishop 1888–1907.
John Briggs (1788–1861), Vicar Apostolic of Yorkshire District from 1836.

16 November 1846 Polding to Priests Embarking for Australia[31]

(*Polding Letters* II.65–66)

London
16 November 1846

My dear children in Christ,
I regret exceedingly that I am deprived of the gratification of accompanying you on board and of imparting to you my blessing. In this exigence, I must endeavour to supply by writing, some of those instructions and suggestions which, in my anxiety for your welfare, I should have given you. These will refer rather to your sojourn on shipboard than to your conduct on landing. For the time of the voyage is most valuable; during it, studies may be matured, attention given to the interior life, habits of order, recollection and piety strengthened in a very discernible degree. . .

[F]rom unaccustomedness with the sea, it is probable that sickness will come on and continue for some days. During this time if, as is often the case, the recitation of the Divine Office be exceedingly burdensome, without scruple substitute the three parts of the rosary or even one if the sickness be very oppressive. The rosary may be said lying in your berth; you will find the recumbent posture most easy . . .

31. The three priests embarking had been recruited by Polding during his stay in Ireland during September 1846:
Michael Andrew Corish (1818–1865) of County Wexford, completed studies for priesthood at St Kieran's College, Kilkenny, and was ordained in 1845. On arrival in Sydney he was one of the few Irish diocesan clergy who joined the Benedictines, taking the name Miletus. He served in Sydney and country missions, dying at Bathurst.
William McGinty (d. 1871) of County Donegal was a graduate of All Hallows Missionary College, where he was ordained in October 1846 and where Polding had stayed in September. In Australia he served in rural missions, dying at Ipswich after many years of ministry there.
Francis Coyle from the United States, whom Bishop Murphy met at Mount Melleray Cistercian monastery, was recruited for the newly created diocese of Adelaide, where he served until 1850. When he was suspended he relocated to New York. He was described as 'American' on Polding's 1859 list of 'disgraced priests'. On Coyle see T. L. Suttor, *Hierarchy and Democracy in Australia 1788–1870*, Melbourne University Press, Melbourne, 1965.

As regards the celebration of the Mystery, this can only take place when the vessel is steady, sailing with the wind on lee beam. To prevent scruples, whenever you doubt whether you can without difficulty celebrate, in all cases of doubt decide you will not celebrate . . .

Cultivate towards your fellow passengers and the officers a cheerful disposition, no familiarity, but all the ease and gentleness and desire to oblige which, constituting the ordinary politeness, becomes, when animated by a supernatural motive, a Christian virtue.

I do not object to your joining, in this spirit, any games that may be played, chess, backgammon, even cards, though from the moment you reach Sydney, these are never to be touched. But on shipboard it is virtue to contribute to the amusement of others, even by these unusual modes of clerical relaxation . . . It will be advantageous to you if you keep a log-book as it is called. I do not mean for the purpose of merely notifying the incidents, trifling or otherwise, which may occur, but more particularly to note down the remarks you have made in the course of the day's reading . . . A day of strict retirement occasionally will be of service . . . [T]ake at least some hours, say four, of active exercise each day. By taking relaxation at proper times, observing silence at other times, you will find the voyage exceedingly pleasant and improving. Your beads, when in health, should be recited, the daily tribute to our good mother, as a matter of course. To her affectionate keeping I commend you, and am,

Your loving bishop and friend,
+John Bede Polding
Archbishop of Sydney

August 1847 Lewis Harding at Polperro, Cornwall

(Thomas Quiller Couch, 'A sketch of the life of Jonathan Couch' in Jonathan Couch, *The History of Polperro: a fishing town on the South coast of Cornwall*, Truro, 1871, p 5.)

The Trelawny family, especially, had not only the fullest confidence in his [Dr Jonathan Couch's] abilities, but admitted him to their intimate friendship at the old mansion of Trelawne, where he often engaged himself in deciphering and transcribing the archives of the house . . . A member of the family [Lewis Harding] had returned from a distant clime in a very imperfect state of health, and it became necessary to prescribe for him a sort and degree of occupation which should direct his mind without overstraining it, and not entail bodily fatigue. Mr. Couch set him such a pleasant task, by requesting him to observe and keep a daily diary of the inhabitants of the old rookery. The result was the improved health of the patient and, for the doctor, a very interesting MS. Volume entitled 'Life in a Rookery'.

Bibliography

Manuscripts, Theses & Websites

Benedictine Journal 1843–1860, Sydney Archdiocesan Archives.

Compton, Margaret E., *A Life of John Bede Polding*, MA Thesis, University of New England, 1977.

Condon, Brian, *Letters and Documents in 19th Century Australian Catholic History* (http://www.library.unisa.edu.au/condon/CatholicLetters).

Correll, Philip, *Lewis Harding: photographer of Polperro*, typescript, 1996 (State Library of NSW, MLMSS 6119).

Harding, Lewis, *Journal of Voyage from England to New South Wales 1835*, Downside Abbey Archives.

Harding, Lewis, *Ship Journal of Lewis Harding on board the ship Ratcliff from Sydney to London 1846*, SAA.

Milford, Frederick, *Reminiscences of Frederick Milford* (V3051/31), University of New England and Regional Archives (AO465), n.d.

Sharpe, Thomas, *Journal on Norfolk Island 1837–1840*, manuscript, State Library of NSW (B 217–B 218).

Skinner, Graeme, *Australharmony* (http://sydney.edu.au/paradisec/australharmony/).

Starkey, Miriam Theresa, *J. B. Polding – Ships*, manuscript, 1977, Good Samaritan Archives.

Published Texts

Abbot of Downside, 'Abbot Gregory Gregory (1813–1877)', *Downside Review*, 89(1971), 191–195.

Anon, 'The Most Reverend John Bede Polding, D.D., O.S.B., First Archbishop of Sydney', *Downside Review* 1(1881), 91–102, 165–175, 241–249.

Backhouse, James, *A Narrative of a visit to the Australian Colonies*, London, 1843.

Barry, Vincent, *Alexander Maconochie of Norfolk Island: a study of a pioneer in penal reform*, OUP, Melbourne, 1958.

Bateson, Charles, *The Convict Ships 1787–1868*, Brown, Son & Ferguson, Glasgow, 1939.

Bayliss, Robert A. and C. William Ellis, 'Neil Arnott, F.R.S., Reformer, Innovator and Popularizer of Science, 1788–1874', *Notes and Records of the Royal Society of London*, Vol. 36, No. 1 (1981).

Birt, Henry Norbert, *Downside: the history of St. Gregory's School from its commencement at Douay to the present time*, London, 1902.

Birt, Henry Norbert, *Benedictine Pioneers in Australia*. 2 vols, London 1911.

Birt, Henry Norbert (ed), *Obit Book of the English Benedictines, 1600–1912*, Edinburgh, 1913.

Bunbury, Thomas, *Reminiscences of a veteran: being personal and military adventures in Portugal, Spain, France, Malta, New South Wales, Norfolk Island, New Zealand, Andaman Islands, and India*, 3 vols., London, 1861.

Butler, J. Brian, 'Jean Gourbeillon: a French Sculptor in Nineteenth-Century Sydney', *Tjurunga. An Australian Benedictine Review*, 67(2004), 35–47.

Cable, K. J., 'Atkins, Thomas (1808–1860)', *Australian Dictionary of Biography*, National Centre of Biography, Australian National University, 1966.

Compton, M. Xavier et al (eds), *The Letters of John Bede Polding OSB*, 3 vols, Sydney, 1994.

Compton, M. Xavier et al (eds), *Adjutor Deus. Documents and resource material relating to the episcopacy of Archbishop John Bede Polding OSB*, 2 vols Sydney, 2000.

Correll, Philip, 'John Cooke Harding's Journal', *South Western Catholic History*, 13(1995), 15ff.

Correll, Philip, *Lewis Harding: Cornwall's pioneer photographer*, Polperro, Heritage Press, 2000.

Couch, Jonathan, *The History of Polperro: a fishing town on the South coast of Cornwall*, Truro, 1871.

Couch, Thomas Quiller, 'A sketch of the life of Jonathan Couch' in Jonathan Couch, *The History of Polperro*.

Daly, Robert A., 'Archdeacon McEncroe on Norfolk Island, 1838–42', *Australasian Catholic Record*, 36(1959), 285–305.

Elliott, Sizar, *Fifty years of colonial life*, Melbourne, 1886.

Forster, M. G. (ed), 'Fragment of a Diary kept by Sister Mary Scholastica Gregory on her voyage from Liverpool, England, to Australia 1847–1848', *Tjurunga*, 26(1984), 52–72.

Fowler, C. F., 'Anti-Catholic polemic at the origins of Australia's first Catholic newspaper', *Journal of the Australian Catholic Historical Society*, 37 (2016), 147–160.

Fowler, C. F., 'Invoking the patronage of St. Bede in New South Wales', *Australasian Catholic Record*, 94(2017), 294–304.

Fowler, C. F., 'Lewis Harding: catechist at Norfolk Island Penal Settlement 1838–1842', *Journal of the Australian Catholic Historical Society*, 39(2018), 13–28.

Fowler, C. F., 'From Cornwall to Norfolk Island: Lewis Harding, Catechist at 'Hell in Paradise', *Journal of the Cornwall Association of Local Historians*, 71(2019), 60–68.

Fowler, Frank, *Southern Lights and Shadows: Being Brief Notes of Three Years' Experience of Social, Literary, and Political Life*, London, 1859.

Haines, Gregory et al (eds), *The Eye of Faith: the pastoral letters of John Bede Polding*, Lowden Publications, Kilmore, 1977.

Hosie, John, 'Letters of Jean Gourbeillon', *Tjurunga* 12(1976), 143–155.

Kavenagh, T. J., 'Polding's Monks', *Tjurunga* 8(1974), Appendix 1, pp i–xviii.

Kavenagh, T. J. (ed), 'My Dear Alphonsus: selections from the Sydney letters of Abbot Edmund Moore', *Tjurunga* 10(1975), 43–60.

Kavenagh, T. J., 'Vaughan and the Monks of Sydney', *Tjurunga* 25(1983), 147–233.

Kavenagh, T. J., 'Profession dates (and others) of the monks of St. Mary's, Sydney', *Tjurunga* 48(1985), 69–75.

Kavenagh, T. J., 'J. B. Polding and the English Benedictine Congregation, 1834–1843', *Tjurunga* 34(1988), 65–69.

Kavenagh, T. J., 'The end of the Sydney Benedictines', *Tjurunga* 52(1996), 31–42.

Kemp, Peter (ed), *The Oxford companion to ships and the sea*, Oxford, OUP, 1994.

Kenny, John, *A History of the Commencement and Progress of Catholicity in Australia up to the Year 1840*, Sydney, 1886.

Lanyon, Andrew, *The Rooks of Trelawne*, The Photographers Gallery, London, 1976.

Maddox, Alan, 'On the machinery of moral improvement: music and prison reform in the penal colony of Norfolk Island', *Musicology Australia*, 34(2012), 185–205.

McEncroe, John, *The Wanderings of the Human Mind in Searching the Scriptures, being a concise history of the origin, progress and condemnation of the principal heresies that have arisen in the several ages of Christianity from the private interpretation of the Holy Bible, in a series of letters to a candid inquirer after truth*, W.A. Duncan, Sydney, 1841.

Moore, Edmund, 'With Dr. Polding to Australia, 1847', *Downside Review*, 32(1913) 69–92, 314–327, republished in *Tjurunga* 6(1974) 109–124, 7(1974) 77–92, 9(1975) 105–119.

Moran, Patrick Francis, *History of the Catholic Church in Australasia*, Sydney, 1894.

Morlok, Franziska and Miriam Waszelewski, *Bookbinding: a comprehensive guide to folding, sewing & binding*, translated by Caroline Waight, Princeton Architectural Press, New York, 2018.

Musgrave, A., *Dr James Stuart: Artist Naturalist*, Sydney, 1955.

O'Brien, Conor, 'Attitudes to St Cuthbert's Body during the Nineteenth Century', *Northern History*, 53(2016) pp. 236–248.

O'Donoghue, Frances, *The Bishop of Botany Bay: the life of John Bede Polding, Australia's first Catholic Archbishop*, Sydney, Angus & Robertson, 1982.

O'Farrell, Patrick (ed), *St Mary's Cathedral Sydney, 1821–1971*, Devonshire Press, Sydney, 1971.

Pender, Graeme, 'The life and contribution of Bishop Charles Henry Davis OSB (1815–1854) to the Catholic Church in Australia' *Journal of the Australian Catholic Historical Society*, 39(2018), 29–44.

Shanahan, Mary, *Out of Time, Out of Place: Henry Gregory and the Benedictine Order in Colonial Australia*, ANU Press, Canberra, 1970.

Spruson, Joseph, *Norfolk Island: outline of its history from 1788 to 1884*, Sydney, 1885.

Steven, Margaret, 'Campbell, Robert (1769–1846)', *Australian Dictionary of Biography*, National Centre of Biography, Australian National University, 1966.

Suttor, T. L., *Hierarchy and Democracy in Australia 1788–1870*, Melbourne University Press, Melbourne, 1965.

Ullathorne, William Bernard, *Autobiography*, London 1891.

Ullathorne, William Bernard, *The Devil is a Jackass: being the dying words of the autobiographer William Bernard Ullathorne 1806–1889* (edited by Leo Madigan), Downside Abbey Publications Bath, 1995.

Vials, Joanna, *The Indomitable Mr Cotham: missioner, convict chaplain and monk*. Gracewing, Leominster, 2019.

Wark, Anne, *Journal of a Voyage to Australia 1855–56: Myles Athy, a recruit for St Mary's Monastery Sydney*, ATF Press, Adelaide, 2017.

Watson, Frederick (ed), *Historical Records of Australia. Series I: Governors' despatches to and from England, 1788–1848*, 26 vols., Library Committee of the Commonwealth Parliament, Sydney, 1914–1925.

Index

C

D

E

F

G

H

CPSIA information can be obtained
at www.ICGtesting.com
Printed in the USA
FFHW021214031019
55349413-61092FF

9 781925 872736